*An Introduction to*

# EVANGELICAL
# CHRISTIAN EDUCATION

*Edited by*

J. EDWARD HAKES

MOODY PRESS
CHICAGO

*An Introduction to*
# EVANGELICAL
# CHRISTIAN EDUCATION

# PREFACE

ALTHOUGH there are excellent books which present surveys of or introductions to Christian education, none of them is written from a
strictly evangelical viewpoint. Yet evangelicals are involved in Christian nurture to an extent unequaled by any other group in American
Protestantism. Teachers and students in our evangelical schools, pastors
of our evangelical churches, and friends of Christian education have long
been aware of the need for a book such as *Introduction to Evangelical
Christian Education*.

In this day of increasing specialization, the probability of one person
having success in writing a scholarly work which surveys a wide field has
been substantially reduced. Multiple authorship is now the prevailing
practice in many branches of educational literature. This principle has
been followed in the preparation of this book. Many of the editor's colleagues in the field of Christian education were polled in order to learn
who, among evangelicals, in their estimation were best qualified to write
the different chapters. The roster of authors pretty much represents the
consensus of their opinion.

When the writers were given their respective assignments, they were
granted freedom to express their own ideas in their own ways. It was the
editor's conviction that an attempt to structure their manuscripts in the
interest of uniformity would not only limit their contributions but would
also be deceptive in that it would hide differences of opinion which actually exist among knowledgeable people, all of whom are deeply committed to Jesus Christ.

The reader must keep in mind that this book is only what its title represents it to be—an *introduction* to Christian education. It does not claim
to be a complete treatment of the whole field or any part of it. As a result
some important areas are not dealt with, and no one area has been treated
exhaustively. Anyone who reads these chapters and does not feel constrained to explore the subject further by supplementary reading in depth
has unfortunately missed the point of the book.

5

May God use the insights and understandings which the writers share with us in the chapters which follow to increase the effectiveness of the service we render to His growing children in the name of His Son, who said, "Learn of me."

J. EDWARD HAKES

# CONTENTS

## PART FOUR—*Organizing the Learner*

## PART FIVE—*Agencies of Christian Education*

With the rapid secularization of state-supported school systems as a result of public pressure and Supreme Court decisions, Christians in America have given increasing attention to private schools with a distinctly evangelical philosophy of education.

# PART ONE

*Backgrounds of Christian Education*

*Chapter 1*

# THE SECULARIZATION OF
# AMERICAN LIFE

## CARL F. H. HENRY

A DISTINCT, even unique, combination of Western cultural traits and trends once characterized American life. And it must be conceded that the United States still towers with manifest distinction above the modern world in many respects: it has staggering material resources and a vast share of world wealth; its advanced technology has shaped a highly industrialized and scientific society; its living standard is probably the highest anywhere; its literacy rate and educational system are remarkable; as a whole, the nation remains the twentieth century's clearest mirror of the democratic way of life. Someone estimated a few years ago that America has 10 per cent of the world's population, 52 per cent of its food, 75 per cent of its clothes, 80 per cent of its bathtubs, 95 per cent of its automobiles, 98 per cent of its radios, and 99.4 per cent of the world's televisions.

Something seems to be fundamentally wrong, however. To scores of Americans the basic meaning of "American way" is unclear. Loss of once-cherished beliefs about the nature of man, about society and the state, and consequent uncertainty about national purpose, yield widely recognized evidence of our decline as a nation. In a recent "Review of Current Religious Thought," Frank E. Gaebelein describes secularism as "simply a respectable way of spelling godlessness." He identifies "the great internal menace of our nation" with "the creeping secularism that has insinuated itself into all areas of national life, religion not excluded," with "the infiltration of our culture by the selfsame atheistic spirit that is integral to dialectical materialism," with "a secularism that amounts to

Carl F. H. Henry, Th.D., Ph.D., is editor of *Christianity Today*.

nothing less than atheism by default."[1] The majority of thinkers today acknowledge the inroads of such disintegration and decay on contemporary thought and life, and they are deeply troubled.

The one hopeful turn in this fearsome drift of American life is our frank recognition of the evil omens that bedevil our day-to-day existence. These assessments are actually value judgments; taken seriously, they could serve to propel us into discerning discussion of our moral and spiritual dilemma. Those students of American history alert to the peculiar influence of Christianity upon the national heritage point out that recovery of perspectives requires much more than merely self-analysis and confession. They find little evidence of that spiritual quest and concern for moral renewal that stirred the heart of early America. Rather, the United States now seems so deeply secularized that, instead of returning to the Judeo-Christian heritage which distinguished much of its past outlook on life, the present generation is satisfied to settle for "faith" of the barest significance, a vague belief in "spirit" whose moral idealism and spiritual earnestness are isolated from the great, enduring realities of revealed and redemptive religion. The historians warn that to rise above the corroding effect of secularism and scientism America must have renewal of a religion specific in its convictions and intense in its commitment. Such was the Christianity of the Pilgrims and of the Puritans. Such was the theism of Jonathan Edwards with whom begins the history of American philosophy.

## THE AMERICAN DREAM

Attempts to isolate the secret of America's greatness have yielded countless materialistic explanations. Among clues cited for her strength are the conflict of class interests and the challenge of the environment. Other analysts speak of the nation's geographic position in the Western hemisphere, of the relatively scanty population, of America's wealth of resources. Still others point to the shifting "frontier" with its accompanying contribution to democratic processes and institutional and cultural development. But deeper scrutiny (as by Ralph Barton Perry) to plumb the real soul of America—the so-called "American mind" or spirit—has often led beyond economic and social factors. In such studies the secret of the American way has been found to lodge in a distinctive union of ideas and ideals.

In a recent essay, "The Kingdom of God in America and the Task of the Church," Robert S. Michaelsen notes how readily the American patriot seems to link "the meaning of history with the fate of his nation. He regards the birth of his nation as a special act of providence or as that occurrence toward which the whole historical development has been

[1]*Christianity Today,* IV (November 9, 1959), p. 43.

moving. Confidently he feels that the future of the world rests with the future of his nation, his political ideology, and his economic system. For him the study of American history takes the form of proving the superiority of his nation and upholding its 'manifest destiny.' "[2] Dr. Michaelsen senses a deep-rooted, traditional American conviction that American destiny is somehow bound up with the religious idea of the kingdom of God in history.

In studying American history, H. Richard Niebuhr traces the influence of this kingdom-idea in various periods of national development and emphasizes the vital role of the Christian community to the larger American society. "American Christianity and American culture," he remarks, "cannot be understood at all save on the basis of faith in a sovereign, living, loving God."[3] Building on this thesis, Dr. Michaelsen reminds us that the eighteenth century deists, whose influence was strong among the founding fathers, placed more emphasis on "nature's God" than on God's activity in history. As a result, God's sovereignty as the guiding factor in history was already compromised in the role of free men who in founding and governing the nation declared that "ultimate power rests in the people."[4]

Early political traditions clearly reflect the emphasis both of Biblical theism as the pervading faith of the great masses and of deism, the speculative philosophy of men like Franklin and Jefferson. While the leaders of the American Revolution may not be clearly termed evangelical Christians, in view of intellectual deviations under way after 1700 in the colonies, nearly all these men were deeply indebted to the Biblical perspective for their political and moral philosophy. While some historians see more of deistic philosophy than of Biblical theology in deriving human rights from nature or natural law, in declaring government to be of human origin, and in formulating the right to revolution as in 1776, they have nonetheless conceded that the Declaration of Independence stands squarely on a Biblical foundation. The light of such Christian heritage is reflected in the Scriptural "doctrine of human rights—to life, liberty, property, and marriage," and even in Jefferson's contention that "government exists to defend these inalienable rights."[5]

Early American Protestants—who represented the great bulk of the population—interpreted history with a lively sense of God's providence; this emphasis is unmistakable in the early political documents. These forebears underscored the great theological conviction that God's sov-

[2]Paul Ramsey (ed.), *Faith and Ethics* (New York: Harper & Bros., 1957), p. 270.
[3]*The Kingdom of God in America* (Chicago: Willett, Clark & Company, 1937), p. xiv.
[4]Ramsey (ed.), *op. cit.*, p. 274.
[5]C. Gregg Singer, "Theological Aspects of the Revolution," *Christianity Today*, III (June 22, 1959), p. 5.

ereign purpose and acts are the key to the course of history; they therefore believed that America's beginnings, development and destiny must be understood "under God." Aware of the spiritual awakenings so recently past, Jonathan Edwards commented: "It is worthy to be noted that America was discovered about the time of the Reformation, which was the first thing God did toward the glorious renovation of the world, after it had sunk into the depths of darkness and ruin."[6]

American clergymen readily proclaimed the political implications of Christianity from their pulpits. "They preached liberty," as Franklin P. Cole reminds us in a volume by that title,[7] in an age when freedom was under fire. The Revolutionary clergy proclaimed that *civil government is of divine institution,* and also welcomed safeguards against centralized federal power and supported the separation of church and state.

Some even saw in Israel's deliverance from Egyptian tyranny a spiritual precedent for America's political independence from the oppressions of the English crown. They stressed the *spiritual* source, nature, and cost of freedom, and found its undergirding supports in Biblical rather than in secular traditions. The later revival movements in American life quickened the need for both spiritual decision and social renewal; revivalism and perfectionism, as Timothy L. Smith observes, "became socially volatile only when combined with the doctrine of Christ's imminent conquest of the earth."[8]

The balance of moral and political power thus remained in the hands of American Christians, who warned against worship of the golden calf, and pled for the golden rule. In the crisis of the Civil War with its slavery issue, spiritual and political themes merged often. America was a showcase to the world of brotherhood; if she rose to moral greatness she would rule the world, not in national pride but in Christian love. The spiritual awakenings, moreover, by heightening the sense of American mission to the world, supplied Protestantism with a vitality that ultimately made the United States the world's main source of missionary personnel.

The spread of postmillennialism (partly in reaction to discredited millennial fanatics) influenced the church's shift from spiritual to social preoccupations. The slavery issue itself had encouraged identification of the progress of liberal democratic culture with the triumph of Christianity. Discoveries of science, multiplication of physical comforts, the extension of benevolence were viewed more and more as signs of Christ's enlarging kingdom. The Civil War had given American evangelicals good cause to question the prospect of a "social millennium" realized through a pro-

---

[6]Jonathan Edwards, *The Revival of Religion,* 1740.
[7]*They Preached Liberty* (New York: Fleming H. Revell Co., 1941).
[8]*Revivalism and Social Reform* (New York: Abingdon Press, 1957), p. 225.

gressing spiritual conquest of personal and social evil. Subsequent withdrawal of evangelical premillennialists from the arena of broader social concerns, together with the rise of the liberal "social gospel" (which distrusted individual redemption as the best dynamic for transforming society, and drew encouragement from speculations about evolutionary development), shaped a new era.

By the time events in the twentieth century had made America a great power, and then a world power, the "spiritual elements" of the American dream had become so diluted that even the churches had largely replaced the spiritual evangel with a social mission, had surrendered the dynamic of regeneration for the devices of propaganda and legislative lobby, even to mistaking quasi-socialist motifs for fundamental patterns of the Christian ethic. American Protestantism has not yet recovered from this theological delinquency; ecumenical effort to weld a giant church from the fragmented denominations gains its semblance of strength more from administrative organization superimposed upon grass roots indifference than from spiritual vitality.

In secular circles where the new religion in America was democracy, churches were a prized platform for proclaiming and implementing the movement. Even proponents of a "pluralistic one world" use an ecclesiastical springboard to decry "the American dream" as a regrettable remnant of prejudiced nationalism. With our nation now poised at a decisive crossroads, the church in America unfortunately sustains a quite ambivalent relationship, not only to the populace (almost half are not in the churches) but to the kingdom of God as well.[9]

## THE AMERICAN DILEMMA

In many respects the American dream has turned into a nightmare, the outcome of which at best is now highly uncertain. Even surface examination of national behavior discloses a deplorable decline in ideals. This is the tragic situation one finds whether he turns to the sphere of the home, of work, or of the state and culture.

[9]Archie J. Baum, assessing "The New Conservatism" (or conformity) in *The Colorado Quarterly* (Autumn, 1959), writes: "Increased church memberships may signify . . . more . . . a reflection of new feelings of insignificance than of a revival of faith in traditional doctrines. Religion, confined largely to church and Sunday, is now a speciality. . . . Whether or not church membership now signifies a retreat from thinking things through for oneself, church management involves its own battery of trained specialists and the churchgoer is inclined to let them perform their specialized functions for him just as he expects them to call upon him to provide his specialized services for them. Little occasion for serious questioning occurs, except where some aspect of the church-management complex (such as sound equipment or bookkeeping machines) overlaps with a member's area of competence."

## MARRIAGE AND THE HOME

That one out of four American marriages now ends in divorce makes obvious the disturbing consequences for the stability of the American home. Pitirim A. Sorokin, the distinguished sociologist, characterizes the American sex revolution as unparalleled in history, one that "is changing the lives of men and women more radically than any other revolution of our time."[10] In reply to those who minimize the seriousness and shame of this tide of sex anarchy, he insists that "in its 'sex-obsession' and 'free' sex-behavior our age has hardly ever been rivaled in the preceding periods of our history."[11]

"Some of the older concepts of marriage, including the firm anchorage of women in the home . . . high birth rate and low divorce—all have been altering more rapidly in the United States during the past half century than in any other nation," comments Dixon Wecter. "This change is now having repercussions, whether for good or ill, among other cultures as widely different as those of Britain and Japan."[12] Of this upheaval of family patterns, Wecter remarks that "no society in history has shown so widespread a shift in so short a time. In ancient Rome of . . . the first century B.C., marked symptoms of family disintegration, chiefly among the leisure class—divorce, refusal to bear children, infidelity, and other symptoms—led to the Julian legislation and an era of stern enforcement, stressing the civic obligations of marriage, parenthood, and family cohesion—laws not repealed until the fourth century after Christ and soon thereafter supplanted by the Christian code of Basil."[13] The phenomena of today's marital infidelity and sexual laxity are flaunted to the world by American movies whose romantic idols are often devotees of unabashed polygamy.

## LABOR AND ECONOMICS

Unions have so one-sidedly indoctrinated labor in terms of mere dollar-and-cents values that the American worker today has scant appreciation for the concept of work as a divine calling or vocation. The turn in national economic affairs involving staggering budgets and staggering debts has done little to encourage among the citizenry a respect for those ordinary monetary virtues entrusted to us by Puritan idealism. By minimizing the sanctity of private property and the determination for solvency, quasi-socialist ideals have subtly engendered a gnawing doubt over the wisdom of industry, thrift, and savings. Disregard for established statutes is evident in the growing number both of merchants and of workers who

[10]*The American Sex Revolution* (Boston: Porter Sargent, 1956), p. 4.
[11]"American Sex Morality Today," *Christianity Today*, IV (July 4, 1960), p. 3.
[12]*Changing Patterns in American Civilization* (Philadelphia: University of Pennsylvania Press, 1949), p. 17.
[13]*Ibid.*, p. 19.

no longer feel impelled to stay "within the law" for financial gain. In the decline of honesty as an economic virtue such phenomena as feather-bedding, shoplifting, and fraud replace the ideal of "hard work" with the yen for a "quick dollar." Mass media, through "strike it rich" programs, have catered to this temptation and nourished the desire for lucre without work.

## THE STATE

Among the disconcerting developments of our century is the abysmal ignorance of American citizens of the political documents serving as the nation's charter. The reasons for this ignorance are not difficult to discover. A mood of evolutionary naturalism in the twentieth century imbued the notion that all past documents because of social change must yield to present and future revision. Furthermore, liberal theology and philosophical idealism of the forepart of the century tended to exalt experience as the primary arena for the understanding of life at the expense of history. In addition, one must consider the lethargy of men in general, despite the high view of the common man projected by the democratic philosophies of the time; tendency to accept human freedoms as automatic and self-sustaining requires little by way of spiritual and political decision. This mood led to an indifference concerning America's past political ideals that enabled social revisionists to make changes in some of the basic patterns of American life with seemingly little awareness of their significance by the populace.

The concept of human freedoms found in the Declaration of Independence borrows more from Biblical theology than is usually recognized. The affirmation of inalienable rights does not stand in isolation even in the early American political documents; it is linked to faith in a supernatural Creator, who not only endows men with rights and stipulates their responsibilities, but also providentially rules the course of history and appoints the destiny of nations. In early American political traditions, the will of God was therefore a significant category, fully as significant as the will of the majority. Anyone familiar with New England history knows how much the atmosphere of the town meeting owed to the democracy shaped within the Christian churches under the Holy Spirit. Among the distressing turns of contemporary life in America is the extent to which popular opinion, or a mere statistical majority, determines the political outcomes of the day, and thereby invites powerful minority pressure blocs and lobbies to create the illusion of the majority will. God's will has ceased to be a significant factor. If George Washington rightly regarded supernatural religion and morality as the twin supports of the republic, neglect of these priorities now threatens to speed the decline of the nation.

The cumulative effect of contemporary developments in the political order is that the American concept of the state grows daily more complex and less cohesive. The average voter stumbles in his effort to interpret national purpose in terms of a controlling rationale. Increased religious illiteracy and ethical indifference have yielded a citizenry deficient both in principle and in dedication, and quite possibly in those very reserves necessary to protect the United States from the national suicide which seems inevitably to cap the roadway of secularism and materialism.

## EDUCATION

From a religiously oriented philosophy, education in the United States has declined to one almost completely devoid of religion. As Frank E. Gaebelein has said: "Any honest appraisal of our public schools cannot blink the fact that the anti-religious philosophy of secularism is pressing for dominance."[14] The staggering influence of John Dewey's philosophy of experimental naturalism in the American school system cannot be minimized. Even the former editor of *The Christian Century*, whose speculative bias at times veered as far left as humanism, complained: "Public education without religion creates a secular mentality faster than the church can Christianize it."[15]

The high expectation of an earlier era, that public education would win the world for democracy and decency, has steadily faded. Frederick Eby declares that "one conclusion is certain: the strong claims of a century ago that a system of public schools would do away with crime now look absurd. . . . The knowledge of moral principles and religious faith is no longer considered essential for the educated man. . . . Not only has public education failed to eliminate crime but it is in some measure responsible for the increase of these various evils. . . . Today practically none of the teachers of America have studied ethics, much less the principles of moral education. A sampling poll of 1,500,000 students in higher institutions showed that less than 5 per cent have studied ethics."[16]

## CULTURE

In *The Crisis of Our Age*, Sorokin points out that medieval painting and sculpture were overwhelmingly religious in topic; secular pictures and sculptures were virtually absent. Since then, however, the religious inter-

[14]*Christian Education in a Democracy* (New York: Oxford University Press, 1951), p. 86. Gaebelein notes that secularism is becoming more openly anti-religious; that while some liberal religious education is now becoming uneasy about its alliance with secularism, many religious educators of the past generation did not even suspect the anti-religious character of secularistic educational philosophy.

[15]C. C. Morrison, "The Inner Citadel of Democracy," *The Christian Century*, LVIII (May 14, 1941), p. 652.

[16]*The Development of Modern Education* (New York: Prentice-Hall, Inc., 1952), pp. 680 ff.

est has steadily lessened until today more than 96 per cent of the subjects
are secular. A similar situation, he says, prevails in music, literature and
architecture.[17]  He asserts both the indivisibility of European-American
culture and the similarity of cultural trends (decline of idealism and
"truth of faith"; rise of sensate philosophy; reflection of these philosophical
currents in art, in painting and sculpture, in music and in literature).
A recent critic appraises the American scene in this fashion: "Our literature is somber and violent; our political life is torn by factionalism; our
philosophy is pragmatic and loosely humanitarian; our total thinking is
inclined to be cynical and often sardonic."[18]

## THE AMERICAN DESTINY

If to recognize the critical state of American affairs indicates that
decadence has not yet totally destroyed the nation and reflects a moral
judgment that may reactivate the question of goals and standards with
new urgency, we should mention another sign. Russell Kirk has summarized it thus: "To do their duty under God; to rear decent families;
to improve their own condition, and that of their community; to educate
themselves; to acquire a home and other property; to maintain the best
in their civilization—these goals continue to attract many millions of
Americans. . . . America is not the nation of the Kinsey Report subjects,
inane television viewers, and Hollywood addicts that Communist propaganda describes."[19] This is a land—where today is there its parallel?—in
which Sunday schools enroll almost twenty-five million Protestant pupils
from cradle to adulthood. We too easily underestimate the courage and
generosity of the United States in this time of international trouble. "If
she is not invariably guided by an exalted justice and benevolence,"
Dr. Kirk continues, "nonetheless she has set her face against the "totalist
ideologies" and "poured out her national wealth in aid of the defense
and the welfare of the free world."

It is only an unbounded optimism, however, that fails to wince at
the stark statistics of social decline. Every trustworthy yardstick attests
our swift decline from earlier heights of moral and spiritual vitality. We
have abundant reason for soul-searching, for repentance and for renewal.
We need a return to those timeless priorities that alone can assure us of
national well-being.

If our institutions, if our way of life, are closely related to the primary
tenets of the Christian religion (students of American history time and
again have so conceded), only a return to these wellsprings can in-
vigorate our philosophy of life, our concepts of right and wrong, of the

[17]Pitirim A. Sorokin, *The Crisis of Our Age* (New York: E. P. Dutton & Co., 1946),
p. 45.
[18]Robert E. Spiller, *Changing Patterns in American Civilization*, p. ix, Preface.
[19]*The American Cause* (Chicago: Henry Regnery Co., 1957), p. 162.

dignity of persons, of the rights and responsibility of individuals. More is required than a welcome for every flash of "faith," more than a "religion in life" emphasis.

Recovery of the Bible will save us from the dangers of a merely subjective religion that lacks objectivity and external authority. To really withstand the assaults of naturalism, of the antichrist philosophies that pervade our era, we need a religion definite in its convictions, intense in its commitment, and fully alert to the threats of scientism and secularism to civilization. Christianity stems from a positive revelation that governs man's total outlook on the total life. George F. Thomas goes partway at least in saying that "since the source of our troubles is spiritual and moral, the only possible remedy is a restoration of faith in God . . . in the moral law established by His will; in the primacy of the spiritual life over material interests; and in the reality of eternal life."[20]

We could learn much from a fair-minded search of our Biblical heritage. Has this great legacy nothing more to teach us? Surely the Bible points the way out of the cultural morass of our century. Modern philosophers know all too well that the dissociation of ontology (the study of reality), epistemology (the study of knowledge), and axiology (the study of values) is the core of our dilemma. To discover that Jesus Christ is the divine agent in creation, in revelation, and in redemption welds these great concerns into the closest possible relationship. Basic to Christianity is the fact that the Supreme Being and His will for man are knowable, that life in this world and in the world to come gains rightness only through a proper identification with Him.

The Bible, moreover, solves the problem of our fragmented approach to freedom. At one time Christians knew that freedom is indivisible; its dissection into "four freedoms" or more disturbs the unity of freedom's basic theological foundations. Each fraction therefore becomes vulnerable to some artificial reconstruction if not to assault. Herein lies the danger of disconnecting political from economic from religious liberty. The Bible does much more than deal with freedom in a comprehensive way; it not only sets the totality of human experience under the sovereignty of God, but within this unifying orbit also defines human *responsibility and rights*.

If we are to recover the best in our American perspective, the Bible can fulfill another strategic function toward that end by renewing and reinforcing those social virtues that guard against totalitarian aggression. Religion, even Christianity, enjoys much regard today simply as a cultural preservative. But to revere Christianity in this way overlooks the fact that true religion refuses to be *used* as a mechanical catalyst for other more popular interests, such as the so-called "American way of life"

[20]*Changing Patterns in American Civilization*, p. 150.

or "free enterprise" or "the democratic outlook." Freedom endures only in a nation whose citizens live by the rule of truth, of justice, of charity, and of generosity. Wherever untruth, injustice, enmity and greed prevail, the strong exploit the weak, might displaces right, social order eventually yields to anarchy. Without the constraints of divine moral law, human life becomes corrupt and human government unjust. Truth, justice, and love of neighbor are the virtues of revealed religion. Where virtues born of redemptive religion are long neglected, freedom itself is soon dissolved. The rule of God in the lives of men is the only enduring alternative to the rule of tyrants.

In the face of our American dilemma, the purpose of this book on Christian education is significant. To know the Word in its power; to recall the inestimable blessing of the Great Commission for soldiers of faith in our times; to realize the essentially Christian element in our national heritage, should fire evangelical vitality to effective combat against secularism. If we meet this challenge in a comprehensive way—in its concern for man and society, for the worker and the economic world, for the citizen and the state, for education and culture—we shall supply all mankind with a needed sense of direction; with a purpose for everyone to incorporate; with universally valid principles and values that push us to a cause beyond our finite selves. To carry forward His work in the world, Jesus left behind only a minority of men, the Holy Spirit, marching orders, and a manual. It could well be the last hour for translating and transplanting the Biblical perspective into the spirits of our fellow countrymen.

## BIBLIOGRAPHY

Bready, J. Wesley. *This Freedom—Whence?* New York: American Tract Society, 1942.

Cairns, Earle E. *Saints and Society.* The Social Impact of Eighteenth Century English Revivals and Its Contemporary Relevance. Chicago: Moody Press, 1960.

Cole, Franklin P. *They Preached Liberty.* New York: Fleming H. Revell Co., 1944.

Eby, Frederick. *The Development of Modern Education.* New York: Prentice-Hall, Inc., 1952.

Gaebelein, Frank E. *Christian Education in a Democracy.* New York: Oxford University Press, 1951.

Henry, Carl F. H. *The Uneasy Conscience of Modern Fundamentalism.* Grand Rapids: Wm. B. Eerdmans Publishing Co., 1947.

Kirk, Russell. *The American Cause.* Chicago: Henry Regnery Co., 1957.

Morley, Felix. *The Power in the People.* New York: D. Van Nostrand and Co., 1949.

Smith, Timothy L. *Revivalism and Social Reform.* New York: Abingdon Press, 1957.

Sorokin, Pitirim A. *The American Sex Revolution.* Boston: Porter Sargent, 1956.

———. *The Crisis of Our Age.* New York: E. P. Dutton and Co., 1946.

Spann, J. Richard (ed.). *The Christian Faith and Secularism.* New York: Abingdon-Cokesbury Press, 1948.

Wecter, Dixon *et al. Changing Patterns in American Civilization.* Philadelphia: University of Pennsylvania Press, 1949.

*Chapter 2*

# THE HISTORY OF CHRISTIAN EDUCATION

## HAROLD CARLTON MASON

R ELIGIOUS EDUCATION was an integral part of the life of God's chosen people, the Hebrews. At Sinai God had given them the decalogue. Instruction in divine truth was so important that in the closing days of their wilderness wanderings God gave them what is known as the Shema, the remarkable basic educational pronouncement of Deuteronomy 6:4-9, including: "And these words, which I command thee this day, shall be in thine heart: and thou shalt teach them diligently unto thy children, and shalt talk of them when thou sittest in thine house, and when thou walkest by the way, and when thou liest down, and when thou risest up. And thou shalt bind them for a sign upon thine hand, and they shall be as frontlets between thine eyes. And thou shalt write them upon the posts of thy house, and on thy gates."

Through the temple rites on the great feast days, the synagogue with its reading and interpreting of the Scriptures, faithful instruction in the home, and emphasis upon teachers and teaching, the faith of Israel was preserved. Religious rites and symbolism were faithfully employed in the home instruction of children. In their great national feasts and the weekly observance of the Sabbath with its ritual in the home, the Hebrews were taught the meaning of sacred history in relation to life while concepts and habits of reverence and worship were being developed.

After the final destruction of the temple and the dispersion of the Jewish nation, remnants were held together in sentiment and understanding by the common continuous emphasis upon the Law, which came to be known as Torah. The time came when the body of Old Testament

---

Harold C. Mason, Ed.D., is an instructor of Christian Education at Grace Theological Seminary, Winona Lake, Indiana.

Scripture and commentaries and other written and spoken traditions and interpretations were included in Torah.[1]

The Jewish teacher, called rabbi during the exile, was honored as no other man. It is probable that synagogues arose during the period of the Babylonian captivity. These were places for instruction, and teaching was included in worship. Thus the homily or sermon in our day has its educational connotations similar to the expositions of the Scriptures in the synagogues, although teaching and preaching are to be distinguished. Each Sabbath morning the Shema, along with other portions of Scripture, was read in the synagogue. While the synagogue service proper was essentially for adults, there came to be elementary schools for children known as "the House of the Book," or *Beth Hassepher.*

## JESUS CHRIST THE TEACHER

Our Lord Jesus Christ came teaching. He not only preached to great multitudes, but also gave much time and attention to individuals and small groups. Since teachers were held in greatest esteem among the Jews, His teaching aroused profound interest.

In the Gospels Jesus is directly referred to as teacher thirty-one times. Five times He refers to Himself as a teacher. He is addressed as Rabbi and Rabboni fourteen times. He is spoken of many times as teaching, and what He said is referred to as His teachings. His followers were called disciples or pupils, and before His ascension He commissioned them to teach all nations.[2] He used a textbook, the Old Testament Scriptures, and said, "Learn of me."

His teaching methods were an incomparable example to His followers. He delivered messages in the open air, notably the Sermon on the Mount and the Olivet discourse; and He taught a select group on frequent occasions. He was a master in the use of the story method; numerous books are still written on the parables of Jesus. He was equally at home in dealing with a crowd or an individual. Among His famous dialogues were those with the Samaritan woman and Nicodemus. His disputations with His enemies were also used to teach divine truth; and His methods of meeting opposition are fruitful means of instruction for modern Christian workers. Our Lord used object lessons on numerous occasions with telling effect. Note, for instance, the lesson on humility taught by means of washing the disciples' feet. He was also an effective propagandizer in the best sense of the term. The three basic elements in propaganda which He utilized effectively were repetition, calling on a higher source of authority, and a clear indication of the activity He expected His followers to engage in.

[1]Lewis Joseph Sherrill, *The Rise of Christian Education* (New York: Macmillan Co., 1944), pp. 31-37.
[2]*Ibid.,* pp. 86, 87.

## CHRISTIAN EDUCATION IN THE FIRST CENTURIES
## OF THE CHURCH

For a time after our Lord's resurrection and ascension the early Christian church worshiped in Jewish synagogues. It is thought that after the synagogues closed to them and the followers of Christ worshiped in private homes, there may have been an afternoon service of teaching, as well as a morning worship service with preaching.[3] The sermons always included the *kerugma* or gospel, that Christ died, was buried, rose from the dead, and appeared unto His disciples. The preaching, or *kerugma*, was distinguished from teaching, or the *didache*. In teaching, the Old Testament Scriptures were interpreted, the content of the gospel was explained, and Christian doctrine was studied in its creedal form. The *Sayings of Jesus* and *The Two Ways*, the *Way of Life* and the *Way of Death*, were materials of instruction. There was a regular meeting of the early Christians known as the "meeting for the Word," in which a part of the service was known as "a teaching."[4] The apostles enjoined parents to instruct their children in the Scriptures and fundamental Christian doctrine.

In the ancient church the threats of false cults were met by teaching. The day came in A.D. 313 when Christianity was accepted by the state in an edict of Constantine granting freedom of worship. Emperor Theodosius in A.D. 381 made Christianity the state religion of the Roman empire. In A.D. 367 Athanasius formulated the canon, and in 397 this was officially recognized in a great church council, the church being the depositum of these revealed writings.

The invasion of barbarian peoples from the north brought chaos to the Roman world, but Christianity proved to be the saving salt of civilization. The invasion of the barbaric Germanic tribes began in the fifth century. The rise of monasteries provided refuge for many literate churchmen, and eventually the chaos accompanying the barbarian invasions was succeeded by medieval culture.

The ancient church, as early as the third century, had instituted and maintained a catechumenal system through which converts were prepared for Christian baptism in a three year course of instruction. Conversion and enlightenment went hand in hand. Catechetical schools arose to defend the gospel and to ground young scholars in the faith in cities where pagan learning and influence abounded. One of these great schools was at Alexandria in Egypt. There Clement and his pupil Origen became famous as Christian thinkers and teachers.

During the Dark Ages, which followed the barbarian invasions in

[3] Arlo Ayers Brown, *A History of Religious Education in Recent Times* (New York: Abingdon Press, 1923), p. 19.
[4] Lewis J. Sherrill, *op cit.*, p. 154.

the early centuries of the Christian era, illiteracy prevailed both among the common people and the clergy. The church resorted to the extensive use of symbols, pageantry, and dramatics to preserve some degree of intelligence in matters of religion.

In the eighth century A.D., Charlemagne of the Germanic empire, himself unable to read or write, brought to his court from England a young scholar by the name of Alcuin to teach the members and attendants of the royal palace. He also directed that abbots and bishops throughout the realm pursue learning, and decreed that schools be established.

Intelligent, eager young men drifted from city to city to sit at the feet of men who had become known as teachers. Groups of scholars assembled until thousands might be found in a single city, forming a student city within the civil metropolis. These migratory students organized themselves into "nations" modeled after the medieval guilds of tradesmen and artisans. The assemblages of students from far and near became known as *studium generale.* Eventually they developed into universities, such as the University of Paris, where the seven liberal arts composing the trivium (grammar, rhetoric, logic) and the quadrivium (arithmetic, geometry, astronomy, music) were taught. The supreme subject in the curriculum was theology, although medicine and law were also included.

The development of towns and guilds and the breaking down of feudalism meant the gradual increase of intellectual interest and hope. In the eleventh century the Papacy appealed to an increasingly restless population to rescue the holy sepulcher in Palestine from the domination of the Muslims. Serfs and peasants by the thousands volunteered for the launching of successive military drives to this end. The returning crusaders caught a glimpse of other lands and culture and were no longer content with the life of the serf, "who had no present because he had no past." Great Greek and Roman classics were being discovered among ancient manuscripts and faithfully studied. These events culminated in what is now known as the Renaissance or revival of learning.

## THE SUNDAY SCHOOL AS A PROTESTANT MOVEMENT

Out of the quickening of mind resulting in the growth of cities and the establishment of universities came the Protestant Reformation in the sixteenth century under the leadership of university professors and clergymen, such as Luther and Melanchthon, Zwingli, Calvin, and John Knox. The basic Reformation principle which crowned the revival of learning was that every person be able to read the Scripture in his own language, for his salvation and spiritual growth. Thus the religious basis for universal elementary education was projected. With the establishment of Protestant schools, the Roman Catholic Jesuit Society founded a system of Roman Catholic elementary schools as a Counter-Reformation movement.

In England, with motives differing from those of the Protestant leaders, the Episcopalian or Anglican church was established by King Henry VIII, with its continuation of certain of the hierarchical and aristocratic traditions of the Roman Catholic church, as distinguished from the Protestant emphasis upon universal literacy as a religious necessity.

During the Wesleyan Revival in the eighteenth century, a portion of the Anglican church accepted the title of "evangelicals" as a group within the church, the "Low Church Party" as distinguished from the highly sacerdotal element of the church. Among these evangelicals was a printer and publisher in Gloucester, England, by the name of Robert Raikes.[5] In 1780, touched by the plight of the children of the poor in Gloucester who were compelled to work in the mines six days a week from sunup to sundown with no opportunity to learn to read, he succeeded in bringing some of them into his home on Sundays to be taught to read. He employed four women teachers to work with the children. The school came to be known as the Sunday school and Raikes's example was soon widely publicized and followed.

John Wesley endorsed the Sunday school, as did many notables, including the Queen of England. The Anglican or established church opposed it as a violation of the Sabbath day and a means for the lower elements of society to become more intelligent, and thus more alert in their destructive practices.[6] Wesley favored the Sunday school as an instrument for teaching religion to the underprivileged with volunteer teachers.

## THE SUNDAY SCHOOL IN AMERICA

The first Sunday school in America was held at the home of William Elliott in Virginia, in 1785. Later the school was transferred to the Burton-Grove Methodist Church in Accomack County, Virginia. The American Sunday-School Union was organized in Philadelphia in 1824 as an outgrowth of more local and limited cooperational endeavors.

The Reformation principle of universal literacy had been brought to America by the Pilgrims in 1620. In the Puritan colonies of Plymouth and Massachusetts Bay the education of children was prescribed by ordinance, and public day schools began to appear in these colonies at an

[5]William Alva Gifford, The Story of the Faith (New York: Macmillan Co., 1946), p. 490.
[6]Arlo Ayers Brown, op. cit., p. 48.

early date. In these early schools much of the teaching was religious. As communities became heterogeneous religiously, however, the problem of sectarian teaching in the schools became acute, and the pluralistic religious situation complicated efforts to provide free public schools. With the establishment of the American public school system early in the nineteenth century, influences from naturalistic European sources affected the curriculum of elementary education. Also, the rise of industrialism put secular demands upon public education. With these influences and changes many new textbooks appeared in the public schools and the Bible was no longer taught in public, tax-supported schools.

So the Sunday school came to be solely a school of religion, or the Bible school, especially among churches which did not maintain parochial schools, whereas originally and at various times and places it was a school for the teaching of reading, with the Bible as textbook. In 1830 the American Sunday-School Union raised $30,000 to send Sunday school missionaries to the Ohio and Mississippi valleys to teach the children of the illiterate frontiersmen of the Midwest to read. These schools were held on Sunday as an implementation of the Protestant principle of universal literacy.

There was direct Bible study in the early Sunday schools. Catechisms, books of Scripture questions, hymnbooks and books containing prayers for memorization were made available to the children.

The Sunday school was largely a lay movement, free of denominational control or domination, but accepted by the denominations as a means of religious intelligence. The movement grew rapidly in America, as in the British Isles.

For many years there was no national or international Sunday school organization as such, the conventions serving as the uniting agencies. Early national Sunday school conventions were held in 1832, 1833 and 1859. The fourth national convention convened in Newark, New Jersey, in 1869, and the fifth national convention in Indianapolis in 1872.

At this latter convention, which was also attended by two delegates from the Dominion of Canada, an International Lesson Committee was appointed to prepare Sunday school lesson outlines for the United States and Canada, the lessons to be drawn from the Bible. This was accomplished over the opposition of certain denominational leaders who were less Biblically inclined and some who favored graded lessons instead of a uniform series.[7]

After 1872, international Sunday school conventions were held every three years until the convention in Chicago in 1914.[8] Meanwhile the

[7]Arlo Ayers Brown, op. cit.
[8]Clarence H. Benson, A Popular History of Christian Education (Chicago: Moody Press, 1943), pp. 188-195.

executive committee of the International Sunday School Convention was incorporated in 1907 as the International Sunday School Association. Marion Lawrance had been made the first general secretary of the International Sunday School Convention in 1899, and thereafter the convention maintained a staff of full-time workers. Many state and county conventions were organized prior to 1907. Among the leaders in the Sunday school movement in those days were John H. Vincent, Dwight L. Moody, H. C. Trumbull, Charles G. Trumbull, Frank Brown, W. C. Pearce, H. M. Hamill, B. F. Jacobs, Edward Eggleston, E. K. Warren, and H. J. Heinz.

The growth of the public school system with normal schools for the preparation of professional teachers heightened the interest of Sunday school leaders in the preparation of lay Sunday school teachers.

## CURRICULUM AND ORGANIZATION OF THE SUNDAY SCHOOL

Early in the history of the Sunday school movement interest in curriculum and organization was evident. The improvement of teaching received attention in the American Sunday-School Union. As early as 1847 the secretary of the Methodist Sunday School Union proposed the training of Sunday school teachers. John H. Vincent strongly advocated such training. At the turn of the century, teacher training courses were being offered. Eventually these courses were formed into series, such as the Leadership Training Series of the Division of Christian Education of the National Council of Churches and the Evangelical Teacher Training Series, instituted by Clarence H. Benson.

In 1874 a summer school for Sunday school teachers was opened at Lake Chautauqua, New York. Emphasis upon the grouping of pupils in age brackets and the arrangement of materials to fit the various groups was furthered by the increasing influence of secular innovators, such as the famed Swiss educator Pestalozzi.

Early Sunday schools consisted of four departments: infant, elementary, Scripture, and senior. Later there came to be three divisions and a number of departments within the divisions, such as the children's, youth's, and adult divisions, and the beginner, primary, junior, intermediate or junior high, senior, young people's, and adult departments. This arrangement now also takes account of the cradle roll, nursery and extension departments. The extension department not only includes those who compose the home department but also all members of the Sunday school who are forced to be absent over extended periods of time.

In the traditional plan of departmentalization, curriculum cycles include the nursery, ages 2-3; beginners, 4-5; primaries, 6-8; juniors, 9-11; intermediates, 12-14; seniors, 15-17. In many larger Sunday schools the public school plan of grading in yearly cycles is followed, and in other schools a two-year cycle is used, instead of a three-year cycle of departmentalization.

For many years a general Sunday school opening assembly was held for devotions, announcements, and special features. This gave rise to what is known as the "Akron" type of church architecture, with a large general assembly room bordered on the main floor by small classrooms or cells, with a balcony of similar rooms. This plan was superseded by the public school type of unit architecture with solid wall partitions dividing the rather large classrooms. Since these rooms were used for so short a time, the problem of utility, or proper investment of church funds, arose out of the rising costs of building construction and maintenance. There is now a return to the conservation of space by the multiple use of facilities and the carefully planned utilization of all available space for activities and instruction.

## THE BEGINNING OF SCHISM

Some denominations made early provision for Sunday school promotion and supervision. In certain denominational circles there developed objection to the Bible-centered curriculum, the evangelistic emphasis, and the lay leadership of the Sunday school movement. The impact of naturalism and rationalism upon Biblical studies in colleges and seminaries gave rise to a persistent protest against the traditional program of the Sunday school. By 1903 there had been organized in the United States what is known as the Religious Education Association, which included liberal Protestant and Jewish elements in its direction and control.

As early as 1908 the International Sunday School Association adopted resolutions at its convention in Louisville, Kentucky, providing for the establishment of an international graded lesson series. Many persons favoring the introduction of graded lessons desired that such lessons include extra-Biblical materials and topics. In 1910 the Sunday School Council of Evangelical Denominations was formed in which the leadership was largely of the clergy, many of them of a theologically liberal bent. By 1918 the educational philosophy of John Dewey and others, known as "progressive education," based on evolutionary naturalism with its emphasis upon "child-centeredness," entered the graded lesson controversy. At all times, however, there were advocates of orthodox graded lessons.

In 1914 the International Lesson Committee was enlarged to include eight members elected by the International Sunday School Association, eight members by the Sunday School Council of Evangelical Denominations, and one member by each denomination represented in the council. Finally, in 1918, steps were taken leading to the merging of the International Sunday School Association and the Sunday School Council of Evangelical Denominations. The new organization functioned for more than a quarter of a century under the name of the International Council of Religious Education.

When the Federal Council of Churches, organized in 1908, changed its name to the National Council of Christian Churches in 1950, the International Council of Religious Education became in effect a commission of the National Council of Christian Churches, changing its name to the Division of Christian Education of the National Council of Christian Churches.

The first world's Sunday school convention was held in London, England, in 1889. At intervals of a few years they have been held in various cities of the world. At the convention in Rome in 1907 the world convention formed the World Sunday School Association, which still functions as such, although in some quarters a change in name and relationships is considered desirable.

During the period from 1922 to 1944 the evangelical Sunday school found itself largely without leadership in the ecumenical sense. Under the auspices of the newly formed National Association of Evangelicals a meeting was held in Columbus, Ohio, in 1944, at which steps were taken toward the formation of an evangelical Sunday school association. In 1945, in Chicago, a temporary organization of the national Sunday school organization was effected. The founding convention of the permanent organization was held in Chicago in 1946. A lesson committee to provide uniform lesson outlines for the newly formed association had been set up by the temporary organization and was made permanent by the convention. The permanent lesson committee adopted the statement of belief of the National Association of Evangelicals. The committee included in its membership Dr. James D. Murch, Bishop Leslie B. Marston, Dr. Henrietta Mears, Dr. Harold C. Mason, Dr. Harry A. Ironside, Dr. H. H. Savage, Dr. R. C. McQuilkin, Rev. Stanley H. Frodsham, and Dr. R. H. Fritsch. Evangelical graded lessons, both denominational and interdenominational, are provided by evangelical publishers.

National and area conventions have been held by the National Sunday School Association across the nation. Various groups, such as the research section composed of professors of Christian education in Bible schools, colleges and seminaries, function within it. The official relation of the National Sunday School Association to the National Association of Evangelicals is through the latter's Church School Commission.

## EDUCATIONAL ACTIVITIES OTHER THAN THE SUNDAY SCHOOL

Other evangelical educational activities than the Sunday school have developed, such as the Christian day school movement based somewhat on the original parochial day school conception.

The daily vacation Bible school had its origin in various states, including Illinois, Wisconsin, and Pennsylvania, but took its place as a movement under the leadership of Dr. Robert G. Boville, superintendent of the Baptist City Mission Society in New York City. There a summer school with a program of Bible study, worship, and recreation was held on summer mornings for the poor children on the East Side. Today the various denominations include in their Christian education programs for the local church what is known as the vacation church school.

The young people's movement in America as distinguished from the Sunday school roots deeply in earlier youth activities, such as singing school, missionary societies, the Young Men's Christian Association, and the Young Women's Christian Association. Having read of the Young Men's Christian organization in the church of Dr. Theodore Cuyler, Dr. Francis E. Clark, pastor of the Williston Congregational Church of Portland, Maine, in 1861, organized the young people of his church into the first chapter of the United Society of Christian Endeavor. This plan of young people's organization was adopted by many denominations either as the United Society of Christian Endeavor, or with denominational names and maintaining strictly denominational relationships.

The type of youth organization now most prevalent is known as the Youth Fellowship, begun in 1936, in which the young people of the Sunday church school function throughout the week in expressional and recreational activities.

Groups for children in the junior or intermediate age brackets corresponding to Boy Scout and Girl Scout groups are becoming a significant part of denominational programs, with such names as Christian Youth Crusaders or Junior Missionary Society.

Another contemporary movement in religious education is the camping and summer conference movement. There are two generally recognized kinds of Christian education camps, the cabin and the dormitory types. The entire corps of full-time workers from kitchen to water front are known as counselors. Classes in Christian education are conducted throughout each camping session. Summer conferences have a somewhat less rustic or primitive setting than camps, being held on college campuses or in well-developed summer teaching centers, with well-known speakers and workers. Such institutions as the American Camping Association devote full time to the development of camping in all of its aspects.

The weekday church school program in religious education began as courses in the life of Christ offered by a pastor at Greeley, Colorado, and accepted as credit in the State Normal School there; and by W. A. Squires at the University of North Dakota, who offered Bible courses for credit in that institution. Several state systems offered credit for prescribed courses in Bible in the public schools. Those who objected to a Bible-centered approach to religious education opposed the development of these Bible courses for credit in public education[9] and succeeded in slowing down and stopping the movement. In its place was instituted the present weekday church school plan in which religious subjects are geared into the public school type of curriculum.

This weekday church school movement had its beginnings in Gary, Indiana, as early as 1913. The American educational innovator, Superintendent W. A. Wirt of the Gary Public School System, and Dr. W. A. Avann, pastor of the First Methodist Church of Gary, developed a plan whereby children were released from public school at certain periods of the day for classes in religion. The movement spread across the country in both city and county programs of released-time religious education for elementary school children.

In the celebrated Champaign case the Supreme Court of the United States decided that public moneys such as are devoted to plant upkeep, janitorial service, time of teachers, utilities, etc., could not be devoted to the teaching of religion in the public schools. This forced the consideration of the dismissed time plan, gained by closing school early one day a week instead of releasing pupils during school hours for weekday church school classes. This arrangement was upheld by the Supreme Court in the Zorach case. Considerable litigation and consequent uncertainty attend the development of the weekday church school movement.

In 1914 Walter S. Athearn proposed that all the educational agencies and activities of the local church be correlated under the name "the church school."[10] It became a matter of national policy on the part of the International Council (later the Division of Christian Education of the National Council) to use that term in describing the specifically educational aspects of the local church program.

Such contemporary movements as Youth for Christ and Youth in One Accord, with educational implications but primary emphasis upon mass evangelism in program and policy, are highly regarded by conservatives in religious education; but the several denominational programs of Christian education in the denominations are the generally accepted distinctively Christian education programs on the youth level.

[9]Arlo Ayers Brown, op. cit., p. 203.
[10]The Church School (Boston: Pilgrim Press, 1914).

## SECULARISM IN RELIGIOUS EDUCATION

The detractors of the Sunday school hold that the answer to the travesty upon education, which for them the Sunday school presents, is a thorough-going organic ecumenicity. Instead of a community employing five preachers, for example, it should employ one preacher and four teachers. The four full-time professional teachers would thus be able to put worth into the otherwise shabby and impossible church educational situation.

More and more higher institutions of learning are providing training for professional leaders in religious education, who in turn train laymen for effective educational service in the local church. The increasing number of departments of Christian education in Bible schools and evangelical colleges and seminaries is providing professionally trained leaders for even the smallest churches. These in turn teach Christian lay leaders to participate in the great program of universal Christian education.

### BIBLIOGRAPHY

Athearn, Walter S. *The Church School.* Boston: Pilgrim Press, 1914.

Benson, Clarence H. *A Popular History of Christian Education.* Chicago: Moody Press, 1943.

Boyd, William. *The History of Western Education.* London: Adam and Charles Black, 1950.

Bower, William Clayton, and Hayward, Percy Roy. *Protestantism Faces Its Educational Task Together.* Appleton, Wis.: C. C. Nelson Publishing Co., 1949.

Brown, Arlo Ayers. *A History of Religious Education in Recent Times.* New York: Abingdon Press, 1923.

Cubberley, Ellwood P. *A Brief History of Education.* New York: Houghton-Mifflin Co., 1922.

Gifford, William Alva. *The Story of the Faith.* New York: Macmillan Co., 1946.

Hardman, Oscar. *A History of Christian Worship.* Nashville: Cokesbury Press, 1937.

Nichols, James Hastings. *History of Christianity.* New York: Ronald Press Co., 1956.

Sherrill, Lewis Joseph. *The Rise of Christian Education.* New York: Macmillan Co., 1944.

Smith, H. Shelton. *Faith and Nurture.* New York: Charles Scribner's Sons, 1942.

*Chapter 3*

# TOWARD A PHILOSOPHY OF CHRISTIAN EDUCATION

## FRANK E. GAEBELEIN

THE WEALTH OF EDUCATIONAL MATERIAL contained in the Bible requires formulation. Just as Scripture presents no organized doctrinal system but rather the inspired data out of which theology is constructed, so with Christian education. The data are there in Scripture; the obligation is for us to derive from them a Christian view of teaching and learning. Ours is the religion of the Book, and nothing short of a philosophy centered in Biblical truth has a right to the name Christian.

But why, it may be asked, should we be concerned with formulating a Christian view of education? Why not simply go on using and teaching the Bible, regardless of this matter of a philosophy based upon it? After all, from time immemorial the Bible has had its place in education. In many schools and colleges today, including some that are downright secular, it is read and studied. Moreover, religious observances, such as chapel services and classroom devotional exercises, are part of the program in large numbers of schools.

There is, however, a vast difference between education in which devotional exercises and the study of Scripture have a place, and education in which the Christianity of the Bible is the matrix of the whole program or, to change the figure, the bed in which the river of teaching and learning flows. For without a Christian philosophy our Protestant education cannot but lack wholeness in God.

Editor's note: While this chapter may seem to be more academically oriented than church-school related, there is much presented here which may be applied to Christian education in the local church. Much of this chapter appeared (some of it in slightly different form) in the writer's Bauman Memorial Lectures for 1962 at Grace College and Theological Seminary, Winona Lake, Indiana, and is used by permission. Cf. *Grace Journal*, Fall, 1962.

Frank E. Gaebelein, Litt.D., D.D., LL.D., is coeditor of *Christianity Today*.

## THE SEARCH FOR MEANING IN EDUCATION

In relation to his educational theory in *The Republic*, Socrates says of the endeavor to find out the nature of justice: "Here is no path . . . and the wood is dark and perplexing; still we must push on."[1] Today, despite the vast accumulation of knowledge in every field, education included, the wood is still "dark and perplexing" to an extent undreamed of in Socrates' day. Nevertheless, we must "push on." Advances in teaching have been numerous; the history of education is the history of new and more effective procedures from the catechetical method of the early Christians through the trivium and quadrivium of the Middle Ages to the modern period beginning with Comenius and moving on through Rousseau, Pestalozzi, Herbart, and Froebel to James, Dewey, Kilpatrick, and Brameld, and reaching beyond these to the language laboratories and teaching machines of the present. Yet through it all the search for meaning has continued. And this search for an over-all frame of reference, for a view of man and his relation to God and the universe that has wholeness, is by its very nature philosophical.

In 1945, the Harvard Report, *General Education in a Free Society*, described the quest in these words: "Thus the search continues for some over-all logic, some strong, not easily broken frame within which both school and college may fulfill their at once diversifying and unifying tasks."[2] Earlier in the same chapter the authors acknowledge that "the conviction that Christianity gives meaning and ultimate unity to all parts of the curriculum"[3] was in the past general in America. But they dismiss this conviction with the statement that "religion is not now . . . a practicable source of intellectual unity."[4] Whereupon they turn to society for the source of a unifying educational philosophy. "It [the over-all logic] is evidently to be looked for in the character of American society . . . this logic must further embody certain intangibles of the American spirit . . . which is to say, belief in the worth and meaning of the human spirit, however one may understand it."[5]

This endeavor to derive the ultimate meaning of education from society, so clearly expressed in the above words, still characterizes secular educational philosophy whether in its life-adjustment, reconstructionist, or other leading contemporary aspects. But there is a fatal flaw in this turning to

[1]B. Jowett (ed.), *Collected Works of Plato* (New York: Greystone Press, n.d.), p. 94.
[2]*General Education in a Free Society* (Cambridge: Harvard University Press, 1945), p. 40.
[3]*Ibid.*, p. 39.
[4]*Ibid.*, p. 39. It is significant that the reason Christianity as the source of educational philosophy is so widely rejected today is not just because it is considered to be untrue, but because the separation of church and state makes its adoption inexpedient.
[5]*Ibid.*, p. 41.

society and to the human spirit for the complete frame of reference. Just as the physical organism must have nourishment from without, so the human spirit is not self-nourished. No soul ever finds sustenance from within itself. If humanity, whether individually or en masse, cannot lift itself by its bootstraps, no more can education. When it comes to the philosophy of education, the alternatives are the same as in the individual search in which man proceeds either upon the assumption that he can save himself, if indeed he needs saving at all, or that he must have a Saviour. The former is the way of secularistic naturalism; the latter that of supernaturalistic Christianity.

Now, it is against all naturalistic and secular philosophies that Christian education stands resolutely opposed. In his Bampton Lectures at Oxford for 1944, entitled *Christian Education*, Spencer Leeson, former headmaster of Winchester and late Bishop of Peterborough, has a chapter on Plato, whom he calls "the first thinker who ever speculated upon the ends and methods of true education; and he lifts us at once to the heights."[6] After an appreciative analysis of Plato's educational thought, he shows its inadequacy as measured against the Christian norm, concluding his critique with these words:

> Again and lastly Plato fails us, as the so-called philosophical religions must always fail us, because he does not satisfy the deepest needs and spiritual instincts of man. . . . We need a living Saviour, who will bring to our sinning souls not only a standard by which to judge ourselves, but a raising and purifying power from God Himself. Augustine summed the matter up in a sentence. The Platonists had taught him, he said, the same doctrine about the Word that he found in the opening verses of St. John's Gospel; but they did not go on to teach him, as St. John did, that the Word was made flesh.[7]

What Spencer Leeson says of Plato applies to all lesser philosophies, including the naturalistic views of our day. Despite their innovations in method and their plausibility, they too "fail us," as all purely human philosophies must in the long run fail, because they do not satisfy the deepest needs and instincts of man.

## THE BIBLICAL BASIS OF CHRISTIAN EDUCATION

Of philosophies of Christian education there has not been the dearth that some writers lament. Roman Catholicism has its Thomistic philosophy of education. The reformers—Luther, Calvin, and particularly Melanchthon,[8] who was in some respects the unsung pioneer of the com-

---

[6]*Christian Education* (London: Longmans, Green & Co., 1947), p. 30.
[7]*Ibid.*, pp. 49, 51.
[8]Clyde L. Manschreck, *Melanchthon, the Quiet Reformer* (New York: Abingdon Press, 1958), pp. 144 f.

mon school—were far from poor in educational theory. And behind both Romanist and Protestant thought there stands Augustine, who also dealt with education. As for modern American Protestantism, since the turn of the century there have been attempts at a philosophy of Christian education on the part of the Missouri Synod and other Lutherans, the Mennonites, the Seventh Day Adventists, the Christian Reformed Church, the Protestant Episcopalians, some of the liberal and neo-orthodox Protestants, and various conservative groups, such as the National Association of Evangelicals and its affiliate, the National Association of Christian Schools with its strenuous promotion of the Christian day school.

By and large, however, the weakness of these attempts at a Christian philosophy of education has been twofold: on the one hand, a parochialism of thought that sees only the distinctive views of the particular group; on the other hand, an eclecticism that would combine Christian philosophy with certain of the secularistic views. The result has been a fragmentization in Christian educational philosophy that has led to a variety of fairly restricted views with consequent neglect of a comprehensive Christian frame of reference. So Edwin H. Rian wrote in 1949: "At the present time there is no comprehensive Protestant philosophy of thought and life,"[9] while in 1957 he could open a published symposium, entitled *Toward a Christian Philosophy of Higher Education* with a chapter on "The Need: A World View."[10] And Perry D. Le Fevre of the University of Chicago in *The Christian Teacher* regrets the fact that "not many theologians have . . . addressed this problem" (the interpretation of the religious meaning of the teaching-learning process).[11] Moreover, Herbert W. Byrne, writing out of the Bible college movement, remarks in his volume, *A Christian Approach to Education:* "Little effort . . . has been made thus far to develop a real Bible philosophy of Christian education. The efforts that have been made may be described as Christian-secularism education."[12] This is an accurate comment, as is his further statement: "In other areas of Christian education the efforts at building a true bibliocentric curriculum have been few."[13]

The plain fact is that the same weakness afflicts most Protestant attempts at educational philosophy that mars Roman Catholic educational philosophy—a neglect of full reliance upon Scripture. And, let it be noted, this is true even of the theologically conservative groups; in doctrine they

[9]Edwin H. Rian, *Christianity and American Education* (San Antonio: Naylor Co., 1949), p. 235.

[10]J. P. von Gruenigen (ed.), *Toward a Christian Philosophy of Higher Education* (Philadelphia: Westminster Press, 1957).

[11]*The Christian Teacher* (New York: Abingdon Press, 1958), p. 147.

[12]*A Christian Approach to Education* (Grand Rapids: Zondervan Publishing House, 1961), p. 176.

[13]*Ibid.*, p. 177.

are thoroughly Biblical, but they have failed to see that the great truths of Scripture embrace even the so-called secular fields of knowledge. Despite their adherence to fundamental gospel truth, they have either not seen the unity of all truth in God or, recognizing this unity, have done little to make it a living reality throughout the whole of education. Thus much of evangelical educational thought has yet to move beyond a kind of scholastic schizophrenia in which a highly orthodox theology coexists uneasily with a teaching of non-religious subjects that differs little from that in secular institutions.

If Protestants in general and evangelicals in particular, in respect to a broad and deep Christian view of education, are yet in the "dark and perplexing" wood, the reason is that they are like a man who owns a mine full of valuable ore but who fails to work it because some lesser project has captured his interest.

The time then is ripe for us to work the mine. In a day of revival of Biblical theology, the climate is favorable for the construction of a view of education that, instead of being a patchwork of naturalistic ideas mixed with Biblical truth, will stand under the truth of the Word of God itself.

The relation between theology and a Christian philosophy of education is intimate. And the layman cannot escape it. As Dorothy Leach of the University of Florida says, "The educator is forced by the nature of his work to be in some measure a lay theologian."[14] It is this very closeness of theology to education that makes the construction of a single, over-all Protestant philosophy difficult. Theologies differ—and their differences are not trivial. For example, both the Reformed and Arminian systems are within the framework of Protestantism, yet their divergences are major. Likewise the variations between evangelical, neo-orthodox, and liberal thought are of prime significance.

Is there, then, a watershed, a continental divide, as it were, that separates a consistent Christian philosophy of education from all forms of eclecticism? The answer is a clear affirmative. The great divide is nothing less than the authority of the Bible and its acceptance as normative. To say it plainly, a thoroughly Christian view of education must not only be based upon Scripture; it must also stand under it. And the distinction is not insignificant. Someone said to Adolph Schlatter, the renowned New Testament scholar, that he had always wanted to meet a theologian who stood upon the Word of God. Schlatter thanked him and said: "I don't stand on the Word of God; I stand under it."[15] Sometimes basing a view upon the Bible may mean for the orthodox a rationalistic manipulation of the Bible to accord with his view. But for the view really to stand

[14]"Letters to Laymen," *Journal of the Christian Faith-and-Life Community* (February, 1961).
[15]Cf. E. Earle Ellis, *Paul's Use of the Old Testament* (Edinburgh: Oliver and Boyd, 1957), pp. 25, 26.

under the Word is for it to be seen as subordinate and in subjection to the Word.

In any case, a high view of Scripture is the essential watershed for the ultimate frame of reference. And what is a high view of Scripture? The reply is unequivocal; it is one that must accord with Christ's view of the Bible as the completely irrefragable and fully veracious Word of God. Theories of inspiration aside—and our Lord did not elaborate theories— He who said, "Till heaven and earth pass, one jot or one tittle shall in no wise pass from the law, till all be fulfilled" (Matt. 5:18), who declared at a crisis in His life on earth, "Scripture cannot be broken" (John 10:35), and who said in His most exalted prayer, "Thy word is truth" (John 17:17), used Scripture as the wholly reliable Word.

The thought may seem naive, yet we need to be reminded that the Biblical basis of a Christian philosophy of education is no arcanum, accessible only to the initiated. On the contrary, it is an open secret, available to all who will take the Bible seriously at Christ's valuation. Certain truths plainly set forth in Scripture constitute the framework of our Christian world view. The living God, Creator of all things, Source of all being, Sovereign of the universe; man created in the divine image, an image ruined through sin beyond human power to repair but not beyond God's power to regenerate; the incarnation of the Son of God and His atoning and renewing work through His death and resurrection; the activity of the Holy Spirit in the outcalling of Christ's Body, the Church; and the consummation of earthly history through the "glorious appearing of the great God and our Saviour Jesus Christ"—these are the spacious context of a Christian philosophy not only of education but also of any other area of human knowledge and concern. Nor is there anything sectarian or cultic about this framework; the truths comprising it are in the best sense ecumenical. Although they are and have been clouded by tradition and dogma or weakened by rationalistic concessions, such truths as these remain the essential frame of reference for a Christian world view.[16]

## KNOWING THE TRUTH IN CHRISTIAN EDUCATION

What, then, does it mean to build a philosophy of Christian education upon this basis? First of all, it means a realization of the far-reaching implications of these Biblical distinctives. If God is the Creator of all things, the living Sovereign of the universe, then naturalism is ruled out of our educational philosophy for good and all. If man is a fallen creature, then the sin that so easily besets him has radically distorted his life and thought. If Christ is the only Redeemer, then the distortion that

[16]For the gist of this paragraph, see Frank E. Gaebelein, *The Pattern of God's Truth* (New York: Oxford University Press, 1954), pp. 34, 35.

began with the fall can be corrected only by His truth, and education, along with all else, needs to be set right in Him. If Christ is really coming again, then even the greatest of human achievements must in humility be considered as subject to the judgment of the Coming One. Or to sum it up in a single principle, the God who in His Son is the Truth incarnate, the God whose revealed Word is truth, the God who does all things well, the God "unto whom all hearts are open, all desires known, and from whom no secrets are hid,"[17] the God who cannot lie, is the source and ground of all truth. Everything true is of Him. All truth, anywhere and of any kind, is His truth. For if, as Scripture affirms, God is the God of truth (Ps. 31:5), if His Son is the Lord of truth (John 14:6), if His Spirit is the Spirit of truth (John 14:16, 17), then the truth in its boundless dimensions, unknown and undiscovered as well as known and discovered, must be at once the context and the goal of our education. At the heart of a Christian philosophy of education there must be sound Biblical theology wedded to unremitting devotion to the truth and openness to it in every field of knowledge.

At this point, some critical thinking is required. How do we know the truth? Let us consider this epistemological question humbly and honestly. There are some—and they are in both camps theologically (liberal as well as conservative)—who are afraid of the truth. They suffer from a species of "aletheiophobia,"[18] to coin a word. When an evangelical is afraid of the truth, it may be because he has equated some particular human formulation with final truth. (This is not, however, to suggest that the great historic creeds based on Scripture are not actually true.) Therefore, when he sees some newly apprehended scientific truth, some breakthrough into wider knowledge as a threat to the system to which he is committed, he may react in fear and, sometimes, even in anger. But, as Socrates said, "No man should be angry at what is true."[19] To do so is to be angry at God.

On the other hand, those of more liberal persuasion theologically are prone to another kind of "aletheiophobia." Priding themselves upon their openness to everything new, they may see in old yet unwelcome truth a threat to their breadth of view. Theirs is not so much the fear of the expanding aspects of truth as it is the fear of the particularity of truth. But what if old truths that have been discarded as outmoded, mythological, or unhistorical suddenly come to life? Adjustment to truth cuts both ways. So the undoubted trend of archaeology corroborating the historicity of many a Biblical passage discarded as unreliable; the overthrow of critical strongholds like the Graf-Wellhausen theory of the

[17]*Book of Common Prayer.*
[18]Cf. "Some Corollaries of Biblical Scholarship," Frank E. Gaebelein, *Christianity Today*, May 11, 1962.
[19]B. Jowett (trans.), *The Republic* (New York: Greystone Press, n.d.), p. 137.

Pentateuch; the demolition of the idea of the perfectibility of man through new revelations of the depths of human sin; the return to the one basis of man's justification by God through the redeeming work of Christ—these are a few of the particular areas of truth with which liberalism must come to terms.

For *hubris* is not the sin of the ancients only. As Emile Cailliet has shown, man has an innate tendency to be a pseudo-maker.[20] And nowhere is this tendency more evident than in his pursuit of the truth. The blasphemy of secular, intellectual man is to think that, because he has reasoned out some of the truth, he has "made" or "originated" it. Against this Promethean impiety there must be opposed a Christian epistemology. For, despite the fullest and freest exercise of man's God-given powers of intelligence and reason, truth retains an ultimate revelational aspect. It is not something we make up; it is rather something that, in the most profound sense, "happens" to us. When we come to it, we find that it is already there. The history of science, as Cailliet points out, abounds with examples of the sudden unveiling of truth, as in the case of Newton and the apple or Poincaré's apprehension of a key mathematical concept while getting into his carriage.[21]

Should we not, therefore, take a further step and say that the "hunches" of the patient scientific researcher that lead to further grasp of the truth and the sudden intuitions of thinkers in other fields are not mere luck but are part of God's disclosure of truth[22] in His common grace?

Now if truth "happens" by way of revelation, then faith has its vital function in knowing the truth. Augustine put the relation of faith to knowledge thus: "*Nisi credederisti, non intellegisti*" ("Unless you believe, you will not come to know").[23] Anselm of Canterbury set down the same epistemological principle even more succinctly in these three words, "*Credo ut intelligam*" ("I believe that I might know").

The application to Christian education is plain. If all truth is of God, as indeed it is; if the disclosure of truth has its deep revelational basis, then the Christian teacher and the Christian student, provided they maintain a posture of humble faith, are standing on the very ground where truth may indeed "happen."

Lest someone confuse this principle of faith with irrational mysticism, let us turn to its application to education. But before doing so, it should

[20]*The Christian Approach to Culture* (New York: Abingdon Press, 1953), pp. 138 f., 146, 147.
[21]Emile Cailliet, *The Recovery of Purpose* (New York: Harper & Bros., 1959), p. 104.
[22]The Greek word for truth (*aletheia*) means literally "without a veil." Cf. Albert C. Outler, "Quid Est Veritas?" *Christian Century*, LXXVI (March 4, 1959), p. 258. Cf. also J. J. Von Allmen, *A Companion to the Bible* (New York: Oxford University Press, 1958), p. 430 f.
[23]Cf. E. Harris Harbison, *The Christian Scholar in the Age of Reformation* (New York: Charles Scribner's Sons, 1956), p. 14.

be plainly understood that nothing that has been said here of faith has been meant to decry the place of reason in apprehending truth. If the rational side of epistemology has not been elaborated, it is simply because it has been taken for granted as an essential, although not the sole, element in knowing. The application of the principle of "*Credo ut intelligam*" does not for a moment do away with the patient exercise of the mind in the ordinary discipline of learning. But it does mean that, as every experienced and discerning teacher knows, there enters into the learning process every now and then the sudden flash of illumination, when something of the truth really breaks through to the student.

What the psychologist might call the emergence of meaning is really the deeper epistemology of Christian education, of all education in fact, for insofar as any education is communicating truth, to that extent is it under the God of all truth. And let us also see that no teacher, above all no Christian teacher, is teaching to the full unless there are times when this intangible process of sudden illumination is happening to those under his instruction.

But what, it may be asked, of the daily round of teaching when nothing much seems to happen and when the moments surcharged with insight seem discouragingly absent? Is the faithful going-on in classroom routine mere humdrum routine and nothing more? Certainly not, provided a teacher's best efforts are being put forth as unto the Lord. The fact is that, although God does indeed reveal truth by way of the illuminating flash, He more generally uses at His appointed time truth that has been quietly and undramatically implanted. The truth of God, faithfully taught, often works by delayed action. At the appointed time, it will come to life.[24]

## DOING THE TRUTH IN CHRISTIAN EDUCATION

The title of this chapter, "Toward a Philosophy of Christian Education," reminds us of its limitations. So far we have been occupied chiefly with essential matters of background and principles. But we cannot close without exploring, if only briefly, the application of the central principle of Christian education that all truth is of God. John Bunyan's statement in *The Pilgrim's Progress*, "The soul of religion is the practical part," applies to Christian education of which Bunyan's allegory is in good part a picture. It is a key principle, too generally overlooked, that the Bible is not concerned with abstract truth; on the contrary, it always sees truth as related to life. "He that doeth truth," wrote John, "cometh to the light" (John 3:21).

Protestant Christian education has yet to realize the full import of John's words. Actually to "do truth" means a much more thoroughgoing

[24]Cf. "Religion and the Independent School," Frank E. Gaebelein, *Independent School Bulletin*, April, 1962.

integration of our education with God's truth than has yet been achieved. This is not to suggest that Christian education will ever have arrived, short of the millennium, at a perfect and unclouded practice of the truth. For surely in respect to a consistent doing of the truth in every corner of the educational program, we have far to go.

That this gap between theory and practice in Christian education is being honestly recognized is one of the hopeful signs of the times.

A recent book, *Christian Faith and the Liberal Arts*, explores step by step the integration of Christianity with the college curriculum in direct response to the charge made at a meeting of the Association of Lutheran College Faculties "that Lutheran colleges in America operated according to no distinctive Lutheran or even Christian philosophy of education, but had simply imitated secular patterns to which they had added church services, religion classes, and a religious atmosphere"[25]—a charge which might be leveled at most denominational schools and colleges.

Notable among attempts to effect greater correlation of Christian truth with the various fields of learning is the series of studies published under the auspices of the Hazen Foundation, although these reflect less of a direct Biblical orientation than a philosophical one. The National Union of Christian Schools, closely related to the parent-controlled schools of the Christian Reformed Church, has done effective work in God-centered education, even to the extent of the publication of textbooks based upon a consistent Calvinist position; while the National Association of Christian Schools has, under the stimulus of the writings and lectures of Dr. Mark Fakkema, also gone forward in the application in elementary and secondary schools of a God-centered curriculum. Likewise certain of the evangelical liberal arts colleges, such as Wheaton, Houghton, Westmont, and Gordon, have applied themselves to these problems through special faculty studies, as have the Bible institutes and Bible colleges also. But despite these hopeful efforts, all will agree that, while a promising beginning has been made, much more is yet to be done.

Therefore, we go on to consider in brief outline four main principles that must be more fully practiced if our education is to achieve effective integration with the truth of God.[26]

The first is that Christian education can be done only by Christian teachers. Because this principle is generally accepted by most evangelical schools and colleges, it need not detain us long. Let us simply be very sure that our teachers are Christians in depth, Christians whose faith reaches into their intellect, who are on guard against the persuasive

[25]Harold H. Ditmanson, Howard V. Hong, and Warren A. Quanbeck, *Christian Faith and the Liberal Arts* (Minneapolis: Augsburg Publishing House, 1960), Preface.
[26]For an elaboration of the first two principles, see Frank E. Gaebelein, *The Pattern of God's Truth* (New York: Oxford University Press, 1954), chap. 2.

secularism of present-day thought, and who are genuinely concerned in presenting their subjects as part of a Christian world view.

The second principle is that of the Bible as the very heart of the curriculum. For, as we have already seen, the road to the integration of every subject with the truth of God must take as its starting point the Word of God. Now, to teach the Bible as one among many subjects, even to require it of all students, is not enough. If no more than this is done, even with the best of intentions, the result may be a kind of isolationism of which the chapel at the Massachusetts Institute of Technology is an illustration. At this great engineering school, the chapel stands within a water-filled moat, an architectural device that, whatever its aesthetic effectiveness, expresses exactly the place that religion on a campus should not have. Far better to have the center of worship and spiritual activities in close relation with libraries, laboratories, and lecture halls than off by itself. So with the study of Bible. The moat must be drained; in new and living ways, the influence of Biblical truth, radiating from required classes in the Scriptures, must come alive in the so-called secular curriculum from mathematics to economics.

How this may be done is one of the challenging fields for research in Christian education. That it must be done is an imperative confronting every school and college determined to go all the way in the truth.

Considering the classroom in particular—and it must never be forgotten that the truth must also be done in extracurricular activities, in counseling and discipline, and in the administrator's office—there is a way in which a long stride may be made toward delivering the Bible from a place of isolation. That way is through the policy of assigning, whenever possible, some Bible teaching to teachers whose main work is in other fields or assigning to Bible teachers some work in so-called secular subjects. While such crossing over of departmental barriers is easier on the elementary or secondary levels, where study of the Bible is less specialized than in college, nevertheless it is not impossible in higher education, given the occasional teacher who combines competency in another discipline with deep knowledge of Scripture.

But the main attack upon the problem of integrating the whole curriculum under a Biblical world view is being made through the identification and development of correlations of Christian concepts with the subject matter in the various fields of study. Useful as this approach is, it has certain pitfalls, chief among them being that of a false integration through forced correlations that are not truly indigenous to the subject in question. Such lugging in of stilted correlations, even though motivated by Christian zeal, is liable to do more harm than good through giving the impression that integration of specific subjects with God's truth is a put-up job.

What may be needed is a more relaxed attack upon the problem and a clearer realization of the limits under which we are working. Here a suggestion of Emil Brunner[27] is useful. Speaking of the distortion brought into our thinking through sin, he sees it at its greatest in such areas as theology, philosophy, and literature, because these are nearest man's relation to God and have thus been most radically altered through the fall. They therefore stand most in need of correction, and in them correlation with Christianity is at its highest. But as we move from the humanities to the sciences and mathematics, the disturbance through sin diminishes almost to the vanishing point. Thus the Christian teacher of the more objective subjects, mathematics in particular, ought not to seek for the detailed and systematic correlations that his colleagues in psychology, literature, or history might validly make.

But there is a third and broader principle whereby education may be integrated with a Christian world view. And that is through excellence.[28] In a day when the aims and purpose of education are under searching scrutiny, the pursuit of excellence in schools and colleges has become a shining goal. One of the encouraging trends in present-day education is a growing intolerance of the slipshod and mediocre, a tightening of the reins in demands being made upon teacher as well as pupil.

This trend has its implications for Christian education, which is above all obligated to excellence. It was Jonathan Edwards, the greatest of American philosophers, who said: "God is the head of the universal system of existence from whom all is perfectly derived and on whom all is most absolutely dependent, whose Being and Beauty is the sum and comprehension of all existence and excellence."

When a teacher or a pupil, a department of study or a whole school achieves some real measure of excellence, then integration with the truth of God is well on the way. There is a clear equation between excellence and truth. Nothing false, shoddy, or vulgar is really true. Only the first-rate is worthy of companionship with God's truth. Therefore, standards of excellence are of fundamental importance for Christian education.

But a caution in the form of a fourth principle must at once be voiced, lest the concept of truth through excellence be too narrowly interpreted. Christian education along with secular education too readily confines excellence only to the higher levels of academic achievement and limits it to the more gifted students. In doing so, it may forget that Christian education, broadly considered, must be democratic in a Scriptural sense.

---

[27]Cf. Emile Cailliet, op. cit., p. 101.
[28]For a fuller discussion of the obligation of Christian education to excellence see "The Christian's Intellectual Life," Frank E. Gaebelein, Christianity Today, May 8, 1961, and "The Obligation of Excellence in Christian Education," by the same writer, Gordon Review, Winter, 1962.

The danger of the pursuit of excellence in education lies in narrowing opportunity only to the more able of our youth at the risk of a snobbery that looks down upon those who are less gifted. On this point Spencer Leeson speaks incisively:

> But to the Christian all souls are God's. No true Christian may feel contempt for anybody, and the pride of superior intelligence is as dangerous to its possessor as any form of that most deadly sin. . . . The fundamental principle for the Christian . . . is that all men and women . . . are of equal value in the sight of God and are therefore entitled to equal respect from all other men and women. Our Lord died for them all, the divinely appointed means of grace are open to them all. . . . A Christian community . . . will train its artisans and clerks and laborers as carefully as it trains its doctors and lawyers and priests. . . . And the gravest of its responsibilities will be to provide that all its children shall be taught the faith . . . so that all of them may become children of their Father in heaven.[29]

The position so well advocated rests on firm Biblical ground. In addition to Ezekiel 18:4, "All souls are mine," to which Dr. Leeson alludes, there come to mind certain of Paul's words, notably Acts 17:25-28: "He giveth to all life . . . and hath made of one blood all nations of men . . . for in him we live, and move, and have our being"; and Colossians 3:11: "There is neither Greek nor Jew, circumcision nor uncircumcision, Barbarian, Scythian, bond nor free: but Christ is all, and in all."

## BIBLIOGRAPHY

Byrne, Herbert W. *A Christian Approach to Education.* Grand Rapids: Zondervan Publishing House, 1961.

Cailliet, Emile. *The Christian Approach to Culture.* New York: Abingdon Press, 1953.

———. *The Recovery of Purpose.* New York: Harper & Bros., 1959.

Ditmanson, Harold H., Hong, Howard Y., Quanbeck, Warren A. *Christian Faith and the Liberal Arts.* Minneapolis: Augsburg Publishing House, 1960.

Ellis, E. Earle. *Paul's Use of the Old Testament.* Edinburgh: Oliver and Boyd, 1957.

Gaebelein, Frank E. *The Pattern of God's Truth.* New York: Oxford University Press, 1954.

*General Education in a Free Society.* Cambridge: Harvard University Press, 1945.

Harbison, E. Harris. *The Christian Scholar in the Age of Reformation.* New York: Charles Scribner's Sons, 1956.

[29]Spencer Leeson, *op. cit.,* pp. 45, 46.

Jowett, B. (ed.). *Collected Works of Plato*. New York: Greystone Press, n.d.

Leach, Dorothy. "Letters to Laymen," *Journal of the Christian Faith-and-Life Community* (February, 1961).

Leeson, Spencer. *Christian Education*. London: Longmans, Green & Co., 1947.

Le Fevre, Perry D. *The Christian Teacher*. New York: Abingdon Press, 1958.

Manschreck, Clyde L. *Melanchthon, the Quiet Reformer*. New York: Abingdon Press, 1958.

Outler, Albert C. "Quid Est Veritas?" *Christian Century*, LXXVI (March 4, 1959).

Rian, Edwin H. *Christianity and American Education*. San Antonio: Naylor Co., 1949.

Von Allmen, J. J. *A Companion to the Bible*. New York: Oxford University Press, 1958.

Von Gruenigen, J. P. (ed.). *Toward a Christian Philosophy of Higher Education*. Philadelphia: Westminster Press, 1957.

### FOR FURTHER READING

Ferré, Nels. *Christian Faith and Higher Education*. New York: Harper & Bros., 1954.

Fuller, Edmund (ed.). *The Christian Idea of Education*. New Haven: Yale University Press, 1957.

Gaebelein, Frank E. *Christian Education in a Democracy*. New York: Oxford University Press, 1951.

Gaebelein, Frank E., Robinson, Earl G., Jr., Swing, William L. (eds.). *Education for Decision*. New York: Seabury Press, 1963.

Ginzberg, Eli (ed.). *The Nation's Children* (3 vols.). New York: Columbia University Press, 1960.

Jaarsma, Cornelius. *Fundamentals in Christian Education*. Grand Rapids: Wm. B. Eerdmans Publishing Co., 1953.

Livingstone, Sir Richard. *On Education*. New York: Macmillan Co., 1945.

Smart, James D. *The Teaching Ministry of the Church*. Philadelphia: Westminster Press, 1954.

Strachan, Malcolm, and Beardslee, Alvord (eds.). *The Christian Faith and Youth Today*. Greenwich, Conn.: Seabury Press, 1957.

Trueblood, Elton. *The Idea of a College*. New York: Harper & Bros., 1959.

Whitehead, Alfred North. *The Aims of Education*. New York: Mentor Books, 1948.

*Chapter 4*

# AIMS AND OBJECTIVES OF CHRISTIAN EDUCATION

## C. B. EAVEY

M EANINGS AND VALUES are basic to aims. This is equivalent to saying that philosophy determines aims, for philosophy is the critical work of the mind of man dealing with facts and therefrom developing meanings, making choices, and deciding values.[1] Accordingly, whatever aims, objectives, goals, or purposes one has for Christian education, they are the outcome of one's philosophy of Christian education.[2] Everyone has such a philosophy because it is impossible to know even a little in any area and not develop—perhaps quite inarticulately—some sort of philosophy concerning it. And one's philosophy is influenced by his theology.

Therefore a correct conception of the nature of Christianity is essential to the formulation of right aims in Christian education. Usually in a phrase like "Christian education" the noun is the key word, but in this case the adjective is of greater importance.[3] Christian education has no existence in its own right; it is wholly dependent upon Christianity and exists solely for the sake of Christianity.

And Christianity is not just one among a number of religions. It is more than a mere religion. A religion is any system of faith in and worship of a supreme being, or a god or gods. Christianity is this, but it is also much more than this. Comparison of its Founder with the founders of other

[1]Robert L. Cooke, *Philosophy, Education and Certainty* (Grand Rapids: Zondervan Publishing House, 1940), p. 45.
[2]Paul H. Vieth, *Objectives in Religious Education* (New York: Harper & Bros., 1930), p. 45.
[3]Frank E. Gaebelein, *Christian Education in a Democracy* (New York: Oxford University Press, 1951), pp. 13 f.

C. B. Eavey, Ph.D., now retired, was formerly professor of Christian Education at Wheaton College, Wheaton, Illinois.

systems of worship proves Him to be much more than they; He is divine, not human. He who lived on earth as man was God in the flesh. And God is not just "a supreme being, or a god" among gods; He is the absolute, personal Spirit, dependent upon Himself alone, and the source of all that is.

Christianity is Christ, a Person, the eternal Son of God, who not only has the life of God in Himself, but who is also the Source of this life in all who are redeemed through faith in His atoning work.[4] Being the manifestation of God to man, He is the center of the philosophy of Christian education, for He is the reality wherein men find the meanings and the values they seek.

There is a vast difference between Christianity as it is and Christianity as it is practiced, even in some circles called Christian. Actually, Christianity is the life of God in the soul; Christianity as practiced is often an imitation of the genuine—a product of corrupted views of men tinctured with some of the symbols of Christianity.[5] There are educators who take this faulty Christian practice and further dilute it to suit their human thinking. As a consequence, much of what is called Christian education is not at all a fruit of genuine Christianity.

Numerous and very diverse philosophies of education have been developed. However, all can be divided into two classes: those that make man their center and those that center in God.[6] Along with the entrance of sin into the life of man, there began to run through human history two ways of thinking.[7] The former was the way of man in reaction against God, the way of self-will, of man proud that he knows and can do so much. The latter was the way of total dependence upon God, the way of wholehearted submission to His will, the way of man humble in the recognition that in God alone are knowledge and wisdom and redemption. There is that in the nature of every human being, however holy and Christlike he may be, which can succumb to the effect of the former, even without his being aware of its influence.

Eve was but the first of a long line of human beings who, setting their own thinking over against the revealed will of God, became enamored with the deceitful beauty of knowledge originating solely in human capacity for reason and insight. Through the centuries the principle of the creativity of human thought has held sway among men, being present often in their thinking on the subject of education. The

[4]Ibid., p. 25.
[5]Edwin Wilbur Rice, The Sunday-School Movement and the American Sunday-School Union (Philadelphia: Union Press, 1917), p. 410.
[6]Edwin H. Rian, Christianity and American Education (San Antonio, Texas: Naylor Co., 1949), p. 66.
[7]Erich Sauer, The Dawn of World Redemption (Grand Rapids: Wm. B. Eerdmans Publishing Co., 1951), p. 63.

philosophy founded upon this thinking assumes an indefinite number of forms, but all agree in their emphasis upon the sufficiency of man to cope with his own problems and to live his own life. Always, as it was in the beginning, there is conflict between the two ways of thinking, the man-centered and the God-centered. Every person's philosophy of education, whether it be considered Christian or not, has for its center either man's ideas or God's revealed truth.

The way of man is not in himself; the finite does not have sufficiency in itself; the goodness of man does not extend to God. Without God, man's experience and life are meaningless; apart from God he can perceive no true values. With all their ability to think and reason, men cannot by intellectual seeking come to know God. The meanings and the values of life are rooted in revelation. True Christian education is education that centers in God, not in man. It is education that begins with God and is carried on under the direction of God. He who created man and who loves man in spite of his waywardness and sin has never ceased to work in and for and through man, education-wise as otherwise.

## PHILOSOPHY OF CHRISTIAN EDUCATION AND PURPOSE

True Christian education is not something of interest to a few people engaged in a particular movement or belonging to some organization.[8] No single group of people have a monopoly upon Christian truth. The term "Christian" is rightfully applied to any and every person, church, denomination, organization, institution, and movement that is true to the plain, simple teachings of the Bible. The doctrines enunciated originally by the majority of Protestant churches are in accord with such teachings. All who today accept these doctrines probably agree that the aims of Christian education rest upon meanings and values such as the following:

God is the Creator and the Sustainer of the universe which shows forth His handiwork; God, a personal and moral Being, created man as a personal and moral being in His own image, responsible to God for his conduct, so the fear of the Lord is the beginning of knowledge and wisdom; in Adam man sinned, so all men are sinners by nature and in deed, under the wrath of God and the condemnation of eternal death; God in infinite love provided in Christ, His own Son, salvation for all who by simple faith accept the righteousness thus made available; the Bible is God's revelation of Himself and His will given men that they may become alive in Him through Christ by the power of the Holy Spirit; upon those who have come to know God rests the responsibility of making known to others the grace of God that they also may, by the Holy Spirit, come to experience

[8]Gaebelein, op. cit., p. 14.

God through faith in Christ;[9] every human being is a never-dying spirit who, through the teaching of the Word of God, may be born into the kingdom of God; it is the concern of Christianity that all men be prepared for living in this world as God would have them live and afterward live eternally with Him in heaven; the end result of true Christian education is individuals rightly related to God, to themselves, and to others, mature persons, obedient to God in all things, who bear the fruit of the Spirit.

It is in God and in His Son that the life of man has meaning; it is interpretations of facts in the light of the revelation of God that gives man a sense of true values. This necessitates the relating of all of life to God so that it may be lived in fellowship with Him to His glory. True education keeps paramount this relationship, seeking to bring all of man's experience under the control of God.[10] That is to say, education deals with persons who are essentially and fundamentally spirits, and it deals with them for the spiritual purpose of preparing them to live with God, the Father of all spirits.[11]

Whitehead says, "The essence of education is that it be religious."[12] Though fallen, man is still definitely tied, in every aspect of life and experience, to the reality and the knowledge of his origin. Knowledge comes from God; man, though capable of much and though proudly lifted up by reason of what he is capable, actually knows nothing of himself. It is in God that he lives and moves and has his being. The Bible, though it makes no claim to being the total of all knowledge, definitely is the basis of all reality.[13] Education is an essential part of the dealing of God with man. Therefore, education, in the ultimate sense of the word, must be Christian education.

Nothing exists for itself alone; everything that is serves some purpose beyond itself. Contrary to Dewey, the educational process does have an end not contained in itself; its continual reorganizing and reconstructing are not "its own end."[14] Since God is the source of all truth and reality[15] and since education therefore is inescapably Christian, its purpose must be Christian. That is, its purpose is inherent in Christianity, God's revela-

[9]Wesner Fallaw, Church Education for Tomorrow (Philadelphia: Westminster Press, 1960), pp. 38-52.
[10]Cornelius Jaarsma, Fundamentals in Christian Education (Grand Rapids: Wm. B. Eerdmans Publishing Co., 1953), p. 444.
[11]H. F. Cope, Religious Education in the Church (New York: Charles Scribner's Sons, 1918), p. 35.
[12]Alfred North Whitehead, The Aims of Education (New York: Macmillan Co., 1929), p. 26.
[13]Rousas J. Rushdoony, Intellectual Schizophrenia (Grand Rapids: Baker Book House, 1961), p. 18.
[14]John Dewey, Democracy and Education (New York: Macmillan Co., 1924), p. 60.
[15]H. W. Byrne, A Christian Approach to Education (Grand Rapids: Zondervan Publishing House, 1961), p. 105.

tion of His will given man in the Bible. God gave man this revelation that each individual to whom it is made known may live as he was created to live and become what his Creator intended him to be. The sole purpose of true Christian education is one with the sole purpose of man's life, namely, that man may become like God.[16]

## THE RELATION OF PURPOSE TO AIMS

With its purpose single and clear, Christian education is ready to develop aims for achieving that purpose. Aims are absolutely necessary, for education carried on at random is useless. Christian education must have aims; it is to no avail that it aim at nothing even if that be hit with accuracy. To shoot into the air with no thought as to where the landing ought to take place is folly. Success is not always certain but never should work be done aimlessly.[17]

The purpose of man's life and education is of too great significance for Christian education to ignore aims, to be satisfied with low aims, or to carry on with indefinite aims. Only as its work is done with right aims will that purpose be realized. It is not sufficient that there be results, however satisfying these may be, if the purpose is not achieved. What must be done is to set conditions that will bring about the operation of the grace of God in the heart and in the life of the pupil, transforming him into the likeness of God.

In Christian education, as elsewhere, there are goals within goals. As lesser goals are attained one after the other, the large inclusive goal is ultimately reached. This final goal, or purpose, must always be kept clearly in mind, and everything that is done, whether it is great or small, must contribute in some way to its attainment.

## THE NATURE OF AIM

An aim is attention brought to focus to make possible expenditure of energy for achieving a predetermined purpose. An aim implies activity directed in an intelligent and orderly manner toward the realization of some end.[18] To aim is to see beforehand what is to be done and then so to concentrate attention as to direct energy to accomplish what is in mind. From the nature of aim it is obvious that aim permeates every aspect of the program of Christian education. Without aims it is impossible to determine what should be taught, how it ought to be taught, or the outcomes to be sought from teaching. When it is not mere beating of the

[16]C. B. Eavey, *The Art of Effective Teaching* (Grand Rapids: Zondervan Publishing House, 1953), p. 14.
[17]Peter P. Person, *An Introduction to Christian Education* (Grand Rapids: Baker Book House, 1958), p. 68.
[18]C. B. Eavey, *Principles of Teaching for Christian Teachers* (Grand Rapids: Zondervan Publishing House, 1940), pp. 42 ff.

air, Christian education starts with aim, proceeds on its way with aim, and ends with aim.

The more complex the process, the more are aims, great and small, intermingled. Each step or stage in such a process grows out of the preceding one and is a link in an unbroken chain of steps leading to the achieving of the ultimate goal or purpose. For each single step of a properly ordered course of procedure there must be a clear and definite aim.

The purpose and the goal of true Christian education is the man of God perfected in character and conduct until he is like Christ. Under this ultimate purpose fall certain aims and within these are other aims. Each lesson, each class session, must have an aim and always there are still further aims for meeting the needs of individual pupils. In other words, aims are immediate steps taken one after the other in class sessions toward goals which keep the teacher and the pupil moving on the way to achievement of the final goal or purpose.[19]

The educational process may be likened to the climbing of successive flights of stairs to reach the top of a building. To arrive at this destination is the ultimate, or final, goal, but it can be attained only as the first, second, and perhaps other flights of stairs have been ascended. Moreover, ascending in the normal manner necessitates the climbing of each step in any given flight.

This means that aims are both general, or comprehensive, and specific.[20] Chave expresses the commonly agreed distinction between the two: "Some objectives are general and only indicate the direction one may choose to go, while others are specific and describe both the immediate and ultimate goals."[21] To illustrate, keeping in mind the analogy of climbing flights of stairs to get to the top of a building, it could be said that the development of a kindly spirit is one level or stage to come to for transformation into likeness to God. This level, or general aim, is reached as a number of lessons are so learned that they are reduced to practice in performing deeds of kindness. As one step after another is climbed—as the specific aim of one lesson after another is reached in life and in practice—the level of a kindly spirit—the achievement of a general aim—is realized. Then, as the development of other general aims, such as love, purity, holiness, etc. proceeds apace, likeness to God, in so far as this is produced educationally, is the ultimate outcome. Such is an attempt to explain a very complex process.

As Chave's statement suggests, there is no sharp line of demarcation

19Fallaw, op. cit., p. 146.
20Vieth, op. cit., p. 32.
21Ernest J. Chave, Supervision of Religious Education (Chicago: University of Chicago Press, 1931), p. 46.

between general and specific aims. Like all analogies, that of climbing flights of stairs as descriptive of the educational process breaks down at certain points. Specific aims have a way of becoming more general, and general ones may become more specific; the two are then so closely related that they are practically indistinguishable each from the other. Neither is to be preferred above the other; only as the two are taken together is it possible to think accurately about the process of Christian education. Always, however, the general aims must be developed before anything can be done right with respect to the specific.[22] One must have a flight of stairs if he would install steps.

## FUNCTIONS OF AIMS

General aims have functional value. It is for this reason that they are so essential. Vieth presents these as the functions of objectives: (1) to give direction to the processes through which desirable changes are to be realized; (2) to give proper sequence to educational activities; (3) to serve as guides to activity through which desirable changes may be produced; (4) to guide in the selection of content to be taught; (5) to serve as means for evaluating the effectiveness of the educational process.[23]

Speaking generally, aims give direction to all activity involved in the educational process. In addition to the above functions it may be said that aims motivate and stimulate learners. It is not necessary to tell pupils what the aim is, but the fruits of experience borne as a result of the presence of right aim soon become evident to all involved in the educational enterprise. Right aim is also a source of inspiration to the teacher, for it brings a sense of destiny and a challenge to persevere when the going is difficult.[24] Finally, satisfactory aim saves from harm, for education carried on aimlessly or with bad aim is dangerous. When the blind lead the blind, both may come to disaster.

## THE HISTORY OF AIMS IN CHRISTIAN EDUCATION

Our Lord's last command, "Go . . . and teach," made Christian education mandatory. Implicit in His command are three aims: to teach that men may be brought into fellowship with God; to teach that those brought into such fellowship may be built up in God; to teach that those thus brought into fellowship and thus built up may become teachers of others. In His command our Lord made every Christian a teacher as the means for continuing among men the nurturing of the life of God He had begun.

The apostles were obedient to the command. They taught everywhere

[22]Vieth, op. cit., p. 34.
[23]Ibid., pp. 20, 21.
[24]S. L. Roberts, Teaching in the Church School (Philadelphia: Judson Press, 1927), pp. 40-44.

they could, using every possible occasion to make known in public and in private the truth they had received from the Lord. Empowered and led by the Spirit, their first aim was to bring men through repentance of sin to salvation by faith in Christ, and their second aim, to nurture believers unto godliness in character and life. These two aims prevailed during the early centuries of the history of the church. Leaders taught catechumens the truths of the gospel for three years before admitting them to church membership.

Then for ten or twelve centuries, from Constantine to the Reformation, the chief aim was the ecclesiastical one. The people were neglected while those destined for the priesthood were trained with the purpose of perpetuating the church and enhancing its glory. Though there were among the many a few who stood for God instead of church, the interests of the church were in general held to be paramount.

The Reformation made education for all a necessity and brought about a change in aim. The Bible, often through creeds and catechisms, became the basis of instruction, and the aim was to know doctrine and the Bible. True, this aim did not always exist for itself; often knowledge of the Bible was conceived to be only a means for achieving a higher aim, namely, to bring men to God through Christ. The coming of the Sunday school made more important the aim of evangelization, especially after the modern missionary movements began.[25]

With the impact of general education upon religious education in the latter part of the nineteenth and the early decades of the twentieth centuries, the validity of the knowledge aim began to be called into question. The outcome of the conclusions expressed on the subject of aims led to the publication in 1930 of Paul H. Vieth's well-known statement of the objectives of religious education.

These seven deal with a consciousness of God and a sense of personal relationship to Him, an understanding of Christ, the development of Christlike character, the building of a good social order, the formulating of a life philosophy on a basis of Christian meanings, participation in the church, and the use of religious racial experience for personal guidance.[26] This list of objectives has been used for the past thirty years by most Protestant agencies; the only change in it was the addition in 1940 of an eighth objective on appreciation of the meaning and importance of the Christian family.[27]

Through these years work has been carried on in connection with determination of the objectives for the various age groups. Modifications of

[25]J. M. Price, et al., Introduction to Religious Education (New York: Macmillan Co., 1932), pp. 24, 25.
[26]Vieth, op. cit., pp. 80-88.
[27]Marvin J. Taylor (ed.), Religious Education, a Comprehensive Survey (New York: Abingdon Press, 1960), p. 71.

Vieth's objectives have been made with a view to adapting them to the requirements of curriculum makers. Rearrangements and various combinations have been found necessary; sometimes rewording of the original statements had to be made. Some Protestant groups have taken these objectives as a starting point for formulating statements of aims in accord with their particular interpretations.[28]

In 1952 the Commission on General Christian Education of the National Council appointed a special committee to study objectives. After working five years this committee submitted its report in the form of a study document, recommending that this be made the basis for continuing work on objectives.[29]

In its statement of objectives the committee gives as the supreme purpose of Christian education the bringing of individuals to awareness of and response in faith to the love of God. For achieving this purpose it sets forth five aims: to assist persons to realize their highest potentialities as beings created by God and to become mature Christians; to help individuals in their social relationships, leading them to recognize that all human beings are loved by God; to aid persons to gain a good understanding and awareness of the natural world, the creation of God, and to use it in the service of God and of man; to lead persons to an increasing knowledge of the Bible, inculcating obedience thereto, and to help them use well other elements in the heritage of Christianity; to enable persons to see and to fill helpful roles in home and foreign missionary activity of the church.[30]

Few evangelicals, either individually or collectively, have ventured to state aims for Christian education. Some, such as Murch and Schultz, have stated an over-all purpose. The former says this is to fit "men to live in perfect harmony with the will of God,"[31] and the latter says: "Thinking the thoughts of God was and should be the great educational objective."[32] In *Christian Education in a Democracy*, a book published under the sponsorship of the National Association of Evangelicals, Gaebelein says that Christian education "must recognize a twofold objective: seeing clearly the primary necessity for leading youth first of all to personal commitment to Christ, it must at the same time accept the responsibility for the nurture of those who are already committed."[33]

Sherrill lists eight general goals that most evangelicals would likely find

[28]*Ibid.*, p. 74.
[29]*The Objectives of Christian Education: A Study Document* (New York: Commission on General Christian Education, National Council of the Churches of Christ in the U.S.A.), p. 6.
[30]*Ibid.*
[31]James DeForest Murch, *Christian Education and the Local Church* (Cincinnati: Standard Publishing Co., 1943), p. 128.
[32]Jaarsma, *op. cit.*, p. 179.
[33]Gaebelein, *op. cit.*, p. 30.

acceptable. These deal with knowledge and love of the Bible and making it the guide for daily living along with proper appreciation of extrabiblical materials; fellowship with God; salvation through Christ and Christian conduct out of love for Him; the Holy Spirit and His power to bring to Christlikeness; the ideal of the fatherhood of God and the brotherhood of man as the basis for right Christian attitudes in all social relationships; the church and its nurturing by means of fellowship; evangelistic and missionary responsibility in the light of the Great Commission; and a Christian interpretation of life with acceptance of and conscious effort to carry out God's plans for life.[34]

## THE AIMS OF CHRISTIAN EDUCATION

Christian education is an aspect of the plan of redemption God is carrying out through the ages. Whatever is of man—kingdoms and empires, civilizations and cultures, philosophies and programs—have their day and cease to be. God is Lord of all. His kingdom is an everlasting kingdom, stretching from eternity to eternity. Time is but a little span between two eternities. God is above time and overrules the events of time. Therefore, God alone can explain the meaning of these events.[35]

He explains this by revelation, of which the Bible is the record. God reveals Himself and His plan in words. He reveals Himself also in His Son, the personal Word of whom the written Word testifies. The Bible is inspired by the Holy Spirit. It is a living book, not merely a written word but a spiritually living word, not just cold print but the message of the Spirit of God to the heart.

God's Son, the personal Word of whom the written Word testifies, is the Person by whom, through the operation of the Spirit who inspired the written Word, men come into fellowship with God. Those in such fellowship are used of God to bring to other individuals the revelation of Himself. All men are created for fellowship with God. The function of Christian education is to mediate to men God's plan of redemption revealed in Christ that it may become operative in souls. That is, Christian education is essentially spiritual. Whatever other aims it has, spiritual aims are both basic and ascendant. It can, and should, use the best of methods and employ every worthwhile technique to achieve for each pupil the mediating of God's grace and his nurture in grace, but its aims are always spiritual aims.[36]

All mediating and all nurturing has to be done in and through the fellowship of those who have been redeemed by faith in Christ. Those who

[34]Lewis J. Sherrill, *Lift Up Your Eyes* (Richmond: John Knox, 1949), pp. 100, 101.
[35]Erich Sauer, *From Eternity to Eternity* (Grand Rapids: Wm. B. Eerdmans Publishing Co., 1954), p. 97.
[36]Austen K. DeBlois and Donald R. Gorham, *Christian Religious Education* (New York: Fleming H. Revell Co., 1939), p. 110.

minister through Christian education must have in themselves the life of Christ and be possessed by the Spirit of God. Christian education is no matter of mere human activity but one of individuals meeting God in Christ. It is Christ being experienced by persons who, as a consequence, are born again and grow into the likeness of the Person they meet.[37]

But consideration of the philosophy, the nature, the functions, and the history of aims makes evident the necessity in Christian education of a clear and well-defined aim on the part of those who mediate and nurture. The question these may well ask is, What should constitute this clear and well-defined aim? And a related question is, Where seek for an adequate aim?

The sources used by seekers through the years in dealing with the second question have been many. From them have come excellent statements of aims. The Christian teacher recognizes values in these but is careful not to lose sight of what is basic. In the Bible, God's revelation to man, are to be found the aims of education that are truly Christian; from the Bible it is possible to construct for every pupil and every group of pupils a set of aims sufficient for meeting the basic demands of life, individual and social. What man devises suffices neither for redemption of self or of others nor for spiritual nurture. Only the truth revealed in the Bible can transform life and build Christian character. Both the inclusive and the specific aims of Christian education are found in the Bible, the revelation of God to man concerning his state, his need, his salvation, and his destiny.

This is not to say that knowledge of the Bible is the inclusive aim of Christian education. Subject matter is never an end in itself but always a means to an end; it is the basis for activity through which the pupil may grow and develop. What the pupil becomes as a consequence of using that which he studies is far more important than knowledge of content. Knowledge of the Bible is no more an end in itself than is any other knowledge. The great purpose of teaching the Bible is that the content thereof may have its intended effect in the life of the one taught. So the teaching of the Bible cannot be the sole aim of Christian education.

Only one who has been made a new creature in Christ can mediate to others God's grace or nurture others in that grace. To a Christian teacher, the Bible is the inspired Word of God and, with spiritual understanding, he turns to it to find an inclusive aim for mediating and nurturing. As a teacher he has one inclusive aim which has within it numerous specific aims. The practical question is, What is a clear and definite aim for Christian education that is sufficiently inclusive to comprehend within itself

[37]Fallaw, op. cit., p. 80.

all other aims? The direct answer is "that the man of God may be perfect, throughly furnished unto all good works" (II Tim. 3:17). All that is done in Christian education has the one final aim of bringing those taught to perfection in godly life and character. It was for achieving this end that the Word of God was given "for doctrine, for reproof, for correction, for instruction in righteousness."

Subordinate to this comprehensive aim are the various specific aims, the attainment of which result in the achieving of the final inclusive aim. The foundational aim in Christian education is the bringing of the individual to Christ for salvation. Before a man of God can be perfected, there must be a man of God to perfect; without the new birth there is no man of God. First of all, the teacher, already in fellowship with God, under the direction and guidance of the Holy Spirit, so teaches the Bible as to bring the pupil to realization of the righteousness of God and the sinfulness of man.

The Christian teacher acquaints the pupil with the fact that he is a lost, guilty sinner; then presents Christ and His atoning work as availing for him that he may be accepted by the righteous God. Only as he is convicted by the Holy Spirit can any person lay hold on salvation. As the Christian teacher presents Bible truth, he makes clear the way of salvation as revealed by God, prays earnestly for the pupil, and seeks in loving, tactful manner to influence him to a definite, voluntary acceptance of Christ as his personal Saviour.

Once this aim is achieved, the aim of the Christian teacher becomes that of having the pupil make a complete surrender of himself to Christ as Lord. To be saved from sin is one thing; to be saved from the power of sin is another thing. Christ died for sin's penalty but He died too that the saved soul might be freed from sin's power to live for Him. The Christian teacher so brings home to the new-born pupil the truth of God that he is constrained to consecrate himself to Christ, who must be Lord of all if He is to be Lord at all.

Another specific aim of Christian education is to build each pupil up in the Christian life. Born of the Spirit, the pupil needs both the written Word and the living Word that he may grow. To become perfect, the new life must be nourished and sustained. The pupil needs thorough and correct understanding of his being in an evil world, of his having a corrupt nature, of there being an enemy to God and righteousness, of his position in Christ, and of God's provision for holy living. Comprehensive instruction in what the Bible teaches, its requirements and standards for normal Christian living, God's means for fulfilling these, and understanding of God and His ways will prepare the young Christian to move forward on the road to perfection.

Inasmuch as all education is social as well as individual, Christian education has as one of its aims development of each individual for effective social serviceability.[38] The Christian teacher therefore so presents Bible truth as to establish ideals and habits of Christlike living in common life and in all human relations. He endeavors to develop wholesome attitudes toward the individual's place in the social group, as well as in regard to government, political life, social problems, other races, and the various areas of life as men live it collectively.

Another aim Christian education has is to bring those taught to an understanding of and an appreciation of God's gracious and glorious purpose for His children. "Eye hath not seen, nor ear heard, neither have entered into the heart of man, the things which God hath prepared for them that love him" (I Cor. 2:9). Under the guidance and with the help of the Holy Spirit, Christian teaching opens to view the undreamed glories of a marvelous eternal existence. The more abundant life concerning which Jesus taught is the wonderful theme of Christian education. And this life goes on and on, making it possible for men cursed by sin to have the unspeakable glory of living in the eternal kingdom God has for those who will forsake sin and turn to Him for pardon and redemption.

In this connection, Christian education aims to train in worship to develop proper attitudes of the soul toward God. It cultivates reverence, praise, love, gratitude, and faith. It requires that pupils have opportunity to worship. It instructs in the value of daily devotional reading and private prayer. It stimulates and guides in the forming of daily habits of reading the Bible and communing with God. For the forming of such habits, pupils are taught how to read the Bible for devotional purposes and how to pray effectively. The spirit, not the mere routine, of worship is stressed.

As did Jesus, Christian education aims to show those taught God's glorious plan for His children. Jesus said, "Fear not, little flock; for it is your Father's good pleasure to give you the kingdom" (Luke 12:32), and "In my Father's house are many mansions: if it were not so, I would have told you. I go to prepare a place for you" (John 14:2). As was Jesus, so Christian education is concerned about the life that is eternal. It presents the vision of a timeless eternity and the necessity of being prepared to enter it, that God's plan not be in vain so far as one is concerned.

Christian education aims to teach the way of life and Christian living, as well as a system of theology. It is not concerned nearly so much with theories as it is with actualities. It deals not with the Bible from the standpoint of argument but from that of its life-giving power. Following the example of Jesus, it presents God and points men to God, the source of life and righteousness. It sets God forth as a very present and real

[38]Jaarsma, op. cit., pp. 185-187.

Being, a loving heavenly Father who takes deep personal interest in man, His highest creation.

Also, as Jesus did, Christian education trains for witnessing. At various times Jesus commanded those who received Him to tell others of the blessing they had experienced. Moreover, He chose twelve and trained them patiently and persistently to teach and to evangelize. The winning of souls is for all time a work entrusted to those in fellowship with God. These new-born persons who are growing in Christ toward perfection are part of a host in whose souls the kingdom of God began. They live for and work in the interests of this kingdom which is always coming but which has not fully arrived—a kingdom that is both in time and beyond time. Christian education aims to impress upon these the obligation not to live unto themselves but unto Christ, and to prepare them for effective work on behalf of those who have not yet entered into fellowship with God.

## BIBLIOGRAPHY

Byrne, H. W. *A Christian Approach to Education.* Grand Rapids: Zondervan Publishing House, 1961.

Chave, Ernest J. *Supervision of Religious Education.* Chicago: University of Chicago Press, 1931.

Cooke, Robert L. *Philosophy, Education and Certainty.* Grand Rapids: Zondervan Publishing House, 1940.

Cope, H. F. *Religious Education in the Church.* New York: Charles Scribner's Sons, 1918.

DeBlois, Austen K., and Gorham, Donald R. *Christian Religious Education.* New York: Fleming H. Revell Co., 1939.

Dewey, John. *Democracy and Education.* New York: Macmillan Co., 1924.

Eavey, C. B. *The Art of Effective Teaching.* Grand Rapids: Zondervan Publishing House, 1953.

———. *Principles of Teaching for Christian Teachers.* Grand Rapids: Zondervan Publishing House, 1940.

Fallaw, Wesner. *Church Education for Tomorrow.* Philadelphia: Westminster Press, 1960.

Gaebelein, Frank E. *Christian Education in a Democracy.* New York: Oxford University Press, 1951.

Jaarsma, Cornelius. *Fundamentals in Christian Education.* Grand Rapids: Wm. B. Eerdmans Publishing Co., 1953.

Murch, James DeForest. *Christian Education and the Local Church.* Cincinnati: Standard Publishing Co., 1943.

*Objectives of Christian Education: A Study Document.* New York: Commission on Christian Education, National Council of the Churches of Christ in the U.S.A.

Person, Peter P. *An Introduction to Christian Education.* Grand Rapids: Baker Book House, 1958.

Price, J. M., *et al. Introduction to Religious Education.* New York: Macmillan Co., 1932.

Rian, Edwin H. *Christianity and American Education.* San Antonio, Texas: Naylor Co., 1949.

Rice, Edwin Wilbur. *The Sunday-School Movement and the American Sunday-School Union.* Philadelphia: Union Press, 1917.

Roberts, S. L. *Teaching in the Church School.* Philadelphia: Judson Press, 1927.

Rushdoony, Rousas J. *Intellectual Schizophrenia.* Grand Rapids: Baker Book House, 1961.

Sauer, Erich. *The Dawn of World Redemption.* Grand Rapids: Wm. B. Eerdmans Publishing Co., 1951.

———. *From Eternity to Eternity.* Grand Rapids: Wm. B. Eerdmans Publishing Co., 1954.

Sherrill, Lewis J. *Lift Up Your Eyes.* Richmond: John Knox Press, 1949.

Taylor, Marvin J. *et al. Religious Education, A Comprehensive Survey.* New York: Abingdon Press, 1960.

Vieth, Paul H. *Objectives in Religious Education.* New York: Harper & Bros., 1930.

Whitehead, Alfred North. *The Aims of Education.* New York: Macmillan Co., 1929.

## FOR FURTHER READING

Clark, Gordon H. *A Christian Philosophy of Education.* Grand Rapids: Wm. B. Eerdmans Publishing Co., 1946.

Edge, Findley B. *Teaching for Results.* Nashville: Broadman Press, 1956.

Elliott, Harrison S. *Can Religious Education Be Christian?* New York: Macmillan Co., 1940.

Fiske, George Walter. *Purpose in Teaching Religion.* New York: Abingdon Press, 1927.

LeBar, Lois. *Education That Is Christian.* New York: Fleming H. Revell Co., 1958.

Little, Lawrence C. *Formulating the Objectives of Christian Adult Education.* Pittsburgh: University of Pittsburgh Press, 1958.

———. *The Future Course of Christian Adult Education.* Pittsburgh: University of Pittsburgh Press, 1959.

Lotz, Philip Henry, *et al. Orientation in Religious Education.* New York: Abingdon Press, 1950.

Smart, James D. *The Teaching Ministry of the Church.* Philadelphia: Westminster Press, 1954.

Vieth, Paul H., *et al. The Church and Christian Education.* St. Louis: Bethany Press, 1947.

Wyckoff, D. Campbell. *The Task of Christian Education.* Philadelphia: Westminster Press, 1940.

Audio-visual materials play an increasing role in training teachers and in instructing pupils.

(Courtesy of Bell and Howell)

# PART TWO

*Preparing to Teach*

*Chapter 5*

# THE LEARNING PROCESS

## CORNELIUS JAARSMA

THAT PEOPLE LEARN is a commonly observed fact. When one has learned, he can do something he could not do before, he knows something he did not know before, he feels for or against something he felt differently toward before, and he wants something he did not want before. In short, some change has taken place in one's behavior in general that influences him in his relationship to future situations confronting him. This is in accordance with the daily experience of all of us. When we turn to a study of the learning process, we are not questioning the validity of this common experience. Rather, we want to understand our common experience a little better so that we can understand Christian education more clearly.

The learning process is frequently passed by or but briefly referred to in many articles and books on Christian education. There are several reasons for this omission. For example, it is assumed that everyone understands what learning is and how it takes place. Also, learning is not thought of as a process, as an on-going experience in the person. Learning is "getting" what one did not have before, it is thought.

What takes place in a person's experience when he learns, and how learning takes place is *not* common knowledge. For answers to these questions many people, including many teachers, depend on ideas that prevailed prior to a scientific, experimental study of learning. But as we surely would not turn to pre-scientific ideas in medical practice today, neither should we be satisfied with pre-scientific ideas about learning. Experimental studies and clinical observation and analysis have been so fruitful in the study of human development including learning, that we want to profit from them in Christian education the best we can.

---

Cornelius Jaarsma, Ph.D., is professor of education at Calvin College, Grand Rapids, Michigan.

## *LEARNING AS A PHASE OF HUMAN DEVELOPMENT*

THE DYNAMICS OF HUMAN DEVELOPMENT

It has been said many times that one cannot speak meaningfully about education without raising the question, what is man? This is just as true of human development, for education is the directing of human development.

Is man a dualism of mind and body, or soul and body, that is, is he composed of two substances that somehow interact in his behavior? Or is he a biological organism of like constitution as animals but infinitely more complex, especially in his neural structure? If the former, then the focal point of education is the mind or the soul, for the body is the instrument of mind or soul. If man, on the other hand, is a biological or behaving organism, then the focal point of education is man's mental behavior, for it is the mental capacity of the nervous system, especially the brain, that makes for uniquely human behavior.

But are these the only answers we can give to the question, what is man? The former, that man is a dichotomy, flies into the face of all evidence of the behavioral sciences (psychology and sociology), which clearly point to the functional unity or wholeness of man. The latter fails to recognize in man what the Bible speaks of as the image of God, or spirit, or heart of man.

Does the Bible teach a dualism? Hardly. The Scripture does not address itself to the structure of man and the functions of that structure. Students of Scripture are increasingly coming to understand that the Bible refers to man in his godlikeness as a creature, in his destitute condition as a sinner, in his need of redemption, and in his restoration in Christ, rather than setting forth the structure and function of the structure. The Scripture adopts prevailing terminology in referring to man to make clear these great truths. Hence, we cannot appeal to the Bible for evidence of man's dualism. On the other hand, it is equally clear from Scripture that a biological or behavioral monism is a wrong view of man.

What, then, is man? Man is a functional unity. By this we mean that in his behavior man is an inherent unity. He is an organic unity, which means that he sustains and reproduces himself by inherent power; that he functions as a whole, not as an aggregation or assemblage of parts interacting with one another. The power is in the whole rather than in the parts. However, man's functional unity is not merely of an operational nature as in plant and in animal life, but his is the functional unity of a godlike being by creation. In his psychophysical structure, the godlike man comes to expression. Man is not a dualism of two distinct substances. He is not a monism of behavior patterns in a biological structure.

Rather, man is a godlike being by creation who in a psychophysical structure functions as a whole in relation to his environment.

On the basis of this organic unity of man we can speak of the dynamics of human development. The person enters the world an organic unity of his godlike (image of God) being in a psychophysical or mental-physical structure. His life is that of his godlikeness, which may be called the ego or I. It is this godlikeness as the life of the person that infuses his structure. The structure is adapted to man's godlikeness or ego for functioning as man. Man as man, then, is unique and distinctive from all organic beings, not so much in psychophysical structure but in what structure can do, and how structure can function as expression of the godlike life that innervates it.

We might diagram the organic unity of the person as follows:

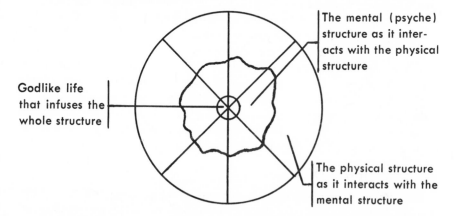

The mental (psyche) structure as it interacts with the physical structure

Godlike life that infuses the whole structure

The physical structure as it interacts with the mental structure

Operationally, that is, in behavior, the infant is subject to the processes of development characteristic of all organic life. He begins in immaturity, that is, dependent upon others for normal functioning. Motivated by inherent, indigenous impetus which we might call a developmental urge, he develops to maturity. The environment furnishes the wherewithal or means and ends for the subject's self-fulfillment or realization of his godlikeness in every dimension and function of life as he lives it.

This is called the dynamics of human development because it seeks to explain what man is and how he matures as man.

There is more to be said about his development. Man is subject to the characteristics of organic development. The inner urge toward maturity is inherent. Two basic factors direct development to maturity. First of all, the ancestral line, called heredity, furnishes the person a given equipment. Second, the environment provides opportunity. These are often referred to as nature and nurture.

The interplay of these forces explains all aspects of the development of animals, but is not adequate to account for the making of man. Early in life the person takes over in the making of himself. Both heredity and environment provide limitations as well as opportunities, but the self or ego does take over and begins to direct his course of development. In part we are born, in part we are made, and in part we make ourselves, as the late Dr. Herman Harrell Horne was wont to say.

Heredity, environment, and self function as an integrated whole in the organic unity of the person. Though we must distinguish them as concepts in human development, they are integral in their functioning of the whole. The inner, inherent drive to maturity, referred to as the developmental urge, gives rise to tensions that call for satisfactions which contribute to continued progress to maturity. These tensions are felt needs that provide a sense of direction in which the needs can be satisfied. In their search for satisfaction, goals as satisfiers are perceived. Goals that can satisfy on given levels of maturity contribute to further development.

The hungry infant in his crib illustrates these factors for all levels of development to maturity. His apparent aimless squirming suddenly takes on direction upon the first evidence of food. He gets hold of the nipple with zest and draws his food as he experiences a successful outcome. This low level, primitive act can be recognized in higher level development when one is confronted by a situation that gives direction to the feeling of curiosity or holds promise of providing what one is seeking.

STAGES OF HUMAN DEVELOPMENT

Development to maturity is continuous, that is, there are no breaks, though degree of development may vary at different levels and at different times. Development is also total; it embraces the whole person, physically, emotionally, socially, and intellectually. One or more of these dimensions of the personality can affect the person favorably or adversely. Their rate of development may differ at a given level. The continuity of development, however, remains a fact.

Characteristics of development are especially evident at certain levels. Hence, educational psychologists speak of early childhood, childhood, early adolescence, adolescence, and other classifications of developmental stages.

GENUINE LEARNING

The dynamics and stages of human development are important to an understanding of learning because learning is an integral phase of development. What is true about development is true of learning. Genuine human learning is change that contributes to a person's development to maturity, to independent and responsible behavior. There is learning which achieves little or no progress in development to maturity, such as momentary memorizing of a telephone number or house number, parroting a phrase or passage or idea for reproduction at a given time, practicing a routine that is appropriate for a given occasion. Learning, however, which involves one in an endeavor with a feeling of completeness or wholeness changes his behavior. The result is that he faces subsequent situations with a changed outlook. This is genuine human learning.

## VIEWS OF LEARNING

How one views learning makes a difference with reference to what one observes in the learning process. Two persons may observe the same facts but come up with varying interpretations because their outlooks are quite different. In current discussions of learning two widely held views color the observed facts. One is the biological view; the other the social or cultural view. We should take account of each and ask, can we have a Christian view in distinction from these two views?

### BIOLOGICAL VIEW OF LEARNING

There are students of learning who view man as a behaving organism capable of complex and high level modes of adjustment. High refinements of this view refer to man's nervous system as conceptual in its functioning. They mean that the nervous system, especially the brain, is capable not merely of many interrelations among the constituent parts, but of performing as a whole and taking over as a whole where function of parts fail. In any case, it is the nervous system that does the learning. The learning process to be understood must be traced to and demonstrated in terms of the nervous system and its functions.

In this view adaptive behavior and adjustment are of major concern in education, for they are the outcomes of learning. It is the coalescence of behavior patterns that is observed in the formed or shaped personality.

### SOCIAL OR CULTURAL VIEW OF LEARNING

Among researchers in learning theory are others who recognize a uniqueness in human learning that cannot meaningfully be traced to or be explained in terms of behavior patterns. A human being, it is observed, early in his development reaches a level of accomplishment that is creative in character. He soon is capable of behavior uniquely his. As he gains experience, his way becomes of a more reflective kind. As he meets new situations on a reflective level, a level of thought and reason, he brings forth his ideas which he can organize and reorganize. Man is capable of a culture. He can learn from a cultural product and contribute to it. He is said to be capable of acculturation.

According to this view, the learning process in man is not adequately described in terms of adaptive behavior or adjustments in one's environment. Man as man learns by reasoning and creative expression. He should be viewed as exploring a perceptive (perceivable) situation for desired goals and the ability to give his achievement resourceful expression.

A Christian View of Learning

Man is not merely a biological being who has the mechanism to make mental and physical adjustments in relation to his environment. His psychophysical structure does not constitute the fullness of his being. On this subject the Scripture is clear when it says in Genesis 1:27: "So God created man in his own image, in the image of God created he him. . . ." Likewise we read in Genesis 2:7: "Then the Lord God formed man of dust from the ground, and breathed into his nostrils the breath of life; and man became a living being" (R.S.V.).

Learning as a phase of human development is, therefore, not adequately viewed as the making of progressive adjustments in a psychophysical structure. The godlike life that infuses the whole gives human learning a dimension a mere biological structure is incapable of possessing.

To say that man as man in his organismic whole is capable of making achievements in his development that enable him to solve problems and give resourceful, creative expression to his attainments, in other words, is capable of producing and transmitting a culture, is to view learning as a uniquely human enterprise. It should be observed that in this view of man the vehicle or carrier can hardly shoulder the load. An organismic structure and function is hardly adequate to account for the amazing outreach of reasoning and creative expression. Furthermore, according to Scripture, the pride and glory of man is not his amazing creative ingenuity, but the fear of God or the wisdom that is the very embodiment or personalizing of the true, the good, and the beautiful.

Where does the Christian turn for a right view of learning? The dichotomies of earlier days, mind-body or soul-body, failed to do justice to the organic unity of the person clearly evident in our consciousness, demonstratively set forth in the wholeness in human behavior, and presupposed in Scripture. Learning is not to be viewed as a passive process of filling a container, the mind, or as a process of setting a dynamo in action to produce power. Learning is a phase of human development. It is that phase in his development which points to achievements made by the person in the forming of his personality. The Christian views learning as the self-active process of a person exploring reality perceptively for meaning, and thus coming to grips with truth that forms him as a son of

God to mature self-fulfillment. Learning so viewed can be described as a process that is distinctively human, yet embodying the biological and the cultural in experience.

## THEORIES OF LEARNING

### FROM DEDUCTIVE TO INDUCTIVE

Attempts to describe learning as a process in experience are of comparatively recent origin. Until about a hundred years ago the dictum of medieval pedagogy, *repetitio mater studiorum* (repetition is the mother of learning), prevailed. In keeping with the view that mind or soul is a substance or power in itself, propositions in one form or another were presented for memorization. Memorized answers were considered a storehouse of power for future use.

In the middle of the nineteenth century, when the substance theory of mind or soul had all but disappeared, except in conservative theology, the association of ideas began to take the place of repeating, verbalizing or parroting prescribed propositions. Ideas to be learned were simplified so they could be assimilated by the learner, and associated with his present ideas. The process of association was called apperception, and the body of ideas with which the association was to be made was called the apperceptive mass. Learning thus became a process of apperceiving and assimilating. The well-known Herbartian formal steps were based on this description of learning. But this concept of ideas as constituent unitary elements in learning has also been discredited. It was when the study of learning proceeded inductively and experimentally rather than deductively that new insights demanded a revision of both the learning and teaching processes.

### SIGNIFICANCE OF THEORIES

Theories of learning have multiplied to the extent that entire books are devoted to them. Since the early experiments with animal learning by Bechterev, Pavlov, and Thorndike, theories have been revised, restated, and extended to all levels and areas of human learning. Theories are descriptive statements of scientific findings which try to explain the process of the phenomena observed. In the case of learning, a theory seeks to explain what takes place as the student observes the process. Hence a theory is always subject to an experimenter's point of view or reference of thought. There is no such thing as "let the facts lead where they will." Facts as isolated events are meaningless. The experimenter relates the facts into a meaningful relationship. But he always does this in the framework of his world and life view. Hence, the importance of how we as Christians view learning. The Christian considers the experimental data and techniques, but he does this as a Christian. As a Christian he hears the voice of God, verbally in the Scriptures, and providentially in history, in nature, and in conscience and culture.

Teachers should be primarily interested in how a pupil learns in a formal educational program of instruction, whether it be in the day school or church school. For this purpose note three groups of theories that are helpful from an educational point of view.

## Learning as Connection

Learning, according to this school of thought, is the process of linking stimuli to certain responses by establishing pathways of conduction in the nervous system. Practice with a feeling of satisfaction tends toward stamping in initially accomplished neural connections, so that stimuli become permanently linked to produce certain responses, and desired responses are linked to certain presented stimuli. This process holds for the most complicated and superior kinds of human behavior. Select desired stimuli to be linked to desired responses. Practice with satisfying results the connecting of them. The outcome will be a large degree of permanency in behavior. The human mechanism is so constituted that it undergoes a coalescence of conduction units to constitute a larger unit of behavior.

This description of learning as a process of achieving permanent connections by practice and satisfaction points up many aspects of learning regardless of how learning is viewed. A degree of freedom in the selection of responses generates a feeling of satisfaction. Repetition is essential for retention. The curve of forgetting, however, indicates that the greatest amount of loss comes after the first learning, and is less meaningful than in rote learning. Learning does not follow an even curve to perfection, but an irregular curve to maximum possible achievement. Irregularities call for revitalizing effort through incentives or reinforcement. Effort in learning is triggered by felt needs calling for a goal to consummate the need. Felt needs generate expectancy, set, or anticipation for appropriate ends to be reached. Motivation, therefore, is important in learning. One learns what he sets out to learn, not necessarily what others expect of him.

Yet in spite of the many valuable aspects of learning evident in this process, some of the most distinctively human characteristics of learning are not given consideration. Because man is viewed as a behaving organism in his biological structure and function, the rational, moral, social, aesthetic, free, and responsible behavior of man is hardly considered. Yet these are the functions of which man is distinctively capable.

## LEARNING AS WHOLENESS IN EXPERIENCE

A second group of theories does not view man other than a biological being. This group makes some important corrections in the description of learning of the connectionists however. These theories find ground for a greater wholeness than a stimulus—conduction unit—response mechanism can adequately describe. In observing behavior they recognize an interrelation of the inner function of organismic structure and the environment. The environment provides a situation that the organism can relate to established ways of behavior to the degree that new ways of behavior can be achieved. The new behavior often comes, not by trial-and-error response, but by sudden flash or what this group calls insight. In the interaction through insight a pattern of behavior has been enriched and extended. Repetition reinforces the achievement, but patterning by insight is the really potent element.

These theories are often spoken of as field theories. The concept is borrowed from modern physics which emphasizes the interrelationship of forces operative in a given situation. It is in a field relationship that new elements in experience take on meaning. An object becomes perceptive, that is, one perceives or relates in experience. Genuine learning has its rootings in perceptivity of experience. Only what one has perceptively experienced can be meaningful. Meaning and understanding are of the essence of human learning.

The field theories provide a basic ingredient in all human learning, namely, that to make learning meaningful the learner must be able to explore a situation perceptively. But this very important ingredient of the learning process hardly reaches what we look for in the learning process of man as a religious being, as godlike, the image of his Creator.

## LEARNING AS REASONING AND CREATIVE EXPRESSION

When we consider how human beings learn by an inductive process of first-hand observation and analysis of concrete distinctly human learning situations, we discover that those factors involved in learning which are emphasized by the connectionists and field theorists promote human learning but do not describe the process adequately. Confront a person with a learning situation, and what do we observe? Triggered or activated by a felt need for attacking a problematic situation, he explores it, perceptibly anticipating, expecting to find suggested directions and solutions; possible goals or solutions come into view; new ideas or meanings, concepts are born. Successful achievement issues forth into expression which is not prescribed, is genuine, is the fruit of his own search, and is communicable.

## HOW WE LEARN

We view man, in light of the Bible, as a religious being, that is, as an organic unity of psychophysical structure infused by godlike or God-image reality. Man's functions are biological, cultural, and spiritual. We recognize, from the studies of human development and learning, ways of behavior and the change and improvement of behavior, important phenomena and factors that enter into genuine learning, namely, the changes in the person that mature him as a son of God, that form him as a godlike personality. According to Scriptural teaching, we recognize too that a person is formed in the potential expression of his godlikeness by truth as revealed to him verbally in the Scriptures and providentially in God's works and human culture. If, therefore, we would describe learning as we as Christians should understand it, the Christian view of man, scientific studies of learning, and the Scriptural estimate of man's potential must be our directives.

A definitive description of learning in keeping with these concepts may now be set forth under the following eight headings. Each must not be understood as a single step or stage, but as a facet of the entire process overlapping more or less each of the others.

### FELT NEEDS

Since learning is an achievement in the development of a person from immaturity to maturity, the dynamics of development apply to learning. The power and potential for development are indigenous. The fulfillment of the potential takes place through nurture from the environment. Nurture makes essentially two contributions to fulfillment of potential: activating the indigenous urge or drive (developmental urge we have called it) and the media in and through which potential is realized.

The development of a plant may serve as an analogy. The drive or impetus toward a full-grown plant is inherent in the seed or bulb and in the structure that springs from it. Warming ground, moisture, light, etc., can trigger or activate latent power but not produce it. Nourishing soil, sunshine, and water provide nurture in the way of food for the plant. There is an important difference, however, in human development. The plant never becomes aware of its power or potential, nor purposes to seek its food, nor reflects on its potential with a feeling of what it ought to do with its potential. There are three, not merely two factors, that integrate in human development, as we have seen: in part we are born, in part we are made, and in part we make ourselves. The person is engaged in self-fulfillment. It is at the basis of all his striving and goals which he sets for himself.

The drive or impetus involved in the indigenous motivation of self-fulfillment gives rise to a feeling of imbalance called need. Needs are tensions arising in this feeling of imbalance. Felt needs set the organism into action. Hunger, or felt need for food, is an illustration. The absence of nourishment for a growing body structure sets up a feeling of imbalance. The infant becomes restless and cries. Similarly, a developing person explores his environment in response to the novelty of a situation.

Felt needs may be classified as primary and secondary, according to their basic contribution to development. Food, for example, is a primary need.

For purpose of formal learning, we must reckon with six primary needs, basic more or less at various stages in a person's development to maturity: affection, adult approval, peer approval, self-respect, independence, and commitment. The felt need for affection, to be loved and to love, for example, is an expression arising out of the indigenous motivation for self-fulfillment. The need manifests itself variously on different levels of development and is satisfied in various ways, but the activity generated is basic to all development. The same can be said for the other needs.

Secondary needs arise in response to external situations. The felt need to read, for example, is triggered early in a child's life by books around the house and by seeing others read. He too can secure adult approval for his reading. He feels that he is growing up.

The activity in a person's development called learning is the result of felt needs, as is all other activity involved in development. Important questions with reference to formal education are: What are the primary felt needs of a person and how do they manifest themselves at given levels of maturity or immaturity? What felt needs can be triggered or activated at given levels that initiate formal education?

We do not have to make a youngster want to learn, nor can we. He is an indefatigable learner. What we can do is interpret rightly primary needs, and understand what secondary needs can be activated in a child on a given level so that he will seek to learn what he ought to learn.

DIRECTION

Felt needs do not only generate activity involved in learning, but set the person in search for meeting the needs in an external situation. They generate a set, expectancy, or anticipation, even a sense of direction. Many factors determine the expectancy or anticipation, or the direction of search for meeting needs. In general they are a person's past experience, environmental opportunity, and self-determination.

EXTERNAL SITUATION

The external situation provides form and content which the person activated to felt needs can perceptively explore in his expectancy toward desired ends with satisfaction. Freedom of the learner is presupposed, reinforcement may be necessary on the way, a feeling of adequacy and achievement should be attainable, interrelatedness of constituent parts should be at hand, and insights should be achieved.

In school the subject matter provides form and content. Whether the subject matter is appropriate for the learner depends in part on his perceptivity. The learner must be challenged by it, explore with anticipation in and through it, and achieve self-assurance through successfully pursuing his course.

EMERGING GOAL

If the exploratory process in an external situation is perceptive to the learner and his efforts are reinforced chiefly by initial success, ends which promise to satisfy felt needs come into view. These are goals or purposes. As goals and purposes are clarified and attain significance in the experience of relating them to desired ends, they gain in the impact they make upon the person. The learning activity increasingly becomes purposeful, goal-directed. This is what is called motivation in learning and teaching. We read that a teacher should motivate learning. Actually all learning is motivated; that is, felt needs are constantly operative to drive a person in a given direction in the course of which purpose is generated. What the teacher wants for his students is right and desired goals, for if he understands learning he knows that pupils learn what they set out to learn, not necessarily what a teacher tries to teach.

MEANING—IDEAS OR CONCEPTS

In the exploratory process of a learning situation, a pupil begins to see new relationships among facts and previously acquired understandings. Facts do not merely increase, but attain a setting, an enriched relationship. The learner generalizes from the more specific to the more abstract. New and enriched ideas or concepts are achieved. Meanings are enriched and attained. In the formal learning situation a graduated body of concepts is achieved which becomes an integral part of his total mental life.

In a learning situation that a pupil can perceptively explore to gain new meanings and understanding, the drive of purposeful endeavor grows more potent. The dynamics of the learning process are intensified. In this sense we may say that meaning is the key to genuine learning. A learner gives meaning to a learning situation before he can achieve meaning in it. If the situation is not perceptive to him, he cannot relate the factors involved according to the intent of the situation; he cannot get meaning or purpose from it. Parroting or repeating of external form and content is not learning. Repetition, review is an essential corollary to learning, not its source. Meaningful experience is the source.

TRUTH

Learning, we have seen, is the achievement a person makes in his development to maturity. In Christian thinking it is viewed as self-fulfillment of a person as son of God. The son of God, the godlike creature called man, comes to self-fulfillment as he lives the truth. As God is the truth, the godlike man lives the truth made knowable to him in God's self-revelation in His Word and in providence. The truth, however, is not received by man as a container, but achieved in active pursuit of it. God makes it knowable, and He created us with capacity and power to achieve the knowledge of it.

As a learner achieves ideas, concepts, meanings, and understandings, truth is disclosed, uncovered, perceived. Man as a religious being is created to live the truth. It is native to his being. The distortions of sin have not erased the religious nature of man. He lives even today by what he alleges to be true. In his fractured, distorted spiritual condition, he can develop to maturity only what he holds to be true.

Christian education, Christian teaching in a formal learning situation especially, should be very conscious of the fact that a learner achieves truth that forms his personality in a meaningful learning experience. Too frequently indoctrination in the Christian religion is interpreted to mean that we hand down ready-made adult ideas in religion in simplified form on the child level. This easily results in parroting and taking the repeating of prescribed statements for the reality of Christian experience. Indoctrination is necessary. But the truth to be transmitted is achieved only in meaningful exploration by the learner in a perceptive situation that discloses truth to his consciousness.

CHANNELING OR FORMING

Genuine learning brings about change in a developing person's behavior that can be described as more mature, that is, increasingly self-determining, independent, and responsible. Truth meaningfully disclosed to the learner in an exploratory process in which he experiences a feeling of successful achievement, a feeling of adequacy, channels behavior out of the inner resources of a self-determining person.

Channeling, or forming of behavior, can be accomplished on a biological level of adjustment. Behavior patterns acquired by practice are internalized in attitudes. Or it can be accomplished on a cultural level.

Insights and meanings of the culture are attained in a problem-solving way and given desirable expression. This is known as acculturation. But man is not merely a behaving organism, not merely a culture-producing and culture-transmitting organism; he is also a religious being who attains self-fulfillment in living the truth. Attitudes are not enough. Convictions and commitments pattern man's behavior. Truth or alleged truth, ultimate concerns, are native to his being.

## CREATIVE EXPRESSION

Behavior channeled, formed, out of the inner resources of the self-fulfillment of a developing personality is self-expression. It is the expression of the self, the self living the truth. This is creative expression in distinction from representative expression. One may represent truth in a formal way without its being the self-expression of the person. Creative expression is self-expression according to truth. The former can be attained by parroting and repetition; the latter is achieved in meaningfully exploring reality.

Creative expression is native to man as a religious being. He is like the Creator. However, creative expression not representative of truth, God's self-revelation, lacks the norm or standard for self-fulfillment of man as a son of God.

## FACTORS FAVORABLE TO LEARNING

Many factors which are not specifically stated in the process contribute to the promotion or advancement of genuine learning: an atmosphere alive with classroom appearance that suggests and concretizes learning; a teacher-pupil relationship that radiates affectionate communication; provision for incentives to reinforce learning; effective routinization of peripheral and more mechanical necessities; periodic review and drill; recognition of spurts and lapses in learning progress; well-selected tools and sources; firm direction and supporting discipline. These and others do much to facilitate genuine learning.

## LEARNING PROCESS SUMMARIZED

How does a person viewed as a religious being learn? A person learns by being involved in a challenging situation that is meaningful and purposeful and calls forth ideas and concepts that disclose truth to channel behavior as self-expression and self-fulfillment.

Learning so understood by teachers will give them a perspective of their task. Rather than being lecturers, disciplinarians, imposers of formal tasks, hearers of lessons, examiners and reporters, they will see themselves as directors of the learning process. Though none of these factors are excluded, they find their proper place only when viewed as a phase of directing learning.

## FOR FURTHER READING

Blair, G. M., Jones, R. S., and Simpson, R. H. *Educational Psychology.* New York: Macmillan Co., 1954. Part III.

Coladarci, A. P. (ed.). *Educational Psychology.* New York: Dryden Press, 1955. Chapters V and VI.

Cole, L. E., and Bruce, W. F. *Educational Psychology.* Yonkers-on-Hudson, N.Y.: World Book Co., 1950. Part III.

Cronbach, L. J. *Educational Psychology.* New York: Harcourt, Brace & Co., 1954. Chapter IV and Part C.

Crow, L. D. and A. C. *Human Development and Learning.* New York: American Book Co., 1956. Part IV.

Gates, A. I. *Educational Psychology* (3rd ed.). New York: Macmillan Co., 1949. Chapters IX-XV.

Jaarsma, C. *Human Development, Learning and Teaching.* Grand Rapids: Wm. B. Eerdmans Publishing Co., 1961.

Jordan, A. M. *Educational Psychology* (4th ed.). New York: Henry Holt & Co., 1956. Chapters V-VII.

Morse, W. C., and Wingo, G. M. *Psychology and Teaching.* New York: Scott, Foresman & Co., 1955. Chapters VIII-XI.

Mursell, J. L. *Psychology for Modern Education.* New York: W. W. Norton & Co., 1952. Chapters VI-X.

Peterson, H. A., Marzolf, S. S., and Bayley, N. *Educational Psychology.* New York: Macmillan Co., 1948. Chapters VIII-XI.

Remmers, H. H., Ryden, E. R., and Morgan, C. L. *Introduction to Educational Psychology.* New York: Harper & Bros., 1954. Chapters IX and X.

Skinner, C. E. (ed.). *Educational Psychology.* Englewood Cliffs, N.J.: Prentice-Hall, Inc., 1955. Part II.

Sorenson, H. *Psychology in Education* (3rd ed.). New York: McGraw-Hill Book Co., 1954. Chapters XVI-XIX.

Stephens, J. M. *Educational Psychology* (rev. ed.). New York: Henry Holt & Co., 1956. Chapters IX-XIV.

Witherington, H. C. *Educational Psychology* (rev. ed.). New York: Ginn and Co., 1952. Chapter VIII.

*Chapter 6*

# CURRICULUM

## Lois E. LeBar

T HE CURRICULUM OF CHRISTIAN EDUCATION may be defined as the specific plans of a church agency for accomplishing its aims, or as the
activities of teachers and pupils in relation to Scripture for the purpose
of leading pupils toward maturity in Christ.

Literally a racecourse, the curriculum of the past has often been conceived as the content covered by pupils with little attention paid to their
needs and interests. Recently some curricula have veered to the other extreme of conceiving the course to be the activities of pupils as they run,
allowing their choices and interests to determine the process and the
goal. In the former concept we visualize the pupils goaded by teachers
to sprint straight for the prescribed goal over a narrow track that is clearly laid out for them. In the latter we see the pupils strolling through wide
fields, stopping to study the flowers and birds that interest them.

### NATURE OF THE CURRICULUM

An authentic curriculum of Christian education incorporates insights
from both these extremes. A curriculum is not Christian unless it involves
interaction with the Word of God; it is not educational unless this interaction results in spiritual growth for the pupil. Since God has disclosed
Himself in closed special revelation, this is an essential body of knowledge
for which nothing can be substituted. But handing it out piecemeal regardless of the particular pupils or their immediate situation may harden
them against the truth rather than provide growth thereby. If this essential content is to produce spiritual changes in pupils, the curriculum must
give large place to their readiness, needs, and capacities.

We are not treating Scripture as God's special revelation unless through
our teaching God reveals Himself personally to our pupils. Much of

---

Lois E. LeBar, Ph.D., is professor of Christian Education at Wheaton College, Wheaton, Ill.

Scripture is historical, and much is doctrinal. And often Scripture is taught merely as Bible history and as Bible doctrine. But it is not primarily history, nor primarily doctrine. The purpose of the history and doctrine as well as the biography and poetry is to reveal God to people. Through Scripture God wishes to speak a personal word to individuals today.

"Out of life, for the life, should the Word of life be understood." What intimate dealings God had with His chosen nation Israel. How many details the Bible gives of men like David, Moses, Joseph. How personal are Paul's letters, affording help in concrete existential situations. And of the life of the Central Figure of the great drama of redemption, we have been given close-up glimpses in four filmstrips, so that we may view Him from four points of view. Through doctrine also God desires to communicate His own life to men, for doctrine deals with basic human needs—regeneration, security, self-fulfillment, wisdom, power, freedom.

Christian teaching is preeminently Person to person, then person to Person. God conveys His own life to men, then seeks response from them. He has communicated Himself in writing as well as in a God-Man; He has provided His own Holy Spirit to be the divine Teacher; He ordains human teachers to work with this Guidance Counselor. The Holy Spirit is ever wooing men to God, but human teachers have not always learned from Him His methods. In their use of Scripture, they sometimes hinder men from dealing with the Lord. They sometimes get pupils bogged down in the written Word without getting them through to the living Word. They sometimes make Scripture an end in itself rather than the means to the end of Life Himself. For Christianity is nothing less than Life, the life of Christ, eternal life, fullness of life. All our talking about life is to produce life. It is easy to substitute verbalizations for real understanding and the personal relationship. The only way we receive life and truth and wisdom and power is by receiving Christ, who is life and truth and wisdom and power. In intimate union with Him all things are ours.

Sometimes we make teaching extremely complicated by analyzing the many factors involved. It surely can be refined indefinitely. But before we teach its complications, it should be viewed quite simply as the process of making connections between the learner and his Lord. It is the Lord Himself who imparts life, who changes life. The curriculum must leave room for Him to come in as He pleases. If we make this definite provision in the process, something happens. As we pray and plan, we expect something to happen. Pupils come with expectation, which is a prelude to faith.

Why shouldn't great things happen in the Christian curriculum if human teachers work with the Holy Spirit, using the sword of the Spirit?

Our pupils come to us with great needs, deep gnawing drives that cry out to be met. These furnish the motivation for change. If we can help our pupils discover that Christ is the answer to these needs, our session begins to move. The Word provides the goal, the content, and the power. The response of pupils determines the immediate pattern and the methods. As pupils interact with the Word, the Holy Spirit lifts up the risen Christ of the cross, who draws the learner to Himself. Then the Lord God of the universe becomes the great I AM in personal experience; He is no longer conceived as the remote HE WAS. Facts are used to clarify understanding, then understanding is transcended by decision and worship. Life is transformed in the process. Plans are made for carrying out the vision in tomorrow's workaday world.

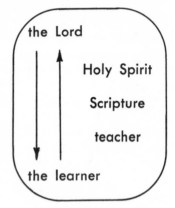

In our curriculum we ought to see God at work in our world today. A Bible lesson ought to be viewed as a part of daily life, not apart from life. It ought to be an incident closely related to the rest of the week, often a highlight that enriches and enhances the rest of the week, or that interprets it. When pupils come to Bible class, we don't propose to take them out of their world, but add to their world a new dimension that will raise it to a new level. We teachers prepare, not by bringing to them a simplified version of *our* world, but by entering *their* world and becoming a naturalized citizen of it. Then we will have eyes to see what eternal truth and experiences they are ripe for, what is the next step for them to take in their upward spiritual climb. Our purpose will not be to entice them to swallow a predigested capsule of knowledge, or to entertain them with gimmicks or bags of tricks.

Our purpose will be to set up a situation in which students can communicate in depth with each other, with the teacher, with God through Scripture and His Spirit, with the great personalities of Scripture. Bible class should be known as a place where insecure persons can take off their masks, can break down barriers of all kinds, can express their fears and frustrations, and find God's ways of releasing their tensions. Of course the teacher is the key factor. The Word must again become flesh in the life of the teacher. He must represent God aright, must embody Scripture, must be filled with the Spirit. If he is open and honest with respect to his own and others needs, he can furnish the spiritual climate in which pupils will acknowledge their sin, feel free to ask questions about the Source of life, and make creative plans for practicing God's commands.

## STRUCTURING THE CURRICULUM

The two elements that constitute the curriculum may be expressed as content and experience, or factors outside the pupil and factors inside the pupil. Both are necessary. Christian content without experience is empty; experience without content is blind. The way in which these two elements are related to each other determines the results that will be achieved.

Through the centuries content has been given greater emphasis than experience. It is more natural to think of a course of study as essential content that is passed on from one generation to the next. But educators through the centuries have realized that what the pupils are thinking and feeling and doing is as significant as what the teacher is doing. To teach content transmissively by considering only the selection, organization, and accuracy of the material to be passed on may not actually transmit it. To teach authoritative content in an authoritarian manner in the sense that pupils are expected to accept without question the pronouncements of the teacher may not result in the content becoming truly authoritative for the learner.

The ancient nations taught content impersonally by rote memory and outward imitation in order to preserve the status quo. The Greeks, on the other hand, aimed at well-rounded harmonious development of the individual through self-activity. Old Testament education balanced knowing with doing, as did Christ, who taught His disciples eternal truth in life situations. The apostolic age also was characterized by a wholesome balance of doctrine, worship, fellowship, and holy living.

But in the early church, as theology and church organization were systematized, instruction grew formal until the common life was externalized in sacramental worship. The trend continued in the Middle Ages. Intellectual deductive logic acknowledged the shell of Scripture without penetrating to the kernel or applying it to the problems of man and nature. When the authority of the church was transferred to the authority of Scripture in the Reformation, personal salvation and judgment were recovered. But the quicker method of preaching soon replaced the slower method of teaching, and rote memorization of the catechism replaced the study of Scripture.

In colonial America the child in his home practiced holy living as well as prepared for holy dying, but as a miniature adult rather than a child in his own right. The Sunday school era in the latter part of the eighteenth century stressed knowledge of the Bible and conversion with little relation to the Christian life, little appreciation of the laws of growth and the unity of the educational process. In the twentieth century religious liberals followed in the train of John Dewey's progressive reconstruction of experience until neo-orthodox theology reemphasized God's revelation in history and in experience. Evangelicals have been slowly moving to regain balance once more, to teach authoritative Scripture in the power of the Spirit to effect the complete Christian life.

Though both content and experience are generally ackowledged to be necessary in structuring any curriculum, one of these elements becomes the source of authority which takes priority over the other; one becomes the organizing principle upon which the other depends. If the Bible is made the center, the curriculum tends to stress factual knowledge. If the curriculum is organized around the pupil or his experience, it is man-centered, rather than God-centered, and sub-Christian. The Bible cannot be taken out of the center, and yet the Bible as an end in itself is contrary to God's intention for His written revelation. As Charles Hodge wrote: "Superior knowledge enhances the guilt of sin, and increases the certainty, necessity, and severity of punishment, without in itself increasing the power of resistance." The written Word was given to reveal the living Word. In all things Christ should have the preeminence. Yet He can be known only through Scripture. Therefore the Christian curriculum is centered in the Word of God, written and living. What other center can possibly be as dynamic as Life Himself! The curriculum is centered in the Person for whom everything was created and in whom it will culminate.

Yet experience as the secondary element is absolutely essential to the Christian curriculum. It cannot be treated casually or left to happenstance. It does not result automatically from knowledge. It must be definitely provided in the curriculum. Still today Christ comes down into our world; He seeks to talk with us in the temple, and to walk with us by the way. He enters our life just as it is, He makes our hearts burn within us, and gives us first-hand experience of Himself. He understands us altogether and shows through Scripture how He wishes to transform our lives here and now. His power in others' lives shows us what He can do in ours. We ourselves must see our present need, discover His higher ways of working, and begin to practice that quality of life.

As we begin to move in the direction of maturity in Christ, there is progressively less of self and more of Christ. His life becomes our life. The content of our curriculum merges with experience. This is spiritual reality. What was originally outside is internalized. It is the peculiar ministry of the Holy Spirit to make the outer Word inner experience for the pupil. The human teacher works with Him to effect this direct experience. We are not content to accept shortcuts that are spurious or the vicarious end-products of others' experience.

## THE PLACE OF EXPERIENCE

Evangelicals who accept the authority of Scripture have little problem making the Word of God central in their teaching. They are deeply grateful that the way of eternal life has been made so plain in words. They teach special revelation as rational, since it is not contrary to reason though some of it may be beyond reason; as historical, since God used decisive historical acts to disclose Himself; as objective, since God has provided us the security of a permanent verbalized expression of truth about Himself; as personal, since the purpose of the Bible is to bring about personal dealings with God Himself (John 5:39). Evangelicals teach "thus saith the Lord" with a ring of authority. But too often through their teaching, pupils fail to hear the voice of God speaking to them. Scripture does not seem relevant to their lives, they cannot fit it into their patterns of thinking, they do not know how to put it in practice.

Thus the pupils' self-activity is necessary if the pupils are to discover insights that they can use and appropriate in their own lives. The emphasis will be on pupils learning the Word of God rather than on teachers teaching. The teacher will help them catch a vision of the vitality of full-orbed life in Christ, of the satisfaction of self-fulfillment in Him, and of the exciting adventures that are awaiting them in relation with God and others when they are free from self. It is not easy in a technological age to go through the slow process of helping learners take each step in the ascent toward maturity. But the genuine Christian product is not turned out wholesale at the end of any assembly line.

In practical terms, content and experience are most effectively related in units of work. The teacher's first step is to pray and ponder the needs of his pupils until he can feel with them and see with them; then when he goes to the Scripture, he thinks of what he reads in terms of these needs. He saturates himself with the Scripture portions that relate to the pupils' problems until the Word dwells richly in him in all wisdom. This enables him to use it flexibly as occasion demands. He then helps his pupils formulate their problems and discover what they already know and are doing in relation to them. The pupils participate as much as they are able in organizing the attack, securing source materials, and deciding upon methods. Their questions and suggestions determine the actual procedure. The teacher serves as stimulator and guide. The pupils continually evaluate their findings and revise their plans accordingly. When the problem is successfully solved, they make definite plans for using their conclusions. They expect to meet the Lord in the process and to change their ways as a result.

Initially, continuity of experience is more important than continuity of content. At first the pupils are concerned about their own personal needs, which constitute the thread that ties their experiences together and determines what content is selected and provides the carrying power. Later in the process, when they have experienced God's working, their problems become also content problems, and truth becomes organized systematically in doctrine and theology. However, even when content is approached experientially, it should be organized at the end of units, for generalization aids transfer to new situations after experience has demonstrated its reality.

## THE PLACE OF THE LOCAL CHURCH IN CURRICULUM MAKING

While educational specialists prepare printed *curriculum materials* for typical situations, only the local church can provide *a curriculum* that effectively relates the experience of its own members to the Word of God. Each pupil, each church, each community has particular needs and particular opportunities that ought to be reflected in the curriculum if it is life-changing rather than dull routine. The manuals prepared by experts should be respected as an invaluable tool, but the members of any class must be taught by teachers who know them as individuals and lead them as fast or as slowly as they are ready to go.

Teachers in the local church need to be trained to use their manuals properly, neither to cast them aside as impractical nor to follow them slavishly. Each month department superintendents should conduct a preview of the next month's lessons, analyzing why the writer suggested what he did and how the suggestions should be adapted to the local situation. This requires insight into the principles of lesson planning. Because of the many untrained teachers, ideas in lesson manuals are often very specific, so that the teachers will be able to visualize the possibilities. Many teachers need self-teaching manuals, for they are not privileged to receive supervision. But as soon as possible they should be encouraged to make their own creative plans and try experiments on their own.

One's own church therefore has a responsibility in the process of curriculum making. It should furnish a warm, friendly atmosphere in which spiritual attitudes may be caught; an exhilarating climate in which nobility of life is exemplified, in which the members are reinforcing each other in maintaining high standards. Its own beliefs and policies will be studied whenever relevant to the aim of a lesson.

The homes of the pupils also play a large part in the actual curriculum. Current problems furnish the starting point for units of work; the insights achieved are carried back into the home for implementation. A teacher should visualize a pupil not as an isolated figure but as a member of the groups that are important to him. It should make a difference in the curriculum whether or not a mother is employed outside the home, whether or not television is a problem, whether things are valued materialistically, whether both self-acceptance and self-denial are considered practical. Personal crises often furnish remarkable opportunities for speeded-up learning.

If workbooks are to be done at home to enrich the learning process, they should help the pupils make practical decisions and translate insight into action. If used before a lesson, they should motivate Bible study and provide some of the facts on which the class study can be built. If used after a lesson, they should guide in actual use of the truth.

The local community too has a part in curriculum building. It acquaints its members with its own kind of social relationships, furnishes good or poor examples of interaction, conditions many kinds of habitual response, prompts civic action for the improvement of conditions, provides specialists in various fields who can be called upon as resource persons. The Christian teacher needs to know to what extent the public schools are teaching character values, leisure time is being profitably used, civic government is operated altruistically.

## INTEGRATING THE CURRICULA OF VARIOUS AGENCIES

When people are challenged to attend several agencies in the church, these agencies must be planned cooperatively to afford each individual a balanced program without overlapping or omission of essentials. A balanced program consists of instruction, worship, service, and fellowship. Some agencies include all four of these elements, such as camp and vacation Bible school, while others major on one or two elements. Together they should accomplish the comprehensive aims of Christian education for each individual: worship of God the Father, receiving of Christ as Saviour and Lord, submitting to the guidance and empowering of the Holy Spirit, knowing and obeying Scripture, formulation of a Christian philosophy of life, progressive growth in grace toward maturity, making one's contribution to the edification of the church, reaching lost men wherever they are, and assuming responsibility as a Christian citizen in community groups.

Each agency has a distinctive contribution to make because it has a distinctive purpose. The Sunday school is usually considered to be the core agency with the basic curriculum that is supplemented by other agencies. For young children it has time to provide all four elements; for older persons, primarily Bible instruction, with at least a few moments for worship to clinch in the presence of God the impulses that are aroused. Nursery, beginner and primary church, that are expanded sessions of Sunday school, can reinforce the Sunday school aim by creative supplementary activities. Junior church can train in worship and churchmanship by directing the juniors in planning, practicing and conducting their own church service on their own level. The training hour on Sunday evening can carry out the implications of the Sunday school lesson in the form of discussion of practical problems and service projects, can afford insight and practice in aspects of leadership, such as public speaking, personality development, development of talents, group dynamics, personal witnessing, and the like.

The consecutive hours of vacation school concentrate on a specific need or interest that is developed largely in terms of expressional activities. Weekday church school relates Christianity to secular school experience during the week. Weekday clubs help young people put Christ in the center of all the activities of life. Camp has a unique opportunity to help young people discover God's secrets in nature and tackle personal problems of living and working together.

Evangelism, missions, and special days should also be integrated in the curricula of the various agencies. Evangelism is not considered to be a mere element of the program, because it is thought of as the very breath of Christianity. If a program is not evangelistic, it is not Christian. Although special evangelistic crusades and missionary units have a place, God's gracious invitations and our response should be integrally woven into every curriculum. People are only frustrated if they are taught God's requirements without being led to appropriate His life and power. If a curriculum is to stay close to the experience of its pupils, it will also make provision for special days, not to repeat the emphasis of the previous year, but to raise new questions and explore new horizons at each developmental level.

## BIBLIOGRAPHY

A *Guide for Curriculum in Christian Education*. New York: Division of Christian Education, National Council of Churches, 1955.

Hanna, Lavone A., *et al. Unit Teaching in the Elementary School*. New York: Rinehart and Co., 1955.

Henry, Carl F. H. (ed.). *Revelation and the Bible*. Grand Rapids: Baker Book House, 1958.

LeBar, Lois E. *Education That is Christian*. Westwood, N.J.: Fleming H. Revell Co., 1958.

Vieth, Paul H. (ed.). *The Church and Christian Education*. St. Louis: Bethany Press, 1947.

Wyckoff, D. Campbell. *Theory and Design in Christian Education Curriculum*. Philadelphia: Westminster Press, 1961.

## FOR FURTHER READING

Cantor, Nathaniel. *The Teaching-Learning Process.* New York: Dryden Press, 1953.

Cully, Iris V. *The Dynamics of Christian Education.* Philadelphia: Westminster Press, 1958.

Edge, Findley B. *Teaching for Results.* Nashville: Broadman Press, 1956.

Gaebelein, Frank E. *The Pattern of God's Truth.* New York: Oxford University Press, 1954.

Jaarsma, Cornelius. *Fundamentals in Christian Education.* Grand Rapids: Wm. B. Eerdmans Publishing Co., 1953.

Miller, Randolph Crump. *Education for Christian Living.* Englewood Cliffs, N.J.: Prentice-Hall, Inc., 1956.

Rozell, Ray. *Informal Talks on Sunday School Teaching.* Grand Rapids: International Publishers, 1956.

Sherrill, Lewis J. *The Gift of Power.* New York: Macmillan Co., 1955.

Taylor, Marvin J. (ed.). *Religious Education: A Comprehensive Survey.* New York: Abingdon Press, 1960.

*Chapter 7*

# TEACHER TRAINING

## D. K. REISINGER

A LOCAL CHRISTIAN EDUCATION PROGRAM will be no stronger than its administrative officers and leaders. Its over-all success is determined largely by the quality of the teachers who teach the Word of God. Many churches are seriously handicapped by a lack of trained leadership. A basic reason for failure lies in the fact that many leaders cannot lead, and many teachers do not know how to teach.

This conclusion is at once a discouragement and an encouragement. It is discouraging to realize that so few Christian teachers take seriously the command of the Lord Jesus: "Go . . . teach . . . teaching them to observe all things whatsoever I have commanded you" (Matt. 28:19, 20). By the same token it is encouraging to know that there is a remedy, not a quick cure, but a sure treatment: "Study to show thyself approved unto God, a workman that needeth not to be ashamed, rightly dividing the word of truth" (II Tim. 2:15).

Proper teaching methods and deep personal spirituality are not mutually exclusive; they are compatible. Sunday school leaders and teachers need a thorough knowledge of God's Word, but they must also know and use God-given methods and techniques, so that the Bible will be learned, experienced, and practiced. The transforming effects of God's grace are experienced through the Holy Spirit's ministry. To accomplish His work, the Holy Spirit usually seeks out, commissions, and uses teachers who are well trained, adequately prepared, spiritually motivated, and God-ordained. Such teachers produce challenging and permanent results, and their ministries honor the Lord Jesus Christ.

Teacher training is a vital factor in leadership education. It is involved

The Rev. Mr. D. K. Reisinger, a graduate of Wesley Theological Seminary, is director of Leadership Education at Gospel Light Publications in Glendale, California.

in and directed by the church's basic philosophy and outline of Christian education. To be valid and dynamic, a broad training program must be planned, promoted, and conducted as a long-range, progressive, perennial, integral function of the church. It should be structured into every church-related educational level—the local Sunday school and church; the entire denominational concept; the Bible college, college, and seminary; the Christian elementary and secondary school. The pastor, missionary, director of Christian education, and lay leaders all share responsibility for the church's over-all training of its active Christian service personnel. A rich training program will focus and bless the individual witness of each believer.

## THE CHURCH NEEDS TRAINED LEADERS

SUNDAY SCHOOL IS A FAMILY AFFAIR

The Sunday school is not limited to children. It should encompass every age level—cradle roll, nursery, kindergarten, primary, junior, junior high, senior high, young adult, the middle-aged, the senior citizen.

Sunday schools reach all types of people—rich and poor, educated and noneducated, married and single, professional and non-professional, parents and children, those on both sides of the proverbial railroad tracks, saved and unsaved, church members and nonchurched. Consequently, Sunday schools must be graded to meet the need of all ages, types, and kinds of people. The teacher's constant thrust must aim to teach, train, and win every pupil for Christ. Should Sunday schools fail in this objective, they may well go out of business. When Dwight David Eisenhower was President of the United States he said, "To build faith in our children, take them to Sunday school."

THE CHURCH IS AN EDUCATIONAL AGENCY

Illustrations of the church as an educational agency could be multiplied from every level or cross section of Sunday school pupils. The public school will demonstrate a sampling of this truth for all areas.

Today's public school pupil is involved in an educational process that is, in most cases, superior to that of any previous generation. The elementary, secondary, collegiate, and graduate student never before had so many advantages. The student rides to school in a modern, safety-featured school bus. He attends classes in elaborate school buildings that are functionally designed, with adequate classrooms and laboratories, with comfortable seats and desks. He studies textbooks that are educationally correct in content and up to date in format. He enjoys approved heating, lighting, and ventilation. He is motivated by teaching tools and equipment, including the most scientific audio-visual aids and other teaching-learning devices. In his research he uses source materials that are scholarly and widely available. He learns in an ideal situation, with many media for impression and expression. Yesterday's pupils "never had it so good."

Today's well-educated schoolteacher is thoroughly trained in content and teaching methodology. He knows how to evaluate and catalog age groups, characteristics, and personality differences. He has the advantages of professional counsel in medicine, psychology, psychiatry, testing, and grading. He knows all about IQ's and learning levels. Five days each week, during the school term, today's children are taught by a corps of supertrained teachers, who impress their pupils with the importance and the urgency of getting a good education.

On Sunday morning these same children come to Sunday school. What a difference! What a contrast in almost every area! There is abundant evidence that this problem is serious. Examine the typical Sunday school. Evaluate the building, equipment, environment, sanitation, textbooks. By comparison with public schools, most Sunday schools are substandard.

## SUNDAY SCHOOL REFLECTS THE TEACHER'S TRAINING

Evaluate the teacher in Sunday school. How does he rate? Probably he lacks formal training. He is usually a volunteer. He may have only meager knowledge of his subject or his textbook, the Bible. He may be unaware of modern teaching methods. Frequently he is apologetic or indifferent about his ignorance of what to do and how to do it. He may practice outmoded techniques such as, "I'll read the questions and you find and read the answers." He may stick close to the teacher's quarterly and never refer to the Bible. He may fit the little boy's description, "My teacher is a quarterly, wired for sound."

Thank God, most evangelical teachers confess that "God and the Bible are important." But some may unwittingly insist that their pupils "sit still and be serious, for this is God's house." They may urge their pupils to study their lessons. But what these teachers believe and say may be entirely different from what they teach. By nonverbal communication the pupils observe their teachers' lethargy and poor preparation. They are led to believe that the truths spoken in Sunday school are not nearly as important as the secular truths taught in the public school. This is a sad situation, and the tragedy becomes more deeply entrenched in each advancing age level.

Actually the Sunday school may not be a school. The result is that thousands of children, young people, and adults are robbed of vital knowledge of God's Word. They may never be urged or trained to "search the Scriptures" for themselves. So the Christian testimony is vitiated and hosts of church members do nothing more than "play church." The Sunday school needs trained teachers. It needs more trained teachers—many more of them—in order to reach and teach its constituency.

## TRAINED LEADERS DETERMINE THE CHURCH'S OUTREACH

Churches that do not grow usually fail to reach their communities. They are probably understaffed or they have poorly trained teachers and officers. "Where there is no vision, the people perish." The church must be aware of its area of responsibility. It must ask largely, and then fully implement every plan, or it will not discharge its responsibility.

J. Edgar Hoover, director of the Federal Bureau of Investigation, wrote this brief statement relative to the value of trained teachers:

> The qualified teacher is a basic factor in strengthening the Sunday school and, ultimately, in promoting the spiritual strength of the nation.
>
> The fundamental wisdom of the Bible does not become available to the individual by some automatic means. It must be made accessible to him; that is, it must be taught to him in understandable form. The Sunday school teacher must have the capacity to convey the real meaning of the Biblical lessons; to reveal the great truths which glow forth when properly presented; and to bring alive the exciting drama in the greatest Book ever written. And the teacher must be competent in other ways. The methods of presenting Biblical lessons to children of primary age necessarily differ from those afforded adults.
>
> In all of these things, training is material; for the problem confronting Sunday school authorities not only is the one of finding persons who know the basic material, but also finding teachers who know how to present it in an interesting and understandable manner.
>
> We are today witnessing a tremendous struggle between the material and the spiritual. The outcome of this ideological war is vital. It must determine the course of civilization for centuries to come. We can progress in a world which assures the sanctity of the individual only if the spiritual forces which form the foundation of freedom remain strong and constant. The competent, trained Sunday school teacher is a real factor in renewing and preserving those forces.[1]

*Present outreach.* A series of concentric circles will help to visualize the church's responsibility and to focus attention on the importance of trained leaders. The first circle may represent the over-all program of any Sunday school. The figure "100" indicates the current enrollment or average attendance. (See figure 1.)

In most churches the present fragmentary program is hampered by

[1]*Apt to Teach* (Wheaton and Chicago: Evangelical Teacher Training Association and National Sunday School Association, 1957).

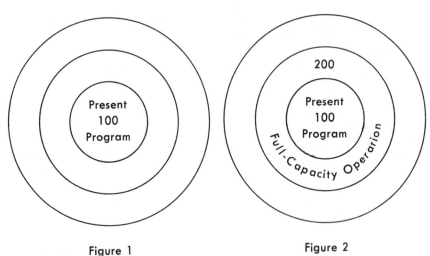

Figure 1          Figure 2

lack of consecrated, well-trained leaders. Few churches have a surplus or a waiting list of good teachers. If a Sunday school only maintains its status quo, it needs a growing corps of young people and adults who are in process of training. These should be enrolled in formal training classes. They should be assigned to serve as practice teachers, or as associate teachers.

*Full-capacity operation.* The typical church is not using all the physical faculties that are available. A careful survey of many buildings will reveal unused space, furniture, and material. After checking the actual equipment, it is a simple matter to establish a Sunday school's maximum capacity. This is entered in the second circle. It may be possible to double the present enrollment, if the building is filled every Sunday. Such growth demonstrates better stewardship and good business methods since it cuts the per capita cost of operation.

Figure 2 now represents a full-capacity operation. Is it double the present activity and enrollment? Or triple? Such a full-capacity program will require redoubled effort in leadership education. This is the Sunday school's immediate need. A Sunday school can never expand in quantity or quality without a larger, more efficient staff. An accelerated training program will develop the required personnel, will challenge new recruits, and will provide in-service training for present teachers. This is a "must" if the church is going to do its best with the equipment that is available.

*Total responsibility.* Another and even larger expansion program must be faced and studied. It is important to make an impact on the total community through the Sunday school's ministry. No church can be satisfied to "reach, teach, train, and send" only those who are enrolled presently. The Sunday school is not a closed corporation, responsible only for its

*Prepare job description.* The board of Christian education should exercise creative vision in establishing a clear, concise job analysis for each position in the church, Sunday school, and related agencies. The correlation of all responsibilities is important. Prepare a list of the basic requirements in each area. Define clearly any extracurricular requirements. List all other regular functions which the worker is expected to attend, including church attendance, visitation, teachers and officers meetings.

*Establish a schedule of training classes.* Teacher training classes are more likely to involve *all* the teachers and officers if the schedule is set up months in advance. Arrange the dates, sequence of courses, place of meeting, and clear the calendar so that conflicts will be avoided. After preparing a long-range yearly plan, submit this program to the board of Christian education and the general church board for approval and adoption. This will guarantee the assigned dates and will eliminate the common excuse, "I have other meetings scheduled."

Prepare an explicit list of all courses to be offered for a year or two in advance. This will enable workers to schedule courses that will fill out their required subjects. With today's multiple demands, most people are already overloaded with meetings. Careful planning will help to ease this load and lead to complete cooperation in the training program. Classes should be scheduled to meet the convenience of the corps of workers. The following suggestions should prove helpful. Classes may be scheduled at any of these periods:

1. The hour immediately preceding Sunday school.

2. During the regular Sunday school period. This eliminates the active teachers and officers, but reaches a wide list of prospective workers. Entire classes can study teacher training for one or more quarters each year. Prospects can be handpicked from the various youth and adult classes.

3. Preceding the Sunday evening worship service, or at the same hour as the youth and adult group activities.

4. After the Sunday evening service.

5. On a regular training night each week, kept clear of any other meetings.

6. Before, during, or after the regular midweek prayer meeting.

7. During a two-week training session, with one or more classes every evening. This can be scheduled on the same basis as evangelistic meetings. An intensive period of training should result in a spiritual quickening of the whole church.

8. A teacher training class included in vacation Bible school.

9. An extended summer camp program.

10. Workers may register for evening classes at a local or nearby Bible

institute or Bible college. The church might pay the tuition of those who satisfactorily complete courses.

11. In cooperation with other churches of the same denomination in an area-wide training school.

12. In an interdenominational school in the local community.

*Secure the best available instructor.* A competent instructor will increase the enrollment. Local pastors or directors of Christian education are usually "apt to teach." A neighboring pastor or an outside director or Christian education specialist may stimulate interest. Public school teachers are well qualified for methods courses. Businessmen with administrative or professional training may be available for specialized courses. In each case the instructor himself should demonstrate good teaching in each class session.

*Examine and select the most adequate curriculum.* The evaluation and selection of a curriculum and curriculum materials are most important. Textbooks should be doctrinally sound, pedagogically correct, and interestingly written. Methods courses should reflect the latest findings of Christian education leaders. Courses should be graded for lay workers. Highly technical or professional vocabularies will discourage the typical volunteer Sunday school worker. Materials are available from a number of sources:

1. The denominational board of Christian education or denominational publishing house or bookstore.

2. Agencies, such as the Evangelical Teacher Training Association. The ETTA curriculum is produced on two levels—a Preliminary Training Course and an Advanced Training Course. Each of these includes six units of twelve lessons each, for a total of seventy-two sessions. There are standardized awards leading to the Preliminary Teachers certificate and the Advanced Teachers certificate.

3. Correspondence courses are offered by several leading Bible institutes and colleges. (Moody Bible Institute, Barrington College, Biola College are examples.) These courses may be studied by individuals or by classes.

4. Some interdenominational or nondenominationally related publishers produce training materials adaptable to local needs.

5. A tailor-made series, including selected courses from many sources, may be prepared by local leaders. This procedure has the disadvantage of not being standardized.

*Advertise and publicize the courses.* "To the person who has never heard of your product, it does not exist." The best laid plans will fail without a balanced emphasis on advertising, promoting, and publicizing the training courses. Every legitimate means should be used to sell the program of training opportunities. All advertising should be undergirded with prayer and spiritual discernment. Here are some suggested mediums that have proved effective:

1. Personal letters—preferably a series of communications.
2. Personal interviews, to handpick prospective leaders and teachers.
3. Preregistration for enrollment.
4. Testimonies by students who have completed former courses.
5. Pulpit and platform announcements and dramatizations.
6. Posters, bulletin boards, etc.
7. Newspaper, radio, and TV.
8. Emphasis during teachers-officers meetings.
9. Promotion by a wide-awake committee.

## THE CHURCH CONDUCTS THE PROGRAM

Teacher training involves preparation, publicity, and promotion by the sponsoring agency or by individuals. It means *work* for all students enrolled. It presupposes regular attendance, constant study, careful research, challenging practice teaching, high standards, and the actual completion of the course. Some teachers and officers will rebel at such a program, but any Christian worker worthy of the name will be challenged by the opportunity to be "approved of God."

Thorough training requires complete records of attendance, class participation, and grades; the issuance of certificates of credit and other course awards; assignments and follow-up of practice teaching; placement of those who are qualified to serve; the selection and use of a standardized course of study that will motivate the students; and a program of in-service training that magnifies the teacher, office, and function.

The local church should conduct a perennial cycle of approved courses. Workers should also be encouraged to take courses in a nearby Bible college or in other schools. They should be advised of courses offered on a community, cooperative plan. If no class is available, well-established correspondence courses should be suggested to broaden the scope of the training.

There is an old alibi that "teacher training costs too much in terms of time and money." This is certainly not true; for *teacher training does not cost, it PAYS.*

## THE CHURCH CONSERVES THE RESULTS

Many Sunday schools capitalize on their high standards and advertise the fact that their teachers and officers are well trained. Teacher training certificates may be framed and displayed in the classrooms or in the church foyer. Promotional literature and verbal announcements should stress the program of teacher-officer education. A public commencement program will motivate the entire church by demonstrating the value of training, and its relationships to the over-all program of Christian education. The use of a covenant will dignify the assignment of the teaching staff.

The church should involve its trainees in active Christian service. Vacation Bible school, weekday Christian education, and all age-group activities should be staffed by trained personnel. Community projects, such as Scouts, Boys Brigade, Pioneer Girls, Jet Cadets provide opportunities for in-service training and experience. Every person who is being trained should be used.

Teacher training must be a major emphasis in a growing church and Sunday school. Trained teachers are more likely to succeed. And successful teachers make a successful Sunday school.

## BIBLIOGRAPHY

Benson, Clarence H. *The Sunday School in Action.* Chicago: Moody Press, 1932.

——. *The Christian Teacher.* Chicago: Moody Press, 1950.

Eavey, C. B. *Principles of Teaching for Christian Teachers.* Grand Rapids: Zondervan Publishing House, 1940.

Hodges, Vern R. *Christian Education Bibliography.* Salem: Conservative Baptist Association of Oregon.

Leavitt, Guy P. *Teach with Success.* Cincinnati: Standard Publishing Co., 1956.

Murch, James DeForest. *Christian Education and the Local Church.* Cincinnati: Standard Publishing Co., 1943.

Person, Peter P. *Introduction to Christian Education.* Grand Rapids: Baker Book House, 1958.

Reisinger, D. K., and Risley, Clate. *Apt to Teach.* Wheaton and Chicago: Evangelical Teacher Training Association and National Sunday School Association, 1957.

Rozell, Ray. *Informal Talks on Sunday School Teaching.* Grand Rapids: Grand Rapids International Publications, 1956.

Soderholm, Marjorie. *Understanding the Pupil* (three vols.). Grand Rapids: Baker Book House, 1956-57.

*Sunday School Encyclopedia.* Chicago: National Sunday School Association.

Teacher training textbooks of the Preliminary and Advanced Courses (12 subjects). Wheaton: Evangelical Teacher Training Association.

Weidman, Mavis Anderson. *Charting the Course.* Harrisburg: Christian Publications, 1955.

Wymore, Leonard G. (ed.). *Christian Education Handbook.* Cincinnati: Standard Publishing Co., 1960.

# Chapter 8

# AUDIO-VISUAL MATERIALS

## Ruth Haycock

SOME TIME AGO the advertising department of *Parade* magazine gave an unusual assignment. To each of three top artists they handed the following description, asking that he draw a picture of the animal portrayed. Since the men were professional artists and the description of an aardvark was an accurate one, taken from *Encyclopaedia Britannica,* it seemed that the sketches should be quite authentic. As you read the description below, study the sketches to see the accuracy with which each artist followed instructions:

> The body is stout, with arched back; the limbs are short and stout, armed with strong, blunt claws; the ears long; and the tail thick at the base and tapering gradually. The elongated head is set on a short, thick neck, and at the extremity of the snout is a disc in which the nostrils open. The mouth is small and tubular, furnished with a long extensile tongue. A large individual measured 6 ft. 8 in. In color it is pale sandy or yellow, the hair being scanty and allowing the skin to show.

Yet the three drawings are so different! What does an aardvark look like? An actual photograph, when compared with the sketches made from verbal descriptions, points out the inadequacy of even carefully chosen words to convey to trained adults the meaning of the word *aardvark.* So also in Christian education, words alone cannot do the job. Even a carefully developed curriculum, with content chosen from Scripture and vocabulary adapted

**THIS IS AN AARDVARK**

Ruth Haycock, Ed.D., is professor of Christian Education at Baptist Bible Seminary, Johnson City, New York.

From "Three Artists Couldn't Draw an Aardvark." Courtesy of Bausch and Lomb, Inc., Rochester, N.Y.

to the ability of the pupil, may fail to accomplish the purpose of its writers if it depends only on words.

The fact that Jesus was a great teacher—the Master Teacher, *the* Great Teacher—is recognized even by those who do not accept Him as God or as Saviour. The apostle John says of Him, "He knew all [men]; and He did not need that anyone should witness concerning man—needed no evidence from anyone about men; for He Himself knew what was in human nature. [He could read men's hearts]" (John 2:24, 25, Amplified New Testament). Here was the greatest teacher of all time, the One who understood man best, yet a study of His teaching methods reveals much use of illustrative material. When He was asked, "Is it lawful to give tribute to Caesar, or not?" He might merely have replied, "Yes, we have a duty both to God and to Rome," but He did not. He asked for a coin and referred his questioners to the image and superscription (Mark 12:14-17). Again, to teach His disciples about true greatness, Jesus used a child as an object lesson to mature men (Mark 9:33-37; Matt. 18:1-14). He knew what some present-day teachers fail to recognize, that people, even adults, learn better when visual materials are used in the teaching process.

The Lord Jesus was not the only one who used illustrative material in Scripture, nor is such use confined to the New Testament. Over and over again, God commanded His prophets to perform some act to teach an important truth, or to provoke people to ask questions (Jer. 13:1-27; 18:1-10; 19:1-13; 24:1-10; Amos 7:1, 7, 8; 8:1-3; 9:1; I Kings 11:29-39). God knows man's heart; He knows how difficult it is to get man's attention, and to make him understand abstract truth. Someone has rightly said that the use of visual materials *is* God's way of teaching, and that if we would teach Biblically we must teach visually.

## THE EFFECTIVENESS OF AUDIO-VISUAL MATERIALS

Since man's view of God and the world affects every area of his life, it is of utmost importance that those who present the teachings of the Bible use methods and tools which make learning as effective as possible. Teaching time in the church suffers from competition with many outside activities, and is therefore limited to a few hours per week—too few when one considers the enormity of the task of teaching eternal truth. Christian leaders should be concerned to know how much help and what kinds of help can be gained from using audio-visual materials in the classroom and assembly.

Much research has been done in this field. In 1950, Hoban and van Ormer reviewed and summarized the findings of more than two hundred

studies relating to films alone.[1]    Paul R. Wendt,[2] interpreting for the
National Education Association what audio-visual research says to the
teacher, concludes that audio-visual materials can do the following:

1. Teach facts at all grade levels and in most subjects.

> Furthermore, in most cases the teaching of facts has been accom-
> plished more efficiently than by traditional teaching methods. For
> one thing, less time was taken for pupils to learn with the help of
> these materials than would have been used without them. The sav-
> ing of time has sometimes been spectacular. Any materials or meth-
> ods that can increase the efficiency of our teaching by 20 per cent
> deserves serious consideration.

2. Cause pupils to remember significantly longer than when taught by
purely verbal means.

3. Arouse and sustain interest in the learner.

4. Cause vocabulary growth.

> Rich experiences are a solid basis of a good vocabulary, and ex-
> perience is precisely what audio-visual materials provide. . . . Both
> school librarians and public librarians can recall instances where
> the demand for printed materials on a certain topic had exhausted
> the library's supply soon after a film on that topic was shown locally.

5. Change opinions and attitudes. This is particularly true when pupils
are exposed to a series of films over a period of time, or when films are
used which have an emotional appeal. Films are also valuable in reinforcing attitudes already held by an audience.

6. Stimulate thinking and problem-solving.

> We are mistaken when we think that audio-visual materials, es-
> pecially films, have a stigma of "passive" learning attached to them.
> The pupil does not sit in the classroom watching a film like an empty
> cup collecting the drippings of facts from the film. On the contrary,
> he is able to use the facts obtained from the film in forming concepts
> and drawing generalizations based on these facts. Even though the
> teaching film is different from the theatrical film, some comparison
> with the theatrical film is useful. The motion picture theaters would
> have few customers if the enjoyment of a theatrical film were a pas-
> sive activity. The very ability of a film to absorb the complete at-
> tention and feelings of the viewer underlies the success of the theatri-
> cal film business.

[1]Charles F. Hoban, Jr., and Edward B. van Ormer, *Instructional Film Research,*
*1918-1950.* Technical Report SDC 269-7-19, United States Department of the Army
and United States Department of the Navy (Port Washington, L.I., N.Y.: Special
Devices Center, 1950), pp. 1, 2.
[2]Paul R. Wendt, "Audio-Visual Instruction," *What Research Says to the Teacher,*
*No. 14* (Washington, D.C.: Department of Classroom Teachers and American Educational Research Association of the National Education Association, 1957), pp. 10-
15. (Used by permission.)

7. Speed up the learning of skills.

While it is true that most of the experimentation in the use of audio-visual teaching tools has been related to public school subjects and to the training of personnel in the armed services, the conclusions are nonetheless relevant to Christian teaching. Here too we have a body of facts to teach, facts to be used by the pupil as a basis for thinking and problem-solving, dealing with relationships between God and man, and between man and man. Here too it is important that at every age we teach accurately and that pupils form attitudes which are in conformity to the Word of God. Since religious vocabulary is not taught in the public school, Christian teachers must be doubly sure that their pupils learn Christian terminology. The events of the Bible took place in a country and at a time foreign to modern Americans and need the clarification which illustrative materials provide.

When a teacher of teen-agers steps to the blackboard, draws a time line, using simple drawings or words to represent familiar events in Bible history, then locates David on the chart, the interest of the class is stimulated and the fact thus represented is likely to be remembered. Likewise, when a teacher in the junior department uses a picture or flannelboard to show Peter praying on the housetop, not only is interest increased, but children are less likely to imagine Peter praying on a sloping American roof. Arousing interest by means of illustrative material may well be the first step in transferring attention to the Bible content itself.

## BASIC PRINCIPLES FOR THE USE OF AUDIO-VISUAL MATERIALS IN TEACHING

With all the evidence available concerning the usefulness of these teaching helps, it would be a mistake to assume that because a teacher uses a variety of visual materials he is doing an effective job. Too many illustrations may confuse rather than help the pupil. It is also possible to use material which makes thinking more difficult, rather than less difficult. Some basic principles of utilization may help in the selection and presentation of materials:

1. The value of a given teaching tool is not absolute, but depends on many factors.

2. The use of any illustrative material must be thoroughly integrated into the total teaching situation.

3. The total teaching situation, including audio-visual utilization, must be set up to follow proved principles of teaching.

### VALUE NOT ABSOLUTE

In a beginners' department one Sunday morning, Mrs. James used several songs and prayer before sending the children to their classes. In each class of about five youngsters, the teacher told the Bible story and directed her pupils in related activities. When the department reassembled, Mrs. James explained that the children were to see a film which, she said, they would be interested in. The projectionist, who had quietly set up his equipment before the service, started the projector. For about fifteen minutes these four- and five-year-olds watched the film. The story began with a boy building a model airplane. Soon the plane flew off through the window and became the main character in the film. The narration emphasized the fact that unless boys and girls obey God's rules, their lives will be wrecked, as the plane was at one point in the story. When the film was ended, Mrs. James spoke rather weakly, "I know we did not understand all of that picture, but I am sure we all enjoyed it. Will Mrs. Knight please lead us in our closing prayer and ask God to keep us through another week." Obviously, this use of a film left much to be desired. What was wrong?

The value of any teaching material depends on several factors: on the material itself, on the group, and on the purpose of the teacher. This film presented truth about salvation and obedience in a symbolic form more suitable for an older group. For beginners the relationship between a life and a plane was not clear. Since these children were not yet interested in making models, the plane did not serve even as a good attention-getting device. The leader's purpose in using the film was not evident; the film story had no relationship to the Bible lesson or to the application of that lesson. Perhaps some other group in the church had obtained the film and had passed it on so that the church would be sure to get its money's worth out of the rental. However valuable the presentation might have been for another situation, it did not contribute to an otherwise good teaching session for beginners.

A map of Palestine may or may not be valuable. If the class is of at least fourth grade level, the children will have had some experience with maps and will be interested in geographical relationships. Most young people and adults in Bible-teaching churches could profit greatly by the wise use of maps to help relate their present Bible study to events previously studied, or to current happenings. But the value of a map depends not alone on the age and experience of the pupils. It depends also on the lesson series being taught and the purpose of the instructor in teaching a given section, and on the particular map which is available. For instance, in teaching the conquest of Canaan to an older group, a teacher may want to show how Israel was victorious over certain areas. Finding only a small map with too many fine-print names, the instructor might decide to use a hand-drawn map locating pertinent cities to be circled as each conquest is studied. Thus both the progress and the incompleteness of the conquest could be emphasized, and at the same time a portion of the book of Joshua would take on life.

A teacher considering the use of a picture with a particular class must consider these factors:

1. The *picture* itself—its size, clarity, content, accuracy.

2. The *purpose* in using the picture—whether to show Bible customs or dress, illustrate the meaning of a word, lead pupils to discuss an event previously studied.

3. The *group*—ages, backgrounds, experience, previous study, present needs.

4. The *way* in which the picture is to be shown—posted on a bulletin board, held before the class, passed from one to another, displayed at an interest center for pre-session study, or projected by an opaque projector.

All these factors enter into the value of a picture, and similar considerations into a decision concerning the use of any illustrative material. It is often impossible to state that particular material is good or poor without knowing the teaching situation; the value is not absolute.

ILLUSTRATIVE MATERIAL THOROUGHLY INTEGRATED INTO SITUATION

Perhaps the most frequent error made in the use of projected materials arises out of the feeling that, since the film or filmstrip is a unit in itself, the use of it *is* the lesson. Again and again one hears a teacher say, "I would like to borrow a film [or filmstrip] because I don't have time to prepare," or "Since I'm using a filmstrip in my weekday class, I don't have to study this week." In actuality, whatever teaching method is used, the method and the material used must be worked into the total situation, if real teaching is to be accomplished.

When an instructor merely shows a film, or tells a flannelgraph story, or has a discussion, or delivers a lecture, he has not necessarily taught. Each of these activities may well be part of a teaching period, but seldom is any one of them complete in itself. A group should be prepared for a film. Following the presentation should come discussion of what was portrayed, or summarization of the points made or steps shown, or planning for further study or activity in the light of the material presented. A second showing may be valuable if there are unanswered questions after the discussion, if the film contains many difficult concepts, if the students differ in their interpretation of the film, or if it seems a repetition will reinforce the learning enough to make it stick.[3] In both the preparation and the follow-up a teacher can often use a blackboard as points are listed. Here then is a combination of film, blackboard, discussion or

[3]William H. Allen, "Audio-Visual Communication," *Encyclopedia of Educational Research* (3rd ed.; New York: Macmillan Co., 1960), p. 127.

summarization, and perhaps other activities, all planned to accomplish one purpose.

A teacher may use a recorded story to capture the attention of a group of primaries or juniors and lead them into the Bible lesson; a few Bible word flashcards in teaching new vocabulary to first and second graders; or a diagrammatic chart built on the flannelboard in an adult class—whatever it is that he uses, he must consider the material as part of a larger teaching process.[4]

PRINCIPLES OF TEACHING FOLLOWED

Considerable research and the experience of thousands of teachers have shown that an instructor must follow certain principles if learning is to take place. These principles include motivation, understanding, participation, repetition, and immediate application. Regardless of what materials a teacher uses to apply these principles, the principles must be carried out. The fact that a second grade teacher uses a wood model of Rahab's house in teaching the story of the spies does not in itself guarantee that the children will be motivated to believe God, or even to know more about the Bible story. The model may result only in greater understanding of the type of houses and the way in which Rahab could hide the men on the roof, but this is not enough. If the teacher also uses clothespins to represent Rahab and the spies, a bit of dry grass for a covering, and a red cord hung from the window, performing the actions as the story is told, interest becomes greater and each child tends to identify himself with the people in the Bible story. If in addition the children are encouraged to manipulate the materials and retell the story, the teacher has provided for added participation and the kind of repetition which causes youngsters to remember an important Old Testament event.

But even this is not enough, for many a student leaves class feeling that what he has learned has little or no relevance to his own experience. Pupils at every level need help in seeing the relationship of Bible teaching to their lives. They must leave class able to make applications of truth. Perhaps the emphasis desired is that Rahab believed that God would do what He promised because she knew He had already done so much. A teacher can lead even seven-year-olds to think of the wonderful things that God has done and of promises that they can make their own. Just as Rahab saw that she needed to be on God's side, so present-day children can see their need.

At a more mature level, an instructor cannot forget basic principles of teaching and assume that his use of illustrative material insures student

[4]For an excellent example of the integration of a variety of audio-visual materials into a lesson series on the shepherd theme, see Lois E. LeBar, "All Bible Vacation School Series," *The Primary Teacher* and *Primary Workbook* (Wheaton: Scripture Press, 1962).

learning. It has been said that learning involves a change of behavior, and that unless learning takes place, no teaching takes place. The failure of Christian teachers to realize that principles of teaching are basic and cannot be ignored is an important reason for so many class sessions with so few changes of attitude or behavior. If people at any age are to change, there must be motivation; if they are to study the Word, they must see some reason for studying; if they are to participate in class discussion, they must be motivated to take part. But they must also be helped to understand the Bible; be provided with enough repetition and review to fix facts and clarify relationships; be helped to make the changes in their lives which obedience to the Word of God demands. Telling alone will not accomplish these things; neither will abundant use of audio-visual materials, valuable as they are. Lesson planning is needed that is based upon sound principles and that uses the best material available for a given situation.

## PROBLEMS RELATED TO USE OF AUDIO-VISUAL MATERIALS

In a recent survey[5] of sixty churches, pastors listed the following as their most serious audio-visual problems: (1) lack of workers trained to use materials effectively, (2) lack of recognition of the value of such materials, (3) expense, (4) need of a better system of classification. This listing indicates basic problems—problems of attitude, training, and administration.

Perhaps most basic is the problem of attitude or lack of the recognition of the value of audio-visual materials. When people are convinced of the value of better teaching materials, they learn how to use them; they are willing for their church to spend the necessary money to provide them; and they find out how to administer materials effectively.

Even in schools of education, a major stumbling block for student teachers is the gap between the methods of teaching taught to them and the methods which they have seen used by their instructors. In churches the condition is often more serious because so many who teach have never been exposed to better methods in teacher training. The example then of the pastor or some other leader who makes effective use of audio-visual materials can stir others to see the possibilities as perhaps nothing else can. This is particularly true if such a person has varied opportunities to teach in the presence of other teachers.

The problem of attitude is not solved by demonstration alone, however, though such demonstration may serve as a valuable eye opener. A

[5]Ruth C. Haycock, "A Survey of Sixty Churches in Respect to Audio-Visual Utilization" (unpublished report, 1954), p. 11.
See also Edwin J. Swineford, "Facing Obstacles in the Use of Audio-Visuals," Education Screen and Audio-Visual Guide, January, 1959, p. 19.

good example may even cause others so to feel the inadequacy of their own teaching that they become discouraged. A church must help its teachers to see the possibility of their *personal* use of visual teaching materials. A combined program of making materials available and training workers in their use is needed.

The training should be part of a larger leadership training effort, but should be sufficiently explicit to be effective. In regular teacher training classes, workers should be instructed and shown how to use pictures in teaching a song; how to tell a flannelgraph story; how to make simple charts, diagrams, and time lines and use them with older groups; how to prepare a lesson plan in which audio-visual materials are used to accomplish a specific objective; how to use a chalkboard in a variety of ways.

In departmental meetings workers need to review methods and materials particularly suitable for their age group. They should prepare materials to be used in the next month or quarter or look over what is already available and make plans. In monthly conferences for all teachers and officers, workers can learn what kinds of helps are available; they should see some demonstration of effective use in the conduct of the conference sessions; and there can be an occasional work session when small groups mount pictures, make flannelboards, or sort materials.

Churches ought also to take responsibility for furnishing adequate teaching materials for their teachers. If a church provides only lesson manuals, the implication is that the teacher needs nothing else! A visit to a public school will quickly convince a skeptical person that books are but one of many kinds of materials used by alert teachers.

Adequate planning and administration are essential if a church is to provide and conserve illustrative materials. One person should be given administrative responsibility to accomplish the following tasks:

1. Collect what the church already has.

2. Find out what is available that is related to the curriculums being used.

3. Make recommendations concerning equipment and materials needed.

4. Set up a workable library of instructional materials.

5. Help train teachers to use what is available and to prepare handmade materials as needed.

One person, however, cannot change the teaching methods of a church. A director of audio-visual materials will need the backing of a sound financial plan and of a committee representing all age groups and agencies of the church. He will need the enthusiastic cooperation of the pastor, officers, and teachers. A director will want to begin where people are, teaching them to use what is easily available; then introducing them to other helps which meet local needs. Equipment should be purchased only after a need is felt by those who would use it.[6]

The Bible is the Word of God to men. If men, women, and children are to be saved through the Word, and then grow in the Lord, their interest must be aroused; their understanding must be enlightened; and their convictions must be deepened. Through the history of mankind, God has been pleased on many occasions to do these things by the use of that which man can both see and hear. Good teachers in all ages have *shown* their pupils as well as told them.

## SUMMARY

| Values of A-V Materials | Basic Principles in Utilization | Problems to Be Overcome |
|---|---|---|
| 1. Teach facts. | 1. Value is dependent on many factors. | 1. Lack of recognition of values. |
| 2. Improve retention. | | |
| 3. Arouse and hold interest. | 2. Use must be part of total teaching situation. | 2. Failure to train workers in effective utilization. |
| 4. Cause vocabulary growth. | | |
| 5. Change attitudes. | 3. Total situation must follow proved principles of teaching. | 3. Inadequate availability of materials in the church. |
| 6. Stimulate thinking. | | |
| 7. Speed up learning. | | |

## BIBLIOGRAPHY

Allen, William H. "Audio-Visual Communication," *Encyclopedia of Educational Research.* (3rd ed.) New York: Macmillan Co., 1960.

Hoban, Charles F., Hoban, Charles F., Jr., Zisman, Samuel B. *Visualizing the Curriculum.* New York: Dryden Press, 1944.

Hockman, William S. *Projected Visual Aids in the Church.* Boston: Pilgrim Press, 1947.

Swineford, Edwin J. "Facing Obstacles in the Use of Audio-Visuals," *Educational Screen and Audio-Visual Guide,* January, 1959.

Wendt, Paul R. "Audio-Visual Instruction," *What Research Says to the Teacher, No. 14.* Washington: National Education Association, 1957.

## FOR FURTHER READING

*General Discussions*

Dale, Edgar. *Audio-Visual Methods in Teaching.* (rev.) New York: Dryden Press, 1954. Primarily for the day school teacher.

Eboch, Sidney C. *Operating Audio-Visual Equipment.* San Francisco: Howard Chandler Publishing Co., 1960.

  Excellent instructions and diagrams relating to use of all kinds of projectors, record players, tape recorders.

[6]For further information on administration in churches, see Gene Getz, *Audio-Visuals in the Church* (Chicago: Moody Press, 1959), Chapter 13.

Getz, Gene. *Audio-Visuals in the Church.* Chicago: Moody Press, 1959.
Covers preparation and use of all kinds of materials, presented from evangelical viewpoint.

Kinder, James S. *Audio-Visual Materials and Techniques.* New York: American Book Co., 1950.
Day school viewpoint.

Minor, Ed. *Simplified Techniques for Preparing Visual Instructional Materials.* New York: McGraw-Hill Book Co., Inc., 1962.
A well-illustrated book which includes techniques, materials, and sources of materials for many preparation methods.

Rogers, William L., and Vieth, Paul H. *Visual Aids in the Church.* Philadelphia: Christian Education Press, 1946.
The earliest general discussion in the church field.

Rumpf, Oscar J. *The Use of Audio-Visuals in the Church.* Philadelphia: Christian Education Press, 1958.

Thomas, R. Murray, and Swartout, Sherwin G. *Integrated Teaching Materials: How to Choose, Create, and Use Them.* New York: Longmans Green and Co., 1960.

Tower, Howard E. *Church Use of Audio-Visuals.* New York: Abingdon-Cokesbury Press, 1950.

Waldrup, Earl. *Using Visual Aids in a Church.* Nashville: Broadman Press, 1949.

*Preparation of Materials*

East, Marjorie. *Display for Learning.* New York: Dryden Press, 1952.
Valuable classic dealing particularly with non-projected materials for day schools.

*Flannelgraph Helps.* Wheaton: Scripture Press.
Brief pamphlet dealing with values, preparation, presentation and selection of materials for churches.

*A Guide for Use with the Indiana University Film Series in the Area of Preparation and Use of Audio-Visual Instructional Materials.* Bloomington, Ind.: Indiana University Audio-Visual Center, 1958.
A manual containing a wealth of information related to the preparation of many kinds of materials; valuable even without the films.

Haas, Kenneth B., and Packer, Harry Q. *Preparation and Use of Audio-Visual Aids.* New York: Prentice-Hall, Inc., 1950.
Prepared primarily for the use of industry but with many applications to church use.

Liechti, Alice O., and Chappell, Jack R. *Making and Using Charts.* San Francisco: Fearon Publishers, 1957.

Chart methods for elementary school use, many of which may be adapted.

Meeks, Martha F. *Lettering Techniques.* Austin, Texas: University of Texas, Visual Instruction Bureau, 1956.

Clear instructions for person without art training.

Meeks, Martha F. *Models for Teaching.* Austin, Texas: University of Texas, Visual Instruction Bureau, 1956.

Teaches use of various materials, including plaster, rubber molds, papier-mâché; slanted to elementary school use; includes extensive bibliography.

Nelson, Leslie. *Instructional Aids: How to Make and Use Them.* Dubuque, Iowa: William C. Brown Co., 1958.

Suggestions and instructions on models, charts, bulletin boards, lettering, boards and easels, puppets, and simple projection equipment; elementary school emphasis.

Rogers, Fay. *How to Use Flannelgraph.* Cincinnati: Standard Publishing Co., 1950.

Descriptive information and instructions for preparation of boards, easels, backgrounds, and figures, for church use.

Thompson, David W. *Bible Box Talks.* Cincinnati: Standard Publishing Co., 1954.

Patterns and instructions for making models of Bible objects, using boxes.

Weselah, Anne Douglas. *E-Z Bulletin Boards.* San Francisco: Author, 2263 Union St., 1959.

Excellent suggestions for layout, 3-D effects, sources of prepared letters.

*Available Projected Materials and Records*

*Audio-Visual Resource Guide for Religious Education.* New York: Department of Audio-Visual and Broadcast Education, National Council of Churches, published periodically.

*Educational Film Guide.* New York: H. W. Wilson Co.

A periodical similar to *Reader's Guide,* available in many libraries; indexes motion pictures for educational and religious use.

*Educational Media Index.* Washington, D.C.: U.S. Office of Education and Educational Media Council.

A valuable extensive index to many kinds of educational material.

*Filmstrip Guide.* New York: H. W. Wilson Co.,

A periodical index to filmstrips, both secular and religious.

An important part of teaching children is to discover how to in-volve them most effectively in the classroom situation.

(Courtesy of Luoma Photos)

# PART THREE

*Understanding the Learner*

## Chapter 9

# THE CRADLE ROLL

## BERNICE T. CORY

THE CRADLE ROLL DEPARTMENT of the Sunday school is gradually being recognized as an outstanding *service* agency. For no other department in a well-functioning Sunday school so effectually links church and home and brings entire families into the Sunday school and church. The cradle roll is the foundation of the Sunday school, for it starts where life itself starts—at birth—and maintains interest in a baby till he is two and is "promoted" to the nursery department. However, though *babies* are the subject of and reason for the cradle roll, the literature taken by visitors into the home at stated intervals is slanted to their *parents,* young adults.

The potential of the cradle roll ministry has hardly been tapped. Relatively few churches have taken advantage of its unique ministry. Perhaps this is because of its name, *cradle roll.* This often evokes a nostalgic picture of an inactive list of names on dusty cardboard cradles, dangling on a church wall. The title was apt when it was given back in 1884. But its originators could not foresee the far-reaching possibilities of ministering to babies and parents, first in the home and in more recent years also in the church itself.

Actually, the cradle roll was never planned to be; it just happened. In 1880, a little boy, whose name we do not know, dropped one penny into the birthday bank in a Sunday school in Elizabeth, New Jersey, for his baby brother. This inspired the teachers, Mrs. Alonzo Pettit and her sister Juliett (Mrs. J. M. Dudley), to compile a list of other babies too young to attend Sunday school. Thus the cradle roll was born.

Little is known concerning its growth and history. One looks in vain

Bernice T. Cory, Litt.D., is editorial director of the Children's Division, Scripture Press, Wheaton, Illinois.

through histories of religious education to find evidences of activity in the cradle roll department of the Sunday school. Most educators ignore it. Some make no distinction between the ministry for infants (from birth to two) and nursery children (two's and three's), and that for beginners (four's and five's).

However, in 1921, nearly fifty years after the cradle roll's founding, Jessie E. Moore, a far-visioned graduate of Teachers College, Columbia University, and an earnest Sunday school teacher, wrote a *Cradle Roll Manual*.[1] Her hope was that "through the cradle roll the uplifting arm of the church could be thrown around mother and father and child, that through this influence a Christian atmosphere might be created for the child in the home." She said: "More and more fully educators are coming to understand the importance of infancy as a formative period. Because of the great plasticity of the infant it is inevitable that habits shall be formed. From a baby's first hour, every moment counts for good or ill in the making of character. . . . At birth the baby begins to react to the outside world, the world of material things and of folks." To substantiate this, she quotes Patterson DuBois:

> The infant is a suckling in the fullest sense of the term, and the whole life is not sufficient to efface that which is absorbed during these earliest years when the receptive powers are so great and the powers of resistance so weak. At this time the germs of character, especially of the emotional life, are developed. Antipathies and likings are acquired which cannot be explained in later life. While memory can recall nothing of the events of these years, many characteristics are gained at this time.

Also, Jessie E. Moore cited Froebel's saying, "Train the mother and you train the child."

The modern attitude, which recognizes the cradle roll as the first ally of the church in providing a spiritual ministry for new parents, is represented by Mattie C. Leatherwood. She says:

> With the years have come an ever-enlarging vision of the possibilities of the cradle roll and a change in its emphasis from sentiment to service. Thus it has long since ceased to be merely a list of babies' names and has become a department of the Sunday school charged with responsibility for the definite ministry of the church to babies. . . . "Train up a child in the way he should go," said the wise man of old. He might well have said, "Begin at birth and train up a child in the way he should go," for the importance of the first years of a child's life cannot be overestimated. . . . The cradle roll department

[1] *Cradle Roll Manual* (New York: Methodist Book Concern, 1921).

is the fountainhead of a stream that blesses and refreshes and constantly flows into the Sunday school.[2]

## PURPOSES OF A CRADLE ROLL MINISTRY

Cradle roll workers are true missionaries, for they visit homes, show keen interest in the infant members of families, and tactfully try to establish a close bond between parents and Sunday school and church. Some other purposes of the cradle roll workers are:

To leave with parents attractive, helpful literature at a time when their hearts are responsive and they will most appreciate practical help and loving concern.

To establish a continuing contact that will win parents to Christ if they are not yet Christians, that will attract indifferent Christian parents back to the Lord, and will strengthen those who are earnest Christians.

To help parents realize that their baby is a gift from God and that they must be godly character-builders and pattern-setters so that their child's earliest recollections are of Christian influences.

To help parents, especially with their first baby, to carry out the demanding roles of husband-father and wife-mother. To alert them to the high calling of Christian parenthood by educating them for their role in Christian nurture.

To woo them into God's Word, encouraging daily family devotions. To furnish motivation and guidance in maintaining family worship.

To train parents to train their child to relate the Lord naturally to everything in his life—his home, family, food, clothes, toys, pets, nature, friends.

To interest parents and entire families in the fellowship, instruction, and opportunities for service which the church affords.

In every way to fulfill the cradle roll slogans: "A Christian home for every baby" and "Christ-centered homes for times like these."

## IMPORTANCE OF A CRADLE ROLL MINISTRY

Physicians, psychologists, and school administrators agree that a child learns more new things in his first three years than in any other like period of his life. Thus, no time is as fruitful in laying the groundwork for rich spiritual growth as during a baby's highly impressionable years.

According to J. D. Ratcliff, baby's first year is "the growingest,"[3] for he progresses from utter helplessness, with all faculties dormant, to semi-independence. In no other year does he traverse such difficult and dangerous ground or encounter so many new experiences.

[2]*The Cradle Roll Department of the Sunday School* (Nashville: Sunday School Board of the Southern Baptist Convention, 1941), pp. 12, 20.
[3]"The First Year Is the Growingest," *Parents' Magazine*, XXXV (September, 1960), p. 44.

Among the 1960 White House Conference reports on the family is the finding that there has been a shift in focus in American standards. Housing, feeding, and educating children are not enough. Today, parents are also keenly interested in their personality development and warm-hearted relationships with each other.[4] This conference affirmed the importance of personal faith in God and of moral and religious values. They recommend "that families place greater emphasis on family worship and family participation in organized religious activities." For years both Hebrews and Christians have recognized God's command for such instruction of children in Scriptures such as Deuteronomy 6:5-9 and 31:12, 13. God instructs parents to teach their children diligently day and night, indoors and out, through both seeing and hearing and in every relationship of life.

But few fathers today know how or where to begin spiritual training. Statistics on marriage inform us that in 1960 nearly half the married couples were twenty years of age or under, many of them in the stress-and-strain situation of trying to adjust from living as a pair to living as a trio, and striving to stretch low salaries to meet mounting expenses. A cradle roll visitor is in a unique position to witness to them, and to invite them to fellowship with other Christian couples who are experiencing the joy and relief of believing the promises in God's Word and trusting Him for practical help and guidance.

The visitor, too, can take an interest in all members of the family, and let them know that the Sunday school has classes for each one. Pastors and Sunday school leaders who have diligently carried on a cradle roll ministry have found it to be the best of all church-building agencies. Dr. George Truett, for years pastor of the First Baptist Church of Dallas, Texas, said many times that his cradle roll department had meant as much to the growth of his church as any other human element.

## ORGANIZATION OF CRADLE ROLL WORKERS

Cradle roll officers are important members of the Sunday school staff. They attend Sunday school workers' conferences and submit reports. Officers needed are a superintendent, a secretary, and as many visitors as are necessary to contact homes (one to each six to ten babies).

All cradle roll workers are alert to enroll babies. Naturally, they begin with babies of their own church members. They also contact expectant mothers, follow up birth announcements in the newspapers, get courthouse records and hospital lists, depend on Sunday school pupils to notify them of new babies in their families, and conduct "baby hunts" with door-to-door canvasses. In addition, an "interest center" in the church

[4]Reuben Hill, "The American Family Today," *The Nation's Children* (New York: Columbia University Press, 1960), p. 84.

foyer will not only bring in new babies but will publicize the cradle roll. This can be a table or even a wall shelf, attractive with baby things such as a wall roll or chart, magazine pictures of babies, or actual pictures of cradle roll babies.

RESPONSIBILITIES OF THE SUPERINTENDENT

To cooperate with the pastor and general Sunday school superintendent in enlisting cradle roll helpers, and in overseeing the entire program. If necessary, appoint one or more associate superintendents.

To hold regular meetings with the workers, to pray for their needs and for those in the homes to be visited; to study from the Bible the Scriptures they should know to be able to answer key questions intelligently; to call for visitation reports; to preview letters to parents and literature for other family members; to share experiences and encourage one another; to discuss best visiting techniques, bearing in mind that no two visits are alike. Such training begets confidence.

To maintain an up-to-date file on parent-baby information and ideas for making the cradle roll ministry sparkle. Clip newspaper and magazine articles and pictures.

To zone the community so that visitors call in the areas as close to their homes as possible.

To assign new babies to visitors for first visit and regular follow-up.

To visit every home on the entire cradle roll list at least once each year. Though each visitor calls regularly on the assigned six to ten babies, the superintendent should occasionally call, to strengthen further church-home ties.

To appoint a cradle roll photographer, and mount pictures of the babies, to be displayed where they will attract notice, perhaps in the church foyer at the cradle roll interest center.

To contrive original ways to keep the cradle roll ministry before the church. To supply the church secretary with birth notices and pertinent cradle roll information for the church bulletin. To place a flower bud on the pulpit or interest center when a baby is born, and afterward give it to the father for his baby's book.

To supervise planning of all social activities of the department.

RESPONSIBILITIES OF THE SECRETARY

To file complete and accurate records of each baby which are turned in by visitors. Records take time, but they also save time. A simple system that functions is much better than an elaborate one that does not or is not used. Provide a folder for each child. Record specific data reported by visitors, such as conditions in the home, any help needed or given (financially, spiritually, etc.), number and ages of other children, parents' religious affiliations or preferences, etc. This confidential information is valuable not only to the whole cradle roll staff but to the Sunday school superintendent, church officers, and pastor.

To make out two sets of enrollment cards, one with birthdays filed in chronological order, the other with family names filed in alphabetical order. Each visitor needs duplicate cards of his or her assigned babies.

To send birthday cards to babies (unless the visitor does this).

To send out announcement of meetings to workers.

To send invitations for all social events to parents and workers.

To order and distribute cradle roll letters, Sunday school papers, etc., to visitors.

To compile monthly reports of all meetings.

To keep up-to-date names and pictures of babies on a wall chart.

RESPONSIBILITIES OF THE VISITOR

To establish a friendly beachhead for Christ in the home as soon as possible after the baby's birth. A visitor may pave the way by mailing a card of congratulations either to the hospital or the home.

To deliver personally a cradle roll message addressed to *Mr. and Mrs. Parent*. When the visitor enrolls the baby, she may give the parents a binder and silk cord to insert the letters they will be getting from time to time. Also, the visitor fills out the certificate of enrollment; then writes the baby's name, birthday, and the parents' name and address on the packet envelope.

To pass out to other family members appropriate literature, such as Sunday school papers, home department magazine for shut-ins, etc. Though a visitor calls to see the *baby*, yet she can graciously invite all in the family to Sunday school.

To mail, or deliver, birthday cards on time (unless the secretary cares for this).

To keep accurate records on the packet envelope for each baby. To give the secretary additional written data, any pertinent information necessary for future contacts, that should be added to a baby's folder.

To leave a church bulletin in the home, especially if the cradle roll letter calls attention to it.

A cradle roll worker's visit may be the first evidence to parents that Christians *care* about them. No two visits, even to the same home, are alike. A visitor may find both sexes, all ages, Christians and non-Christians, interested and indifferent, well-to-do and underprivileged, all in the same neighborhood.

Cradle roll visiting is not restricted to women. Men are finding that visiting *fathers* is one of the best ways to witness for Christ and to add to their church rolls. Actually, the ideal plan is for married couples to visit together. When men see that other *men* are interested in the work of the church, they will much more readily accept an invitation to that church.

## QUALIFICATIONS OF ALL CRADLE ROLL WORKERS

### KNOW AND LOVE CHRIST AS SAVIOUR AND LORD

At the beginning of his first epistle (I John 1:1-3), the apostle John authenticated his writings by declaring that he himself had *heard* and *seen* and *touched* the Lord Jesus. Therefore, he could accurately tell others about Him so that they too could realize and enjoy similar fellowship. Knowing Christ as one's own Saviour and desiring to make Him known to others must be the experience of every cradle roll worker. Only then can he recommend to those in the cradle roll member's family that *they* believe in Christ and receive Him for themselves.

### KNOW AND LOVE GOD'S WORD AND DEPEND ON THE HOLY SPIRIT IN PRAYER

No human zeal, no matter how fervent, can take the place of absolute dependence on the Holy Spirit and searching God's Word for Scriptures that will induce heart-searching and conviction of sin; that will instruct parents in becoming Christians, and will comfort and encourage them through trials. The Christians who can help and strengthen others are those who have undergone similar experiences and have found the Lord to be not only their Saviour, but their Guide, Strength, Helper, Wisdom, Comforter—their All (Ps. 32:8; 18:1, 2; Heb. 13:6; I Cor. 1:30; II Cor. 1:3, 4; Col. 3:11b).

### KNOW AND LOVE CHILDREN

A cradle roll worker must have a mother-heart, but need not necessarily be a mother. Young grandmothers with few household responsibilities often make ideal visitors. They have been mellowed with both children and grandchildren and have perspective that begets confidence in a young mother. They have well learned that children are not robots with dials set which cause them to teeth and talk at a stated time, but that each baby is different, unique in his own way.

### KNOW AND LOVE PARENTS

The wise writer of Proverbs compared the close heart-response of kindred friends to a face mirrored in a pool (Prov. 27:19). A sympathetic and tactful cradle roll worker can, on succeeding visits, gradually move from being a stranger to an acquaintance, then to a friend, and finally to a confidant. Young fathers and mothers appreciate talking out problems with someone who cares and will listen, someone whom they respect and feel they can trust. Love begets love. Unselfish interest and a friendly, cheerful spirit will many times do more to make Christ known than preaching.

## THE CRADLE ROLL MINISTRY IN THE CHURCH BUILDING

Young parents prefer to attend a church which provides competent attendants for their baby, as well as feeding, sleeping, and playing facilities. This enables the parents to attend services, or be freed to teach Sunday school or sing in the choir, assured that as they do so their baby is well cared for. If parents have to stay home till the baby is "old enough," the next baby usually arrives, and home-church ties may be completely broken. But if the baby is brought to God's house and is well cared for, so that his first impressions are pleasant, he may early acquire a secure sense of "belonging" that will last through the years.

It is not optional nowadays but practically mandatory that a church wanting to grow, provide well-equipped rooms for babies, preferably in charge of a registered or practical nurse, on duty through both Sunday school and worship service. If this is not possible, an experienced mother may take charge. She will need enough helpers to feed and care for the babies—one for each five or six. These attendants may serve on a rotating basis, so that they can take turns attending church. A young father may also be a great help, especially with the older babies who often respond more readily to a man than to a woman.

As each baby is brought in, his feeding and sleeping schedule should be written down and his bottles labeled with his name on adhesive tape. Toddlers' helpers may be more than baby-sitters. They can help the older babies to appreciate God's creation, love and care with books, such as *Rhyme-Times for Wee Ones* and the eight *Tiny Question Books*.[5]

STANDARDS OF THE IDEAL BABY ROOM

1. Actually there should be two separate rooms, one for the tucked-in babies and one for the toddlers.

2. The rooms should be light and airy and large enough to accommodate all the babies brought.

3. Pastel walls, attractive pictures and curtains, washable rugs will give eye appeal.

4. A Dutch door will enable parents to leave babies without having to enter the room.

5. The room should be near the adult department.

[5]Marie H. Frost, *Rhyme-Times for Wee Ones* (Wheaton: Scripture Press); and Ruth M. Hinds, *Who?, What?, Where?, Why?, Do You Know When?, Which Child is Helping?, See the Colors?, I Wonder How?* (Wheaton: Scripture Press).

6. It should be soundproof and be equipped with intercommunication or PA system.

7. It should have a thermostat to regulate the temperature, and have good ventilation.

8. Provide enough beds with firm comfortable mattresses. Cribs 20×35×18″ may be built to hold standard-size crib mattresses. Crib rails should be washed with antiseptic in water each week, and sheets and blankets washed after each use.

9. A special bin or box should be used for each baby's diaper bag, wraps, etc. This should be labeled with name.

10. A coat rack may be placed outside the door for older children's wraps.

11. Have at least one rocking chair and a play pen.

12. Have counter tops or tables, for changing babies.

13. A linen cabinet or drawers will be useful.

14. A medicine cabinet with first-aid kit is a necessity.

15. Have a bathinette or comparable bathing facility.

16. A washroom with child's toilet seat must be close at hand.

17. Have a refrigerator and a stove or bottle warmer.

18. Duplex electrical outlets should be near the counter, out of toddlers' reach.

19. Suitable washable toys for each age level should be provided, as well as books for the older babies.

20. Storage space for toys is needed, either drawers or cabinets or boxes, preferably on rollers; or use plastic stackable vegetable bins with suction cups for stability.

21. Provide a book in which to register names, addresses, and, if desired, babies' birthdays.

22. A department bulletin board will be useful for current announcements, pictures, etc., and a Baby Book for recording "cute" doings and sayings.

Relatively few churches can have the *ideal* quarters and equipment here listed. But that should not deter them from starting with what they have and adding needed facilities as rapidly as possible.

## SPECIAL OCCASIONS TO PROMOTE THE CRADLE ROLL

CRADLE ROLL DAY

The Sunday school should set apart one day each year, usually in May after National Baby Week,[6] to recognize and specially honor their cradle

[6]This annual observance takes place at the end of April and the beginning of May.

roll babies. The service should be held during the Sunday school hour or during the morning church service. Each department of the Sunday school helps—ushering, pinning a flower on each mother's dress and on each father's coat lapel, providing special numbers on the program, taking the offering, or running the movie camera. The main feature may be a short but pertinent message by the pastor, directed to parents, stressing the joy and privilege of being *Christian* parents.

## PROMOTION DAY

Promotion day for the entire Sunday school is usually held the last Sunday in September. Each department then graduates pupils to the department higher up. In the cradle roll department, however, babies are usually promoted into the nursery when they become two years old, and at that time they receive their promotion certificates, regardless of the time of year. All babies who have become eligible for the nursery department during the past year may be present with the parents on promotion day and have their names read. A small gift may be presented to each cradle roll "graduate."

## SOCIAL OCCASIONS

Afternoon parties for mothers and babies, and an evening banquet for both parents may occasionally be held. Purely social gatherings, which may include a brief but well-planned and well-prayed-for devotional message, do much to get people acquainted and appreciative of the Sunday school. Workers may care for the babies during afternoon parties. Attractive refreshments and flowers will make the occasions festive. Fathers may be featured on the banquet program, as toastmaster, child trainers, etc.

## A MOTHER'S CLUB

No feature of the cradle roll ministry has contributed more to its success than a mother's club. The mothers usually meet each month, to discuss mutual problems of child care, and either study the Bible together or hear a Bible message. Such fellowship instructs, strengthens, and encourages the young women. Furthermore, it starts a chain reaction. Mothers transmit their enthusiasm to fathers, and soon fathers are in a Sunday school class. Before long, couples are joining the church.

Topics for discussion spring from the cradle roll letters, current magazines, and home situations, and range in interest from the birth of babies to adolescence.[7] Educators warn that the time to start meeting adolescent

[7]For a nominal cost you may secure bulletins and pamphlets from Childhood Education International, 1200 Fifteenth Street, N.W., Washington, D.C.; also Public Affairs Committee, 22 East 38th Street, New York, N.Y. Ask for the publications that deal with the ages in which you are particularly interested.

problems is during infancy. Discussion of child training should always be followed by a message from God's Word which should be the highlight of the program.

## THE CHALLENGE OF A CRADLE ROLL MINISTRY

Demographers (students of populations) forecast a "population explosion." They foresee a doubling of world population from three billion to six billion at the dawn of the twenty-first century. What are Sunday schools and churches doing to provide for the spiritual welfare of these coming babies? If Christians, both men and women, will wholeheartedly engage in this ministry which so effectually links the home and the Sunday school and is such a profitable feeder for the church, there is no telling what they can accomplish. For the cradle roll ministry follows the pattern set by the early church of going from home to home (Acts 2:46, 47). Can there be a more effectual way of obeying the command of the Lord Jesus to go and bring forth fruit that will remain (John 15:16)?

### BIBLIOGRAPHY

Brandt, Henry R. Keys to Better Living for Parents. Chicago: Moody Bible Institute Correspondence School, 1959.

Brandt, Henry R., and Dowdy, Homer E. Building a Christian Home. Wheaton: Scripture Press Foundation, 1960.

Brenneman, Helen Good. Meditations for the New Mother. Scottdale: Herald Press, 1953.

Brim, Jr., Orville G. Education for Child Rearing. New York: Russell Sage Foundation, 1959.

Bueltmann, A. J. Happiness is Homemade. Parent-Guidance Series No. 3. St. Louis: Concordia Publishing House.

Coiner, Harry G. Parents are Teachers. Parent-Guidance Series No. 6. St. Louis: Concordia Publishing House.

Cross, R. T. Making the Home Happy. Chicago: Moody Press, 1952.

Dean, Horace F. Visitation Evangelism Made Practical. Grand Rapids: Zondervan Publishing House, 1957.

Dolloff, Eugene Dinsmore. The Romance of Doorbells. A Guide to Effective Pastoral Calling and Visitation in General. Philadelphia: Judson Press, 1951.

Frank, Lawrence K. The Fundamental Needs of the Child. New York: The National Association of Mental Health, Inc., 1952. Distributed free by the State of Illinois, Department of Public Welfare, Springfield, Ill.

Gerber, Maxine Ethel. How to Organize and Conduct the Cradle Roll Department. Cincinnati: Standard Publishing Co., 1952.

Ginzberg, Eli. *The Nation's Children.* The 1960 White House Conference on Children and Youth. New York: Columbia University Press, 1960.

Gunderson, Edith M. *Training Your Child for Christ.* Chicago: Moody Press, 1945.

Harrison, Eugene Myers. *How to Win Souls.* Wheaton: Scripture Press Foundation, 1952.

Hymes, Jr., James L. *Enjoy Your Child—Ages 1, 2, and 3.* Public Affairs Pamphlet No. 141. Springfield, Ill.: State of Illinois, Department of Public Welfare, 1950.

Latham, Joy. *Baby Days in the Church.* Kansas City: Lillenas Publishing Co., 1958. Program materials for cradle roll days.

Leatherwood, Mattie C. *The Cradle Roll Department of the Sunday School.* Nashville: Sunday School Board of the Southern Baptist Convention, 1941.

Moore, Jessie Eleanor. *Cradle Roll Manual.* New York: Methodist Book Concern, 1921.

Orr, William W. *Bible Hints on Rearing Children.* Wheaton: Scripture Press Foundation, 1955.

Pollock, Edwina, and Stoner, Lou Bina. *Manual for Workers in the Cradle Roll of the Sunday School.* Springfield, Mo.: Gospel Publishing Co., 1950.

Simon, Martin. *Pointers for Parents.* St. Louis: Concordia Publishing House.

Spock, Benjamin, and Reinhart, John. *A Baby's First Year.* New York: Duell, Sloan and Pearce, Inc., 1956. Pictures with comments.

Wolf, Anna W. M., and Stein, Lucille. *The One-Parent Family.* Public Affairs Pamphlet No. 287. New York: Child Study Association of America, 1959.

Wolf, Anna W. M., and Dawson, Margaret C. *What Makes a Good Home?* New York: Child Study Association of America.

## Chapter 10

# TEACHING PRESCHOOL CHILDREN

### Mary E. LeBar

### PRIORITY OF THE HOME

BEFORE A CHILD begins his formal education in the first grade, his learning has been rapid and remarkable in quantity and scope. "By the age of six a child has been initiated into most of the major forms of experience that can befall a human being during his lifetime."[1] The home is obviously the chief agency in guidance; for one hour, or even a whole morning, in church is but a minute fraction of the Christian education of the young child. Oscar E. Feucht points out that the home is the primary institution of God, the cradle of personality, potentially the greatest teacher, the agency of evangelism, a transmitter of culture, a barrier to evil, a bulwark of the church, and a cornerstone of the nation.[2] The home has the first opportunity to train the young child, and the most persistent over-all influence.

Family life education for young people and parents may therefore be considered basic for effective preschool teaching. The church should help parents to understand typical phases of child development, to accept the task of Christian parenthood seriously, and to take time to savor its special joys. Parents teach both verbally and by example in day-by-day training, through family altar and grace at meals, through spontaneous prayer and worship as well as regular attendance at church, through answers to questions, and through the atmosphere of trust in the home. Joy in Christ can be communicated long before the doctrine of Christology.

[1]A. Jersild and associates, *Child Development and the Curriculum* (Teachers College, Columbia University, 1946), p. 58.
[2]*Helping Families Through the Church* (St. Louis: Concordia Publishing House, 1957), pp. 61-68.

Mary E. LeBar, Ph.D., is professor of Christian Education at Wheaton College, Wheaton, Illinois.

The peace of the Holy Spirit pervading home activities can be felt. Though there be surface storms, parental trust in the undergirding everlasting arms makes for deep security.

With the rise of adult electives in the Sunday school curriculum, a recurring request has come for help in parental tasks. When will the church adequately meet this need, which is both a real need and a felt need? Does the laggard pace of past years mean that the church has failed to grasp the significance of the first years of life?

## THE BIBLICAL CONTRIBUTION

Scripture does not offer much direction for child guidance that can be allocated to a definite age level. The incident when Jesus called the children to Him in opposition to the decision of the disciples is a clear word. That these were young children is indicated by the fact that He took them up in His arms (Mark 10:16). Though Scripture gives a limited view of Jesus as a child, even the one verse, in Luke 2:52, has depth better understood in the light of today's knowledge of child development than ever before. Growth in wisdom (mental) and in stature (physical) and in favor with God (spiritual) and man (social) is the all-round development sought today. The word "wisdom" needs particular stress. Are we aiming at "sound judgment and sagacious use of facts" (Webster) rather than mere knowledge of facts in mental development?

However little Scripture may say to enlighten educators as to preschool education, the Christian leader must be aware that all so-called laws of human development are God's laws. The discovery of the process of wholesome maturation should be the province of the Christian who is thinking the Creator's thoughts after Him. Using discrimination and testing, the Christian can therefore gratefully accept the findings of secular research, and build on them.

## CONTRIBUTION OF EDUCATION AND PSYCHOLOGY

The first half of the twentieth century saw an unprecedented interest in the preschool child in education and psychology. Intensive research and many developmental studies established the crucial importance of the first years of life. Normal wholesome growth, or the seeds of insanity, of delinquency, of an unhappy home life, have close relationship with the early years of life.

With increasing knowledge of the developmental process has come increasing awareness of the great diversity between individuals. Nonetheless there is a typical order of development of various abilities and processes, even though there is no average child. A normal three-year-old has three-year-old limitations; he is not a miniature adult. He must be accepted as he is, and helped to take the next step in his growth as he is ready for it.

Physically, small children are active, yet tire easily. A teaching program must therefore incorporate both movement and quietness. Lack of space, unsuitable available materials, and lack of understanding on the part of local church leaders often conspire to involve small children in activity which is frustrating to them or which must actually be done by the teachers. Incomplete muscular development does not ask for adult help in intricate handwork or for small materials requiring sustained coordination, but for the elimination of such materials in favor of activities with which the child can successfully cope. The delicate constitution of the young child calls for a healthful environment in the church. A sensitive nervous system makes small groups a requisite, and thus affects architectural planning for educational buildings.

Mentally, small children must be thought of as having concrete, literal thought processes; limited concepts of time, space and number; a short interest span; sensory curiosity; limited vocabulary; and a lack of experience. Trained workers are needed to adjust Biblical teaching to these demands and to make Bible stories relevant to the small child's experience. Because chronological and geographical considerations are wasted energy, curriculum makers organize Bible material thematically or psychologically without concern for definite time or place. The wealth of symbolic materials in Scripture does not convey its richness of spiritual truth to the young child; but the same truth can often be expressed in literal simplicity through stories. Songs and Bible verses must pass the same test of being literal and simple.

At nursery level the young child is not ready for group games or cooperative action. Socially he is still operating individualistically, playing alongside rather than "with" other children. He is also likely to pass through a negativistic phase which can be trying unless the leader senses the growth of conscious selfhood. As the child becomes aware of the group, he is easier to teach as a member of a group. This fact and his imitative nature allow for fewer teachers at upper preschool levels. But imitation of the words, acts and attitudes of the teacher as the child grows ever more admiringly suggestible, impose heavy responsibility on the teacher. Broadening his field of vision to include other people near and far is a worthy aim, but it must not be done more rapidly than growing powers admit. Consequently missions are usually beyond the scope of the nursery child, and require careful presentation for the four- and five-year-old. Because of the social nature of the children, the individual work of the nursery teacher becomes the group work of the beginner department.

## BASIC NEEDS

Psychology has brought to focus basic needs, variously labeled, but identifiable as the need for love or affection, for security or belonging, for recognition or success, and for new experiences. To these the Christian adds the needs for forgiveness, and joyously proclaims the ability of the Christian gospel to meet all needs abundantly.

The love of God is basic in Christianity. It is first mediated to the child through his parents or his teacher. The little child who is grounded and established on a foundation of God's faithful unmerited love can stand many stresses from the world as he grows. Where else can security be so perfectly found as in the only One who fails not? God's laws provide the security of boundaries needed for true freedom. "Belonging" is the very heart of the *Koinonia* (fellowship) of the New Testament church. The little child can feel this fellowship long before he understands it.

What of success? In God's sight, happily, it is not measured by intelligence quotient or monetary affluence or talents, but by faithfulness. Nor is the Christian left to achieve this faithfulness in his own inadequate strength; divine help is offered to insure success. New experiences are surely the portion of one who walks with God, yet the nursery child rarely needs more of the new. He can profit from repetition of a few meaningful spiritual activities in which he can feel at ease. A preschool program is more likely to become monotonous at the five-year level. The sensitive leader will find the path between boredom and overstimulation that brings continued growth.

Forgiveness treats the problem of guilt, so often found by psychiatrists at the root of adult problems. When the little child breaks the rules set up by parent or teacher, he feels guilt. To learn the path back to the smile of those he loves is a vital necessity. Leaders and parents must be careful here that they never lead the child to think he loses God's love by his behavior. God's faithful love ever woos the human heart to return, like the prodigal, and confess wrongdoing.

## CONTRIBUTION OF THEOLOGY

The secularist has done little in terms of spiritual ability and development at the various age levels. But the Christian educator has done little more. Such research, difficult though it may be, beckons the evangelical scholar today. Developmental tasks in the spiritual area are needed to set goals for Christian education. It seems logical to expect that as the young child is reaching out physically, mentally, and socially in growing power, his spiritual nature too is active; he must have a hungry, seeking soul, created in God's image, seeking to find rest in Him.

It is evident that the preschooler's Christian education lies more in the realm of attitudes and atmosphere than in concepts and facts. This is not the period for learning doctrine. Yet if the early years are so vital in other areas, is there less reason to suppose that the spiritual attitudes being learned are less significant? Little children respond readily to the spiritual. "A child's recognition of an Unseen Presence suggests an intuitive knowledge of God."[3]

Does the child's response to God mean he is ready and able to make a life decision of allegiance to Jesus Christ? The evangelical rejects Bushnell's doctrine that the child should grow up not knowing himself other than a Christian, for being "born again" requires a definite time. Yet experientially many young people from Christian homes do not know the time of their rebirth. A recent study of 1,272 college young people, all but four of whom professed to be saved, found that nearly 25 per cent of them did not know the date of their salvation. And 8.8 per cent of the men and 12.5 per cent of the women dated their salvation from the preschool period, some stating exactly when and where it occurred at that age. Several indicated confusion regarding its reality.[4] Of course one can deny that any of these experiences were truly salvation and call them only "childhood religious experiences,"[5] but the fact remains that most of the young people considered them a true salvation experience. Certainly at least a minimum of knowledge is necessary for intelligent acceptance of Christ as Saviour. Innate ability and a strong Christian environment may be expected to influence the age of decision. But that the average preschool child is ready for this great decision is contrary to the experience or expectation of most Christian educators who sensitively work with young children.

One of the greatest dangers for the evangelical worker who is concerned about the child's salvation is that of gaining verbalized answers without understanding, or with too superficial an understanding. The small child can quickly learn to repeat sounds, especially those for which he receives approval and attention from adults. To teach the child to say John 3:16 is not difficult. But what does the "world" mean to him, with his limited concept of space and number? What does "believeth" mean? What should it mean? What must it mean? What does "perish" signify? Or "eternal" in the light of the child's very limited time concept? What is "life" or "death" to him?

If the young child is learning to love the Lord Jesus, can we conceive that he will say "No" when he is old enough to grasp the essentials of

[3]Margaret Bailey Jacobsen, The Child in the Christian Home (Wheaton: Scripture Press, 1959), p. 38.
[4]V. Elaine Thomas, "The Relative Effectiveness of Various Agencies in the Salvation of Children and Youth" (unpublished Master's thesis, Department of Christian Education, Wheaton Graduate School, Wheaton, Ill., 1960).
[5]Gideon G. Yoder, The Nurture and Evangelism of Children (Scottdale, Pa.; Herald Press, 1959), p. 119.

the plan of salvation? Or stray away from One who loves him and whose love he returns? If the decision is premature, is any harm done? What does prematurity imply in other areas of life? Is there danger in going through the forms without reality? Workers with children must face these serious questions when they move upon such holy ground. And the worker should ever remind himself that no man effects regeneration; the Holy Spirit Himself must be working in the heart of the child.

Interestingly enough, almost all theological positions regarding the state of the young child merge into unity as far as actual Christian education is concerned. The person who baptizes the baby into covenant relationship, or into church membership, as well as the firm exponent of infant dedication and believer's baptism, all treat the child very much the same in practice.

## CONTENT

Curricula among evangelicals generally agree on the types of experiences to be given and the information that is suitable for the preschool child. Because of his limited experience and mental development, he profits from repetition of carefully selected basic spiritual ideas. God the Creator who loves and cares for him personally is made explicit in the person of the Lord Jesus. That the child uses "God" and "Jesus" interchangeably is of little concern, since the truths he is learning are true of each Person of the Godhead. The Bible becomes a special book to the child, a source for stories about God and Jesus, as well as the criterion for conduct. Thus is laid a foundation for ethics and for realization of the need of a Saviour. The church is a happy place, where he fellowships with God and with his friends. Response to truth is guided into conduct and the beginnings of stewardship; response in love, into expressions of prayer and praise.

## METHODS

The child's nature and ability give ample directives to a Christian teacher as to methods to use. In first place must come the spiritual character of the teacher himself. The young child absorbs the unexpressed attitude and senses the focus of the adult personality before he learns to give attention to verbal communication.

The Bible story is the chief vehicle for conveying spiritual truth concretely in words. While few Bible stories can communicate a message to the nursery child, many more are helpful in adding facets to basic truths for the four- and five-year-old. Simplification of the Biblical tale may involve elaboration of details for vividness, and omission of details which would distract the child's mind from grasping the truth. Until natural law is understood, the miracle of the feeding of the five thousand does not mean much; but the hungry boy's gift of his lunch is impressive to the young child. Acts of violence or punishment may only alienate a young child who cannot hold in balance the love and judgment of God.

A widespread philosophy in evangelical circles advocates teaching Bible verses even if a child does not understand them, with a view to future use. This is a problem that needs resolving in the light of God's own laws of learning. What accompanies the glib repetition of meaningless phrases? Is this the best preparation for the future? Is it the best use of present efforts of both child and teacher? The preschooler can learn to repeat many long Bible verses, but is in real danger of failing to learn the responsibility incumbent upon the person who knows truth (James 4:17). If a verse is to be applied to life, the young child requires more than one lesson to make fruitful associations. Should not even the initial acquaintance with Scripture verses mean necessary response on the child's part? "Be ye kind" thus becomes a difficult verse to "learn." More attention also needs to be given in the area of Bible teaching to the key role played by the emotions in both learning and application of truth. What is the effect on the child's attitude toward Scripture by being bored with a Bible story?

Physical movement must frequently be utilized if the child is not to be frustrated and repressed. So the teacher leads the child in "playing" positive actions, entering into others' experiences and feelings vicariously. He becomes Jacob, walking and walking and walking, feeling alone, until he hears God's promise, "I am with thee, and will keep thee in all places" (Gen. 28:15). The teacher leads the child also to express the very motions that will be a part of his exemplary conduct at home, so that kinesthetic involvement will aid the carry-over into daily life.

Application of truth to life for the young child cannot be left in the abstract, but must be translated into the specific and literal. To admonish the child to "be good," may be interpreted erroneously by him as meaning to sit still and restrain his God-given impulses to exercise his growing muscles. To help Mother by picking up his toys, or to share toys with brothers and sisters, is tangible. Calling upon the Lord for help in such difficult situations makes prayer vital. Generalizations are built upon specifics. That Jesus loves all the children must first be, "Jesus loves Sally and Joe and Hugh and Linda."

As much as possible primary experiences need to be supplied so that the young child is doing as well as hearing, using the senses rather than being completely dependent upon words. Objects and pictures are important tools. Verbalization always requires sufficient experience to give it meaning. And repetition of pleasant experiences serves to give a feeling of achievement and mastery as well as a deeper comprehension because there is time to savor the full breadth of the experience. The concept of "our church" may include going outside to look at the building, to feel the smooth painted boards or touch the rough-hewn stone. Service becomes real through planting flowers, or wiping feet on the doormat to save the caretaker work.

Music and prayer are both valuable worship experiences for the young child. While the nursery child's vocal cords may not be fully developed, so that he cannot be expected to attain proficiency, he does enjoy rhythm and appreciates the teacher's frequent use of music. He joins in, as he is ready, in his own way. For the four- and five-year-old, singing comprises a large share of worship. Songs that they can understand and experience will go with them through the week to help make the lesson a part of life. Criteria for selecting songs must be based on mental characteristics, voice-range ability, and spiritual experience. Choruses used for young people may qualify in terms of length and easy music, but usually do not express a young child's experiences or feelings. And though composed of one-syllable words, such choruses are often symbolically far beyond the comprehension of the young child.

Because of the very nature of prayer, a young child may enjoy a rich experience of fellowship with God. He can learn, at least during beginner age, many different forms, ranging from silent prayer to a memorized prayer poem in which the group join. He can be led to engage in petition, thanksgiving, confession, and the beginnings of adoration and intercession. For him indeed the command to "pray without ceasing" may be a reality.

Stewardship has its roots even in early years. The care of the nursery or beginner church room and the materials there, widening to a concern for the appearance of the church lawn and the corridors, is groundwork for responsible churchmanship. Giving may often be most vital if it is expressed in tangibles such as clothing for needy children. To experience real giving, a small child must be strongly motivated, for he is perhaps just learning the experience of possession. Physically the infant learns to clutch before he can release an object; a sense of personal ownership is necessary before a person can truly give. Stewardship of time and talents may have elementary expression in the "helping" which the preschooler is practicing. Missions follows the Biblical order of Acts 1:8 even in its development for young children. The "here and now" world of the young child is the place to begin; his horizons may be extended as fast as he can appreciate the need of those beyond his view. The five-year-old can sympathize with the child "far away" who has no Sunday school, but feels little concern for a generalization about distant children; geographical location means little or nothing.

## PHYSICAL SURROUNDINGS
To achieve the kind of teaching indicated requires an environment set up specifically for the young child. Allocation of space should follow the rule, "the smaller the child, the more space," rather than the inverted idea often followed by church boards in planning. Choice locations for health conditions, including cleanliness, light, ventilation and even heat, on the first floor should be given the small children. Materials for teaching are not necessarily large, but they are sturdy and manageable by hands or feet that are as yet incompletely coordinated.

## GRADING
"Preschool" is not sufficient grading even in a small church. The nearer one comes to the beginning of life, the more tremendous are the differences each month makes in development. To group two-year-olds with five-year-olds is a span that dismays teachers who know the abilities comprised within such a grouping. One of the greatest problems of working with the young child is to keep pace with his developing capacities—neither lagging behind so that he associates the church with boredom, nor pushing him so that his Christian education becomes a superficial verbalizing that means nothing to him, and that may all too easily lead him into a "form of godliness" without the power thereof (II Tim. 3:5). Even when groups are divided into nursery (two and three years) and beginner or kindergarten (four and five years), the teacher will find great individual differences within the group. Anything less than this division asks more than many teachers would dare to attempt. Trying to tell a story to three-year-olds with toddlers under two years in the group is to risk failure. Trying to tell a story to five-year-olds with a few two- or three-year-olds in the group may be equally frustrating. It is difficult to generalize about the age span "preschool." For while a two-year-old can stand almost limitless repetition, a five-year-old would be bored very quickly by so much exact repetition. Grading by departments becomes the least that can be advocated.

## IN CONCLUSION
Of one fact adults may be sure: the young child is plastic and impressionable spiritually. In a calm, loving atmosphere each child feels accepted and valued for himself. He is helped to make a distinction between a person and a person's act, which may or may not be acceptable. Gradually he becomes oriented to group behavior and learns consideration for others. Deeply he imbibes the attitude of the adults who speak to him about God; he associates God with their words and ways. This fact

in itself makes teaching the preschooler a task of great magnitude and awesome responsibility.

## BIBLIOGRAPHY

Bushnell, Horace. *Christian Nurture.* New York: Scribner and Armstrong and Co., 1876.

Feucht, Oscar E. *Helping Families Through the Church.* St. Louis: Concordia Publishing House, 1957.

Gesell, Arnold L., and Ilg, Frances L. *Infant and Child in the Culture of Today.* New York: Harper & Bros., 1943.

Jacobsen, Margaret Bailey. *The Child in the Christian Home.* Wheaton, Ill.: Scripture Press, 1959.

Jenkins, G., Shacter, H., and Bauer, W. *These Are Your Children.* Chicago: Scott, Foresman and Co., 1953.

Jersild, Arthur, and associates. *Child Development and the Curriculum.* New York: Teachers College, Columbia University, 1946.

Jersild, Arthur. *Child Psychology.* Englewood Cliffs, N.J.: Prentice-Hall, Inc., 1960.

LeBar, Lois. *Children in the Bible School.* Westwood, N.J.: Fleming H. Revell Co., 1952.

*Nursery School Portfolio.* Washington: Association for Childhood International, 1961.

*Portfolio for Kindergarten Teachers.* Washington: Association for Childhood International, 1951.

Thomas, V. Elaine. "The Relative Effectiveness of Various Agencies in the Salvation of Children and Youth." Unpublished Master's thesis, Department of Christian Education, Wheaton Graduate School, Wheaton, Ill., 1960.

Yoder, Gideon G. *The Nurture and Evangelism of Children.* Scottdale, Pa., Herald Press, 1959.

## FOR FURTHER READING

Allstrom, Elizabeth. *Let's Play a Story.* New York: Friendship Press, 1957.

Cook, Melva. *Bible Teaching for Four's and Five's.* Nashvillle: Sunday School Board of the Southern Baptist Convention, 1960.

Cully, Iris. *Children in the Church.* Philadelphia: Westminster Press, 1960.

Dillard, Polly Hargis. *Improving Nursery Departments.* Nashville: Convention Press, 1959.

Heron, Frances. *Kathy Ann, Kindergartner.* Nashville: Abingdon Press, 1955.

Ilg, Frances, and Ames, Louise B. *Child Behavior.* New York: Dell Books, 1955.

LeBar, Mary E. *Living in God's Family.* Wheaton, Ill.: Scripture Press, 1957.

Shields, Elizabeth. *Music in the Religious Growth of Children.* Nashville: Abingdon-Cokesbury, 1943.

Trent, Robbie. *Your Child and God.* New York: Harper & Bros., 1941.

Weill, Blanche. *Through Children's Eyes.* New York: Island Workshop Press, 1940.

Whitehouse, Elizabeth. *Opening the Bible to Children.* St. Louis: Bethany Press, 1945.

*Chapter 11*

# TEACHING PRIMARY CHILDREN

## Gordon G. Talbot

Primary children, six to eight years of age, or grades one through three, are at a most interesting stage in their development. Young enough to retain their innocence and pliable personalities, they are old enough to be more active physically and more alert mentally than beginners. A new world is opening up to them as they begin first grade in school. They are now allowed to venture farther from home during playtimes and when running errands. Spiritually, they are now approaching the place where they will understand the plan of salvation through Christ. Work done well at this point will pay eternal dividends.

## CHARACTERISTICS AND CONTROL

*Physical.* The primary child likes strenuous activity, but he must be given a program which does not cause him to overdo. Activities which alternate between fast and slow projects are best.[1] Since he now attends school, he is susceptible to contagious diseases, and should he show up at church with a cold, for example, he ought to be isolated from the others.[2] Perhaps an assistant could guide him in personal study. His first teeth are coming out, a fact which may cause him some embarrassment, but this can be counteracted by pointing out that he can take pride in his growth.

*Mental.* The primary child is interested in the fairy tale, which he

[1]Marjorie Elaine Soderholm, *Understanding the Pupil, Part II, The Primary and Junior Child* (Grand Rapids: Baker Book House, 1956), pp. 10 f.
[2]*Ibid.*, p. 11.

Gordon G. Talbot, M.A., is instructor of Christian Education at Detroit Bible College, Detroit, Michigan.

knows is make-believe, and the true story.[3] He still thinks very literally, and teachers must use concrete terms and facts he can understand.[4] The usual concentration span is up to twenty minutes in length, so a varied program is still required for a one- or two-hour period.[5] The reading and writing ability of these children will vary from one individual to another, so the worker must help all to have successful experiences when these skills are used.

*Social.* The primary child is concerned about group acceptance, so he should be included as much as possible in all class activities.[6] Pliable and sympathetic to interested adults, he will offer the worker an opportunity to mold his character in the Christian way. He is concerned about the opinions of his teacher, so a good example must be set for him. If he misbehaves, he should see that the teacher disapproves of his actions; if he is good, he should likewise note the teacher's approval.[7] He is not helped by the teacher who ignores his mischief for fear that he might not come back to class again. Primary workers are tempted to "talk down" to the children sometimes, but this should be avoided because of their feeling of growing independence. As these children are still self-centered, personal references to individuals by name are appreciated.

*Spiritual.* The primary child is somewhat insecure as he moves out into the larger world,[8] but he generally trusts people. This is good with the right people but dangerous with the evil. In any case, he should learn to trust God in all situations, for God is unchanging. He is developing more discernment between right and wrong,[9] so Bible standards must be presented clearly to him. He is approaching the age of accountability, which varies from child to child; but even though he may not yet understand the whole plan for his salvation through Christ, the basic truths should be presented carefully at this age. Some primaries, and even some beginners, are certainly capable of salvation, and the testimony of many adult Christians will verify this because of their own experiences of salvation at an early age. However, no pressure should be put on the primary child to make a mere profession of salvation. If the workers are faithful in a simple presentation of the plan of salvation, the Holy Spirit will bring individual children to the crisis at the proper time.[10, 11]

---

[3]Lois E. LeBar, *Children in the Bible School* (Westwood, N.J.: Fleming H. Revell Co., 1952), p. 161.
[4]Soderholm, *op. cit.*, p. 18.
[5]*Ibid.*, p. 15.
[6]*Ibid.*, p. 22.
[7]*Ibid.*, p. 24.
[8]*Ibid.*, p. 28.
[9]*Ibid.*, p. 32.
[10]*Ibid.*, p. 31.
[11]Frank G. Coleman, *The Romance of Winning Children* (Cleveland: Union Gospel Press, 1948), p. 48.

## TEACHING AIMS

The primary teacher should have knowledge of that which primaries *can* be taught; otherwise, his work will be in vain. Some of the basic concepts given below are within the scope of a primary child's understanding.

*God.* God, our heavenly Father, is holy, powerful, loving, and forgiving. He can work through us and with us. He wants us to pray to Him, giving thanks for His blessings and making our needs known.

*Jesus.* Jesus can be a personal Saviour.[12] He did many interesting things while on earth, and we learn about these in the Bible. He is our best Friend and Example to follow.

*Bible.* The Bible is God's personal message to us. It contains the standard for right conduct. It has many stories suitable for children to understand. Selected verses and passages may be memorized. The chief Bible customs should be taught, for many differ from customs today. Introductory work may be done in teaching the use of books, chapters, and verses.

*Church.* Churches help people to know God. Each primary child is part of the church family and should feel the need for participating in it. Baptism, communion, and other ceremonies important to the church should be explained. The church is not just a building, but it is a group of people who are saved and want to please God in every way.

*Conduct.* There ought to be a growing consideration for the sufferings and needs of others. Sorrow for sin should be more and more apparent. Obedience to God should be seen as the basis for obedience to parents, teachers, and others.[13]

*Philosophy of life.* God is related to every activity of life, and He has the answer for each problem that arises. He must be trusted.

## PROGRAM

Teaching aims need a program to serve as a vehicle. A basic program is absolutely essential to the work of the primary department, and it should be an all-inclusive one.

*Four elements of a balanced program.* A good Christian educational program includes instruction, worship, fellowship, and service (or evangelization).[14] Properly balanced, these will give the primary child a well-rounded experience in the church and out of it.

[12]David J. Fant and Addie Marie French, *All About the Sunday School* (Harrisburg: Christian Publications, Inc., 1947), p. 131.
[13]An interesting book to read on the subject of discipline is Regina H. Wieman, *Does Your Child Obey?* (New York: Harper & Bros., 1943).
[14]James DeForest Murch, *Christian Education and the Local Church* (Cincinnati: Standard Publishing Co., 1943), p. 127.

*Sunday school.* The Sunday school, begun by Robert Raikes in England in 1780, was not at first a part of the regular churches.[15] However, when religious content was eliminated from the public school curriculum, the churches embraced the Sunday school and made it their chief agency for Christian education. Satisfied primaries like to come to Sunday school, and the right program will keep them coming.

*Primary church.* Some ministers want a "full house" during the adult worship hour every Sunday morning, but the more enlightened ones realize the tremendous value of graded worship for children. Materials are now available for use in the primary worship hour, which is held at the same time as the adult worship service.[16] This is an excellent way to redeem the time which before was often lost in an adult service where the children could not fully profit by "sitting under the sound of the gospel"— a gospel too often presented in adult terminology and concepts not understood by primaries.

*Daily vacation Bible school.* Two weeks of daily vacation Bible school, or vacation church school, as some call it, can be as worthwhile as a whole year of Sunday school periods, if the school is administered well. The continuity from day to day is a great aid to the teachers, and the fact that all four elements of a balanced program can be made possible at one time is one of the advantages of such a school.

*Missionary club.* Primary children may not understand history and geography very well, but they do appreciate interesting stories of missionary activities. A weekday club, which meets one day after school or on Saturday, can be another agency for reaching primaries with gospel truths.

*Fellowship times.* To provide fellowship for the primaries, there will have to be concentrated efforts which produce parties, picnics, and special celebrations for them. Fellowship cements their relationships as much as it does adults'; and it draws in other children who want to have a good time too.[17]

*Service projects.* Some may wonder what services primaries can perform. As an example, they might make a sunshine basket for a sick friend. It may be only the delivery of a church bulletin each week to a shut-in. The primary worker who keeps his eyes open will see many opportunities for his children to serve the Lord on their own level of ability and interest, and thus they will find strength in Christian action.

[15]Clarence H. Benson, *A Popular History of Christian Education* (Chicago: Moody Press, 1943), p. 119.
[16]Examples: Flora E. Breck, *Church School Chats for Primary Teaching* (Boston: W. A. Wilde Co., 1950); *Primary Worship* (a series by Gospel Light Publications, Glendale 5, Calif., 1960).
[17]Marion Leach Jacobsen, *Good Times for God's People* (Grand Rapids: Zondervan Publishing House, 1952), p. 12.

*Religious education in the home.* Primary workers will find it helpful to visit the parents of their pupils and solicit their cooperation in training the children. Daily devotional readings and attention to memory work will produce coordinated results between church and home efforts.[18] There are also books for parents to use in answering children's questions about life.[19]

*Christian day school.* The Christian day school movement is growing in certain parts of the country, especially in California. While many Christian leaders and parents seem to think it is better to send children to the public schools, no categorical answer can be given to this question, because each school must be studied separately to determine its worth. It does seem logical to say, however, that a primary child who is sent to a first-rate Christian day school will receive a good preparation for facing the challenges of the world in which he must live. As to the criticism that he will become a "hot house Christian," it must be remembered that not all children in Christian schools are "angels," nor does the Christian child escape contact with non-Christians when he is out of school.

## TEACHING METHODS

The best buildings and equipment in the world will not produce the best teaching automatically. Teachers must develop a basic philosophy of teaching and then work it out with a variety of methods.

*A basic Scriptural philosophy.* The essence of the Scriptural method has been well defined by Dr. Lois E. LeBar of Wheaton College. Briefly, the teacher must set up interacting experiences which will take his pupils to the Word of God with their needs and problems, find guiding principles there, and then bring those principles to bear on everyday real-life situations.[20] By means of this cyclic process, the pupils are drawn to the Lord at every turn in an attempt to find solutions to their problems by intimate contact with the living Word (Christ) by way of the written Word (the Bible).

*The threefold approach.* Another way to look at the basic method is to show the necessity for a progression with the following terms:

---

[18]Dorothy Grunbock Johnston, *Pete and Penny Know and Grow* (Wheaton: Scripture Press, 1957), p. 7.

[19]Examples: Dena Korfker, *Can You Tell Me?* (Grand Rapids: Zondervan Publishing House, 1950); Korfker, *Questions Children Ask* (Grand Rapids: Zondervan Publishing House, 1951).
See also Alverta Breitweiser, . . . *And God Cares for Me* (Anderson, Ind.: Warner Press, 1957); Robbie Trent, *Your Child and God* (New York: Harper & Bros., 1952).

[20]Lois E. LeBar, *Education That is Christian* (Westwood, N.J.: Fleming H. Revell Co., 1958), pp. 118, 206.

Intellect → Emotions → Will
Head    → Heart    → Muscles
Know    → Love     → Do[21]

Pupils must be guided in knowing what the Bible says, in feeling and loving personally the underlying principles of it, and then in going out to do what it says. Too many teachers in our churches merely teach the facts and feel their job is done, when actually the most important part of teaching is the application. Telling is not teaching, for in order to say teaching has taken place, learning must have occurred. And no learning takes place until pupils have changed in attitude and/or behavior.[22] The instruction should come in the Sunday school hour, worship in the primary church hour, and an appeal to the will at the end, climaxed with prayer for God's help in doing what should be done.

*The place of storytelling.* Storytelling is the principal tool for use in teaching little children. Fortunately, the Bible has many stories which can be used to teach children as well as adults. This is why teachers begin with the narrative sections of the Word and seek to implant their facts and principles firmly in the minds and hearts of their pupils.[23] There are many books, of course, which provide the teacher with extra-Scriptural stories. As a general rule, however, the *main* part of a teacher's lesson should be straight from the Word of God. God has promised to bless His Word, and extra-Scriptural aids should be used only as supplements to that Word.

*Other useful methods.* Teachers often get into the rut of using only the one or two methods with which they have become familiar. With extra effort they could bring new vitality to their teaching and to the pupils' reception of their material. Demonstrations, short but well-prepared lectures, simple discussions, dramas, audio-visual materials (including pictures, flash cards, flannelgraph, slides, films, and filmstrips), question-and-answer sessions, projects, exhibits, and field trips could be used. It goes without saying that music, prayer, and memorization of Bible verses are integral parts of educational work.[24] Helpful tips on how to make these more effective can be found in Dr. Lois E. LeBar's book, *Children in the Bible School.*[25]

[21]Murch, *op. cit.*, pp. 145-148.
[22]C. B. Eavey, *Principles of Teaching for Christian Teachers* (Grand Rapids: Zondervan Publishing House, 1940), pp. 162 ff.
[23]Jeanette Perkins Brown, *The Storyteller in Religious Education* (Boston: Pilgrim Press, 1951). Excellent for learning how to structure, present, and make good use of stories.
[24]Books which provide good songs for primaries, rather than choruses ladened with symbolism, include: *Primaries Sing in Church and Home* (Wheaton: Scripture Press, 1959); *Primaries Worship* (Glendale, Calif.: Gospel Light Publications, 1960); Elizabeth McEwan Shields, *Worship and Conduct Songs: 5-8 Years* (Richmond: John Knox Press, 1957); *Songs for Primary Children* (Cincinnati: Standard Publishing Co.); *Hymns for Primary Worship* (Philadelphia: Westminster Press).
[25]See also Mildred Morningstar, *Reaching Children* (Chicago: Moody Press, 1944).

## EQUIPMENT

Whenever a church builds a new educational unit, it should set aside about 10 per cent of the cost of the building for equipment. This would be in line with the usual cost of equipping an elementary school.[26]

*Rooms.* Rooms for primaries should be located in one of the better sections of the church building or educational wing. Primary children can take stairs quite well and so they may be located on upper floors, if necessary. Heating, ventilation, lighting, cheerful walls, and proper flooring are all important in providing adequate rooms, and experts in these fields should be consulted. These outer factors of a primary child's environment *can* be controlled by the church, thus making it possible for the teachers to concentrate on their all-important task of dealing with his inner emotional and spiritual factors, which are less tangible and controllable.

Space and privacy are two of the greatest needs in Christian educational programs today. It is easy to say that Christian educators are too idealistic in this regard, when many churches still have only one room or are located on such a small lot that they cannot expand. It must be realized, however, that there *is* no solution to the space and privacy problem in many churches except that of plant renovation or erection of facilities in a new location. Churches must be realistic about this matter.

*Furnishings.* A typical primary room should be bright and cheerful. A light pastel shade of paint on the walls, an acoustical tile ceiling, tiled floor, and large windows will provide a happy meeting place.[27] To this should be added sturdy tables 22 to 24 inches high and posture-type chairs 12 to 14 inches from the floor to the seats. The room should include low-level coat racks with shelves for hats, mittens, and other items, and perhaps another lower rack to keep overshoes off the floor; bulletin boards on the children's eye level; at least one locked, steel, three-shelf cabinet for supplies; a portable chalkboard with flannel on the other side; two or three pictures on religious themes for the walls; a departmental Bible stand; a departmental Bible with large print and many illustrations; and one or two wastebaskets. A good piano is always a welcome addition to such a room, also.

*Curriculum materials.* The board of Christian education should review periodically the curriculum materials being used for primary children. A curriculum calendar can be easily drawn up to show what the primaries are studying in Sunday school, daily vacation Bible school, primary

---

[26]Personal interview in 1960 with Richard Pigott of Pigott's, Inc., School Suppliers, Des Moines, Iowa.
[27]See C. Harry Atkinson, *Building and Equipping for Christian Education* (New York: Office of Publication and Distribution, National Council of the Churches of Christ in the U.S.A., 1956).

church, and the missionary club. This will guard against teaching them the same subject several times each week. Churches should not be bound by their own denomination's curriculum offerings, for each case is different. There may be times when an independent publisher's material will better suit the needs of a particular church. Generally speaking, however, it is usually best for a church to order from one publisher for all departments of the Sunday school, because the pupils have the right to study a series which covers the whole Bible in a given cycle of years. The primary department should also have its own library or a section in the church library for supplementary reading of books which may be checked out.[28]

*Miscellaneous items.* The steel cabinet in each primary room will provide the teacher with a place where valuable materials may be stored without fear of others "borrowing" them. Flannelgraph stories, backgrounds, items for object lessons, hand puppets, models, props and costumes for dramatizing stories, simple offering envelopes for primaries to use, chalk, erasers, pictures, construction paper, round-ended scissors, paste, and many other things can be kept here. Teachers would no doubt buy more materials of their own accord *if* they could be assured of their availability when needed.

## ORGANIZATION AND ADMINISTRATION

*In the smaller church.* In the church of three hundred or less, the primaries would probably be best organized and administered in a departmental system. If there are forty primaries, for example, they could have five classes of eight pupils each. One of the teachers would serve as superintendent for the department. One large room might be used for the primary church and also serve as the space for classes, if properly subdivided by folding curtains or some other means.

*In the larger church.* In the church of over three hundred, the primaries would probably best fit into a graded system. Following the public school grading system, the first graders would have a room of their own, and the same would be true of the second and third graders. A teacher-superintendent would take charge of up to thirty pupils, aided by assistants.

*What about opening and closing exercises?* Dr. Mary E. LeBar, in a very provocative article which hits hard at the practice of opening exercises, shows them to be in many cases time-wasters.[29] Actually, the primary teachers should be given the full period for class activities during the first hour. Singing, birthday recognitions, announcements, and many

[28]Lois E. LeBar, *op. cit.,* p. 143.
[29]Mary E. LeBar, "We've Been Doing It Backwards," *Eternity Magazine,* X (February, 1959), p. 26.

other activities which ordinarily take place in opening exercises should be reserved for the primary church hour. Too many of our children are getting only twenty-five or thirty minutes of class time because the period is taken up by activities of secondary importance.

*Place of the primary department.* Where does the primary department fit into the total church organization? It is the fifth department from the bottom of the age scale, preceded by the cradle roll, toddler, nursery, and beginner departments. The primary department is extremely important in that it deals with pupils who are awakening intellectually and spiritually. In the number of children attending Sunday school, it also ranks high in comparison to other departments.

All the miracle stories of the Bible should be taught to primaries, before the cold doubts of scientific skepticism begin to creep in. Each primary should know the simple plan of salvation so that the harvest may be made, particularly in the junior age, when the children usually seem to come to the place of accepting Christ as their Saviour. The primaries should be represented in the church organizational structure. The primary department superintendent and teachers naturally should have a voice in the Sunday school council or executive committee. In this way, the primaries can be assured that they are important, and their needs will be considered by the highest administrative board in the church.

## EVALUATION

Evaluation is a necessary part of making progress, and the two main means by which a program may be evaluated are the use of records and tests.

*Records.* It is taken for granted that workers with primaries will have on file the vital statistics regarding each child. The real progress for which they look, however, will be in the children's spiritual growth. One way to keep track of this is for the individual teacher to have a personal notebook, in which he will jot down from time to time the improvements in attitude and behavior of each pupil. If his teaching has had an impact throughout the year, it will show up in the notes. Such information will also be invaluable to the next teacher on promotion day.

*Tests.* Churches seem to shy away from giving pupils tests, but this is a mistake. Just as the public school checks up on what the children learn by means of tests, so the church should administer simple oral tests to the primaries periodically. One thing to avoid, however, is the parroting back of material learned by rote memorization. If the teacher has really taught, he should find that his pupils have not only learned *words* but understandable *concepts* and *applications*, as well.

## REVISIONS

The ability to be flexible enough to change, when change is necessary, is an important characteristic of leadership.

*Who does the revising?* The department superintendent, teachers, assistant teachers, and other workers with primaries will naturally be expected to get together to suggest changes. The Sunday school leaders should offer to do what they can to help in making the revisions. The board of Christian education will be concerned with this. The church board itself will take an interest in improvement.

*How often are revisions made?* Generally speaking, revisions should be made whenever they become necessary. Realistically, however, it must be admitted that any major shift in organization, curriculum, or emphasis would have to wait for six months or a year to go through regular channels. The board of Christian education cannot be expected to move as fast on these matters as the individual department may desire. At least once a year each department ought to be closely examined to see if any major changes must be made.

*Revision problems.* What should be done to transfer the unsuccessful teacher out of his class situation? One thing that appears to be basic to such a change is the establishment of a teacher's covenant, which each teacher is required to sign and keep. In this covenant he promises to attend church services regularly, prepare and teach his lessons faithfully, take teacher training courses, use good teaching methods, set a good example for children to follow, and visit the homes of all his pupils. If he falls down in any of these obligations, he should understand that the board of Christian education reserves the right not to renew his teaching position for the next year. The director of Christian education, or the pastor, should look for another job in the church which he can tactfully suggest this person assume.

What can be done to change the curriculum materials in the primary department when it is deemed necessary? This is a matter for the board of Christian education to consider, for it must be remembered that lessons run in cycles of years so that the whole Bible will be covered. If some other materials seem superior to the ones being used, they should be carefully studied and measured objectively against a set of criteria. (See evaluation at end of chapter.)

A true Christian conservative is one who conserves the truth by means of the most modern facilities and methods available to him!

## BIBLIOGRAPHY

Atkinson, C. Harry. *Building and Equipping for Christian Education.* New York: Office of Publication and Distribution, National Council of the Churches of Christ in the U.S.A., 1956.

Benson, Clarence H. *A Popular History of Christian Education.* Chicago: Moody Press, 1943.

Breck, Flora E. *Church School Chats for Primary Teaching.* Boston: W. A. Wilde Co., 1950.

Breitweiser, Alverta. . . . *And God Cares for Me.* Anderson, Ind.: Warner Press, 1957.

Brown, Jeanette Perkins. *The Storyteller in Religious Education.* Boston: Pilgrim Press, 1951.

Coleman, Frank G. *The Romance of Winning Children.* Cleveland: Union Gospel Press, 1948.

Eavey, C. B. *Principles of Teaching for Christian Teachers.* Grand Rapids: Zondervan Publishing House, 1940.

Fant, David J., and French, Addie Marie. *All About the Sunday School.* Harrisburg: Christian Publications, Inc., 1947.

Jacobsen, Marion Leach. *Good Times for God's People.* Grand Rapids: Zondervan Publishing House, 1952.

Johnston, Dorothy Grunbock. *Pete and Penny Know and Grow—Devotionals for Boys and Girls.* Wheaton: Scripture Press, 1957.

Korfker, Dena. *Can You Tell Me?—Answers to Questions Children Ask.* Grand Rapids: Zondervan Publishing House, 1950.

————. *Questions Children Ask.* Grand Rapids: Zondervan Publishing House, 1951.

LeBar, Lois E. *Children in the Bible School.* Westwood, N.J.: Fleming H. Revell Co., 1952.

————. *Education That Is Christian.* Westwood, N.J.: Fleming H. Revell Co., 1958.

Morningstar, Mildred. *Reaching Children.* Chicago: Moody Press, 1944.

Murch, James DeForest. *Christian Education and the Local Church.* Cincinnati: Standard Publishing Co., 1943.

*Primaries Sing in Church and Home.* Wheaton: Scripture Press, 1959.

*Primaries Worship.* Glendale, Calif.: Gospel Light Publications, 1960.

Soderholm, Marjorie Elaine. *Understanding the Pupil, Part II, The Primary and Junior Child.* Grand Rapids: Baker Book House, 1956.

Trent, Robbie. *Your Child and God.* New York: Harper & Bros., 1952.

## FOR FURTHER READING

Bryan, Allene. *Primary Sunday School Work*. Nashville: Broadman Press, 1941.

Byrne, Herbert W. *Christian Education for the Local Church*. Grand Rapids: Zondervan Publishing House, 1961.

Edwards, Mildred Speaks. *ABC Stories of Jesus*. Anderson, Ind.: Warner Press, 1949.

Ellinghusen, Esther. *My Bible Stories Series*. Glendale, Calif.: Gospel Light Publications.

Erb, Alta M. *Christian Education in the Home*. Scottdale, Pa.: Herald Press, 1963.

Fairly, John and Arlene. *Using the Bible to Answer Questions Children Ask*. Richmond: John Knox Press, 1958.

Faris, Lillie A. *The Primary Bible Teacher and Leader*. Cincinnati: Standard Publishing Co., 1943.

Filmer, Edmund. *The Story of Jesus*. London: Marshall, Morgan, & Scott, 1958.

Gesell, Arnold L., and Ilg, Frances L. *The Child from Five to Ten*. New York: Harper & Bros., 1946.

Getz, Gene. *Audio-Visuals in the Church*. Chicago: Moody Press, 1959.

Hall, Arlene. *Your Vacation Church School*. Anderson, Ind.: Warner Press, 1956.

Haynes, Marjorie. *When We Teach Primary Children*. Philadelphia: Westminster Press, 1957.

*Helping Children Toward God*. Objectives in the Christian education of children. Chicago: Covenant Press, 1957.

Hoyer, Dorothy. *The Birthday of Jesus: Sacred Art Bible Stories*. St. Louis: Concordia Publishing House, 1958.

Hunter, Edith. *Conversations with Children*. Boston: Beacon Press, 1961.

Jacobs, J. Vernon. *Teaching Tools and How to Use Them*. Grand Rapids: Zondervan Publishing House, 1963.

Jones, Elizabeth B. *Round About Me*. Devotional Thoughts for Little Folks. Anderson, Ind.: Warner Press, 1953.

Knight, Alice M. *1001 Stories for Children and Children's Workers*. Grand Rapids: Wm. B. Eerdmans Publishing Co., 1952.

Korfker, Dena. *The Story of Jesus for Boys and Girls*. Grand Rapids: Zondervan Publishing House, 1954.

LeBar, Mary E. *Living in God's Family*. Wheaton: Scripture Press, 1957.

Lee, Florence B. *Teaching Primary Children*. Philadelphia: Judson Press, 1951.

Lewis, Hazel A. *The Primary Church School*. St. Louis: Bethany Press, 1951.

Little, Lawrence C. *Foundations for a Philosophy of Christian Education.* Nashville: Abingdon Press, 1962.

Lorensen, Larry. *Spiritual Home Training for the Child.* Chicago: Moody Press, 1954.

Martin, Mary Grace. *Teaching Primary Children.* Philadelphia: Judson Press, 1937.

Murch, James D. *Teach or Perish!* Grand Rapids: Wm. B. Eerdmans Publishing Co., 1962.

Murray, Andrew. *The Children for Christ.* Chicago: Moody Press, 1952.

Pettey, Emma. *Guiding the Primary Child in the Sunday School.* Nashville: Convention Press, rev. 1952.

Shields, Elizabeth McEwan. *Worship and Conduct Songs: 5-8 Years.* Richmond: John Knox Press, 1957.

Smither, Ethel. *Primary Children Learn at Church.* Nashville: Abingdon-Cokesbury Press, 1944.

Taylor, Kenneth N. *Stories for the Children's Hour.* Chicago: Moody Press, 1953.

Wyckoff, D. Campbell. *How to Evaluate Your Christian Education Program.* Philadelphia: Westminster Press, 1962.

Material . . . . . . . . . . . . . . . . . . . . . . Name . . . . . . . . . . . . . . . . . . . . . . . . . . .

## EVALUATION OF CURRICULUM MATERIALS

Good   Fair   Poor

A. *Use of Content*

   1. Is it centered in the Word (written and living)?     . . . . . . . . . . . . . .

   2. Are Bible facts accurate and complete?     . . . . . . . . . . . . . .

   3. Are Biblical essentials emphasized (such as salvation, growth in grace, service, etc.)?     . . . . . . . . . . . . . .

   4. Does extra-Biblical content seek to make the Bible practical to daily living?     . . . . . . . . . . . . . .

   5. Is extra-Biblical material in accordance with the Bible?     . . . . . . . . . . . . . .

   6. Is the stated aim carried out in the lesson?     . . . . . . . . . . . . . .

   7. Does the text of the specific lesson fit into the overall cycle of lessons?     . . . . . . . . . . . . . .

   8. Does the content provide for Christian anniversaries?     . . . . . . . . . . . . . .

B. *Use of Experience*

   1. Are spiritual elements in the pupil's experience stressed as *primary*, and physical, psychological, and social elements as *secondary?*     . . . . . . . . . . . . . .

   2. Are suggestions given which encourage pupils to make principles taught personal in their own lives?     . . . . . . . . . . . . . .

   3. Are suggestions given which encourage expressional activities in class?     . . . . . . . . . . . . . .

Good  Fair  Poor

C. *Relation of Content and Experience*
   1. Is the material graded to meet the needs, interests, and capacities of its stated age level?  . . . . . . . . . . . . . .
   2. Is provision made for the needs of home, church, secular school, and community?  . . . . . . . . . . . . . .

D. *Meeting the Needs of the Individual*
   1. Is the material appealing, challenging, and vital?  . . . . . . . . . . . . . .
   2. Is an attempt made to meet the psychological needs of the individual (such as security, affection, sense of belonging, new experiences, and freedom from guilt)?  . . . . . . . . . . . . . .

E. *Meeting the Needs of the Teacher*
   1. Is the material self-explanatory, practical, and definite?  . . . . . . . . . . . . . .
   2. Is the material flexible enough to meet the needs of teachers in small and large churches?  . . . . . . . . . . . . . .
   3. Does the material provide inspiration, Biblical backgrounds, and teaching principles in addition to specific suggestions for the particular lesson?  . . . . . . . . . . . . . .
   4. Is an attempt made to guide the teacher in using the real-life situations of his pupils for making the Bible real to them?  . . . . . . . . . . . . . .

F. *Mechanical Features*
   1. Is the literary form of suitable quality considering the importance of the teaching?  . . . . . . . . . . . . . .
   2. Is the printing and art work of good quality?  . . . . . . . . . . . . . .

## Chapter 12

# TEACHING JUNIOR CHILDREN

## Marjorie Soderholm

### WHO IS THE JUNIOR?

HE CERTAINLY IS A TYPICAL JUNIOR," someone may say as he sees Johnny scuffling in the yard with his friend George. While Johnny may be a typical junior in one aspect of his life, he may not be typical in another. Actually there is no such thing as a typical junior, for juniors vary in physical development, interests and abilities.

The junior is in the fourth, fifth, or sixth grade in the public school, and most juniors are from nine to eleven years old. Some of the characteristics often mentioned by child psychologists[1] as being common among juniors are usually followed by comments as to how these traits relate to the spiritual training of the child.

*He likes to do.* Do, do, do—that is the junior. He wants to read the story; he wants to take the offering; he wants to hand out the song books. Let him do. Let him pray, lead singing, and plan and carry out missionary projects. He may want to do more than he is able; thus he needs guidance in the choice of his activities. Leaders must take care that handwork projects and other activities are neither too easy nor too difficult for him.

*He is inquisitive.* The junior's world is expanding as he meets others in school, club, church, and neighborhood. He begins to make comparisons as to the way things are done in his home and the way they are done in others' homes. This makes him ask questions. He wants to know why he can't watch TV late at night when Barry Howe can. He wants to know

[1]See Bibliography.

---

Marjorie Soderholm, M.A., is associate professor of Christian Education at Trinity College, Chicago, Illinois.

why he has to take piano lessons when Charlie Gray doesn't have to. He is also inquisitive in his Sunday school class. He wants to know why God let Jesus die. He wants to know how God can be a perfect God if He is a jealous God. He has many questions. His teacher must give him opportunity to ask them and must be alert and ready to answer. However, the teacher must not bluff his way. If he does not know, he should say so, adding that he will find the answer during the week. Then he should keep his promise, for the junior will not forget. Bluffing and breaking promises cause the junior to lose confidence in his teacher.

*He likes "really happened" stories.* "Is it true?" is a question the teacher often hears when telling a story to juniors. The junior is interested in people, and he likes to hear what actually happened to real people. Stories of Adoniram Judson's prison experiences, Charles Haddon Spurgeon's conversion, Stephen Paxson's Sunday schools, and modern day missionary adventures can be couched in the child's language and have a vital ministry in the life of the junior.

*He is eager to learn.* This may sound contrary to what some teachers experience, but it is true nonetheless. He is eager to learn, but he wants to learn what is important to him. Teaching the Bible cannot be the mere telling of cold facts if the junior's interest is to be captured. He must see the Bible characters as real people with real problems, with experiences similar to his own. "How would you feel if you were told to go see how someone who hated you was getting along?" will be of more interest to the junior than "Jacob sent Joseph to see how his brothers were faring." In the first instance, the junior senses a problem, and it isn't long before he is looking at a map to see how far Joseph had to go to find his brothers, checking the Bible to see if Joseph found them there, and how they treated him when he arrived. All this has to be directed by the teacher, of course, but the junior will be discovering for himself an example of one who obeyed his father and who displayed no evil feelings toward his jealous brothers.

*He has a strong sense of justice.* He wants everything to be done fairly. "He handed out the books last time," or "He held up his hand before he found the verse," or "They have one more on their side than we do," are common complaints of the junior. The teacher must see that all have opportunities and responsibilities. The junior's sense of justice also helps him to understand that God must punish sin.

*He is a hero-worshiper.* He admires the strong and the just and the person who does what he would like to do. He changes heroes whenever a person appeals to him for some particular feat. His hero may be his father, his teacher, or some leader in sports. This loyalty to a person can be directed to Christ as Saviour, Leader, and Example.

*He likes competition.* Relays and team games are popular with the junior because they satisfy the desire for the group feeling and for competition. Bible games and drills, and records as to attendance, prepared lessons, and memory work make profitable use of the competitive spirit of the junior. However, the teacher must be careful that the competition is not emphasized to the extent that the junior is always comparing himself to others. He may feel so inferior that the easiest way out is to take on a don't-care attitude and to find other ways to get attention, thus becoming a discipline problem.

*He wants to be recognized by his peers.* He wants those in his class, in his grade, in his group to think highly of him. This gives him a feeling of belonging. If it takes good behavior or bad to get this recognition, he will behave accordingly. If using slang is the accepted thing in his group, he will use slang. If showing off wins approval, he will show off. If doing a job well causes the group to admire him, he will do a good job. A group of juniors desiring to accomplish something each time they meet, will not tolerate one who makes a nuisance of himself and thus hinders the work they are doing. This is an important factor in the disciplining of juniors. If group approval is won by good behavior, the junior is not so likely to be a problem.

*He feels responsible for his own actions.* While a younger child may blame the kitty or an imaginary playmate or say, "Look what you made me do," the junior's sense of justice causes him to feel responsible for what he says and does. Because of this he feels more accountable for his own sins than the younger child does. As he is at an age where he can reason quite well, he can see that sin must be punished and that Christ took that punishment. Many accept Christ during the junior years. The teacher of juniors should emphasize strongly the need of accepting Christ as Saviour.

The following summarizes some of the characteristics of the junior and their significance to the teacher.[2]

| *Because he is like this:* | *The teacher should do this:* |
|---|---|
| PHYSICAL | |
| He is active, and he likes to do things. | Provide a variety of constructive things for him to *do*. |
| He is strong and healthy. | Expect regular attendance; let him do "difficult" jobs. |
| He is noisy, and he loves to fight. | Arrive before he does; give him something to do as soon as he comes. |

[2]Marjorie Soderholm, *Understanding the Pupil, Part II, the Primary and Junior Child* (Grand Rapids: Baker Book House, 1956), p. 56.

He loves the out-of-doors.

Go on hikes with him.

He likes the difficult and competitive.

Challenge his ability with projects and Bible games.

## Mental

He likes history and geography.

Teach him the chronology and geography of the Bible.

He likes to collect.

Interest him in a worthy hobby.

He is inquisitive.

Help him to answer his own questions.

He likes to read and write.

Provide good books for him to read; give him Bible studies that require some writing.

He can think and reason.

Provide opportunities for making right decisions.

He has a good memory.

Encourage him to memorize Scripture.

He does not understand symbolism.

Avoid using object lessons which confuse his thinking.

## Social

He can accept responsibility.

Organize his class with officers who have special duties.

He does not like an authority over him.

Be a guide, not a dictator.

He likes the "gang."

Let his class be a club.

He dislikes the opposite sex.

Avoid situations that intensify the feeling of dislike.

He is a hero-worshiper.

Be an example; present Christ as his Hero.

## Emotional

He has few fears.

Teach him what to fear and what not to fear.

He may be quick tempered.

Avoid the cause of flare-ups.

He dislikes outward display of affection.

Avoid such display.

He enjoys humor.

Teach him what is funny and what is not.

Spiritual

| | |
|---|---|
| He recognizes sin as sin. | Point to Christ who saves him from sin. |
| He has questions about Christianity. | Answer truthfully; help him find the answers in his Bible. |
| Emotions play no part in his religion. | Avoid emotional appeals. |
| He sets high standards for himself. | Meet high standards in your own life. |
| He needs encouragement in daily devotions. | Provide devotional helps for him. |

## WHAT SHALL WE TEACH THE JUNIOR?

The basic truths which should be taught the junior center in the subjects of God, Christ, the Holy Spirit, the Bible, the church, prayer, character and citizenship, home, and missions. Though the following is not exhaustive, it is a core of what should be emphasized:

*What the junior should know about God*

1. God is the great Creator who uses persons, juniors too, to do His work in the world which He has created.
2. God is holy and righteous; He hates sin.
3. God loves active boys and girls.
4. God wants us to be like Him.
5. God is a person.
6. God keeps His promises which are recorded in His book, the Bible.
7. God has a plan for the life of each one of His children.
8. God provides for His children; He has given us all that we have.
9. God doesn't force us to be saved; He lets us choose.

Of course, no one lesson will cover all these truths. One lesson should stress only one main idea. The teacher should study the lesson carefully to determine what the main truth is and center the entire lesson on it. He should occasionally check through this list to see just what he has emphasized or omitted in his teaching.

*What the junior should know about Christ*

1. That Jesus is a Friend who is always with him, a Friend who is interested in the things he does, the friends he makes, and the work that he does at home or at school.
2. That Jesus reveals God.
3. That the only way to God is by accepting Jesus as Saviour.
4. That Jesus will help him in times of temptation.
5. That Jesus will help him in his attitudes toward others.
6. That he should trust Jesus to guide him every day.

7. That he should judge his conduct by the example and teachings of Jesus.

8. That Jesus is a person, the second person of the Trinity.

The main aim of Christian education is to lead the pupil to Christ, to train him up in Christ, and to send him out to serve Christ. In examining curriculum materials, the teacher should make sure that this threefold aim is stressed.

## What the junior should know about the Holy Spirit

1. That the Holy Spirit is the third person of the Trinity, and that He is just as personal as God or Christ.
2. That the Holy Spirit guided those who wrote the Bible.
3. That the Holy Spirit helps him to understand the Bible.
4. That the Holy Spirit helps him to live to please God.

Before the junior age, the child will have had little teaching about the Holy Spirit. He should begin to study the relationship between the three persons of the Trinity. He should also realize that only those who know Christ as Saviour have the Holy Spirit as a guide.

## What the junior should know about the Bible

1. The books of the Bible in order.
2. The chronology of the Bible.
3. The geography of Bible lands.
4. The customs of people who lived in Bible times.
5. That the Bible is inspired by God.
6. That the Bible is the message God has for him.
7. That God expects him to obey the teachings of the Bible.
8. That the Bible is the final authority in all matters.

The Sunday school manual or any other guide book should not take the place of the Bible in the teacher's preparation or in the classroom. The teacher should teach directly from the Bible, and the junior should have his Bible open. Each child should have a Bible of his own with large type. Educators say that the junior's Bible should be printed in 11 point type (this size).[3] The child should understand what he reads and what he memorizes from the Bible. Getting the junior involved in questions and answers is more profitable in helping him understand the Bible than for him to quote words verbatim.

## What the junior should know about the church

1. That the church is *his* church; it is not just for grown-ups.
2. The history of the church.

[3]Marian E. Breckenridge and E. Lee Vincent, *Child Development* (Philadelphia: W. B. Saunders Co., 1955), p. 284.

3. The doctrines of the church, not only to know what they are, but what they mean.

4. The difference between the universal church and the local church.

5. The requirements for church membership.

6. The meaning of the ordinances kept by his church.

7. How to act during the church service.

8. The significance of the various parts of the church service.

Since there is some difference among denominations as to doctrines, their church history, and requirements for membership, lesson materials do not deal in detail with what should be taught about the church. Nevertheless, the junior should be informed on this important subject.

It would be well for the leaders of every aspect of the children's work, Sunday school, club program, children's church, Sunday evening junior fellowship and others, to meet together periodically to go over the listings under each topic in this section to see in which phase of the work each should be emphasized. If the teachings about the church are covered in the youth fellowship, duplication should be avoided. Such a meeting of leaders held once a month would make for an effective integrated program.

### What the junior should know about prayer

1. That God answers prayer, but that the answer does not always come immediately, nor is the answer always "yes."

2. That Jesus prayed, and that it is God's will that he pray.

3. That he can pray any time, in any place, and about anything.

4. That he should pray for those who do not know Christ as Saviour.

5. That only those who have accepted Christ as Saviour can pray in His name.

6. That it is not enough to pray only when he is in trouble.

If the junior is to pray, he must recognize his teacher as one who prays. It is not enough to tell him to pray. He must have opportunity to pray. He should be helped in making his own prayer list, encouraged to give prayer requests as he meets with others, and allowed to pray for the requests of others in his group.

### What the junior should know about character and citizenship

1. That the Bible is his guidebook for living.

2. That God wants him to be like Christ.

3. That God expects him to choose the right and stand for it even in opposition.

4. That some of the traits God expects of His children are these:
Honesty in all things, including school work and play.
Thinking of others first.
Obedience to parents and teachers.
Respect for civil law.
5. That God expects His people to be good citizens.
6. That he should pray for those in authority.

The child should not grow up thinking that being a Christian consists of a list of five or six don'ts. Rather he should be familiar with the Scriptural teaching on such qualities as honesty, freedom from anger, and love for others. He should also realize that whatever he does should bring honor to God.

*What the junior should know about his home*

1. That he should respect his parents.
2. That he should share in the responsibilities at home.
3. That he can be an example to others in his home.
4. That everything he does at home should be pleasing to the Lord.

The subject of the junior and his home cannot be handled by teaching the junior alone. The church must provide classes or meetings for parents to help them in establishing Christian homes, in understanding their children, and in conducting family worship. Family nights at church also give the family a feeling of togetherness. The church calendar should not be so full that the home is divided to the extent that some member must always be at church. Grouping several activities on one night helps to leave some nights for families to be together at home.

*What the junior should know about missions*

1. That work in America as well as that on the foreign field is missions.
2. That every Christian should be a missionary, telling others about Christ.
3. That he can give to missionary work now.
4. That bringing others to Sunday school, church, Bible club is actually missionary work.

If the junior is to be missionary-minded, he must become acquainted with missionaries and their work. When a missionary couple is home on furlough, they should be invited to spend some time with the juniors. The husband, not just the wife, should visit the children's departments. Children often say, "I want to be a doctor," or "I want to be a policeman." What junior boy says, "I want to be a missionary," if he sees only women in that work? Clubs and other organizations afford opportunity for missionary projects, such as collecting used stamps for the purchase of tracts in Japan,[4] preparing flannelgraph materials for use in a children's home, and setting up displays for the missionary conference.

## HOW SHALL WE TEACH THE JUNIOR?

The key to success in working with the junior is the teacher's preparation. Work with the junior cannot be taken lightly; it takes time and effort. Take, for example, the preparation of the Sunday school teacher. He should study the lesson, not only for the pupil, but for himself. He should note from the quarterly the passage on which the lesson is based, and then study the passage. One guide which is helpful in studying the Scriptures for one's own profit is as follows:

1. Read and reread the passage.
2. Outline the passage.
3. Summarize the passage.
4. Write out applications (examples, warnings, promises).
5. Choose one application to work on during the week.
6. Select the most meaningful verse.
7. Note a point for prayer on the basis of the study.

After the teacher has studied the lesson for himself, he can determine the main point he wants to get across to the junior. This point is the aim. Too often the aim has been to cover the quarterly, to fill up the time, or to keep the class quiet. The aim should relate a point in the Scripture to a need in the junior's life. The quarterly will help in this, as most study helps state an aim for each lesson. The teacher must, however, be sure that the aim he uses fits the needs in his particular class.

After the aim is chosen, the teacher will need to determine how to begin the lesson, the method of teaching it, and how to close. The approach may be an attention-getting question, a problem, or perhaps a headline from a newspaper. It should not be, "Now, who can tell me what the lesson was about last week?"

Many methods are effective with juniors. The teacher will have to choose the method most suitable for each lesson. Some of the methods to use with juniors are these:

*Discussion.* The junior loves to get in on things. Telling the junior a lot of facts is not necessarily teaching him. The teacher may prepare questions on the Scripture passage, asking them as the junior searches for the answers. Questions such as these are suitable: How old was Joseph when he received his coat of many colors? What did his brothers think when he got the coat? How did they act? Do people today ever

---

[4]Stamps sent to the following address are sold and the money used to print tracts in Japanese: Kenny Joseph, Japanese Evangelical Overseas Mission, c/o L. W. Hudson and Co., P.O. Box 4015, Fresno 4, Calif. Like projects are conducted by missionaries in other lands.

become jealous when someone has something they would like to have for themselves? How do jealous people act? How did Joseph treat his brothers?

*Maps.* The junior is studying history and geography in school, and he likes to point out places on a map. One group of juniors made a map of the Exodus journeys, with pictures representing the experiences of the Israelites arranged around the map and with lines from each picture to the location at which it happened.

*Charts.* A chart comparing the miracles of Christ could be used. A chart such as this is simple enough for juniors to use:

| Scripture Passage | Person(s) on Whom the Miracle was Performed | What Jesus Did | What Happened |
|---|---|---|---|
|  |  |  |  |

*Dramatization.* If a Bible story is familiar, the group will enjoy dramatizing it rather than listening to it as a story again. For instance, in the story of Samuel's anointing of David, the class would need to open Bibles to answer such questions as these: How many people will we need? What will Samuel say when he hears God's voice telling him to go anoint a new king? How many brothers did David have? Preparing for dramatizing a story can develop into a fascinating and adventuresome Bible study for juniors.

*Workbooks.* Workbooks should serve as guides to Bible study rather than substitutes for it. If the workbook for juniors is not sectioned into parts to do each day of the week, the teacher can make a suggestion for dividing up the work. This is not done just to spread the work over several days, but to help the junior develop the habit of daily studying the Word of God. The teacher can help the junior see that doing his workbook is important by delivering it to his home and explaining it to him and to his parents; by looking into the workbook with the pupil to help him understand what he is to do the next week; by referring, sometime during the lesson, to what he has written in his book; and by grading the workbook at the end of the quarter.

Other methods suitable for juniors are storytelling, projects, puppets, chalk drawings, memory drills, pictures, and models.

Every teacher of juniors should be able to lead his pupil to Christ as Saviour. One study made at a Christian college showed that a high percentage of the young people in that school had accepted Christ when they were juniors.[5] If a child says, "Mr. Thomas, I want to be a Christian," the teacher should not have to reply, "Well, you'd better see the pastor." He should be able to handle the situation himself. These verses are helpful in leading the junior to Christ:[6]

Romans 3:23—shows him that he is a sinner.

John 14:6—shows him that he cannot make himself a Christian.

John 3:16—shows him what God did so that he can become a Christian.

Luke 13:3—shows him what he must do to become a Christian: repent.

Acts 16:31—shows him what he must do to become a Christian: believe.

John 1:12—gives him assurance that he is a Christian.

Romans 10:9—shows him that it is necessary for him to tell others that he is a Christian.

The following principles should be followed in leading a child to Christ:[7]

1. If it is possible, deal with the child individually.

2. Take plenty of time. The child should not feel that you are in a hurry.

3. Be sure that he knows why he needs to be saved.

4. Be sure he understands what it means to be saved.

5. Use a Bible, and let him find the answers for himself.

6. Use a few verses rather than many, but be sure they are appropriate for the situation.

7. Lead him to pray.

8. Make sure he knows what took place when he asked the Lord to forgive him.

9. Show him a verse that will give him assurance of his salvation.

10. Select verses to be memorized that will help him confess Christ to others.

11. Provide opportunity for him to tell what Jesus did for him.

12. If he does not have a Bible, help him obtain one.

13. Show him that a Christian needs to pray and to read his Bible every day.

14. If he does not attend church encourage him to do so.

After the child makes his decision to accept Christ, the teacher must not

[5]Study on conversion experiences conducted at Trinity College and Theological Seminary, Chicago, by Marjorie Soderholm, 1958. The greatest per cent were saved between 9-11 years; 60 per cent of all who replied were saved before or at 12 years of age.

[6]Marjorie Soderholm, *The Junior, A Handbook for His Sunday School Teacher* (Chicago: Moody Press, 1956), pp. 66, 67.

[7]*Ibid.*, p. 66.

feel that his work is finished. Indeed, a new work is just begun, that of follow-up in training the child in the Christian life, in teaching him to study the Bible, and in giving him encouragement. All of this is a part of the great task of Christian education, to bring the pupil to Christ, to train him up in Christ, and to send him out for Christ.

## BIBLIOGRAPHY

Breckenridge, Marian E., and Vincent, E. Lee. *Child Development.* Philadelphia: W. B. Saunders Co., 1955.

Clay, Daisy Jenny. *The Junior Leader.* Chicago: Moody Press, 1951.

Edge, Findley B. *Teaching for Results.* Nashville: Broadman Press, 1956.

Gesell, Arnold L., and Ilg, Frances L. *Child Development.* New York: Harper & Bros., 1949.

Lambert, Clara. *Understand Your Child from Six to Twelve.* Public Affairs Pamphlet No. 144. New York: Public Affairs Committee, Inc., 1948.

Narramore, Clyde M. *Understanding Our Boys and Girls.* Pasadena: Narramore Publications, 1954.

Soderholm, Marjorie. *The Junior, A Handbook for His Sunday School Teacher.* Chicago: Moody Press, 1956.

———. *Understanding the Pupil, Part II, The Primary and Junior Child.* Grand Rapids: Baker Book House, 1956.

Strang, Ruth. *An Introduction to Child Study.* New York: Macmillan Co., 1951.

*Your Child from Six to Twelve.* Children's Bureau Publication No. 324, U.S. Department of Health, Education, and Welfare, 1949.

## FOR FURTHER READING

Clay, Daisy Jenny. *The Junior Leader. Chicago: Moody Press,* 1951.
    Many short chapters giving specific suggestions on such subjects as juniors and the Bible, juniors and Jesus, the offering as worship, birthday Sunday, making juniors missionary-minded, and evaluating contests and awards.

Edge, Findley B. *Teaching for Results.* Nashville: Broadman Press, 1956.
    Excellent help for teachers who want to teach with purpose and see results from their efforts. Good on setting aims and reaching them. Gives practical suggestions and illustrations to help reader see the difference between specific and general aims.

Narramore, Clyde M. *Understanding Our Boys and Girls.* Pasadena: Narramore Publications, 1954.
    A 61-page pamphlet giving characteristics of each age group from before entering school through high school. Takes kindergarten through

eighth grade one year at a time, pointing out physical growth, actions and reactions, special needs, and how adults can help each grade.

Soderholm, Marjorie. *The Junior, A Handbook for His Sunday School Teacher.* Chicago: Moody Press, 1956.

A manual dealing with these subjects: Why teach the junior? What is he like? What are we trying to do? How shall we teach him the Bible? How shall we lead him to Christ? How shall we help him worship? Who shall teach him? Includes a sample worship service, check lists of teacher qualifications, and guides for measuring the spiritual growth of the junior. Has an annotated bibliography.

————. *Understanding the Pupil, Part II, The Primary and Junior Child.* Grand Rapids: Baker Book House, 1956.

The second of a series of three manuals dealing with the characteristics of the pupil from the cradle roll through college age. For each age group characteristics are discussed in five areas: physical, mental, social, emotional, and spiritual. A summary chart of the characteristics and their significance to the teacher closes each chapter (see chart in this chapter).

————. *Explaining Salvation to Children.* Minneapolis: Beacon Publications, 1962. A 32-page booklet dealing with such subjects as the proper use of stories in explaining salvation to children, giving invitations, and what to do when a child wants to accept Jesus Christ.

*Your Child from Six to Twelve.* Children's Bureau Publication No. 324, U.S. Department of Health, Education, and Welfare. Washington: U.S. Government Printing Office, 1949.

Discusses what the children are like; how they are influenced; play in the child's life; home and school working together; fears, worries, frustrations and their outlets; caring for the sick child; and many other subjects.

*Chapter 13*

# TEACHING JUNIOR HIGH SCHOOL YOUTH

## Milford Sholund

TEACHING JUNIOR HIGH SCHOOL STUDENTS is challenging and decisive. The challenge comes from understanding persons who are going through a developmental period called the "storm and stress time of life." The decisiveness arises in the far-reaching effects of the relationship of environmental influences and personal choices in the destinies of these young lives.

### WHAT ARE THEY LIKE?

Junior high students are twelve, thirteen and fourteen years of age,[1] and are usually enrolled in the seventh, eighth and ninth grades. There were approximately ten million as listed in the 1960 U.S. census. These young people are generally enrolled in school.

Junior highers today were born after World War II. In the United States they lived in a decade (1950-1960) of peace amid the "cold war"; an era of prosperity while millions were unemployed; a period of unprecedented home building while 200,000 families were moving from one house to another every week. In short, these teen-agers live in a revolutionary period with the world in transition. While they experience rapid, disturbing changes around them, they also experience a revolution within themselves. Early adolescence is a period of three to five years when the storm and stress of life exerts considerable pressure and brings many changes.

[1] Nevin C. Harner, *Youth Work in the Church* (Nashville: Abingdon-Cokesbury Press, 1942), p. 189.

Milford Sholund, Litt.D., is director of Biblical and Educational Research at Gospel Light Press, Glendale, California.

Some of these changes are physical in nature. Physical change known as puberty involves the sex glands, with considerable variation in the onset of the first period of menstruation in girls and the onset of puberty in boys. Rapid changes take place in the whole body. Junior highers are awkward and unpoised because of the rapid skeletal growth. They are all legs and arms.[2]

Girls tend to mature physically before boys. Seventh grade girls are often taller and heavier than boys. Girls find difficulty in accepting one another and boys during this period. The changes have physical, psychological, and social significance involving self-conscious feelings intimately associated with adolescent maturation.[3] Boys experience a "change of voice." The deepening of the voice often brings embarrassment. Boys who have enjoyed singing often become self-conscious about their voices.

There is a variety of psychological involvements in the early adolescents. They grow in intellectual powers. They develop ability to grasp relationships and solve more complex problems. They grow in practical wisdom, in judgment and common sense. This increased mental development needs to be directed. The great need is for self-understanding. There will be varying degrees of realism. Generally the early adolescent will vacillate in his interests and urges. He may seek knowledge at the same time he resents advice. He may overestimate himself at the same time he underestimates himself. This variation of urges and surges in the psychological outlook is a significant part in the growing person's outlook on life.

The junior high student grows in his ability to deal with abstraction. He begins to handle symbolic ideas in addition to concrete things. This power increases gradually; it does not spring up at once. The Christian teacher should appreciate this ability to discern since he teaches truths that require spiritual understanding.

Along with the internal development of conceptual and perceptual abilities, there is the growing power to make decisions for himself. The historic phrase called the age of accountability blossoms in early adolescence. Now the youth usually is aware of "self." He thinks and says, "I am I," "I am not somebody else," "I can decide." This is a period of awesome realization of "myself, others, and God." The junior higher does not possess adult qualities of responsibility but he knows he is responsible.

His feeling of responsibility involves ideas about what is right and wrong. A great deal of his evaluation of what he should do or what he should not do will depend on what he has learned from his family and

[2]F. L. Goodenough, *Developmental Psychology* (New York: Appleton-Century Co., 1935), p. 467.
[3]Clarence H. Benson, *An Introduction to Child Study* (Chicago: Moody Press, 1927), p. 174.

friends. His associations mean more to him now than during any previous period of his life. He is aware of what others think and do. "Others" in his world of values include the family and particularly his closer friends.

## SOCIAL ACCEPTANCE

His own friends[4] exert a tremendous influence on his life. This awareness of a group apart from his family is one of the most significant features of early adolescence. Although the junior higher leans on his parents for counsel and support, he is peculiarly susceptible to what his peers think, feel, and do. He wants social acceptance. The pressures of the peer group may be more determinative than adult influences.

The peer group will influence his habits, his dress, his leisure time, his interests, his viewpoints, his mannerisms and his speech. In short, it can be said that "if you tell me what his peer group is like, I will tell you what a junior higher is like."

This tendency to conform to the group is often a problem to parents and teachers. More satisfying relationships in the parental-child adjustment are found when parents spend time learning what to expect of the early adolescent. Too often parents expect too much. At least, the teen-ager thinks and feels so. Thus, the emotional factors involved in this conflict are as important as the physical, mental, and social features of maturation.

Adequate research is lacking in the emotional development of early adolescence, but one thing is sure: the way a teen-ager *feels about an experience* is important. He internalizes his experiences. He has feelings of love, hate, pride, anger, and fear.

The sharing of emotions can be a bewildering process to the parent, who is often a spectator. The whisperings, the secretiveness, the silence, the moodiness, and many other reflections of the inner life are difficult for adults to understand and to handle. The teacher who is understanding, however, and concerned with the emotional features of early adolescent experiences will have a high rating among junior high students.

The Christian teacher has a special obligation for the spiritual growth and decisions of the junior higher. There is more to life than physical, mental, and social development. Luke, the biographer of Jesus, tells of the developmental pattern in the life of Christ. He said, "Jesus increased in wisdom and stature, and in favor with God and man" (Luke 2:52).

The Perfect Youth, Jesus Christ, grew spiritually. There is a spiritual quality to the well-rounded person. Modern literature on adolescent development minimizes the religious and spiritual aspects of growth. The

[4]Robert J. Havighurst, *Human Development and Education* (New York: Longmans, Green and Co., 1953), p. 123.

early adolescent is too often bereft of the spiritual heritage essential to strong faith in God. He is too often spiritually starved in childhood. He enters tumultuous years of adolescence with little skill or strength to utilize the powers with which he was endowed by his Creator.

To grow spiritually, youth needs to know God. Along with cultural qualities which he has acquired through social experiences, he needs the true understanding of life as God has revealed it in the Bible. The dynamics and patterns of growth in the whole person are God-given. "God created man in his own image, in the image of God created he him; male and female created he them" (Gen. 1:27).

As surely as a youth responds to food for his body, to wisdom for his mind, so he will respond to guidance concerning the truth of God. Teaching a junior high student what the basic relationships and requirements for spiritual growth are, constitutes a major task of a Christian teacher.

The junior high youth is eager to learn. He is sincere and serious about his desire to know more about God and his relationship to the world in which he lives. His conscience is telling him that he has a responsibility to God and to others.

The junior higher is concerned about his life. He often is confused, perplexed, tempted, misled, and challenged; but he is now edging into the period of his life when he wants to know what life is all about.

## GOALS IN TEACHING

The teacher of junior high youth must have a clear conception of the objectives of Christian education. The basic purpose of Christian education is to teach the truth of God in such a way that the student comes to know Jesus Christ according to the Scriptures, and is controlled by His Spirit to fulfill God's purpose through him. This basic goal is threefold: (1) to teach and lead the student to a vital relationship to Jesus Christ as Lord and Saviour; (2) to guide him and to teach him so that he matures in the Christian faith and life; (3) to challenge him and inspire him to commit his life to God so that God can use him.

The junior higher's teacher stands in a strategic position in the developmental process of the early teen-ager's experiences. In this essential period of early adolescence, the teacher should utilize the childhood background and experiences of the student, and prepare him to exert more self-realization and self-control and self-determination in middle and later adolescence. Too often teachers of this age group underestimate the spiritual capacities and interests of junior highers. They are capable of making vital personal commitments to Jesus Christ. Theodore Roosevelt said, "If you are going to do anything for the average man, you have got to begin before he is a man."

Since the framework in which the Christian teacher functions is the Bible and the heritage of the Christian's faith, the teacher should know the interests among the junior highers so that he can guide his students in understanding and using the truth of the Word of God. The basic interests of junior highers include the following significant fields of experiences: adventure, companions, knowledge, exploration, possessions, "good times," right and wrong, philosophy of life, God.[5]

There is no order of priority in these interests. Just as the whole life of the junior higher is a complex maze of many factors interacting simultaneously, so the value of these interests will vary widely with the individual. Nevertheless, the teacher must exercise care and patience to involve the student in the kind of learning that is related to his life. He wants to know how he can make the most of his own life.

As the early adolescent faces the issues of life he is confronted by many questions which constantly challenge and confuse him. What about the opposite sex? What about recreation and fun? What about the problems of science? What about ambitions for life? What about making money? What about becoming successful? What about happiness? What about God? These are a few of the questions that press in on his life and interest. The skillful teacher will locate the problem in the life of the student and will endeavor to guide him to a solution of his problem according to the Bible and the best Christian experience available. The teen-ager will quickly respond to the teacher who is concerned about his growth and welfare. Studies among thousands of junior highers indicate that they place more value in a teacher who is concerned about their interests than the teacher who is skillful without sensitivity for their problems.

When a boy begins to spend more time combing his hair and brushing his teeth, when he calls for a clean shirt and necktie, there is a dawning sex and social consciousness which indicates that he is emerging from childhood.[6] With the onset of puberty, the focus of interest changes from others to himself.

The skillful teacher will recognize that these changes in the junior higher are normal. He will encourage these developments with guidance rather than disapproval and censorship. The teacher who is personally interested in the early adolescent will take time to talk and to counsel with junior highers. The early adolescent is gradually emerging from parental control toward the realization of self-control. As he goes over the bridge of adolescence, he needs help. He will appreciate and follow the adult who is outside the framework of his home. The teacher can provide this "third party" influence in a remarkable way in his life. The

[5]Milford Sholund, "Teaching Junior High Students," NSSA-Link (July, 1960), p. 7.
[6]John Gran, How to Understand and Teach Teen-Agers (Minneapolis: T. S. Denison and Co., 1958), pp. 94-97.

idealism of the Christian teacher based on Biblical principles can often inspire the student to higher aspirations than he often finds elsewhere.

## JUNIOR HIGH CONFLICTS AND EDUCATION

Comprehensive surveys indicate that 80 per cent of America's junior high school students like school. They like school in general, and find a good deal to complain about in particular. The smaller the community the more chance there is for students and teachers to establish an understanding. Success in school is important to most students. One of the best contributions our present teachers can make toward a feeling of success would be to teach their students better study methods.

The teacher's task is not an easy one. The Christian teacher is confronted with a bifurcation in the total scheme of the educational background and experiences of the typical junior higher. Two contrasting areas of education compete in American educational values. The one is secular and the other is Christian in nature. In public schools in the United States, secular education has prevailed for more than one hundred years. The dominance of the worldly view of life has influenced both the typical teacher and the teen-ager.

The Christian teacher finds himself in the minority educational camp. The student finds himself in a bewildering conflict of values. He does not know whom to believe. For many junior highers, the teacher represents adult viewpoints in general. It is easy for the student to believe that *all* adults think, feel, and act the way his teachers do. What they teach is what society in general teaches, in the opinion of the early adolescent.

The student who attends private or parochial school has some advantage in that he is carried along in a group that supports the view of the theistic teacher, but the student who attends only the public school finds that on Sunday, if he attends church and Sunday school, he is confronted with viewpoints often in conflict with the values he was taught in the public school.

Traditionally the planned goals of education in the public school system are academic and vocational. Recent polls among students and teen-agers indicate that they believe there should be more emphasis on personality development. According to this viewpoint, they believe that the art of getting along with people is more important than learning how to live or how to make a living.

The obligation of the Christian teacher is to inspire the student to search for the truth based on the Word of God. Junior high students are adventurous in their desire to learn. They are interested in all areas of truth. In the adventure of learning, they do not limit their activities to the classroom. The development of their glandular system infuses a vitality of life which seemingly has no bounds. Both boys and girls at this age enjoy new experiences. They are looking forward to becoming high school students. They like to feel that they are accepted before they arrive. They enjoy the first professional football game, the first conquest of a mountain top, the first trip to the big city. They especially enjoy these adventures if they can go with their own group.

The Christian teacher has an unusual opportunity in this adventurous spirit. Here is the opportunity of introducing the junior high students to the Lord Jesus Christ as the great conqueror. Generally, they are the first to admit that they have problems which are very real and which they cannot handle for themselves. They are keenly aware of guilt. They are eager to fulfill their aspirations and ideals. They want to know what is right and wrong.

The sensitivity of the junior high student to social approval both by the peer group and adults makes him unusually vulnerable to the feeling of failure. Too many negative concepts of Christian living can do permanent damage to his Christian viewpoint. As he is exploring the untrodden path of adolescence, he needs wholesome guidance by a teacher filled with the Holy Spirit. He is fortunate if he has a Christian teacher to help him.

## PLAY LIFE

Junior highers like to play. They enjoy humor. They have fun living. They are carefree in their confusion. They are happy in their problems. If they cannot have a good time at home, they will find some way of having it outside of the home. Often they do not want to come home after school. Based on childhood experiences, they have developed an image of what they expect will be the reception they will receive at home. Under any circumstances, they will insist on having a good time.

The Christian teacher is challenged to understand the proper balance of a good time and other responsibilities in the school. The Sunday school teacher who limits himself to simply teaching the lesson on Sunday morning and does not make provision for enjoying life with the junior highers during the week will accomplish little. Life-long impressions of Christian truths and practice are found in the association that teachers have with their students in the recreational aspects of weekday activities.

## MORAL STANDARDS

Much of the problem of play and recreation of the early adolescent has overtones of right and wrong. The issues of right and wrong are weighed by the conscience. The conscience is vital to the moral life, and morality is basic to the well-ordered life. In early adolescence, there is a rapid development of the conscience. The emergence to self in the total developmental pattern manifests the distinctive human quality of moral responsibility. The teen-ager is keenly aware of his accountability for his actions. He is reminded of his accountability by the actions taken for or against him by society as he behaves according to the moral standards.

Apart from the Biblical standard as revealed in the Old and New Testaments, there is little foundation for the morality and ethics of the teen-ager. There is little that is fixed and absolute in the cultural and social standards by which the teen-ager can measure his achievements and accountability. A secularistic society with relative values provides little help. If the teen-ager is to have a constant norm by which he guides his choices of right and wrong, he usually finds it apart from the traditional and contemporary pattern of life. Fortunately, guidance and standards are available in the written Word of God.

The Christian teacher has the responsibility of guiding him in the right way according to the Scriptures. The right way is a Person, Jesus Christ, and not simply a code of behavior. The best that society can provide for guidance with teen-agers is a code of standards. Whenever there is a slipping of behavior in relationship to socially approved activities, an alarmed administration in the school or in the church often reacts by suddenly invoking a new set of rules. Temporarily, this may accomplish results in the group, but such an effort does not get to the basis of the problem in the life of the teen-ager.

The teen-ager is not only in need of guidance, but he is also in need of power to accomplish his purpose. He generally knows enough to do good, but he lacks the power to do it. The distinctive contribution of Christian education is to show him that this power is found in Jesus Christ as Saviour and Lord.[7] The surest way to help an early teen-ager to learn how to handle the problems of the "right and wrong" issues is to show him that Jesus Christ living in him will not only give him the direction but also the power to perform that which is right.

The assurance that Jesus Christ is the foundation of the Christian viewpoint of life will make more of a contribution than all the insights of liberal education. The Christian educator necessarily is theistic in his philosophic orientation. He believes that God is and that God makes Himself known to His creatures. Young people in early adolescence want to know more about God. They are constantly searching for an answer to the basic questions of life: Who am I? What am I doing in this world? Where am I going hereafter?

The Christian teacher recognizes the junior higher as a responsible

[7] Findley B. Edge, *Youth Work in the Church* (Nashville: Broadman Press, 1956), pp. 22, 23.

person. Christ did not simply die for the teen-ager's problems, He died for him as a person. It is not only what the teacher presents to him that makes a difference, but how the teacher makes Christ known to him. The test of this effort to teach will be what the junior high student learns. If he is truly learning, he will show it in his changed behavior.

## TEACHING TECHNIQUES

Effective teaching involves methodology. There can be no instruction without some way of conveying the information and message. Thus, the teacher of junior high students must understand the procedures of sound and effective teaching. The fact that a junior higher can be changed, provides one of the real opportunities and challenges for his instructor.

Preparation is essential to effective teaching. One of the chief aids to preparation of the subject is the sense of purpose. The teacher cannot achieve unless he knows where he is going. What is he trying to do? The teacher must learn the subject matter which he expects to share with the students. The best way to prepare is to plan all the work which the students will do. This plan should be shared with the class. Make sure they keep it in mind and, after the work has been completed, look back over it and sum it up. Young adolescents have comparatively limited ability to make long-term plans. They live from day to day, or at best, from one week to another.

*Summary:* Teaching junior high students requires our human best filled with the Holy Spirit. The early adolescent period is challenging and decisive. The student is neither a child nor an adult. He is crossing the bridge of adolescence over which he must pass to assume his rightful place in society as a mature adult. His maturity will depend very largely on the kind of instruction and association and decisions experienced in his junior high years.

## BIBLIOGRAPHY

Benson, Clarence H. *Introduction to Child Study.* Chicago: Moody Press, 1927.

Bowman, Clarice. *Ways Youth Learn.* New York: Harper & Bros., 1952.

Edge, Findley B. *Teaching for Results.* Nashville: Broadman Press, 1956.

Gesell, Arnold; Ilg, Frances L., and Ames, Louise Bates. *Youth, the Years from Ten to Sixteen.* New York: Harper & Bros., 1956.

Goodenough, F. L. *Developmental Psychology.* New York: Appleton-Century Co., 1935.

Gran, John M. *How to Understand and Teach Teen-Agers.* Minneapolis: T. S. Denison and Co., 1958.

Harner, Nevin C. *Youth Work in the Church.* Nashville: Abingdon-Cokesbury Press, 1942.

Havighurst, Robert J. *Human Development and Education.* New York: Longmans, Green and Co., 1953.

Jaarsma, Cornelius. *Human Development, Learning and Teaching.* Grand Rapids: Wm. B. Eerdmans Publishing Co., 1959.

Jersild, Arthur T. *Psychology of Adolescents.* New York: Macmillan Co., 1957.

Sholund, Milford S. "Teaching Junior High Students," *National Sunday School Association—Link* (July, 1960).

Soderholm, Marjorie. *Understanding the Pupil, Part III—The Adolescent.* Grand Rapids: Baker Book House, 1957.

Taylor, Marvin J. *Religious Education.* New York: Abingdon Press, 1960.

Verkuyl, Gerrit, and Garner, Harold E. *Enriching Teen-Age Worship.* Chicago: Moody Press, 1952.

Zuck, Roy B., and Robertson, Fern. *How to be a Youth Sponsor.* Wheaton: Scripture Press, 1961.

Filmstrip: *The Stages of Growth (Late).* Chicago: Moody Bible Institute. In color, 45 r.p.m. record and leader's guide.

## FOR FURTHER READING

Baruch, Dorothy W. *How to Live With Your Teen-Ager.* New York: McGraw-Hill Book Co., 1953.

Bernard, Harold. *Adolescent Development in American Culture.* New York: World Book Co., 1957.

Brunk, Ada, and Metzler, Ethel. *The Christian Nurture of Youth.* Scottdale, Pa.: Herald Press, 1960.

Byrd, Annie Ward. *Youth at Worship.* Nashville: Broadman Press, 1953.

Desjardins, Lucille. *Building an Intermediate Program.* Philadelphia: Westminster Press, 1949.

Fitzgerald, Lawrence P. *One Hundred Talks to Teen-Agers.* Grand Rapids: Baker Book House, 1961.

Garrison, Karl C. *Psychology of Adolescence.* Englewood Cliffs, N.J.: Prentice-Hall, Inc., 1956.

Havighurst, Robert J. *Developmental Tasks and Education.* New York: Longmans, Green and Co., 1952.

Hoglund, Gunnar, and Grabill, Virginia. *Youth Leader's Handbook.* Wheaton: Miracle Books, 1961.

Howse, W. L. *Guiding Young People in Bible Study.* Nashville: Broadman Press, 1961.

Hurlock, Elizabeth B. *Adolescent Development.* New York: McGraw-Hill Book Co., 1955.

Jenkins, Gladys G., Bauer, William W., and Shacter, Helen. *These Are Your Children.* Chicago: Scott, Foresman and Co., 1949.

Lambdin, Ina S. *The Art of Teaching Intermediates.* Nashville: Convention Press, rev. 1955.

Ligon, Ernest M. *Dimensions of Character.* New York: Macmillan Co., 1956.

Menninger, William. *How to be a Successful Teen-Ager.* New York: Sterling Publishing Co., 1954.

Murch, James DeForest. *Christian Education in the Local Church.* Cincinnati: Standard Publishing Co., 1958.

Narramore, Clyde M. *Young Only Once.* Grand Rapids: Zondervan Publishing House, 1957.

Overton, Grace S. *Living with Teeners.* Nashville: Broadman Press, 1950.

Remmers, H. H., and Radler, D. H. *The American Teen-Ager.* New York: Bobbs-Merrill Co., Inc., 1957.

Reynolds, Lillian R., *Pioneer Handbook.* Richmond: John Knox Press, 1957.

Wittenberg, Rudolph. *Adolescence and Discipline.* New York: Association Press, 1959.

*Chapter 14*

# TEACHING HIGH SCHOOL YOUTH
## Vivienne Blomquist

U ntil 1958, it was something of a distinction to be a teen-ager because there were so few boys and girls in this age group, in relation to the rest of the population. The most dramatic changes in store for America in the next few years will be in the increase in the number of teen-agers. There are 20 million boys and girls of this age group now, and there will be 25 million by 1965, if government estimates are borne out.

## TEEN-AGERS FACE A CHANGING WORLD

This boom in teen-agers is having many important social and economic effects upon our country, ranging all the way from a critical need for high school teachers and high school buildings, to a considerably increased market for foodstuffs rich in body-building protein. There is not only a change in the number of teen-agers, but significant changes in world conditions. These youngsters entered the world on a wave of financial prosperity that is still in progress, and have been destined to live in a world that was then at war and has been under the threat of war ever since. Their world has decreased in size as far as means of communication and transportation are concerned, but at the same time has continually broadened politically and geographically. Geographic boundaries are constantly being changed as new nations are formed. Political powers and ideologies change so frequently that the newspapers and weekly periodicals are more accurate sources of information than the most recently published textbooks.

The world of science has made dramatic but conflicting changes in terms of life expectancy. New medicines and drugs make a long life

---

Vivienne Blomquist, M.A., is professor of Christian Education at Wheaton College, Wheaton, Illinois.

possible, while the power of the A-bomb can mean instant annihilation of man. The new technology broadens the intellectual horizons but poses baffling philosophical and moral problems. High school age young people are facing those problems and the answers are not yet in the textbooks nor are the implications fully understood by their teachers.

Not only the outer environment but the inner life of the teen-ager is changing. His physical body has taken on the characteristics and potential of maturity, but without the wisdom to direct that potential. His emotional life is at its peak, yet the American culture limits the ways in which he may express his feelings. Unspoken rules of conformity and adult expectations are confusing. Socially he is cutting the apron strings and identifying with his own generation.

## A NEW APPROACH NEEDED

If the church is to help young people and win them to Christ, it must evaluate anew its role as God's means of reaching changing people in a changing world. There has to be a break away from the traditional adage that "what was good enough for our fathers is good enough for our children." There must be honesty to face people as they are in a world as it is, and confidence to believe that God's plan and provision in Christ are as adequate for this speeded-up changing world as they were fifty or one hundred years ago. The unregenerate society is encouraging its scholars to interpret the world for our young people from its materialistic, pragmatic standpoint. The church needs to awaken to the fact that it needs to interpret the world and man from a Christ-centered, God-planned point of view without apology for faith as a basic cornerstone from which to work.

This has to be done by men and women who can demonstrate by life as well as word the practicality and adequacy of a life completely surrendered to Christ. The key to reaching high school young people is through winsome, dedicated Christian men and women who love Christ enough to give of themselves, and love young people enough to spend themselves as friends and counselors. This goes beyond the traditional Sunday ministry and occasional week-night gathering. It means being available when young people are free, when they feel the need to talk or to listen. It means open church doors where youth are welcome and even the environment says, "We need you; we want you; you are important to us." These are the things that kept the young Jesus in the temple long after His parents left—a group of adults interested in answering His questions, sharing their knowledge with One who was concerned about His Father's business.

Every young person needs to find his place as a member of society and especially as a member of the household of faith. The naturally gifted and outgoing in personality usually find their place easily and bear a large part of the responsibility of leadership. Those with less spectacular gifts and of a quiet, retiring nature become passive observers, and either slip quietly out the back door of the church or are content to become chronic listeners inhibited by the firm conviction that they are not capable of making a contribution.

All young people have God-given talents that need to be challenged and channeled into satisfying avenues of service and growth. There needs to be a re-evaluation of our ideas of leadership qualities and interpretation of those qualities to the young people. The young person who is willing to set up the chairs, make the poster, type the notices makes just as great a contribution as the one who can stand before the group to lead the singing or bring an inspiring message. The latter we compliment and encourage to go on to higher education. The former we ignore or bury under the duties no one else wants to do. The Lord has placed no premium on up-front leadership, but He has placed a premium on faithful stewardship of God-given time and talent. Every young person wants to be accepted and recognized by his contemporaries as an asset to the group and by adults as a worthy maturing person.

During early adolescent years young people are still controlled by the family pattern of attitudes and disciplines. They take tentative steps toward independence, but their beliefs and the limitations of their activity are accompanied with "my mother says" or "my father thinks" phrases, that betray the authority in their lives. As they go into high school they take steps toward independence from parental control and quote more frequently the members of their peer group or a respected teacher. If the peer group is compatible with the home background and the objectives set up by the parents, there is relatively little conflict; but if they are not compatible, there are major conflicts that upset the young person's world and the tranquillity of the home.

There is security in knowing just what is expected of an individual, but when the demands are too rigid, teen-agers rebel; and when no restrictions are set, the young person flounders, not knowing where he stands in the estimation of others. High standards consistently held in the home, in a permissive atmosphere, and with satisfying recognition when those standards are met, usually result in balanced maturity. The church has a responsibility either to provide an opportunity for healthy guided experience in facing problems or, where outer controls are lacking, to help them find inner controls made possible by the indwelling Christ.

Evangelical churches have felt the challenge of reinforcing the Christian home training of their children and have provided classes and fellowships where they can discuss and work together on problems of mutual interest. However, the need of reaching the youth of indifferent adults or casual churchgoers has too frequently been ignored.

For years the tall, stately spires of churches have stood in central, strategic places in growing communities. With attractive stained-glass windows and tolling bells, such churches have testified to the fact that members of the community believe that the presence of God and the worship of God are important. Those who make up the fellowship have provided for their kith and kin, and then to a great extent have trusted the presence of the building to say to neighbors and young people, "Here is the church to minister to you, if you will come within its doors." Many of the neighbors' children have attended the Sunday school, but four out of five have left the Sunday school as teen-agers never having entered the sanctuary of the church.

## ATTRACTING THE YOUTH TO THE CHURCH

Concerned adults interested in young people find it difficult to get teen-agers from non-churched homes and those with indifferent Sunday school training to enter the sanctuary or become a part of the young people's program of the church. As a result, a number of extra-church youth groups have been started in the last decade to minister to those that the church cannot reach. They have realized that the young people do not go seeking Christ; but Christ, through His people, must go seeking youth. They go into the high school, the youth center, attend the football games, invite them into homes, sit with them over a coke in the corner drugstore. The planned meetings, where God's way of salvation is presented, are held when young people have free time and want some place to go. This may be before school in the morning or after school in the afternoon, or on weekends when the pressure of homework is not so great, and in camps and conferences during the summer months. These organizations, with their emphasis on personal and group evangelism through Bible study, recreation, and fellowship, have been successful in winning high school young people to Christ and training them in personal devotion and witness to the Lord.

The church has a lesson to learn and a responsibility to accept as a result of this movement. First, it must go where young people are, to win and attract them first to Christ, and then nurture them as responsible members of the visible Church of Christ.

A busy, happy group of high school young people, working and playing together, joyously anticipating recreation, fellowship, study, worship, or service, and then coming away from the activity with glowing reports of its satisfying consummation, with no regrets in retrospect, will draw other young people as nothing else will. In a survey of Christian colleges and Bible schools made by J. Robertson McQuilkin, and reported in the March, 1954, issue of *Christian Life*, it was found that most of the young people who had a salvation experience before the age of twelve were primarily the product of Christian homes. Those who came to know the Lord in a personal way during high school years were influenced by Christian friends of their own age. During high school years, young people have more influence on each other than at any other time.

A second attraction is a group of active, successful adults with time to share their zest for life and their way of living with young people. This group could include a young housewife who cannot leave her home because of the presence of young children, but who is willing to share her home and afternoon hours with teen-agers eager to talk about their problems or hold a planning committee meeting. It could also include a businessman who travels alone in his car and is willing to invite teen-agers to go along for a few hours, to counsel with them; or a doctor who will spend a Sunday afternoon informally in his living room, answering questions about the training and rewards of his profession. Every church has rich, untapped resources in successful Christian adults who could counsel and share experiences that would enrich and challenge teen-age lives.

A third attraction is an opportunity to be on a crusade that has significance now and in the future. Young people are looking for a dynamic challenge like the one that caused hardy young fishermen to leave their nets to follow One who said with authority, "Follow me, and I will make you fishers of men" (Matt. 4:19).

## ELEMENTS OF A SUCCESSFUL PROGRAM

The program for a senior age group of young people should include instruction, worship, fellowship, and service. These elements should be so closely correlated that it is difficult to specify when one leaves off and another begins.

The church school on Sunday morning is primarily an instructional agency. Young people going to secular colleges out of high school often lose their faith through the anti-religious pressures, indifference, or the lack of reality in their religious experience during high school days. The reason many lose their faith is that they have been merely taught facts. They know a good deal about Christ, about the Bible, and what Christian people should not do. However, they have not been introduced to Jesus Christ in a personal way nor taught how to read the Bible and to use it purposefully. They have no personal convictions about the activities and attitudes of a born-again Christian.

Young people need to be taught the *process* as well as the product of the teacher's study. They need to share in the thrill of discovering truth and seeing relationships for themselves. They need to know how to use the helps that the teacher uses, such as the concordance, commentary, atlas, maps, cross-reference systems, and pertinent discoveries of archaeology that bring light on the Word of God. They need to know before they leave home what other people think of their faith and where they can expect confrontation by those who disagree with their beliefs. They especially need to know how to "give an answer to those that ask," and how to feed daily on the Word to bring strength and fortitude in their lives.

It is much easier to answer the questions of youth out of adult knowledge and experience than it is to go through the process of helping young people find the answers for themselves. Yet this is a necessary procedure if they are to grow into spiritual maturity. A teacher who goes to a class well prepared is usually enthusiastic about the lesson. He sees all the possibilities in it, and is convinced that its truth can make a difference in the lives of the students. To be enthusiastic is not enough; there must be a plan to get across that enthusiasm to others. People will listen when they feel the need or see the value. It is therefore the teacher's task to motivate pupils to want what he has to share with them. Sharing one's own experience, relating the truth to everyday life, posing questions that demand answers are good motivating techniques. Class members may be present in body, but unless the mind is actively involved as well, no learning will take place. If the lesson is keyed to the needs, interest and level of the group, the teacher can proceed with confidence.

It is not enough to know about the Bible, or in a general way what it teaches; there must be the growing ability to find one's way around alone. A good teacher prays and works toward the end of helping students become increasingly dependent upon what God says rather than what he says. It means that adult teachers must believe that Paul's statement is true, not only in adult life, but for youth as well: "All scripture is given by inspiration of God, and is profitable for doctrine, for reproof, for correction, for instruction in righteousness: that the man of God may be perfect, throughly furnished unto all good works" (II Tim. 3:16, 17).

Catherine Marshall writes:

> In my teaching, whenever the reality has been there, there has never been any problem about interest. Conversely, whenever I've tried to teach some truth I haven't lived, or when I've fallen into the pit of not adding my own experience to someone else's material from a quarterly lesson sheet—or even the Bible itself—always interest has waned. . . . It follows that if we want live Sunday schools, we

are going to have to admit into them more of the presence and direction of the Holy Spirit.[1]

The Sunday evening youth fellowship or training hour provides opportunity for seniors to plan and lead their own meetings. It is an opportunity to put into practice the truths and principles they have learned in the morning and in planning sessions during the week. Each young person should belong to a working group that is periodically responsible for a meeting as a group project. Those who are gifted can help those with limited ability, both by example and encouragement. Some churches have found a night during the week more suitable for youth fellowship. Here is where a knowledge of youth needs and readiness is more important than the traditional format of organization.

Christian young people need to play together as well as work and study together. The demands made by the home, school and community often pose a time problem. Christian educators of high school young people should work with the parents in cooperative planning, be aware of school commitments, evaluate community plans and supplement with church-sponsored activities when it is suitable. For example, times of Christian fellowship can be scheduled before or after school sports events. Program planning sessions can take place after school in the home of a young married couple to avoid interference with homework. One Sunday afternoon a month could be set aside for planning sessions. Service for others can be times of rewarding fellowship. Parties planned for younger children or shut-ins in the church, retreats that include unchurched friends, singspirations with young people from other churches give excellent leadership training opportunities.

A midweek prayer service in conjunction with the adult service, or parallel with it on a youth level, brings the needs of the church into focus for young people and the needs of young people into the focus of the church. Before-school prayer meetings are successful and profitable if the meeting place is on the way to the high school.

Church-sponsored retreats, camps or conferences during vacation periods give seniors an opportunity to live in a Christian fellowship and see Christianity at work twenty-four hours a day. Away from the familiar routine and in an environment conducive to Christian living, young people gain new insights and perspective on life that break through the habitual ways of doing and thinking. The church has an opportunity to exemplify in a telling and unique way its concern for its young people that results in deeper Christian experiences. The church camp program has made its greatest impact on the senior.

[1]Catherine Marshall, "They Would See Jesus," *The Sunday School Teacher*, Vol. 1 (Fall, 1960), p. 3.

## NEEDED: A CHRISTIAN WORLD-AND-LIFE VIEW

High school young people need to see the relationship of God's Word to the immediate world of the high school classroom, to the inner longings and desires of their changing bodies, and the shifting moral standards in a world not sure of tomorrow. The secular world is succeeding in interpreting its philosophies of life. The Christian community of believers needs to be just as prepared and ready, both by life and word, to interpret to high school young people a world-and-life view that is Christian.

### BIBLIOGRAPHY

Cole, Luella. *The Psychology of Adolescence.* New York: Rinehart and Co., Inc., 1959.

Finegan, Jack. *Youth Asks About Religion.* New York: Association Press, 1949.

Griffith, Louise. *The Teacher and Young Teens.* St. Louis: Bethany Press, 1954.

Jersild, Arthur T. *The Psychology of Youth.* New York: Macmillan Co., 1957.

Landis, Paul H. *Adolescence and Youth.* New York: McGraw-Hill Book Co., 1952.

Malm and Jamison. *Adolescence.* New York: McGraw-Hill Book Co., 1952.

Marshall, Catherine. "They Would See Jesus," *Christian Herald's The Sunday School Teacher.* Vol. 1, Fall, 1960.

Remmers, J. J., and Radler, D. H. *The American Teen-ager.* New York: Bobbs-Merrill Co., 1957.

Tani, Henry. *Ventures in Youth Work.* Philadelphia: Christian Education Press, 1957.

Taylor, M. J. *Religious Education.* New York: Abingdon Press, 1960.

### FOR FURTHER READING

Bernard, Harold W. *Adolescent Development in American Culture.* New York: World Book Co., 1957.

Farnham, Marynia F. *The Adolescent.* New York: Harper & Bros., 1951.

Gesell, Arnold, Ilg, Frances L., and Ames, Louise Bates. *Youth: The Years from Ten to Sixteen.* New York: Harper & Bros., 1956.

Johnson, Mel. *Everyday Questions Teen-Agers Ask.* Grand Rapids: Zondervan Publishing House, 1957.

Roberts, Dorothy M. *Leadership of Teen-Age Groups.* New York: Association Press, 1950.

Sadler, William S. *Adolescence Problems.* St. Louis: C. V. Mosby Co., 1948.

## Chapter 15

# TEACHING COLLEGE-AGE YOUTH

### HENRIETTA C. MEARS

THE TYPICAL CHURCH is not reaching its share of the growing army of collegians, which numbered 4,800,332 in 1963.[1] Ninety-five per cent of American collegians are estimated to be unaffiliated with Christ and His church,[2] yet the vast majority of tomorrow's world leaders are coming from college and university campuses. The church cannot ignore its responsibility to train this leadership—to produce young men and women who know Christ as Saviour and Lord, and who are prepared to serve God and their fellowmen.

A main reason that college students are largely unreached by churches is that their rate of attendance in Sunday school and worship services is often irregular and unpredictable. A church can be assured of having many of them for no more than four years. Many do not stay for more than a year or six months. Occasionally a student may attend a college Sunday school class only once.

Another problem is the stereotyped picture of the "rebellious" and "unbelieving" collegian. Churches tend to fear the "agnostic" college student who attempts to refute the Bible as being incompatible with science, and who asserts his desire for independence with absurd and extreme practices that range from instantaneous and reasonless riots to

[1]Edith M. Huddleston, *Opening (Fall) Enrollment in Higher Education, 1963* (Washington, D.C.: U.S. Department of Health, Education, and Welfare, Office of Education, 1963), p. 6.
[2]An over-all estimate of 95 per cent is made by Campus Crusade for Christ, directed by William R. Bright. Originated in 1951, Campus Crusade for Christ has over one hundred representatives working on college and university campuses throughout the United States and in several foreign countries. Mr. Bright, who visits up to fifty campuses every year, feels that in many areas the percentage of those who are not consistently active in the church is even higher, at times reaching 98 and 99 per cent.

---

The late Henrietta C. Mears, L.H.D., was editor in chief of Gospel Light Press, Glendale, California, and director of Christian Education at the First Presbyterian Church of Hollywood, California.

unexplained seasonal migrations to pleasure spots to soak up sun on the beach and beer in the bars.[3]

While these problems are real to varying degrees, they can be solved. The nebulous collegian will appear out of the shadows, *if there is a solid program for the teaching of God's Word to draw him.* The "rebellion" of the collegian must be recognized as his natural need for independence that results as he matures. Collegians are seeking answers to the reason for life. They willingly will examine the claims of Christianity in their search for truth and reality. During a visit to Yale University, Evangelist Billy Graham preached four sermons, each attended by 2,400 students. Twenty-six hundred responded to an invitation to learn more about Christ.[4]

The Carnegie Corporation of New York reports that in one survey of 7,000 students at twelve colleges and universities, eight out of ten said they felt a need for a religious faith. Only one per cent described themselves as atheists.[5]

## CHARACTERISTICS AND NEEDS

Who are college-age young people? Their ages may range from eighteen to twenty-five. Many of them are attending a college or university; others already may be in the business world. In or out of college, unmarried young people in this age span are a separate and distinct crowd. If the church tries to place them in a high school group (and this is often done when there are only three or four college-age students), they won't stay there. If collegians are placed with an older adult group, they won't stay there either. Unless the church specifically provides for college-age youth, it is in danger of losing them entirely.

College-age young people have many needs; and the college teacher should learn what some of these basic needs are in order to work effectively.

The college student seeks friends. People always go where their friends are. Most of us would rather go to the beach with our friends and enjoy sand-garnished wieners than eat a ten-course meal at the Waldorf *alone!*

The college student seeks recognition. He wants to feel that he matters. He must have something to do. When a young person is given a task, he feels recognized, that he belongs.

College students are confident. They have a sense of power and of vision. The collegian wants difficult tasks to perform, difficult lessons to learn. One of the chief reasons churches lose college-age men and women is because they are not provided with tasks which they consider worthy of their time and ability.

[3]"Beer and the Beach," Time, LXXIII (April 13, 1959), p. 54.
[4]"Billy Graham at Yale," *Newsweek*, XLIX (February 25, 1957), p. 68.
[5]"The Search," *Time*, LXVI (November 21, 1955), p. 60.

College students seek adventure. There is an urge to follow someone or something—to serve a great cause. Communism capitalizes on this and offers the young person the opportunity to "join with his comrades to win the world." The church has infinitely more to offer youth in the truth of Jesus Christ. The church must present Christianity as a challenging adventure.

## THREE GREAT QUESTIONS

The problems and complexities of college-age life are many, but three questions stand out for the college youth: (1) Does God have a purpose for my life? (2) What should be my life vocation? (3) Whom should I marry?

### A Purpose for Life

College-age men and women ask again and again, "Is it really true that God has a purpose for me?" The teacher of college-age youth should seek to show how God always has dealt providentially with men and women throughout history, and how He is working among them today. The collegian should learn that God has not lost him in the crowd. Every collegian is important to God, more important to God than he is to himself.[6]

### A Life Vocation

In direct connection with God's purpose for each life, college students ponder what they should do for a living. During teen years young people are occupied with physical and social adjustments. As they reach college age, they begin to realize their capacity under the guidance of trained adults, yet they are free of the restraint they experienced in their teens.

Eager to earn that first pay check, many high school graduates choose a job in favor of college. Young people who have chosen career employment still need guidance and counseling. Whether they are in college or out, the church has a great responsibility to guide young people during their vital choice-making years.

### Marriage

The home-founding instinct—a divine impulse—is strongest at this age. Some critics condemn college departments as "matchmaking institutions." In what better place could matches be made? Far better for the church to be concerned with Christian matchmaking than in trying to patch broken homes and hearts. Young men and women are deeply interested in teachings that concern courtship, the home, family, and marriage. The college

[6]Rosalind Rinker, *The Years That Count* (Grand Rapids: Zondervan Publishing Ho···· 1958) p. 17

teacher has both an opportunity and a responsibility to instruct in all these areas through counseling and the direct application of God's Word.

## THE TEACHING PROGRAM

There are numerous methods and programs for teaching any age group. The following program has been developed over a period of several decades in the college department of the First Presbyterian Church of Hollywood, California.[7] Three major principles are incorporated: leadership, fellowship, and scholarship.

### LEADERSHIP

This principle is foremost in building a living department. The teacher of the group must have leadership qualities to be sure; but student leaders must also be developed. A college department continually must produce leaders from within its own ranks, or it will die.

Every year many leaders are taken from the Hollywood college department. Some go to seminary, some get married, others go into the armed services. In a matter of months all the leaders can be lost. The department has to produce replacements rapidly if there are to be qualified leaders to fill vacant positions.

A good college department develops loyalty among its members. The students are loyal to the group and to each other. There are two basic ways to rule—by force and by love. The army can say, "You *must* come and serve," but the church cannot make its appeal on this basis. Instead there must be love between leaders and individuals and among individuals themselves.

Every college department should use men as leaders. The Lord ordained men; use them. Give them big tasks, not unimportant little jobs. Seldom should girls be allowed to hold key leadership positions—to stand before the group, for example, and lead it. In too many churches the typical college department consists of two men and twenty-seven girls. A husky young fellow might come to a meeting and hear a sweet little girl get up and say, "This Friday night we're going to have a party and I wish we had more men." The frightened newcomer says to himself, "I better get out of here." And he does, never to come back.

The Hollywood college department relies on an inner circle of between fifteen and twenty leaders, which is called the board of directors. The board meets every other week for prayer and business matters. Much of

[7]The author has taught the college department in the Sunday school of the First Presbyterian Church of Hollywood for more than thirty years. The group has grown to an active membership of over 600, with an average attendance of 400 in the Sunday morning Bible study hour. For the sake of brevity in subsequent material, the department will be referred to as the Hollywood college group or department. The reader is asked to make mental note of the illustrative context of the material referring to this specific local church situation.

the business handled in these meetings includes reports and recommendations made by committees working under various board members. The members of these committees are called "executives." Once each month the board of directors meets with the committee executives in a general session. The twofold purpose of this monthly meeting is to help the executives feel they are a definite part of the leadership of the college department, and to give them a clearer picture of the far-reaching program of the entire department.

These leaders are trained to recognize the potential of the group they are leading. One group is capable of one activity, another group of something altogether different. College leaders must be able to learn by experience. They must sense the interests and capabilities of their group and respond to them. No two groups are the same. One group may take an idea readily and develop it into a full-scale program or institution of some kind. The next group may lack creative ability and will want just to sit back. College leaders must know what their group is like and what they like.

Another vital concept is never to let a student leader fail. If he does, two adverse effects result. He is discouraged and defeated individually; and the group also suffers. To fail breeds insecurity and lack of confidence; to succeed develops confidence and the fullest leadership potential in an individual.

### Fellowship

This may be called social contact, camaraderie, *esprit de corps*, or just "getting together." Whatever its name or the function assigned it, fellowship is that real, warm, and inviting atmosphere that molds college students together. Fellowship cannot be separated from any part of a college program. This is not to say that a college department is little more than a social situation. Teaching God's Word, expressing its truths, appropriating its message—this is the most important task. But in everything that is done the aura of fellowship must prevail and permeate.

*Cliques:* Whenever fellowship is stressed within a large group, smaller clusters are certain to develop within the whole. These smaller groups are sometimes called "cliques" and are looked upon as distasteful and dangerous. It is true that in their negative sense cliques are a subtle enemy of Christian outreach and witness. There is, however, a positive side to the clique concept. They can help develop individuals according to their abilities and interests, because people naturally associate themselves with others of like interests and ideas.

A Rhodes scholar once came into the Hollywood college group and found Christ as his personal Saviour. He needed to get into a group that would challenge his intellect if he were to grow in his Christian life. He became part of such a group—a small circle of fellows with great gifts and abilities. Because this brilliant young man was part of this "clique," he took tremendous strides spiritually. Each of the fellows in this group could do something for the others.

There is nothing wrong with a clique as long as it does not begin to feed upon itself and retreat within itself. Then it will consume itself and die spiritually. No large group has any power or life unless these smaller subgroups of those of like interests are operating within it. Without these small groups, fellowship becomes so generalized it is hollow and insincere.

## SCHOLARSHIP: A THREEFOLD APPROACH

A typical weekly program in the Hollywood college department includes three meetings: Sunday morning for Bible study; Sunday evening for Christian expression; Wednesday evening for the development of the devotional life. Each of these three approaches is necessary to build an inclusive program; all are based upon study and expression of truths contained in God's Word.

*Sunday morning:* This should be the Bible study hour. Because of the size, the Hollywood college department Sunday morning class is usually a lecture situation. Dramatization of certain Scripture portions by the church drama group has also been done.

Where a college-age class is small, many teaching methods can be used. Collegians love to discuss (this is done in other Hollywood college group studies, particularly on Wednesday night). Role playing can be an excellent method of teaching young people to be articulate in their beliefs. Projected visual materials—filmstrips and films—can provoke a worth-while discussion.[8]

Whatever method is used, the college teacher must know his class and their needs. Specific aims are vital. The teacher should know what he hopes to accomplish during each lesson. Findley Edge has well said, "In too many instances teachers study their lesson, perhaps carefully, getting a general idea of what it is about. They may even plan a good outline of it. But they teach it on Sunday in general terms only. Seemingly, their primary objective is 'to teach the lesson.' "[9]

Edge believes that a teacher should have one of three specific aims for a lesson: (1) to teach knowledge, (2) to seek inspiration, (3) to secure conduct response. He stresses that only *one* of these aims should be

[8]A good summary of teaching methods can be found in a volume by Findley B. Edge, *Helping the Teacher* (Nashville: Broadman Press, 1959).

[9]*Teaching for Results* (Nashville: Broadman Press, 1956), p. 90. Mr. Edge has done a scholarly job of clearly presenting basic pedagogical principles that every student of Christian education should grasp. His chapters on aims are particularly strong.

dominant in a given lesson.[10] In short, the teacher must decide whether he wants his class to know, to think, or to do, and then concentrate on achieving the desired result.

The college teacher should constantly emphasize the authority of Scripture. He should always keep in mind that his students are interested in facts from Scripture, and how these facts affect their lives. College men and women need to see the Bible as a whole—not as a heterogeneous anthology. A panoramic survey of the entire Bible emphasizing its continuity is an excellent pursuit for any college-age class.

*Sunday evening:* This is a time for expression. The college students conduct the entire program. Adult leaders are present only to guide and counsel. Sunday evening should not be the time for another lecture or sermon. Features can include panel discussion, role playing, dramatic presentation, musical programs, films, or guest speakers who can report on timely subjects.

The Hollywood college group, for example, has presented a drama on the trial of Christ and a "broadcast" from a far-off mission field. The broadcast was done by obtaining a tape recording from a missionary on the field and then arranging the meeting hall to look like a radio broadcasting studio. The voice of the missionary, actually on tape, appeared to be coming in right from a microphone. The event stirred the entire church. It did away with the concept that missionary programs have to be dry and stuffy.

Sunday evening programs should be built around doing, making decisions, acting upon what is known. Sometimes the thrust should be purely evangelistic and a decision should be desired. On other occasions Christian service should be clearly pictured and actually developed. Sunday evening should reach the student where he is and challenge him to use what he has available to him.

*Wednesday night:* The day chosen does not matter, but a college program should include a midweek meeting of some kind. With the Hollywood group, the midweek stress is on the devotional life. Two hundred to 250 students are present and the evening opens with a prayer, singing, and a few announcements. Then the large group breaks up into groups of ten, and these smaller groups distribute themselves about the church to study and pray alone. The leaders of these groups are college students who have been trained in Bible study, prayer, and witnessing. Each group has the same Bible study assignment for that evening, outlined on a mimeographed sheet. The students study for forty minutes—reading and discussing the Scripture lesson in a devotional context—then all groups reconvene and the student leader in charge of the Wednesday program ties any loose ends together. This method—the buzz sessions followed by

[10]*Ibid.,* p. 97.

summation—is excellent for teaching collegians as long as adequate leadership is available.

Wednesday night is a good example of how the social can be combined with the academic. Following the meeting there are refreshments for those who wish to stay. The refreshments are simple—just some cookies and punch. These are placed at the front of the room. People have to make their way to the front in order to be served. Instead of the crowd streaming out the back, many work their way toward the front.

Many students remain for hours, to discuss spiritual matters. Many accept Christ. Wednesday night is a spawning ground for much follow-up work. We approach a student and say, "Glad you're here tonight. Tell me, did what you heard make sense? Let's talk about it." They are glad to talk about it. They open up and real progress can be made in dealing with their spiritual questions and problems.

## Advanced Activities

Those working with college-age youth should always be prepared to develop and train those students who show special potential, or those who desire to deepen their Christian experience. Two methods used by the Hollywood college department for accomplishing this are discipleship classes and world deputation work.

*Discipleship classes:* These classes offer further study and practical application of Christian teaching. Each class runs for thirteen weeks and meets on Friday evenings from 7:00 to 10:00. Class members take a vow that absolutely *nothing* of a controllable nature will prevent them from attending the class. To miss once is serious; to miss twice means the student is dropped.

The total enrollment of the class is broken into workable groups of ten for instruction by trained college students. Bible study, Christian discipline, and personal evangelism are stressed. The prime requisite for entry in a discipleship class is but a sincere desire to become a stronger and more effective Christian.

*World deputation:* Hollywood college department students who show promise in developing for extensive Christian work in later life are chosen to make deputation trips to foreign countries. Here they study and experience actual conditions faced by missionaries. The Hollywood church finances these students and has sent them to Europe, the Orient, and the South Seas. On their return they report their experiences to the college department.

Deputation work can be done on any scale. College youth can be sent to needy spots in the local area, the state, or in another part of the country. The goal of deputation work is to develop potential leadership to its fullest through practical experience.

## THE GOAL OF THE COLLEGE TEACHER

The ultimate goal of those teaching college-age youth should be producing Christians who will reproduce more Christians. Lead young people into a definite experience with the Lord Jesus Christ as Saviour and Lord and into the truth of God's Word as it operates in everyday life; then these young people can go out and establish the faith of others. The best way to strengthen one's own faith is to help produce faith in someone else. The college teacher can build faith with teaching that is convinced and convincing; he strengthens that faith by enlisting his students to convince others. Then a college-age group is alive and growing.

Many tools are needed to accomplish this aim, but the Bible—God's holy, inspired Word—is the central force. It may be agreed that the Bible should be the textbook for spiritual teaching, but a careful evaluation is needed. Why is the Bible being taught? Is the goal to present only the bare facts as they are recorded? Young people are interested in facts from Scripture, *but only as these facts can be applied and made operative in their daily lives.*

Bible teaching should portray the centrality of Jesus Christ in the Christian faith. Jesus Christ is the answer for every life. The Word of God reveals Him in all His ability, majesty and power.

College youth must see the reasonableness of the Word of God. They should be led to examine the internal and external evidences that prove its truth and trustworthiness. The college teacher is charged with the vital responsibility of giving young men and women a reason for the faith that is in them.

The teacher of college-age youth is likely to be dumfounded by the limited knowledge of the Bible that the average young person possesses. This lack of knowledge must be corrected, for the Sunday school teacher is not the only instructor of the collegian. His college professors have tremendous influence on him. The collegian is easily led into believing that his secular instructors are the "real intellectuals." If an agnostic professor has a winning personality, he can easily sway a student into thinking that only naive people believe the facts presented in the Bible. Thus the student who is seeking knowledge finds himself with conflicting loyalties. From one hand comes the voice of his church, his pastor, his Sunday school teacher; from the other comes the teaching of another viewpoint from a teacher whom he has learned to admire.

The Christian teacher of college youth can resolve this conflict by positively and confidently pointing to the evidence of Scripture.[11]

[11]See "For Further Reading" (at end of chapter) for list of books on Christian evidences and apologetics with which teachers of college-age youth should be familiar.

## ORGANIZATION CHART FOR THE SUNDAY SCHOOL COLLEGE DEPARTMENT OF THE FIRST PRESBYTERIAN CHURCH OF HOLLYWOOD

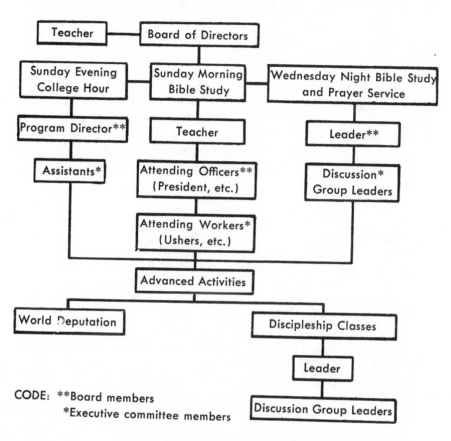

CODE: **Board members
     *Executive committee members

### BOARD OF DIRECTORS

President
Vice-president
Assistant to President
Woman's Vice-president
Secretary

New Members Director
Personnel Directors (four board members who divide department membership among themselves. Main duty: personal service and contact).
College Hour Director (Sunday evening)
Wednesday Night Director (Bible study and prayer service)
Treasurer

Missions Director
Hospitality Director
Publicity Director
Publications Director
Social Director

Winning the young men and women to Christ is half the goal; holding them and building them in the faith is the other. Again it must be emphasized that a program is not enough, thorough and well organized though it may be. Daniel Poling has well-said that youth does not respond to programs, but to personalities. The teacher of the college-age class must attract youth. He must be able to challenge and inspire them, to get them to respond to his teaching.

A college-age Sunday school class is a living organism. It does not grow in a moment. It does not depend on outlines and lists of procedures, necessary as these may be. An effective, witnessing, growing college group is a spirit. It is an experience. It is taking the individual and putting him over against the Lord Jesus Christ. The college department that fails to exert the claims of Christ on the individual will not grow. As Christ enters and controls each young man or woman, then the group grows, is propagated, and lives on.

## BIBLIOGRAPHY

"Beer and the Beach," *Time*, LXXIII (April 13, 1959).

"Billy Graham at Yale," *Newsweek*, XLIX (February 25, 1957).

Cornett, R. Orin. "The Denominational College," *Encyclopedia of Southern Baptists*, Vol. I, p. 297.

Edge, Findley B. *Helping the Teacher*. Nashville: Broadman Press, 1959.

———. *Teaching for Results*. Nashville: Broadman Press, 1956.

Huddleston, Edith M. *Opening (Fall) Enrollment in Higher Education, 1963*. Washington, D.C.: U.S. Department of Health, Education, and Welfare, Office of Education, 1963.

Keegan, G. Kearnie. "What and Why?" *The Baptist Student*, XXXXIX (June, 1960).

Rinker, Rosalind. *The Years That Count*. Grand Rapids: Zondervan Publishing House, 1958.

"The Search," *Time*, LXVI (November 21, 1955).

## FOR FURTHER READING

*Problems and Solutions*

Eddy, Edward D., Jr., assisted by Parkhurst, Mary L., Kayovakis, James S. *The College Influence on Student Character*. Washington: American Council on Education, 1959.

Jeffreys, M. V. C. *Beyond Neutrality*. London: Sir Isaac Pitman and Sons, Ltd., 1955.

Zylstra, Henry. *Testament of Vision*. Grand Rapids: Wm. B. Eerdmans Publishing Co., 1958.

Characteristics and Needs and Three Great Questions

Coleman, James C. Abnormal Psychology and Modern Life. Chicago: Scott, Foresman and Co., 1950.

Hudson, R. Lofton. Growing a Christian Personality. Nashville: Broadman Press, 1956.

Louttit, C. M. (rev. ed. by Gardner Murphy). Clinical Psychology. New York: Harper & Bros., 1947.

Munn, Norman L. Psychology. Boston: Houghton Mifflin Company, 1946.

Narramore, Clyde M. The Psychology of Counseling. Grand Rapids: Zondervan Publishing House, 1960.

———. This Way to Happiness. Grand Rapids: Zondervan Publishing House, 1958.

———. Young Only Once. Grand Rapids: Zondervan Publishing House, 1957.

Rinker, Rosalind. The Years That Count. Grand Rapids: Zondervan Publishing House, 1958.

The Teaching Program

Adler, Mortimer J. How to Read a Book. New York: Simon and Schuster, 1940.

Edge, Findley B. Helping the Teacher. Nashville: Broadman Press, 1959.

———. Teaching for Results. Nashville: Broadman Press, 1956.

Highet, Gilbert. The Art of Teaching. New York: Alfred A. Knopf, 1951.

Smith, Wilbur M. A Treasury of Books for Bible Study. Boston: W. A. Wilde Company, 1960.

The Goal of the College Teacher

American Scientific Affiliation. Modern Science and Christian Faith. Wheaton: Scripture Press, 1948.

Carnell, Edward John. Introduction to Christian Apologetics. Grand Rapids: Wm. B. Eerdmans Publishing Co., 1948.

Feinberg, Charles L. (ed). The Fundamentals for Today, Vols. I and II. Grand Rapids: Kregel Publications, 1958.

Mixter, Russell L. (ed.). Evolution and Christian Thought Today. Grand Rapids: Wm. B. Eerdmans Publishing Co., 1959.

Ramm, Bernard. A Pattern of Authority. Grand Rapids: Wm. B. Eerdmans Publishing Co., 1957.

## Chapter 16

# TEACHING ADULTS

## C. G. SCHAUFFELE

THE INTENSITY OF CHILD STUDY in the 1920's, followed by the zeal for examining teen-age growth in the 40's, is now extending to a deepening investigation in the 50's and 60's to know the possibilities and potentials for adult education. But ever since creation, God, patriarchs, priests and prophets have been teaching adults.

### HISTORY

BIBLICAL TRADITION

Even the casual reader of the Old Testament sees the Almighty teach by theophany, vision and voice the great redemptive truths of salvation by grace to adults, such as Noah, Abraham, Isaac and Jacob. In the Exodus era, Moses, with his spokesman Aaron, was given the tremendous responsibility of training the nation in its moral, ceremonial and juristic law. With the nation divided into tribes, the leaders were responsible for the implementation of adult training to the lower levels.

The high peaks of national life in Judah were correlative with the exercise of kingly responsibility to instruct the people. For example, Jehoshaphat (II Chron. 17:7-9), to promote religious knowledge among the people, sent a commission consisting of five high officials, two priests and nine Levites with the Book of the Law to instruct the people. This was to be done in a "refresher" course every seven years. God's standard to live by was to be reviewed every seven years that the nation, especially the adults, would have purpose and clarity of national goals. Exile came because the priest's mouth no longer contained knowledge (Mal. 2:7), and the adult educational center of the synagogue arose. Wherever the Dias-

---

Charles Schauffele, Th.B., is associate professor of Christian Education at Gordon College, Beverly Farms, Massachusetts.

204

pora poured its orthodox Jewry, there with ten adult males was a synagogue. The pericopes of Law, Prophets and Writings were the lessons, and the Torah was life. Four hundred years without a prophetic voice restricted the adult curriculum of the synagogue. The effect was to fetter the mind, and produce four results:

1. Developed taste for close, critical study
2. Sharpened the wits, even to the point of perversity
3. Encouraged a reverence for law and produced desirable social conduct
4. Formed a powerful bond of union among the Jewish people

To these four enumerated by Davidson[1] can be added the fifth:

5. "Jewish adult education, by its consistent teaching of lofty monotheism and its emphasis, sometimes incidental and sometimes outstanding, upon righteousness and holiness of life as a condition of participation in a future Messianic kingdom, prepared the way for the Christian view of God and the world, set forth in its original distinctiveness of outline and incomparable simplicity in the teachings of Jesus."[2]

Jesus Himself exemplified the Jewish ideal of a teacher. He gathered about Him, as did His contemporaries, a group of chosen disciples to be taught His way, His interpretation of the Law, and His life. He was constantly engaged in teaching adults wherever He could find them, and they would stop to hear and discuss. He trained a group of teachers to carry on His plans after He should leave them. This He did by personalized instruction, teaching Thomas differently from Peter, and Nathanael from John. In Matthew 28:19, 20, He also commissioned His followers to teach, telling them that they should initiate through a teaching ordinance and then continue the teaching process. Christ taught adults to bring light and to change life. Both His message and His methods were divine. His trained leaders carried the good news around the world, yet they were of humble origin, and He was with them only as long as a standard seminary training period.

## MODERN CULTURAL CONTEXT

Beginning with the founding of our nation, a process of adult education began for the development of quite ordinary men and women from subject peoples into rationally self-governing citizens of a republic. The great fundamental truths of human worth and state function were brought from the Bible. The implementing documents were the books of great English and European political libertarians. The spiritual guides were the colonies' Calvinistic theologians. The sermon, the town meeting, and

[1] Thomas Davidson, *History of Education* (New York: Charles Scribner's Sons, 1900), p. 80, quoting Eusebius, *Historia Ecclesiasticas.*
[2] H. H. Meyer, "Education," *International Standard Bible Encyclopedia,* II (Chicago: Howard-Severance Co., 1930), p. 904.

the village store debate provided the matter and the method of American give-and-take.

It was not difficult, however, for secularism to strike its roots deep in the soil of political revolution and frontier development. The industrial expansion, with the imaginative horizons of free enterprise, gave rapid acceleration to informal adult education that far outstripped the spiritual moorings from whence it was launched. The decline of Trinitarianism in New England gave the freedom from theological restraint in which naturalism flourished. The intellectual ferment of the first half of the nineteenth century produced the Boston Mechanic's Institute in 1826, the Franklin Institute in New Haven in 1828, the Lowell Institute in Boston in 1836, the Smithsonian Institute in Washington in 1846, Cooper Union in New York City in 1859, besides public libraries, land grant colleges, and women's clubs. More than three thousand town lyceums by 1835 grew out of the original founded by Josiah Holbrook of Derby, Connecticut, in 1826. Simple demonstration lectures on developments in science were the attractions of town lyceums. "Professors" whose academic claims were sometimes as thin as Ben Franklin's kite string brought similarly "amazing" experiments with electricity to the podium.

At Lake Chautauqua, New York, under Bishop J. H. Vincent, the year 1874 saw an extended summer course for Sunday school teachers established. Vast assemblies gathered there through the years, while the courses were enlarged in scope to include literature and other cultural subjects, and on the latest programs, courses in current events of national and world import.

The adult correspondence course grew from the Literary and Scientific Circle founded in 1878 out of the Chautauqua institution. Today this is still a popular and often necessary way for many adults to whet their intellectual and spiritual appetites. Secondary schools, Bible institutes and universities conduct much larger correspondence departments for home study in hundreds of subjects than eighty years ago. The evening school, begun at first on an elementary level for the underprivileged in New York City in 1889, burgeoned by the end of the century, and today some university extension courses rival the aggregate numbers served by the parent school. In 1926 the American Association for Adult Education was formed for the purpose of coordinating and sharing information in this field. The Adult Education Association of the United States of America was organized in 1951, as a division of the National Education Association, joining many kinds of adult education interests.

Another indicator of increased interest in adult education comes from a study being made by one of the country's leading universities summing up the money being spent on education of their employees by the nation's industries. Several large corporations have begun the practice of sending their top executives back to school to study the humanities. The now famous two-week seminars at Aspen, Colorado, introduce key industrial figures to the classics, ranging from ancient to modern philosophy, the whole gamut of world history, with even an introduction to the fine arts. More money is being spent on education today *inside* business and industry than on all other forms of United States education together. One giant electrical corporation spent forty million dollars on education alone— more than the cost of the entire Boston public school system.

If adults are pursuing education at such a furious pace in industry and through correspondence and evening courses, why are not the adult Bible classes of the local church full of inquiring minds? Against the ideal of 50 per cent of the Sunday school enrollment being in the adult department, why do many church schools feel successful if only 10 per cent of the enrollment is in the adult department? Why is not every adult enrolled in some teaching-learning situation in the local church? Why are not more Christians interested in their own education in the kingdom of God?

## ENCOURAGEMENTS

WHOLENESS OF LIFE

There is a deepening consciousness among Christian adults that life is all one piece. Three decades ago there was still mass compartmentalization among many members of evangelical churches. Another war and the threats of a secularized society have alerted the conscious Christian to the necessity of proving faith by life. The Bible class lesson on James now is more likely to be remembered on Monday morning in the company conference room. The sermon on Hosea is more apt to be reflected on the areas of lingering injustice in the community. The Christian peace of conscience cannot be had with just one foot in heaven. There is a growing realization that grappling daily with the minions of mammon requires proportionate knowledge of the streams of revelation from the Word. Where this new realization exists, new seriousness of Bible study marks the adults. Proofs of this increasing acceptance of a Christian world and life view come in several ways, notably in the rapidly increasing numbers of new Christian day schools organized by parents who want their children at the outset of life to be integrated on one level, the level of a God-centered life.

ADULTS CAN LEARN

Years ago, Edward Lee Thorndike at Columbia University did pioneer experimentation.[3] Since that time many others have advanced studies

[3] E. L. Thorndike, *et al, Adult Learning* (New York: Macmillan Co., 1928).

along similar lines and have successfully exploded the myth that adults lose their ability to learn as they leave the twenties. As Malcolm Knowles points out, "It is not the *capacity* to learn that declines, but the *rate* of learning."[4] The present evidence shifts weight to the *motivation* behind learning. In other words, the highly motivated older adult may be a better learner than the poorly motivated young adult.

The present psychological barometer sees learning ability rise gradually through childhood, adolescence, and on up into young adulthood, reaching its greatest peak around age thirty. The rate of learning begins gradually to decline less than 1 per cent per year from here to fifty, and not noticeably more almost to age seventy. The principal difference between the twenties and fifties is speed of performance, not rate of learning. Older adults can learn just as well as they did when they were younger. Whenever learning ability is measured in terms of power ability, that is, without stringent time limits, the evidence is clear that the learning ability does not change significantly from age twenty to sixty years. An individual at sixty can learn the same kinds of knowledge, skill and appreciation at sixty that he could at twenty. Age as age probably does little to affect the power to learn or think.

Aging brings different values, goals, self-concepts, and responsibilities. Such changes in values, together with physiological changes, may affect performance, but not power. Adults learn much less than they might, partly because of the self-underestimations of their power and wisdom, and partly because of their own anxieties that their learning behavior will bring unfavorable criticism. Thorndike showed that the interests most needed as a basis for adult education, such as interest in books, current events, people, and travel, do not dry up or vanish. Edward K. Strong says that interests of a person at twenty-five will be predictive of interests at forty-five, fifty-five, or later. New interests can be learned and taught. Adults can learn, and even like tasks formerly obnoxious to them.

Psychological and physiological traits change slowly from the twenties to the sixties. Psychologically, the adult at sixty has the advantage over childhood and adolescence in bodily and mental ability. The mature adult has an immense capital of "stored knowledge" and experience which constitutes the wisdom of age. Teachers of adults can capitalize on wisdom and compensate for the physiological changes that time brings to all men. Thorndike discovered that this decline in ability to learn is no more than 1 per cent a year, so that at seventy years of age one's ability to learn is perhaps 60 per cent of what it was at its peak. At sixty-five, one can expect to learn at least half as much per hour as he did at twenty-five, and more than he could learn per hour between eight and ten years of age. Any adult under forty-five can learn faster than a person from ten

[4]*Informal Adult Education* (New York: Association Press, 1953), p. 17.

to fourteen; therefore, no one under forty-five should hesitate about undertaking a new venture because he thinks he is too old to learn. The fact is that age has very little influence upon our fundamental ability to learn.

The average adult Bible class has not begun to take hold of its mental and psychological potential. Worst of all, in most instances no mental or spiritual change is expected. Teachers of adult classes will have to realize that, first, adults can learn throughout life and there is no real obstacle to their taking part in educational activities; and second, that an alert teacher can help provide adults with a continuous experience in learning.

## ADULTS WILL LEARN

*Motivation.* What motivates adults to Bible study? What moves them to join the Tuesday morning prayer group or the Saturday work team at the church? We act to fulfill our needs. We seek physical satisfaction through eating, drinking, playing, and so forth. We may, at the time of the 9:30 A.M. Bible class, be fulfilling our social needs. We want to show that we belong, that we are accepted, and that others respond to us.

The needs so often submerged beneath others, however, are the spiritual. Many people have, by years of habit, buried or repressed these primal basics of true satisfaction. The urge to seek meanings about life and its ultimates is usually the foremost goal of Christian fellowship. Adults may be directed toward their highest Christian fulfillment if they can become aware of their basic motivations.

Motivations can be learned. Just as an infant learns to throw a temper tantrum to get what he wants, so an adult may also continue to do this all his life until he meets someone who will not respond to this kind of exhibitionism. If we could isolate a single motive which would incite the knowledge and practice of Biblical principles among adults, we could stop right here. But motivation is multiple and complex. Much of it is unconscious and is often repressed. It is not a question of providing motivations for unexposed or undirected adults today. Most of us are so multiple-motivated and overstimulated that we need our driving forces to be clarified and isolated, separated and sanctified.

Nearer the surface than basic needs are the interests which impel adults. A catalog of adult interests will be as varied as the cultures and age groupings represented within this category. Adult interests will most certainly converge upon the areas of health, religion, friendship, vocation, politics, aesthetics, economics, and recreation. Any one of these, representing a plethora of related topics, can be a focal point to induce participation in adult group learning.

Motivation begins with interests, since they are near the surface, from which it proceeds to need fulfillment. As the leader of adults analyzes motivation to activity, be it mental or physical, he is invariably impeded by the great roadblock to all learning—*inertia*. This term, from the area of physics, is the tendency of a body to remain at rest or in uniform motion in the same direction until acted upon by some external force. In other words, no one does a thing until he has to do it, and he continues to do it until other causes stop or change the former motion. Applying this to adult education, inertia, representing the status quo, will remain the order of the day until and unless compelling physical, social or spiritual needs become pressing enough to force a change. We all resist change by nature. Evangelical adults are among the most change-resistant people in our world today. They are doubly conservative. Many would much rather have their prejudices confirmed.

The observable tendencies toward balance, growth, and creativity in all human life, however, should be heightened immeasurably in the life called and energized by the power of God. The New Testament speaks of Christian maturity in a number of places. For example, we are told that the purpose of inscripturated revelation inbreathed by the Spirit of God is "that the man of God may himself be complete" (II Tim. 3:17, Weymouth translation). Thus, in a higher sense, the goal of all Christian education, including that of the adult, is the integration of all things into one whole, with God as Ultimate. This conscious absorption of every area of human life and endeavor is the mark of the mature Christian. This godly balance of *knowing* and *doing* the will of God in our culture here and now is the grand object of Christian maturity.

The grown-up Christian adult must not only be able to "bring into captivity every thought to the obedience of Christ" (II Cor. 10:5), but must also be secular-resistant. If the Christian life is "practicing the presence of God," then surely secularism is practicing His absence. Nothing less than the whole man in the whole world serving the Sovereign God should be the aim of Christian adult education.

*Methods.* The pilgrimage of adults from interest through inertia to information and inspiration must be led by completely committed leaders. Much of what has been written about inertia above now applies in a special sense to teachers of adults. The preliminary mountain-moving in adult work begins with the teacher. An effective way to remove some from the morass of stagnation might be through the technique of "complacency shock."[5] This term does not mean personal attack. The process used by Bradford and Sheats to train teachers to use new methods aims to move them "from clutching the status quo to developing an in-

[5]Leland Bradford and Paul Sheats, "Complacency Shock, a Prerequisite to Training," *Sociatry* II, No. 1, 1948.

terest in change." Toward the promotion of desirable changes in leaders, they suggest these analyses:

1. The trainee with a reputation around one form of behavior must be shown that change will improve his position.

2. The trainee with no experience of what could be, must be given a picture of the improved results to be expected of the proposed change and a realization that he can be successful in making such a change.

3. The person who sees only one side of an issue must be helped by stretching the perception of the trainee.

4. When there is individual or group insecurity . . . they must be helped to see that through insight and mastery a trainee can accomplish much more in the future.

Characteristics for adult teachers may be subsumed under the divisions of "being" and "doing" in relation to the revealed will of God.

*Being*

> conscious of God's call to lead and teach
> a consecrated channel of God's redemptive grace to others
> conscious of God's revelation through His Word and His world
> continually growing into Christian patterns of maturity

*Doing*

> seeing continual possibilities beyond the observable in lives of group members, and inciting a holy dissatisfaction with the present state
> opening doors and windows to heavenly breezes and the clear air of truth to dispel prejudices and re-examine the true foundations (including his own)
> providing opportunities for the members of the group to integrate faith with life experiences as an unrelenting holy war against inertia
> leading fellow adults to new plateaus of Christian experience by new routes and timely reminders of the guides for holy living

The leader of adults is often marked by a reticence to consider the unconventional notion. If the group is to be encouraged to adventurous thought, certainly the guide needs to be pioneering in that realm. Someone has said that an educated person is one who can "entertain himself, entertain a friend, and entertain a new idea!"

Since it is an educational axiom that a teacher is 90 per cent of the curriculum, we are not amiss in stressing the qualities of good teaching leadership and methods, but it would be remiss to give the impression that content is not as important as method in adult Christian education. In fact, the content frequently suggests the method. If one studies the life and work of the Great Teacher in the Gospels, he is impressed by the variety of methods used. Demonstration, discussion, question and answer, object and visual aid—all played as important a part as the discourse in His teaching.

For many reasons, method has been most neglected in the adult sector of education. Even in this enlightened day, we can observe in too many adult Bible classes the plodding attempts of the local spellbinder, who may preside by default, droning the group into a comfortable stupor by an unending stream of pious platitudes. Of all teachers, the one who instructs adults most of all needs to be aware that all talking is not teaching and all listening is not learning. Too often the teacher of adults thinks he is supposed to lecture, and if he does, almost always it is only that. Almost never does he think of his function as that of guide, trainer, stimulator, coach, planner, and resource person. His function should determine his method. If no other method is possible because of class size, space available, or subject matter, then with *much* preparation a teacher may lecture if he uses blackboard, maps, charts, illustrations, and asks for questions and comments.

Far more profitable for adult class members is some form of discussion: whole group, panel, or seminar. Many educators of mature individuals see the rewarding possibilities of using interpersonal methods or group work. It is this writer's opinion, however, that most evangelical churches are not yet prepared with either the leadership or the mindset to use these splendid means of group dynamics widely with adults.

In the use of any method of adult training, it is the responsibility of the planning committee or the teacher to prepare the subject, communicate it, and then see if the class has learned it. The preparaton of a lesson by any method requires hard work when it is to be used with adults. It has to be so planned to provide for interaction of the group members with each other and the teacher, in order to approximate learning. The preparation of a lecture requires meticulously clear delineation, with the lucid presentation of the whole piece and all its parts. Rarely should a lesson be given adults by this method without the use of blackboard, charts, maps or objects. The adult teacher has only to view the educational channels on television to see the variety of sensory appeal, including change of tone and expression, used by the expert. Such results did not come without professional briefing and several hours of practice before a half-hour presentation. The failure to communicate effectively leaves most adult Bible class experiences on the level of poor lay sermonettes which drain away whatever readiness was there for the worship service.

In the second place, let the teacher then devise simple and easily administered mechanics of testing. It may be quickly distributed, collected and graded one-word, multiple choice, or true-false lists. Perhaps a half-dozen summary questions at the end of the lecture might be appropriate. It could be duplicated sheets to take home and to return the following week.

The use of any form of discussion done properly requires as much preparation as the lecture, and by more people. One reason some adult classes prefer the sermonette is because they want to listen without working. While the lecture may be given without any visible signs of activity on the part of the class, the discussion cannot. Much of the body of the material may come in a quarterly or other form, but it has to be read at least before it can be discussed, and mastered before it can be applied by discussion. The leader must prepare possible outcomes to problems and their solutions. Good manuals, texts, and filmstrips are available on the technique of the discussion method, outlining the preparatory steps for its use. This, properly used, can insure that the participants will stay awake, will express their own ideas, and will give the leader an indication of whether the facts were received and applied.

The "buzz group" is a very efficient way of enabling everyone to say something on the subject and at the same time coming to a clear con-census on the part of the whole group. There are many benefits to adults in learning together this way. Adults learn more rapidly and efficiently when they are participants rather than spectators. When they see actual conclusions consolidated, interest is greater and learning is longer continued. A number of Christians working together with common interests learn more rapidly than the same persons working alone. If what is concluded by the group is used in application to life, it will be retained. Much good published help is available from the Adult Education Association annual issues of *Leader's Digest*[6] and other publications. The total participation of adults in their respective church groups should be a goal for the next decade. Transforming power can change each life in the group as together they worship, study the Bible, carry out the Great Commission, change the communities in which they live, and while doing these things have the joy of Christian fellowship. Evangelicals in our day must have the white light of God's truth shed on every area of life if they are to maintain the growing edge of testimony for God in secular culture.

## GROUPING

In many adult departments of our Sunday schools an antiquated relic of the past survives in the men's class divided from the women's class. The logical conclusion of this movement was philosophically defended in the second century of the Christian era by the Gnostics and the Mani-

[6]Adult Education Association, 743 N. Wabash Ave., Chicago, Ill.

chees. Practiced through the centuries in the Romanist tradition, it established the monastery and the nunnery. Perpetuation of this unnatural and unrealistic division by evangelical churches today presents a sociological monstrosity and an indefensible unit of Christian education.

Young adults as they emerge from the high school and college classes will naturally want to form their couples' groups for all kinds of church activities. In these days of re-emphasis on Christian family life, what more hopeful group in a church can there be than the young parents banded together for religious and social reasons. Interests reach a changing period around the age of thirty-five, and another logical limit at sixty-five, the age of retirement. So young adults grow into middle-aged adults and on to older adults at sixty-five and over. Three separate interest areas from the standpoint of maturity can thus be the practical foci of these groups in the local church.

For a decade, some adult classes have pioneered in elective courses which cut across barriers of age and sex. Most of these electives are written for a single quarter, and have given new flexibility, zest, and incentive to the adults in our evangelical Sunday schools who know they can do more satisfying things intellectually than to have each one read a verse around in a "canned" lesson.

Many denominational publishers, as well as independent printers of Sunday school materials, have furnished educational and intellectual stimuli in the fields of Bible book study, doctrine, personal evangelism, church history, Christian family life, missions, and other subjects. Some schools award certificates of recognition for the successful completion of prescribed courses. This development is yet in its early stages.

## CHALLENGE

The challenge of adult Christian education is a twofold one. First, the church must build up its young adult groups from "organization men" now swarming into suburbia in unprecedented numbers. Secondly, the church must conserve the mounting resources of experience and untapped spiritual power of our senior citizens. Each church will have to do both in order to give the necessary balance to its whole program of Christian education. The following figures show the comparative growth of the upper bracket of United States population:

1920—4,929,000 persons 65 years or older
1961—16,559,580 persons 65 and over

At the same rate of increase, and with prospects for new medical developments and increased longevity, the estimate in forty more years is

2000—30,000,000 persons 65 and older

Since 1920 there has been an increase of

236 per cent of persons 65 and older
279 per cent of persons 75 and older
920 per cent of persons 85 and older

Many of these people forced to retire in the prime of life have from twenty to thirty years of useful active living to give to multiple kingdom causes. Many are persons of highly diversified skills, who now have fewer home responsibilities and less vulnerability to distraction. Most have judgment and wisdom which comes only from age, with a mature Christian experience which makes them valuable persons in any group.

Their own needs can be met in the *koinonia* of Christian fellowship, and their contribution to the communion of the saints may be large indeed. They can do visitation, mailings, act as church hostesses for special occasions, be librarians, baby-sitters, maintain furniture and grounds, organize mission prayer groups, and an infinite variety of things. Their experience and availability make them the largest and most valuable personnel group in the local church today.

With the findings of the White House Conference on Aging transferred and adapted to the local church, is it too much to expect that shortly we may have a minister of adults aiding in Christian service as much as we have ministers to youth and children? This is the need especially in urban communions. The prospects for development in this sector are unlimited. Christian adulthood is not a penalty; it is an achievement!

## BIBLIOGRAPHY

Barclay, W. C. *Organization and Administration of the Adult Department.* New York: Caxton Press, 1926.

Bergevin, Paul, and McKinley, John. *Design for Adulthood Education in the Church.* Greenwich, Conn.: Seabury Press, 1958.

Blackwood, Carolyn P. *How to Be an Effective Church Woman.* Philadelphia: Westminster Press, 1955.

Bliss, Kathleen. *The Service and Status of Women in the Churches.* London: Student Christian Movement Press, Ltd., 1954.

Caldwell, Irene S. *Adults Learn and Like It.* Anderson, Ind.: Warner Press, 1955.

Case, Lambert J. *How to Reach Group Decisions.* St. Louis: Bethany Press, 1958.

Casteel, John L. *Spiritual Renewal Through Personal Groups.* New York: Association Press, 1957.

Clemmons, Robert S. *Dynamics of Christian Adult Education.* Nashville: Abingdon Press, 1958.

———. *Young Adults in the Church*. Nashville: Abingdon Press, 1959.

Day, Leroy Judson. *Dynamic Christian Fellowship*. Philadelphia: Judson Press, 1960.

Dobbins, Gaines S. *Teaching Adults in the Sunday School*. Nashville: Broadman Press, 1936.

Douglas, Paul. *The Group Workshop Way in the Church*. New York: Association Press, 1956.

Douty, Mary Alice. *How to Work with Church Groups*. New York: Abingdon Press, 1957.

Elliott, Grace L. *How to Help Groups Make Decisions*. New York: Association Press, 1959.

Ernsberger, David J. *A Philosophy of Adult Christian Education*. Philadelphia: Westminster Press, 1959.

Gerber, Israel J. *The Psychology of the Suffering Mind*. New York: Jonathan David Co., 1951.

Gleason, George. *Church Group Activities for Young Married People*. Los Angeles: Privately printed (715 S. Hope St.,), 1937.

———. *Single Young Adults in the Church*. New York: Association Press, 1952.

———. *Horizons for Older People*. New York: Macmillan Co., 1956.

Hugen, M. D. *The Churches' Ministry to the Older Unmarried*. Grand Rapids: Wm. B. Eerdmans Publishing Co., 1958.

Jacobsen, Henry. *How to Teach Adults*. Wheaton: Scripture Press, 1958.

Jones, Idris W. *Our Church Plans for Adult Education*. Philadelphia: Judson Press, 1952.

Koenig, Robert E. *The Use of the Bible with Adults*. Philadelphia: Christian Education Press, 1959.

Little, Lawrence C. *Christian Adult Education*. Pittsburgh: University of Pittsburgh Press, 1959.

Little, Sara. *Learning Together in the Christian Fellowship*. Richmond: John Knox Press, 1956.

Maves, Paul B., and Cedarleaf, J. L. *Older People and the Church*. Nashville: Abingdon-Cokesbury Press, 1949.

Maves, Paul B. *Understanding Ourselves as Adults*. Nashville: Abingdon Press, 1959.

Munro, Harry C. *The Effective Adult Class*. St. Louis: Bethany Press, 1949.

Osteyee, Edith Tiller. *Teaching Adults*. Philadelphia: Judson Press, 1948.

Philips, William P. *The Adult Department of the Sunday School*. Nashville: Sunday School Board of the Southern Baptist Convention, 1935.

Ryrie, Charles C. *The Place of Women in the Church*. New York: Macmillan Co., 1959.

Scudder, D. L. (ed.). *Organized Religion and the Older Person.* Gainesville: University of Florida Press, 1958.

Winchester, Benjamin S. *The Church and Adult Education.* New York: Richard R. Smith, 1930.

Zeigler, Earl F. *Toward Understanding Adults.* Philadelphia: Westminster Press, 1931.

———. *Christian Education of Adults.* Philadelphia: Westminster Press, 1958.

Zerbst-Merkens. *The Office of Woman in the Church.* St. Louis: Concordia Publishing House. 1955.

The minister or Christian education director is often called upon to prepare adults for work in the Sunday school, daily vacation Bible school, and other ministries of the church.

(Courtesy of the Promotion Department of the Moody Bible Institute)

# PART FOUR
*Organizing the Learner*

*Chapter 17*

# THE CHRISTIAN EDUCATION DIRECTOR

## PAUL R. FINLAY

THE MENTION of the title director of Christian education to the average group of evangelical churchmen is likely to bring as many different images of the office as there are people in the group. Diversity of church situations and lack of standardization across denominational lines have contributed to this condition. It is the purpose of this chapter to try to clarify the work of the director, pointing out the value of such an office, identifying the major duties, and listing personal and professional qualifications. In addition, there is a discussion of the importance of good internal relationships, the matter of status for the director, the relative merits of a male and a female director, and some observations concerning the future of such an office.*

## THE DIRECTOR'S CONTRIBUTION TO THE LOCAL CHURCH

Why should a church consider the possibility of employing a Christian education director? The director makes his greatest contribution to the work in the very fact that there is one person, a specialist in the field of Christian education, who is coordinating and giving direction and pur-

*The opinions expressed in this chapter represent the thinking of forty-eight men and women who are or recently have been directly associated with the program of Christian education in local churches. Their ideas were revealed in answers to a questionnaire submitted to them by the author. Most of them serve in the capacity of director of Christian education but because of varying responsibilities and different titles, it is impossible to say that all of them are directors. Sixteen different denominations are represented as well as five independent churches. Geographically they represent thirty-six cities in sixteen states.

Paul R. Finlay, Ph.D., is associate professor of Christian Education at Bethel College, St. Paul, Minnesota.

pose to the church's entire educational program. In the Great Commission Christ doubly admonished His disciples to teach. Unfortunately many of our churches have been trying to operate a "school" without adherence to sound educational policies. What the principal is to the public school, the director ought to be to the church school.

There are also concomitant values. The pastor is relieved of many organizational details in connection with the educational program, allowing him more time to devote to the preparation of sermons and other strictly pastoral duties. From his vantage point the director, as overseer of the total program, is able to evaluate it objectively and direct the training and supervision of teachers and leaders to overcome whatever weaknesses may exist. Furthermore, the presence of a Christian education specialist often encourages more laymen to become active in the work.

## DUTIES OF THE DIRECTOR

Since no two churches are exactly alike in every respect, it would be impossible to present a standardized list of duties for the director in a local church. Each situation demands a different type of ministry, but the extremes of duties now existing in the office betray the lack of definition of the real function of a director. This condition is partially due to the misunderstanding of church members as to the basic needs in the total program.

In the majority of cases surveyed by the author, when a director was hired by a church, there was no job description worked out ahead of time. Sometimes only general areas of operation were suggested, and that in verbal form only. Sometimes the applicant for the position made out his own job analysis in order to protect himself from later misunderstanding. It is conceded that in many churches this is a new office and the duties of the director have not been clearly determined. One director reported, "I was expected to tell them what a director should do." The newness of the position, however, does not excuse a church from making a thorough investigation of its own needs in order to determine how a director of Christian education would best fit into the picture.

One of the foremost duties of a director is the administration of the total Christian education program. The director should not be regarded as an assistant pastor. He is a trained specialist in the field of education and, as such, should be given the opportunity to organize, supervise and coordinate the over-all educational program.

As the administrator and overseer of an important educational institution, certain other responsibilities come under his domain. Much of his time will be spent in seeking out potential teachers and leaders, and assisting them in spiritual growth and development of their understanding and abilities through leadership training courses and institutes. He should serve as the executive secretary of the Christian education board rather than as the chairman of that board, as will be explained later in the chapter. He must often sit in the seat of a counselor, providing guidance in the area of personal problems as well as in the area of problems connected with the implementation of the program.

He must take time for research in the field of Christian education to keep abreast of new ideas in this rapidly developing area. Sufficient opportunities must be granted the director to interpret the cause of Christian education to the members of the congregation and the community.

In most churches, however, it is impossible for the director to remain entirely within the role of an administrator; often it becomes necessary for him to take an active part in the actual running of the program. In the area of youth work, for instance, it may be necessary for him to supervise the groups and do the general planning of the program. It is sometimes his lot to plan youth retreats and special events, including camps, and occasionally to act as adviser to a particular youth fellowship.

Often the director finds himself involved in the area of Sunday school work in such capacities as administrator of the entire program or director of the visitation program. He is obliged to take part in the evaluation of the various curricular materials being used. In some churches he will have to direct the vacation Bible school.

The more time the director spends in taking care of some of these lesser jobs, however, the less time he will have to devote to the administrative aspects of his position. Many directors find themselves doing jobs which they feel laymen might well be performing. This does not contribute to a high level of morale nor is it the most efficient use of the director. If a church wants to hire someone to take care of many miscellaneous jobs which no one else will do, that is its privilege; but if a church employs a person for the position of Christian education director, then, in line with common business sense and proper stewardship of the Lord's money, he ought to be allowed to function in that capacity.

The most frequent complaint of directors is that they are expected to do too much detail work around the church office, such as secretarial service and the handling of bulk mailings. Another complaint is that the director is expected to do too much of the pastor's work, including general pastoral calling and preaching in the absence of the pastor. Some of the directors teach a Sunday school class but actually prefer to be free of any regular obligation at that time on Sunday morning in order to be available for the work for which they are professionally prepared and in which they can make their unique contributions, such as special counseling with superintendents or observing classes in session. In this connection the question arises whether some minor jobs should be left undone until the director can secure and train laymen to fill those positions, or should the director expend his efforts in taking care of these needs immediately?

This leads to another question. How many hours a week should the director be expected to work? It is not uncommon for some directors to spend seventy hours a week in church work. Perhaps a paid church worker ought to donate some of his time to the church, even as laymen do, but how many laymen give more than five hours a week to their church? The director should not be employed with the thought that he will do all the work, but rather with the concept that he will be able to coordinate the work so that more laymen can be engaged actively in the church.

## INTERNAL RELATIONSHIPS

Success in a given task is often contingent upon efficient internal relationships. The effectiveness of the director is similarly often enhanced by good working relationships or, on the other hand, diminished because of petty irritations due to faulty connections. Diversity of church patterns and differences of personalities make it difficult to establish any standard for this area of the work.

Most of the directors responding to the questionnaire indicated that they are directly responsible to the pastor. Some are responsible to the Christian education board, others to the official board, or jointly to the pastor and the official board. In certain instances the Christian education board is directly responsible to the official board.

In indicating the most ideal relationship, there was an almost even division between the concept that the director should answer directly to the pastor and that he be accountable directly to the Christian education board. Responsibility to the pastor seems to be predicated upon the fact that the pastor is a good administrator, understands the field of Christian education and the director's role in it, is generally in agreement with the director theologically, and is willing to delegate authority to him. If these elements are lacking, then accountability to a Christian education board is considered to be more desirable. The plea for more cooperative planning and clarification of duties and relationships was often voiced.

The director's relation to the official board consists in his being an ex-officio member, reporting regularly on his activities, not only to keep the board members informed but also as a means of giving them a better understanding of the essentials of an adequate Christian education program.

There was strong sentiment that the director should be the executive officer of the Christian education board. In this capacity he would serve ex-officio in the role of resource person and adviser, and then carry out the policies of the board. Furthermore, the consensus is that the director should not serve as chairman of the board, but work closely with the chairman in preparing the agenda and discussing other important matters prior to the meeting. In this way a layman presides over the board and the director can play his true role as an adviser and resource person. In addition, if the director should be chairman of the board, it places the board in an embarrassing position if it is not satisfied with his services.

According to the findings of this study, directors seem to have the best relationships with the Sunday school superintendents. In the majority of cases they work together very closely in solving the problems of the school. Here again the training of the director is vital, since he is able to supply valuable information and suggestions.

The director works through the superintendent in dealing with the Sunday school teachers, although he should be directly available as a resource person and consultant in immediate problems. But the director and the superintendent must present a united front to the teachers in policies affecting the operation of the school. The director, in cooperation with the superintendent, works out a program of teacher training and supervision.

Better understanding of the respective duties of the church staff members is often needed to avoid petty friction. Definite scheduling is required with respect to the use of secretaries. Regular staff meetings for planning and prayer ought to be held.

Concerted effort must be made to establish a good relationship between the director and the congregation. The very presence of the director on the platform during public services helps to increase the rapport. Opportunities to explain and interpret Christian education to the church membership in small informal groups serve to strengthen this relationship.

It seems that one of the problems of this area is that of finding ways by which pastors and laymen can be instructed in and challenged by the potential of Christian education.

## PERSONAL QUALIFICATIONS

In view of the duties of a director and the complexities of internal relationships with which he is faced, what kind of person should he be? Of supreme importance is the possession of the basic Christian graces, especially the ability to get along with people. He should have a pleasing and winsome personality and enjoy working with people.

He must love people and be able to lead them—not through coercion but through personal interest in people, initiative, persuasion and challenge. This requires a great exercise of patience and understanding. He ought to be able to detect people's abilities and direct them into the activities for which they are best fitted. He must have organizational and administrative ability, with the perseverance to follow through to successful conclusions. Enhancing this ability is a disciplined and well-ordered personal life.

He should be a person of spiritual maturity, deeply committed to Christ and the cause of Christian education. He ought to have a keen sense of God's leading into this field, rather than using it as a training place or steppingstone toward the ministry. Therefore, he must be willing always to work in the background, taking second place to the pastor with no thought of competing for position or favor.

Other characteristics which should be mentioned include flexibility, reliability, sincerity, resourcefulness, creativity, and enthusiasm. In some situations musical ability and acquaintance with crafts and sports are helpful.

## ACADEMIC PREPARATION

How much formal education is necessary for a directorship? The questionnaire revealed that with one exception all the directors were college graduates. Among this group, the most frequently cited college majors were Christian education, education, psychology and history, with a small representation in philosophy, religion, sociology and Bible. About half of them attended seminary and some had an M.R.E. or an M.A. in religious education.

These same persons were almost unanimous in their belief that a college education is a prerequisite to the position, with the suggestion that concentration in Christian education courses is a definite asset. Courses in education on the college level were said to be highly desirable. Almost half of the group recommended an M.A. in Christian education or an M.R.E. A lesser number felt that seminary training was necessary.

More research needs to be given to the matter of the ideal academic preparation. Since the director's work touches so many phases of learning, where should concentration be made? Since he is the administrator of the educational program, he certainly needs to specialize in Christian education, but he also needs a good grounding in the Bible, the chief textbook of the educational system. Because he deals with the process of human learning all the time, should he not have some background in psychology? Is seminary training, complete with Greek and Hebrew, necessary for the proper administration of his office?

## STATUS

Considerable discussion in Christian education circles is concerned with the matter of status for the director. Should he be ordained? What is an adequate salary for a director? What about housing and automobile allowance? Should he participate in a pension fund and hospitalization plan? Should he have as much vacation as the pastor? These questions are all pertinent, and for lack of definite answers some men are not being attracted to the field. Whether this should figure in a man's call to the directorship is not argued here; the mere fact that it does have an influence demands that some solution be sought. These questions cannot be answered in this present treatment, but some suggestions can be made concerning ways in which status may be raised.

Many directors feel that status will improve as the level of work produced improves. Directors who have the necessary training and background obtain better status when ordained, and are often referred to as minister of Christian education. At any rate, there is need of standardization of titles commensurate with preparation and experience, and a clarification of duties. As denominations work together in this effort and also promote an awareness among their people of the value of the directorship, the matter of status will tend to correct itself.

The demand for higher standards, both in preparation and work produced, will also help. If churches would employ only those who are looking forward to the directorship as a profession, it would tend to lift the standards and status.

The securing of adequate status depends largely upon the support which the pastors give to the position of the directorate. Too long a "one-man ministry" concept has prevailed, and it is necessary for clergymen and laymen alike to realize that the Christian education directorate is just as much a church-related vocation as the pastorate. Seminaries could contribute markedly by requiring all ministerial students to take a course in Christian education in which they could gain an understanding of the field and the place of the director in the local church.

## A MALE DIRECTOR OR A FEMALE DIRECTOR?

Are the demands of directorship more easily met by men or women? Of the forty-eight persons who responded to the inquiry, thirty-eight were men; but both men and women were in substantial agreement concerning the relative advantages and disadvantages of the male and female director.

### MALE DIRECTOR

*Advantages.* A man usually carries more authority and demands more respect when dealing with people of both sexes. Not only does he have greater possibilities in working with youth, especially teen-age boys, but it is easier for him to challenge and inspire men to service. He also has easier personal relationships with the pastor. The fact that he can substitute for the pastor in emergencies can be an advantage.

*Disadvantages.* Apparently the greatest disadvantage is the possibility of professional jealousy between pastor and director. This is a very delicate situation and must be handled with extreme care. Even though the pastor and director have the best of relationships, it is possible for an element in the congregation to favor the director because of some personality attraction. Also, at the present time it is difficult for a married man to live on the salary that many churches expect to pay a director. Yet if the director is a single man, a new set of problems arises.

Another disadvantage for a male director is the fact that his time is often appropriated by the pastor, who, perhaps unwittingly, tends to delegate too many of the pastoral duties to him. Often, too, a male director is using the office only as a steppingstone to the pastorate and, therefore, does not remain long enough in the office to produce lasting results. Whether pertinent or not, the objection is sometimes raised against a male director that he usually does not have sufficient background and experience with those problems associated with work among the smaller children.

FEMALE DIRECTOR

*Advantages.* Many of the advantages of a female director are parallel to the disadvantages of the male. If there is much work in connection with the younger children's departments, then a female director frequently has the advantage. She usually takes to detail work better than a man and is better able to live on the salary offered. There is a reduced chance of professional jealousy. She will not be using the office as preparation for the ministry; therefore, a career in the directorate may be more appealing to a woman.

*Disadvantages.* The female director, however, does not elicit the cooperation from men that a male does. With a female there seems always the temptation to make nothing more of her than a "glorified secretary." A woman in the place of leadership may tend to give the impression that church work is for women. Moreover, some feel that it is unscriptural for a woman to hold a place of authority over men in the church. If she is an attractive, single young woman she must guard herself against getting into situations that would engender gossip.

## OUTLOOK FOR THE DIRECTORATE

Since the support of the pastor is so influential in the upgrading of the directorate, it is heartening to discover that almost unanimously the persons replying to the questionnaire indicated that the pastor had a good attitude toward the field of Christian education. Many expressed the feeling that the pastor was going the second mile in an attempt to promote the cause in his church. It is probably to be expected that in churches employing directors the pastors would be quite sympathetic with the office, and for the most part this is true. However, in some instances the pastor seems to consider the office to be of only minor importance in the church.

Some of the denominations represented in the survey apparently have an excellent attitude toward Christian education and are diligently seeking ways in which to strengthen their program. In others, there is indication of a new awareness of the potential of Christian education and, while these denominations as yet do not have well-developed programs, effort is being made in that direction. The directors of only one church group felt that the denomination they represented did not understand the value of Christian education and held a somewhat indifferent attitude toward it.

In the author's attempt to secure names of Christian education directors in local churches, it was discovered that seven denominations do not have anyone serving in this capacity. Eleven other denominations were able to supply a total of only twenty-five names of directors.

It is conceded that the average size of the churches of some of these denominations is not large, but a majority of those who replied to the questionnaire believed that a church with a membership between 200 and 400 could and should have a director. Furthermore, many indicated that the size of the church membership is not the determining factor, but the vision and foresight of the people.

There are indications from several sources that churches are beginning to see the value of a director faster than the colleges and seminaries are able to produce them. This shows increased interest in Christian education, but Christian schools must accelerate their efforts to train young people for this profession. Yet the responsibility does not rest solely with the schools. Pastors and churches, realizing the great need in this field, must challenge youth with the possibilities of ministering in Christian education.

Thirty-eight of the forty-eight who responded to the questionnaire are younger than forty years of age, and twenty of them are below the age of thirty. This may mean that there is a younger generation arising which sees the need, but it may also mean that the directorate is being used as a training field for other positions of Christian service.

Every effort must be made by schools, churches and Christian workers to promote the concept that here is a field of ministry in which dedicated young people can spend their lives serving God just as much as in the pastorate or on the mission field. When this is done, there will be more qualified young people available and Christian education will gain its rightful place in evangelical churches of America.

## FOR FURTHER READING

Crossland, Weldon. *How to Build Up Your Church School.* New York: Abingdon-Cokesbury Press, 1958. Chapter 2.

Gable, Lee J. (ed.). *Encyclopedia for Church Group Leaders.* New York: Association Press, 1959. Part IV.

Heim, Ralph D. *Leading a Sunday Church School.* Philadelphia: Muhlenberg Press, 1950. Chapters III and V.

Kraft, Vernon R. *The Director of Christian Education in the Local Church.* Chicago: Moody Press, 1957.

Lobingier, John Leslie. *The Better Church School.* Boston: Pilgrim Press, 1952. Chapter 10.

Miller, Randolph Crump. *Education for Christian Living.* Englewood Cliffs, N.J.: Prentice-Hall, Inc., 1956. Pages 277-285.

Munro, Harry C. *Christian Education in Your Church.* St. Louis: Bethany Press, 1933. Chapter X.

———. *The Director of Religious Education.* Philadelphia: Westminster Press, 1930.

Murch, James DeForest. *Christian Education and the Local Church.* Cincinnati: Standard Publishing Co., 1943. Chapter 22.

Taylor, Marvin J. (ed.). *Religious Education.* New York: Abingdon Press, 1960. Chapter 24.

Vieth, Paul H. (ed.). *The Church and Christian Education.* St. Louis: Bethany Press, 1947. Chapter VI.

Vieth, Paul H. *The Church School.* Philadelphia: Christian Education Press, 1957. Chapter 4.

*Chapter 18*

# THE BOARD OF CHRISTIAN EDUCATION

## Dean A. Dalton

### THE EDUCATIONAL MINISTRY OF THE CHURCH

THE CHRISTIAN CHURCH, even the smallest local congregation, is complex when one sees the many essential elements in its program: evangelism, Bible teaching, group and private worship; instruction in church history, doctrine, missions, and stewardship; training in ethics and character; leadership education, parent training; social fellowship; and opportunities for service.

The totality of these experiences provided by the local church reveals that the principal task of the church is Christian education. Each of these essential elements should be properly implemented through the various agencies, such as the Sunday school, children's church, training groups, boys' and girls' clubs, camp programs, vacation Bible school, missionary societies, and the many other endeavors.

If the church is to achieve unity in program, organization, and leadership, there is need for a central unifying body or organization that shall be responsible for supervising and administering the total educational program of the church. That central body is a board of Christian education, authorized by the church, its duties stated by the church, and its work regularly reported to the church.

### THE CHURCH ORGANIZED TO PERFORM ITS EDUCATIONAL MINISTRY

Organization is essential in the life and work of the church, for it makes possible the orderly distribution of responsibility. Murch gives four prin-

---

Dean A. Dalton, B.S. Ed., M.S., is director of the Education Division of Gospel Light Publications in Glendale, California.

ciples for setting up an organization for Christian education in the local church: "The organization is to be Scriptural in principle . . . simple, adequate and practical."[1] Heim says that "adaptability, comprehensiveness, democracy, flexibility, simplicity, and practicability are important factors of an organization."[2] "Another characteristic of good organization," according to Mason, "is that it is indigenous, that is, arising out of the needs of the situation."[3]

The board of Christian education does not relieve the church's central governing group (session, official board, deacons) of its responsibility for all of church life. The board of Christian education gives key people other than members of the central boards a voice in the Christian education program. The church governing group can delegate to the board of Christian education authority for the entire *educational* program. "This means," as Paul H. Vieth says, "more than maintaining what already exists. It means a constant effort directed toward the very best and most comprehensive program of Christian education which the church is capable of maintaining."[4]

## VALUES OF A BOARD OF CHRISTIAN EDUCATION

A board of Christian education appointed by the church makes Christian education responsible to the church. No church is too small or too limited in leadership to have such a board, and to profit by it.

Some of the advantages of a church board of Christian education as suggested by Clarence Stauffer are these:

1. It makes Christian education officially a part of the total program of the church.

2. It unifies, correlates, and coordinates all educational interests of the church, including the Sunday school, young people's work, leadership education, vacation Bible school, and all other educational activities.

3. It provides for continuity in leadership and policies when there is a change of pastor, superintendent or other executive officer.

4. It provides for democracy with authority by electing board members with ample power to act for the church in the board.

5. It gives encouragement to the Sunday school staff (and other educational groups) to have the support of a responsible board that directs their work and hears reports upon it.

6. It makes executive action easier because the board, being impersonal,

---

[1]James DeForest Murch, *Christian Education and the Local Church* (Cincinnati: Standard Publishing Co., 1943), p. 203.
[2]Ralph D. Heim, *Leading a Sunday Church School* (Philadelphia: Muhlenberg Press, 1950), p. 46.
[3]Harold C. Mason, *Abiding Values in Christian Education* (Westwood, N.J.: Fleming H. Revell Co., 1955), p. 84.
[4]Paul H. Vieth, *Improving Your Sunday School* (Philadelphia: Westminster Press, 1930), p. 29.

can deal with delicate problems such as incompetent workers. Also, new programs or procedures considered and adopted by a board are more likely to be accepted by the church and the school.[5]

## THE BOARD'S RELATIONSHIP TO THE LOCAL CHURCH

Some denominations specify the manner in which the body responsible for Christian education in the local church shall be chosen. In most cases, Vieth suggests, "The individual church will have to decide upon its own method. One way is to have the board elected by the congregation. This brings Christian education forcibly before the church, and dignifies it as one of the major tasks of the church. Another plan is to have the board appointed by the governing body of the church. Since this official body may be thought of as representing the entire church program, this plan tends to emphasize and unify that program. Some churches have provided that the chairman of the board of Christian education shall be a member ex officio of the official board of the church, still further assuring unity in the church's program. Whatever plan is adopted, it is important that the board should regularly bring its work to the attention of the governing body of the church."[6]

## ORGANIZATION OF THE BOARD OF CHRISTIAN EDUCATION

### QUALIFICATIONS OF BOARD MEMBERS

Basic to the function of a board of Christian education is the caliber of leadership in its members. The nominating committee of the church should consider capable people, with an interest in Christian education, a desire to learn more, and some understanding of educational methods. These men and women should be responsible persons who are spiritually alive and who are capable of objective, intelligent leadership. It is recommended by some specialists in the field that members be selected for their general interest and capabilities rather than to represent a particular organization. However, it is valuable if the board member is serving on the "front lines" in an educational responsibility. This will enable him to relate his decisions on the board to real needs.

### HOW THE BOARD IS CONSTITUTED

Once the board of Christian education is duly authorized and related to the local church, if it is to be integrated so that it operates in the

[5]Clarence Stauffer, "The Church Organized for Christian Education," *National Voice*, December, 1953, p. 10.
[6]Paul H. Vieth, *op. cit.*, p. 28.

name of the entire congregation, careful attention should be given to its constituency. This is not a committee for only the Sunday school or for any single organization. It is important that the board represent different interests and phases of the total program of the church.

To assure a representative board and one that is vitally related to the church, it is advantageous to have representation from the congregation, from the church governing body, and from the various educational organizations. A practical method, suggested by Lobingier, is to have "one member chosen because of his special ability in the field of children's work, another because of experience in youth work, another as an intelligent parent, another because of special training in teaching and educational method."[7]

It is often wise to elect one young person of high school or college age. He should serve only one year. This is excellent training for future leaders.

The board should be large enough to be representative, but small enough to be effective. Five to nine members are usually desirable. The church with an extensive program may need a larger board with as many as fifteen to twenty members.

Members should serve for a specified time, either on an annual basis, subject to extension up to three years, or for three years with one-third of the members being rotated off the board each year. This approach will help assure continuity in planning.

RELATIONSHIP OF THE PASTOR TO THE BOARD

The pastor, as leader of the total church program, should take an active part in the educational work of the church, and should be an ex-officio member of the board of Christian education. He should be present at every meeting, and where there is no employed director of Christian education he should assume the responsibility for guiding the activities of the board. The amount of personal leadership the pastor will have to give to the program will depend in part upon his own ability and training, and in part upon the abilities of the board members.

RELATIONSHIP OF THE DIRECTOR OF CHRISTIAN EDUCATION

The employed Christian education director will work with all the educational organizations and their leaders to aid them in their work. He is an ex-officio member of the board. The board should look to him, as one trained in the field of Christian education, for information as to what others are doing and for light on the best educational theory and practice. In no sense does the director determine the policies, but if he

[7]John Leslie Lobingier, *The Better Church School* (Boston: Pilgrim Press, 1952), p. 137.

is an effective leader he may influence and guide the policies of the board more than any other person.

The Sunday school superintendent is elected by the church in the annual meeting or is appointed by the board of Christian education. As executive officer of the Sunday school, the superintendent has a vital relationship to the work of the board illustrated in many ways. He may suggest to the board certain policies that relate to the Sunday school. It is his task to see that official policies are carried out. He may be asked to give his judgment in the selection of the curriculum. He is expected to see that the chosen curriculum materials are secured and distributed and used. He helps the board know what teachers are needed each year and recommends certain persons for these positions. He works with newly appointed teachers to see that they have all possible assistance, materials and encouragement. He suggests certain ways of providing training, and he is expected to encourage each teacher to make the most of every opportunity for training.

It is important to note that in the church with an employed director, good working relationships can be established that will make the work of the board, the director, and the superintendent more effective. It should be remembered that the superintendent is primarily responsible for the Sunday school. The director works through the board in the interests of the total educational program of the church.

## BASIC FUNCTIONS OF THE BOARD OF CHRISTIAN EDUCATION

The board of Christian education serves as a clearing house in planning a comprehensive and unified educational program. Its basic functions may be considered fourfold: *integration* of all activities toward a common objective; *correlation* of personnel, time, activities and energies; *unification* of purpose; and *distribution* of responsibility. These functions may be more specifically defined and detailed as follows:

1. *Develop a total educational program.* The general educational policy of the church will be established by the board and it will see to the development of a specific educational program to achieve the purposes set forth in the general educational policy. The program will be studied to see that all needs are being met. Periodic surveys will be made of all organizations within the church doing any kind of educational work to discover overlapping, undue competition, and waste.

2. *Build objectives.* The board will assist in the development of goals and objectives of the various educational agencies of the church. Con-

tinuous study will be given to the implementation of standards for the Sunday school and the development and supervision of the worker's covenant. Through the training program individual workers will be given help in formulating specific objectives in their work, such as aims for the lesson, the worship period, or an activity in the Bible club.

3. *Foster an educational consciousness.* The board is in a unique and pivotal position to develop an educational consciousness on the part of the church membership. This may be realized through its regular activities, reports to the governing body of the church, the annual report to the congregation, newsletters, brochures, and perhaps, most of all, by the enthusiasm and dedication of the board members themselves.

4. *Enlist personnel.* The recruitment of staff members for the educational agencies of the church will be a continuing responsibility of the board. Methods will be developed to discover the church's leadership potential through talent surveys, interviews and other means.

The board will nominate the general and associate superintendents of the Sunday school for election by the church membership or will recommend candidates for these offices to the church nominating committee. Generally the board will appoint to one year terms all teachers, department superintendents and other officers of the Sunday school, training groups, vacation Bible school, and the other educational organizations. When this responsibility rests with the board, ineffective workers may be shifted or removed from office with a minimum of hard feeling.

5. *Train leadership.* An adequate and continuous program of leadership development will be the concern of the board. Supervision of the educational staff will be aimed at achieving a quality program. The program of the workers' conferences, training classes, field trips, demonstrations, observations, book sharing plans, the use of the church library and other training experiences will be provided. These functions will be realized particularly through the leadership education committee of the board.

6. *Provide a curriculum.* Creative guidance and direction will be given to the selection and correlation of curricular materials to assure that the lesson and resource helps used are in terms of the policies, practices and beliefs of the local church. The board will recommend the curriculum materials to be used.

7. *Utilize buildings and equipment.* While in most churches the governing body or a trustee board is primarily responsible for physical facilities, the board of Christian education should be concerned with the proper use of the church plant for educational purposes. It will be the interest of the board to provide good working conditions, to assign space, and to recommend for purchase, adaptation or replacement equipment and furnishings for the educational rooms.

8. *Administer the educational budget.* The board will annually prepare a Christian education budget to be submitted to the church and will administer this budget when adopted. In some churches the board, or a committee of the board, will direct the purchasing of supplies and materials for educational use.

9. *Schedule events.* In projecting an over-all program for the church, the board will plan with the long-range view of accomplishing educational goals. This will necessitate the supervision of the church educational calendar, the programing and observance of special events, such as Christian holidays, family week, Sunday school week, Christian education Sunday, enlargement campaigns, training clinics, workers' conferences, vacation school, camps, retreats, recreational activities, and other programs of the year. This function will prove vital in integrating each activity into the total program of the church.

10. *Develop a balanced program.* The board will regularly study the work of the educational agencies of the church to assure that every needed emphasis is included. This embraces evangelism, worship, fellowship, and service. Included are the missionary and stewardship emphases, and church-home-community relationships to make certain that every individual has an opportunity to share in Christian service.

11. *Study trends.* Educational needs will be studied in the light of newer developments and changing conditions. The board will be alert to the trends in Christian education and to activities and programs, equipment and materials that can be profitably utilized in the local church. These may include, among others, double sessions, extended sessions, children's church, and weekday religious education.

12. *Evaluate and report.* The board will constantly evaluate all the educational work of the church to assure that it is Scripturally sound and spiritually motivated. Instruments of evaluation (including church and Sunday school records) may be used as well as personal observations of the work by board members. The board will prepare a report of the year's accomplishments in Christian education to be presented at the annual business meeting of the church.

## THE BOARD OF CHRISTIAN EDUCATION AT WORK

The board is of no value unless it works. To function effectively the board should organize at its first meeting of the year by electing a chairman, vice-chairman and secretary. It is generally agreed that the chairman should be a person who is able to preside effectively at meetings. He should be able to keep the discussion on the vital aspects of the problem under study and to lead the board to take decisive action. He should be able to lead a discussion without dominating it. The chairman should have sufficient executive ability to be able to assign responsibilities and check up on their fulfillment. He should be capable of providing guidance in developing the work of the board.

The vice-chairman will serve in the absence of the chairman. He should possess those attributes that will mark him as a leader. This position helps assure continuity in board work and provides for the development of other leadership.

A secretary should be elected from the membership of the board to keep a careful record of all actions taken. The secretary may also be responsible for notifying members of the time of meeting. Correspondence with publishers and church suppliers, with denominational and interdenominational agencies to supply the board with information and trends in Christian education will be an important responsibility of the secretary.

A regular time of meeting should be established for the board. In order to give continuous attention to a comprehensive program of Christian education, meetings should be held at least monthly on a stated date. It is advisable to schedule the meeting of the board sufficiently in advance of the workers' conference and following the Sunday school cabinet meeting to enable the best flow of communications to the various groups.

## COMMITTEES OF THE BOARD

The Christian education board is a work group. It will fail in its mission if it assumes an "ivory-tower" position and only issues orders. It has been suggested that every board member should be actively working in the field of Christian education.

Unless the church is very small and the board correspondingly small, it will find it advantageous to divide responsibility by the appointment of subcommittees. Here is where the work will be done.

Two essentially different plans of subdividing responsibility for study and oversight are possible, as suggested by Cummings:[8]

*Functional subdivision:* subdividing for special fields or functions, such as leadership education, curriculum, equipment, etc.

*Age-group subdivision:* subdividing for oversight of age groups, viz., children's division, youth division, adult division.

In the functional subdivision the member may readily become a partialist and neglect the over-all program. In the age-group subdivision the underlying principle is that all phases of Christian education are made to serve the pupil. To preserve the value of both plans, functional and age group, it is possible to give each member an age-group responsi-

[8]Oliver de Wolf Cummings, *Christian Education in the Local Church* (Philadelphia: Judson Press, 1942), p. 61.

bility as a permanent assignment while he may have a functional assignment for a limited time as needs of the church may require. Among the fields likely to need special study are curriculum, leadership training, missionary and stewardship education, evangelism, worship, evaluation, equipment, and special days.

## AGE-GROUP COMMITTEES

A member of the board will be selected to serve as chairman of an age-group committee, of which there are three: children's work, youth work, adult work. For example, all programing and needs in the children's division (cradle roll, nursery, kindergarten, primary and junior age groups) will be the concern of the children's work committee. Considering curriculum, leadership, worship experiences, opportunities for participation in the missionary and stewardship programs, needs in building and equipment—all will come under the close supervision of the age-group committee.

Comparable approaches will be followed by the youth work committee and the adult work committee.

## FUNCTIONAL COMMITTEES

Among other areas that may call for a functional committee, for purposes of illustration we may consider the missionary and stewardship education committee. In addition to the committee chairman, other board members who will serve are the chairmen of children's, youth, and adult work committees. Perhaps working with this committee will be a representative or officer of the youth organization, women's missionary group, men's group, or other related church agency. The pastor, director of Christian education, and the Sunday school superintendent should be ex-officio members.

Obviously this committee should work closely with the financial officers of the church, the church governing body, and other board of Christian education committees to correlate missionary and stewardship education to the total church program.

Activities under the direction of the committee may be missionary projects, observance of missionary Sundays, a reading program, sponsorship of a school of missions, new-member indoctrination in the missionary outreach of the church, tithing emphasis, and the use of the record system of the Sunday school as a teaching medium.

A leadership education committee may be constituted of the committee chairman and other members of the board selected for their preparation or special contribution to the area. Others who may be asked to work with this committee from time to time will be the chairmen of

# CHART PATTERN OF EDUCATIONAL ORGANIZATION

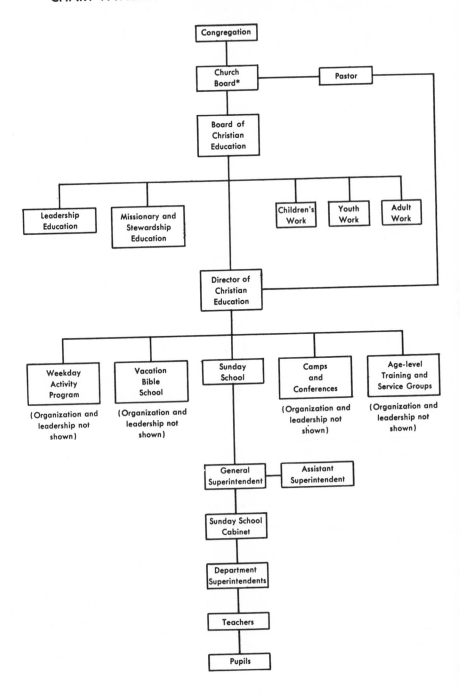

children's, youth, and adult work committees. In addition, the church librarian can play a vital role in the group. Ex-officio members are the pastor, director of Christian education, and Sunday school superintendent.

Emphases that will be the concern of the committee include development of standards for workers, methods of recruitment, processing appointments of personnel, pre-service and in-service training and supervision. Leadership education will be provided through workers' conferences, training classes, clinics, displays, and other experiences. The committee will plan for worker dedication Sunday and other events of the educational year.

Other committees that may be formed to meet needs in the church are worship committee, family life education, evangelism, curriculum, and social education. An organizational pattern may be followed similar to that suggested for the missionary and stewardship education committee and the leadership education committee.

It should be evident that the work of the board of Christian education will be done through functioning committees. While great strength will come to the total program if many people are involved in the work of several committees, the strategic actions of the board will come as a result of collective action and group decision. The regular board meetings should be a planned time of prayer, report, discussion, evaluation, and decision. This is the board at work as a clearing house in which is planned the complete educational program of the local church.

## IMPORTANT CAUTIONS TO ASSURE SUCCESS

The success or failure of the board of Christian education is largely in its own hands. This assumes, however, that the board has been properly constituted, authorized, empowered and respected by the governing body and the congregation of the local church.

The board must not be a "paper board," meeting, talking, but making no real progress. Developments in every phase of the church's program should be evidence that the board is fulfilling its functions.

Lobingier suggests another danger, "that of being dictatorial when it should be democratic. The board must not legislate when it should

*The chart is not to be construed as representing the total program or organization of the local church. The chart diagrams the relationship of the board of Christian education to the program of the church. The term *church board* is used to indicate the governing body of the church (official board, deacons, session, overseers). Consult your denominational manual. See pages 239, 241 for description of the functions of committees of the board of Christian education: leadership education, missionary and stewardship education, children's work, youth work, and adult work. For purpose of simplification, only the basic organization of one agency, the Sunday school, is charted. The weekday activity program may include activities such as Boys Brigade, Pioneer Girls, Bible clubs, weekday religious education. Age-level training and service groups may include the men's and women's organizations, Sunday evening training groups, deputation teams, etc.

advise; it must not issue orders when it should discuss a problem with the workers involved."[9]

The board members, when considering matters of collective concern, should avoid becoming partialists in favoring one phase of the total program. For example, while the Sunday school superintendent is primarily interested in this agency, he will want to make decisions and vote on issues in the best interests of the entire church.

### THE BOARD IN THE SMALL CHURCH

Any church large enough to have a Sunday school is large enough to have a functioning board of Christian education. Many churches with fewer than one hundred members have a board of Christian education that operates effectively.

In the small church the board of Christian education will be small. Three members, one of whom is from the church governing body (session, official board, deacons), will be elected by the church because of their capabilities and interests, while the pastor and Sunday school superintendent will serve as ex-officio members. Each member may be assigned responsibility for certain phases of the work. One may serve as chairman of children's work, another as chairman of youth work, and a third as chairman of adult work. Each member may assume another functional responsibility such as missionary education or leadership training.

The board of Christian education in the smaller church would do well to center its efforts on areas of greatest needs. When properly organized and meeting regularly, the board will offer the same high dividends as the one in the larger church—and perhaps will offer a richer, deeper program because of its simplicity.

### BIBLIOGRAPHY

Cummings, Oliver de Wolf. *Christian Education in the Local Church.* Philadelphia: Judson Press, 1942.

Heim, Ralph D. *Leading a Sunday Church School.* Philadelphia: Muhlenberg Press, 1950.

Lobingier, John Leslie. *The Better Church School.* Boston: Pilgrim Press, 1952.

———. "Why Bother with the Board?" *The International Journal of Religious Education,* XXXII (December, 1955).

Mason, Harold C. *Abiding Values in Christian Education.* Westwood, N.J.: Fleming H. Revell Co., 1955.

[9]John Leslie Lobingier, "Why Bother with the Board?" *The International Journal of Religious Education,* XXXII (December, 1955), p. 16.

Murch, James DeForest. *Christian Education and the Local Church.* Cincinnati: Standard Publishing Co., 1943.

Stauffer, Clarence. "The Church Organized for Christian Education," *National Voice,* (December, 1953).

Vieth, Paul H. *Improving Your Sunday School.* Philadelphia: Westminster Press, 1930.

## FOR FURTHER READING

Carlson, Violet. *The Christian Educator's File.* Chicago: Moody Press, 1954.

Foster, Virgil E. *How a Small Church Can Have Good Christian Education.* New York: Harper & Bros., 1956.

Gwynn, Price H. *Leadership Education in the Local Church.* Philadelphia: Westminster Press, 1952.

Harner, Nevin C. *The Educational Work of the Church.* New York: Abingdon-Cokesbury Press, 1939.

Hoiland, Richard. *Planning Christian Education in the Local Church.* Philadelphia: Judson Press, 1952.

Kraft, Vernon R. *The Director of Christian Education in the Local Church.* Chicago: Moody Press, 1957.

Lotz, Philip H. *Orientation in Religious Education.* New York: Abingdon-Cokesbury Press, 1950.

McKibben, Frank M. *Christian Education Through the Church.* New York: Abingdon-Cokesbury Press, 1947.

Miller, Randolph Crump. *Education for Christian Living.* Englewood Cliffs, N.J.: Prentice-Hall, Inc., 1956.

Risley, Clate A. *The Christian Education Board in the Local Church.* Chicago: Baptist Conference Press, 1958.

Vieth, Paul H. *The Church and Christian Education.* St. Louis: Bethany Press, 1951.

Wyckoff, D. Campbell. *The Task of Christian Education.* Philadelphia: Westminster Press, 1955.

*Chapter 19*

# THE MINISTER'S ROLE IN CHRISTIAN EDUCATION

## C. Adrian Heaton

IN MANY CONTEMPORARY TEXTBOOKS on Christian education the pastor is treated as the administrator of a vast, highly organized agency. He is the "key man" in seeing to it that a program is initiated and carried out. For this task he is given much help. The other phases of his teaching ministry, however, are largely neglected. The purpose of this chapter is to deal with these other aspects of his ministry.

There are at least four responsibilities which a pastor must take seriously if he is to fulfill his role as chief teacher in the congregation. First, he must be able to distinguish clearly, and help his people distinguish, the Biblical meaning of the words "preaching" and "teaching." Second, he must understand the place of clear indoctrination and must further help church workers engage in indoctrination in a way that does not distort high ethical principles. Third, he must help the church develop an adequate educational philosophy rooted in the Scriptures and knowledgeable contemporary educational theory. Fourth, he should function as the director of education in the local church or give supervision to a well-trained director.[1]

## DISTINGUISHING TEACHING AND PREACHING

In most contemporary usage the term "preaching" indicates the formal presentation of a Biblical or topical message from the pulpit. It tends

[1]For a discussion of the relationship between the pastor and director of Christian education, see Chapter 17 on "The Christian Education Director."

C. Adrian Heaton, Th.D., is president of California Baptist Theological Seminary, Covina, California.

to mean an oratorical, persuasive activity in a worship service. On the other hand, in common language, "teaching" is used to refer to those activities carried on within the classrooms of schools. The various methods of lecture, storytelling, discussion, audio-visuals and guiding projects are defined as teaching.

Unfortunately, these contemporary usages miss an important distinction in the Bible. The term "preaching" in the Scriptures means primarily the heralding or proclamation of the gospel. It is the clear affirmation of what God has done in Jesus Christ for the salvation of man. The Biblical preacher must manifest complete fidelity to the One who has called him. He speaks as a representative and gives simply the message which was given to him. His authority has nothing to do with his persuasive power or his personal magnetism, but is solely the authority of the One who gave the message.

In this sense, preaching may be done through pulpit oratory or in the midst of a Sunday school class or in a conversation during a pastoral visit. Preaching may be done not only by the person the church has called to be the minister, but by every child of God who has heard the gospel and can proclaim it to others. Smart says:

> Preaching essentially is the proclamation of this Word of God to man in his unbelief. Both outside and inside the church that definition proves adequate. Preaching is the call to men in their sin and unbelief, to repent and receive the good news; that God is ready to come to them; and that, by the power of His Word and His Spirit dwelling in them, He will establish them in the glad free life of His kingdom.[2]

"Teaching" in its Biblical usage is the interpretation of the Word of God to believers, so that they may see its relevance to the contemporary scene, its inner unity, doctrines, and ethical implications. Teaching may go on within pulpit oratory, the informal activities of the classroom, or the conversations of Christians. While there is a logical priority that one must heed "preaching" before he can receive "teaching," the two activities frequently go on together. For example, it has been found that often the best evangelistic preaching (speaking to man in his unbelief) is carried on in the midst of a sermon prepared to build up the believers in the faith. In our American churches there are probably more unbelievers attending the morning worship service than any other service of the church. Therefore, the minister must keep his preaching and teaching together. So far as youth are concerned, they often hear the preaching

---

[2]James D. Smart, *The Teaching Ministry of the Church* (Philadelphia: Westminster Press, 1954), pp. 19, 20.

Also see article on preaching by Semft in J. J. Von Allmen's *A Companion to the Bible* (New York: Oxford Press, 1958).

of the gospel more effectively in the church school classroom or Christian camp experience than in the large ungraded worship service of the church.

After one makes the distinction between "preaching" and "teaching" he must then recognize that a pastor has an obligation to be both a preacher and a teacher. To engage in the one activity without the other is a tragic failure either in heralding the gospel or building up believers.

## THE ETHICS OF INDOCTRINATION

There has been a long and continuing debate among educators concerning the place of indoctrination in teaching. Some hold that the teacher should not take a specific position but should try to present all sides of important issues and leave to the free decision of pupils the conclusions they are to draw. Others hold that teachers are irresponsible if they do not state clearly what they hold to be the correct position on various points of doctrine. Yet it seems that indoctrination is inevitable. Even those who seek hardest not to indoctrinate are teaching the doctrines of the openness of truth and the freedom of man.[3]

Some years ago, as I entered a conference room in a leading university, some professors were discussing Christian education. The leader of the meeting was suggesting a free presentation of all kinds of religious ideologies. I spoke briefly in defense of some clear affirmations of historic Christianity. With scorn in his voice the leader said, "You are not advocating education, but indoctrination." To him these two terms were opposites. To me they can be harmonized. In his very denial of indoctrination, he was indoctrinating.

We must, however, be careful that in the process of indoctrinating we do not use the coercive techniques of totalitarian governments or churches, or the subversive techniques of brainwashing. Can we indoctrinate in an ethical way? Here are some principles which may be followed.

1. Pastors must help their people differentiate between the great central affirmations of the faith with the weight of Scripture and church tradition, and those matters which are secondary interpretations. For example, the clear affirmation of the deity of Jesus Christ is a far more defensible activity than the authoritative assertion of a particular interpretation of the *kenosis*. In other words, we must be quick to distinguish what we hold as essentials of our faith from those matters which would be of secondary importance and subject to less certainty.

2. Christian educators have an obligation to state clearly the reasons or the ground upon which certain truths are held to be essential. If it is on the basis of a clear statement in the Scriptures, then the Scriptural

[3]See the splendid treatment of this subject by John S. Brubacher, *Modern Philosophies of Education* (New York: McGraw-Hill Book Co., 1950), pp. 201-204.

ground ought to be given. If something is held to be true on the basis of scientific research, the evidence should be cited. If the truth is grounded on our own pragmatic experience, clear witness concerning experience should be given. By such means we enable others to decide whether they will accept the evidences we have accepted.

3. In stating the doctrines, some of the significant alternatives must also be mentioned. These must be presented clearly and without caricature. Furthermore, if students show some genuine interest in the alternative views, further readings giving an exposition of these ideas by those who believe them, should be suggested.

4. In seeking to persuade or indoctrinate students concerning what we consider to be the correct doctrines, there must be careful abstinence from *all use* of ridicule, aggressive humor, or the status position of the preacher, in order to get conformity. Sometimes direct or indirect threats are used in an attempt to keep people from accepting what we consider are false views. The unwillingness to give honest opportunities for differences has often led some of our most thoughtful young people into rebellion against the church. In recent days the tremendous bid for freedom made by the "beat generation" is in part an attempt to be free of authoritarian religion and society. While our Christian doctrine comes with the authority of God, we should not use authoritarian (coercive) methods. We are obligated to respect man's God-given freedom.

5. There must be no impugning the motives of these who hold unsound doctrine. Unless there is a very clear statement of their motives, we are obliged to assume the most sincere motives. Unless our Christian faith and teaching can win responsible people by being fairly and clearly presented, we ought not to seek to teach.

6. Let us remember throughout our endeavor to present sound doctrine that our primary goal is to win people to a deep and personal commitment to Jesus Christ rather than merely to win arguments.

## CHRISTIAN EDUCATIONAL PHILOSOPHY

It is the role of the minister to help the leaders of the church school and the whole congregation develop an education point-of-view based both upon the Scriptures and the best insights of contemporary educational theory. Many slogans have been used to try to point up the emphases of a sound Christian educational philosophy. Let us deal here with some of these.

### THE AIM OF CHRISTIAN EDUCATION IS CHRIST-CENTERED

The sole objective, which includes all other objectives, is to bring people into vital relationship with Jesus Christ. He alone is "the way, the truth, and the life." To lead people into vital relationship with Him is more than to teach them about Christ. At the deepest level our Christian faith is the commitment of a person to the Person.

The methods of evangelism which are richest in interpersonal relationships appear to be the most effective. Since the gospel calls for a personal response, those techniques which are filled with personal meaning lead best to such a response. Christian groups have been tested by asking which of the following were the most basic in leading group members to a commitment to Jesus Christ: radio, preaching, tracts, television, Christian camping, church school classes, personal workers, Christian family life, reading of Christian literature, and the like. Over and over again it has been proved that these methods rank according to the degree of interpersonal relationships. For example, Christian family life ranks ahead of all other means of evangelism; second, small, personal groups; third will come the public services and the preaching of the Word; fourth will come some of the least personal means, such as television, then radio, then tracts.

All of this is true because of the personal nature of the Christian faith. The minister has an opportunity to help people see that the most effective communication of Christian truth is through the family, and then through the small face-to-face groups in the church. Education as well as evangelism follows the same pattern.

## The Educational Approach of Christian Education is Pupil-Centered

We need to keep in mind constantly that we are not merely teaching the Bible, but we are teaching pupils. The dynamic interrelationship we can maintain with people takes precedence over set forms. The key to the educational methods of Jesus, the Master Teacher, is person-centeredness.

## The Curricular Material for Christian Education is Bible-Centered

We have no full knowledge of God as Father and Saviour except through Scriptural revelation. We have no Christ except the Christ of the Bible. The Scriptures interpreted by the Holy Spirit then become our full and sufficient authority in the matters of faith and practice. Other materials may be used in Christian teaching, but they get their validity from their correspondence with Scripture.

We must be careful, however, to distinguish the divine and human elements in the Bible. Some educators emphasize the human elements in the Bible and treat it simply as one among many ancient books to be analyzed by historical and textual criticism. Others accept the Scripture as the miraculously inspired Word of God to be treated quite apart from literary and historical criticism. Of course the truth is, it is the Word of God written through holy men in the literary and thought forms of the ancient world. We must then discern the unity and divine authority of the Scriptures without failing to take seriously the critical study of the documents.

## THE METHODOLOGY OF CHRISTIAN EDUCATION IS EXPERIENCE-CENTERED

Modern educational disciplines have taught that it is the quality of the pupil's experiences through which he learns. Teacher preparation, then, is the planning of a sequence of experiences through which pupils pass as they achieve Christian learning. Teachers should take seriously the wide range of activity suggested in the quarterlies and work books. Most effective church school teaching is not determined by the quantity of Bible covered, but by the quality of relationships the pupils have.

## THE ADMINISTRATION OF CHRISTIAN EDUCATION IS CHURCH-CENTERED

Christian education is the work of the church. Any attempt to segregate it is a failure on the part of the church and a disruption of the unity God intended. The whole congregation must take responsibility for the church school. The church, under the leadership of the minister, must be deeply involved with Christian education. Any agency set up to fulfill a part of the task of the church but without proper recognition of its relationship with the church, is destined to distortion or failure.

# THE PASTOR A TEACHER AND ADVISER

## SETS EXAMPLE AS AN EFFECTIVE TEACHER

Through his pulpit ministry, through his work on boards and committees and in small groups, the pastor is constantly teaching the Word of God. It is his responsibility to become the very best teacher he can. He must learn how to motivate pupils, how to use a variety of methods so that they will have self-involving experiences, how to patiently await the outcomes.

The question often arises whether the pastor himself should teach a Sunday school class. There is no uniform answer, since it depends both on his particular abilities and the needs of the church he is serving. If the pastor is so constituted that he cannot take on the responsibility of the church school class without defeating his pulpit ministry on Sunday morning, then surely it would not be worth it. If, however, he can carry on the classroom teaching situation and engage in the give and take of free discussion rather than merely present a sermonette, and still be effective in leading congregational worship and preaching on Sunday morning, he probably ought to teach.

If the pastor teaches a regular class he ought to have a plan whereby he takes off either one Sunday each month or one quarter out of each school year for visiting other departments. It is important that the pupils and the staff in the various departments come to know the pastor and to be able to interact with him. Also, he will find opportunities for new ministries by meeting the church school members in small groups. As a safeguard, each pastor should be free to decide the question for himself as to whether he should teach or not. No church should stereotype this role and insist that he do what is not feasible for him.

ENCOURAGES ENLISTMENT AND IN-SERVICE TRAINING

1. The pastor should encourage and help the board of education of the local church develop an over-all policy for enlisting and selecting the finest lay people in the church for teaching in the church school. Such a policy ought to include the qualifications needed and job description of workers. As to qualifications, each worker should be a convinced Christian, have a working knowledge of the Bible, be emotionally well-balanced, and quick to learn.

2. The pastor should challenge the entire congregation to exercise the office of teacher when given the opportunity. Parents can learn a great deal about Christian teaching by instructing their own children at home. All people have opportunity to share in some responsibilities of Christian leadership. The joy of learning through teaching should be held up as an ideal. In personal visitation, the pastor should continue to challenge the finest Christians in the church to share their insights with others.

3. A formal service of dedication and installation for new church school workers should be planned for a Sunday morning service each fall. This ought to include a prayer of dedication for these workers, and some litany or response on the part of the entire congregation to undergird the work of the teachers.

4. The regular attendance of workers at the monthly workers' conference, lab schools, training institutes, and other opportunities for in-service training should be encouraged. Frequently a suggestion by the pastor for the church to put some of its budget money into leadership development will make it possible for workers to attend such conferences.

5. Through personal visits and telephone conversations, along with informal chats in the classrooms, the pastor should listen to the problems, burdens and joys of the teachers concerning their work. He should be quick to give appreciation for good work being done, and be patient in understanding the weariness in well-doing which many teachers experience.

6. From time to time the church bulletin should call attention to the

workers of the church school so that the entire congregation gets to know these faithful workers and their special problems.

## SERVES AS A RESOURCE PERSON

The pastor can prove his interest in the board of Christian education and the workers in the field in many ways.

1. He can be quick to note helpful journal articles on special phases of Christian education, and pass these on with a commendation to the appropriate workers.

2. He can help the church school develop a library of suitable materials for encouraging workers.

3. He can help the church keep in contact with the denominational and/or interdenominational agencies producing teaching helps.

4. He can demonstrate a respect for specialists in the field. One of the serious errors of some ministers is to assume that they must pretend to be specialists in every field. The humble minister recognizes that there are dedicated Christians who have spent their lives studying the psychology of learning or in the study of human development or the development of curriculum. There is a place for the pastor to direct the people to depend on the rich research and years of experience of specialists.

Nowhere is this likely to become a problem more than in the field of evaluating and choosing curricula. Often lay workers want the pastor's support of their prejudices regarding curriculum materials. The pastor must recognize that this is a highly specialized matter, and few laymen are qualified to make the necessary discriminations in deciding curriculum. Often when the teaching work is not progressing as well as one would hope, he tends to scapegoat and blame the material. There is no task more needed than for the pastor to enter wholeheartedly into setting up valid criteria and encouraging lay people to examine materials from time to time in the light of these standards.

## ENCOURAGES PROPER PROVISIONS FOR CHRISTIAN EDUCATION

The pastor can help greatly by encouraging the board of Christian education and the church trustees to provide adequate rooms and equipment for Christian education.

1. He must recognize from both the Scriptures and modern educational theory that far from feeling that play activity in the preschool departments is a hindrance to Christian teaching, it is essential. The real world of the child is the world of play and imitation of adult activities. In the midst of these activities, the love of God, responsible concern of others, and response to Jesus Christ can become most real. In the elementary departments, the children still need a great deal of first-hand exploration

of materials and human situations to grasp the great verbal statements of the Christian faith. This means the children need space, freedom, materials, and a colorful, beautiful setting. To insist that they just sit and listen is to miss genuine Christian education.

2. He must resist the temptation to seek to build larger attendance than the rooms and equipment will adequately provide for. In churches of limited facilities it may be necessary to have dual sessions on Sunday mornings. In warm weather more use can be made of the out-of-doors. Crowding children into rooms for hearing only is not education.

3. He must take the lead in helping his church understand the value of educational tools. Some time ago the board of Christian education in a church recommended the spending of three hundred dollars for educational equipment. This request was turned down by the congregation, who thought it merely involved frills and toys. In the same meeting the group passed a motion to spend fourteen hundred dollars for new carpet in the sanctuary, which was not essential but would add beauty to the morning worship services. Apparently these people could not discriminate between the economic values of carpet and the tools necessary for good teaching.

4. He can help the board of Christian education and department superintendents make good use of the equipment they do have. It is not uncommon for American churches to spend large sums for expensive audio-visual equipment and the like, and then use them merely for entertainment or keep them stored because the right use of such equipment involves a great deal of time and effort. In many churches a filmstrip projector and a good supply of filmstrips will be a far better investment than an expensve movie projector. In other cases, an adequate file of flat pictures will be less expensive and just as valuable as projected aids. Great care must be taken regarding these matters.

5. He should be sure that an adequate supply of children's and youth books is provided for each department. These young folk are learning in the public schools how to use reference materials. They delight to do independent research. The church must be in a position to encourage these activities rather than hinder them.

Intelligent pastoral leadership is essential for good Christian education in the church. The pastor must give at least as much time to working in the Christian education field as he does to sermon preparation or pastoral calling. As has been so shockingly pointed out by the Presbyterians, "The church must teach or die."

## BIBLIOGRAPHY

Brubacher, John S. *Modern Philosophies of Education.* New York: McGraw-Hill Book Co., 1950.

Casteel, John L. (ed.) *Spiritual Renewal Through Personal Groups.* New York: Association Press, 1957.

Cully, Iris V. *The Dynamics of Christian Education.* Philadelphia: Westminster Press, 1958.

Dobbins, Gaines S. *A Ministering Church.* Nashville: Broadman Press, 1960.

Forsyth, Nathaniel F. (ed.). *The Minister and Christian Nurture.* New York: Abingdon Press, 1957.

Gable, Lee J. *Christian Nurture Through the Church.* New York: National Council of Churches, 1955.

Gable, Lee J. (ed.). *Encyclopedia for Church Group Leaders.* New York: Association Press, 1959.

Gettys, Joseph M. *How to Teach the Bible.* Richmond: John Knox Press, 1949.

Grimes, Howard. *The Church Redemptive.* New York: Abingdon Press, 1958.

Miller, Randolph Crump. *Education for Christian Living.* Englewood Cliffs, N.J.: Prentice-Hall, Inc., 1956.

Moustakas, Clark E. (ed.). *The Self, Explorations in Personal Growth.* New York: Harper & Bros., 1956.

Sherrill, Lewis Joseph. *The Gift of Power.* New York: Macmillan Co., 1955.

Smart, James D. *The Rebirth of Ministry.* Philadelphia: Westminster Press, 1960.

———. *The Teaching Ministry of the Church.* Philadelphia: Westminster Press, 1954.

Vieth, Paul H. *The Church School.* Philadelphia: Christian Education Press, 1957.

Von Allmen, J. J. (ed.) *A Companion to the Bible.* New York: Oxford University Press, 1958.

Wyckoff, D. Campbell. *The Gospel and Christian Education.* Philadelphia: Westminster Press, 1959.

———. *The Task of Christian Education.* Philadelphia: Westminster Press, 1955.

Wynn, John Charles. *Pastoral Ministry to Families.* Philadelphia: Westminster Press, 1957.

*Chapter 20*

# BUILDING AND EQUIPMENT FOR CHRISTIAN EDUCATION

## GAINES S. DOBBINS

THE BUILDING SETS THE PATTERN."
This statement represents a turning point in the history of those evangelical Christian bodies in the United States that have sought to recover the teaching church. The old-fashioned Sunday school limped along with educational inadequacies that made it almost an absurdity. The adult organized class movement near the beginning of this century broke with the continental tradition that the Sunday school was for children only. The "Baraca" and "Philathea" type of classes for men and women attracted large numbers, and through various promotional means brought phenomenal popularity to the "organized class." Yet by the 1920's this movement had lost its bloom and the Sunday school as an institution was floundering again. A conundrum asked, "When is a school not a school?" brought the answer, "When it's a Sunday school!"

Why could not the Sunday school be a school? It had teachers, pupils, curriculum materials, organization and administration, and obviously met a deep-felt need. The Sunday school had outgrown its original nondescript character and had developed standards and leadership that should have made it a much more effectual educational agency than it was generally found to be. There were those who saw what the Sunday school might become, but they often felt themselves somehow frustrated. Increasingly there was recognized the demand for an educational pattern suitable to the distinctive function of the church school.

An analysis of types of churches to be found in typical American communities indicates a number of distinguishable patterns.

Gaines S. Dobbins, Th.D., D.D., LL.D., is Distinguished Professor, Golden Gate Baptist Theological Seminary, Mill Valley, California.

254

The pattern may be *sacramental*. Salvation may be conceived as mediated by the church through the sacraments of baptism, confirmation, the eucharist, penance, extreme unction, holy orders, and matrimony. The church building, whether it be modest chapel or great cathedral, will of necessity reflect this sacramental concept. Teaching and preaching have a minor place in the formal services of such a church. The Roman Catholic Counter-Reformation revived education but located it in a parochial school.

The pattern may be *ceremonial*. The Protestant revolt from sacramentalism did not involve the repudiation of many of the ceremonies which had been developed through the centuries. Religion in the Old Testament found expression through elaborate ceremonials. While Jesus was not concerned with the maintenance of Jewish ritual, He approved attendance at the temple and taught and preached in the synagogues. There is evidence of the use of the ritual in worship in the Gospels and throughout the New Testament. It would be difficult to conduct a service of worship wholly devoid of ceremony. In the course of time, ceremonies of worship became more or less standardized. On the calendar of the church year were fixed special days and occasions which were celebrated by the use of appropriate liturgies. Eventually the chief purpose of church attendance came to be the performance of and participation in prescribed ceremonies of worship. If a church is a place where rites are performed, the building and its furnishings will be provided accordingly.

The pattern may be *evangelical*. Mark records that "Jesus came . . . preaching the gospel of the kingdom of God" (Mark 1:14). Obviously He was more concerned with announcing "good news" than with administering sacraments or performing ceremonies. The first Christians were tremendously concerned with making known the gospel message. When the saving gospel became identified with sacraments and the saving mission of the church became encrusted with the ceremonial, reformers arose who sought to recover the evangelical nature of Christianity. The priest became preacher, the church service a means of winning the lost and strengthening the saved, the primary function that of preaching. In this evangelical view, the church building is mainly a "meeting house." It may be a residence or a store front, a tent or a tabernacle, or a one-room house with pulpit and pews. Where numbers and wealth make it possible, the church building may be a beautiful and impressive auditorium or sanctuary, seating hundreds or even thousands of persons, its principal purpose being to give maximum opportunity to preach and to hear the gospel. There may be other activities of the evangelical church, but they are subordinate to the high hour on Sunday when the pastor preaches and the people listen and respond.

The pattern may be *educational*. A church may conceive of itself as a school. To be sure, it is more than a school, but its purposes and activities can best be described in terms of teaching and learning. The Gospel records picture Jesus as teacher, His immediate followers as disciples or learners, His method that of the teacher, His results those which come from teaching and training. His preaching contained a large element of teaching; His character and His deeds taught even more effectually than His lips. His early followers saw themselves as preachers and teachers, with healing concern for the sick and crippled. The church as a school of Christian living and witnessing, of learning and serving, needs more than a house of worship or a preaching place—it needs buildings and equipment that will enable it most effectually to "make disciples," learners who become faithful and intelligent followers of Jesus Christ.

## RIGHT RELATION BETWEEN PREACHING SERVICE AND TEACHING SERVICE

In planning the church building, preaching and teaching should be recognized as correlative. The primary purpose of preaching is persuasion; the primary purpose of teaching is instruction. Preaching loses much of its attractiveness and power when it becomes academic; teaching loses much of its distinctiveness and effectiveness when it becomes homiletical. The preacher has a great advantage when he can assume that those whom he addresses have a background of Biblical information and understanding. The teacher is made more confident of results if he can assume that his instruction will find its full fruitage in the preacher's persuasion. There is no sharp dividing line between preaching and teaching, for all good preaching has an element of teaching and all good teaching has an element of preaching, but there is a difference and both preaching and teaching are enhanced when the distinction is observed.

The church building should establish and maintain this supplementary relationship of preaching and teaching. Provision for teaching should, wherever possible, be under the same roof as the auditorium or sanctuary. Officers and teachers of the Sunday school should realize their partnership with the preacher and others who gather about him in the conduct of the service of corporate worship. Care should be taken to provide ample and convenient passageways from departments and classes of the Sunday school to the place of worship. The building itself should in every possible way encourage the conviction that the service of preaching and the service of teaching are not separate but two halves of a common whole. The idea of "staying for church" (meaning the preaching service) should give way to the concept that both services are equally "church," and the building should symbolize and implement this concept.

## CLEARLY DEFINED CHURCH OBJECTIVES

When a church decides to build, it may go about it in several ways.

The approach may be made from the standpoint of location. What factors determine the site of the church? Sometimes the chief consideration may be economic—the cost of the land as within the limited means of the congregation. The result may be a location that handicaps the church for educational purposes. The lot may be too small, making impossible future expansion of space for teaching and training. Or the location may be too crowded and noisy, thus depriving teachers and pupils of the quiet necessary to educational effectiveness. Or the location may be too far away from the center of population in the community, thus losing its appeal to many who might attend if the church school were more accessible. One of the first considerations of a church should be both the present and the future desirability of the location for educational purposes.

The approach may be from the standpoint of materials and costs. Many churches must begin modestly. The decision may be to begin with a basement, covered with temporary roof, in the expectation that a second or third story may be built later. Almost invariably this plan involves disappointment. Experience warns against the basement for a church building. Rarely does it prove to be economical as compared with building above ground. Even so, a basement is highly undesirable for teaching purposes. The church would be well advised to delay building if necessary in order to obtain enough land to dispense with the basement altogether, except for storage and for heating and cooling apparatus. Cheap building materials and cheap construction prove to be most expensive in the long run. The other extreme is that of a building so expensively constructed as to reduce to a minimum space for teaching and training. It is unfortunate when a church permits costs and materials to be the determining factors in erecting the house of God.

The approach may be from the standpoint of the need of a place of worship. In the Protestant tradition, the house of worship with preaching central has been the first consideration. A church may therefore make the building of the sanctuary its first objective. With no less concern for worship, churches today are discovering that the service of worship must have a supporting service of teaching and training. Where a choice must be made, therefore, it has been found wise procedure to build the educational unit first. Within this unit of course will be made provision for the worship service, avowedly temporarily, yet in the conviction confirmed by experience that an adequate and worthy sanctuary can more assuredly be built if the program of the church is undergirded by a strong program of teaching and training.

The wise approach will therefore be made from the standpoint of the church's immediate and ultimate objectives. The determinative question is, What is this church for? If it is true to its New Testament mission, the answer will be:

To reach the multitudes.

To teach them so as to make disciples.

To bring the saved to baptism, church membership and conformity to Christ.

To continue to teach and train and inspire these church members that they will so bear their witness as to reach more of the multitudes.

. . . And so in ever-enlarging circles until the lost have been won to Christ and His kingdom established at home and abroad.

Such a church building, at present and as planned for the long future, will say to the world: "This is our witness to the greatness of God."

## FUNCTIONAL INTERIOR TO MATCH IMPRESSIVE EXTERIOR

It would seem axiomatic that a church should look like a church. True, there is no divinely given design that distinguishes a church from other buildings, but tradition has long established certain distinctive marks of ecclesiastical architecture. A church building should represent a combination of strength, durability, dignity, reality, utility, and beauty. One or more of these qualities may be considered more important than others, but all should be present in such combinations as to leave no doubt that the structure is a church. To the passer-by, the building itself should bear the silent witness: This is a house of God. Something precious is lost if a church building looks like a barn or a store or an apartment house or a school building or a theater.

Yet impressiveness of exterior should not be gained at the sacrifice of usefulness of the interior. Not only should the question be raised, How will this building look? but also, What will be its use? Church buildings occupy valuable land and cost hard-earned money. In their appearance they should be assets to the community and in their usefulness they should serve the community. The building committee and the architect may overemphasize one or the other of these aspects of the building. In the main, the tendency has been to stress exterior appearance to the neglect of interior utility. Occasionally it is the other way around—appearance has been sacrificed to use. Clearly there should be no conflict, for beauty and utility are not contrary to each other.

The educational purposes of the church require a graded building to serve graded teaching and training. This calls for exceeding care in devising the floor plan. A teaching church is one that makes provision for every age group, from the youngest to the oldest. Not only will such provision be made, but the building will implement a sound concept of teaching and learning. If teaching is not to be thought of as telling and learning as listening, classrooms must be provided that give privacy to teacher and pupils. These classrooms should be small enough that the teacher and his teaching will be person-minded. Educators know that learning cannot be divorced from responding, and that responses may take many forms. Classrooms should therefore be not only separate and sound-proof and small enough to encourage togetherness, but so equipped as to stimulate active participation. The kind and quality of teaching and learning will be in large measure determined by the place in which the experiences occur. Consequently it is of first importance in planning any church building to determine that the interior shall be functional in accordance with the educational aims and goals of those who will use it.

## ARCHITECTURAL SERVICE THAT PUTS NEED ABOVE TRADITION

In achieving this ideal of an impressive place of worship together with a useful place of teaching and training, the committee may run into difficulty with the architect. Church designs have been the concern of architects through the ages. Church architecture has developed noble traditions. Pagan temples and Christian cathedrals alike have been notable for their grandeur. Certain types of architecture have long been established as standard and normative. Qualified architects are students of the history of their profession and are disciplined not only in the techniques of design but in the great traditions of the master designers of the past. It would be somewhat unusual, therefore, for the typical architect, called on to draw the plans for a church building, to think in terms first of a floor plan for educational purposes. If such provision is to be made, often it will be as an afterthought and subordinate to the sanctuary design.

At this point, the minister and the planning committee must be appreciative but firm. They must make it crystal clear that the educational purposes of the building are of paramount importance, for in vain will they build for worship if they do not at the same time build for teaching. This, they must explain, is not only a New Testament ideal but a practical necessity in the modern world. With competition for people's time and support never before confronted by the churches and with media of communication that have taken from the preacher his priority, rarely can a church today hope to attract great throngs of worshipers and audiences if listening is the chief appeal. After all, the architect realizes that he is the servant of his client and has no right to impose a preconceived traditional design contrary to the fundamental need of the church. Almost all denominational bodies have consultative architectural service. This aid should be sought and brought to the attention of the employed architect. If he has the church's best interest at heart, the architect will gladly welcome counsel from such an authoritative source and will bring his resources and those of his office to the fulfillment of the church educationally in line with his ideals as to appropriate design.

## ADEQUATE SPACE FOR ALL AGE GROUPS

The Sunday school originated in an effort to do something for the underprivileged children of England. At first it was unrelated to the churches except as church people fostered the movement. Then came tax-supported public schools with their provision of equal educational opportunity for all the children. Gradually the Sunday school was adopted by the churches both of Europe and of America as their chief agency for teaching the Bible. In many parts of the Western world the Sunday school remained an affair for children. In the United States the Sunday school was extended to include adults, with the development of age-group grading that begins with babies in the nursery and continues successively to the end of life. With variations, the age groups are designated as nursery, birth to three; beginners, four and five; primaries, six to eight; juniors, nine to twelve; intermediates, thirteen to sixteen; young people, seventeen to twenty-four; adults, twenty-five and above. More recently, the long span of adulthood has been subdivided as young adults, middle adults, and senior adults.

A church building planned for educational purposes will provide adequate and appropriate space and equipment for each of these age groups. Loving attention will be given to the nursery. Ideally, there will be the reception room where the children are separated from their parents; then at least four other well-lighted and attractive rooms—for the bed babies in their little cribs, and for children one, two, and three years old respectively. The educational importance of the nursery is being more and more realized. Here life is at its beginning and much can be done in these first three formative years to determine the child's future religious life.

Beginners, four and five years of age, need a large, attractive room without partitions, arranged so as to permit maximum learning experiences. Everything in the room should remind the child of God's love in Christ expressed through the church.

Primaries likewise do not always need separate classrooms but can be cared for and taught in a room large enough for them to assemble for common activities, and then separate to go to interest centers where teaching and learning will take into account the active nature of children six to eight years of age. In schools with large numbers of primaries separate rooms for each age or grade have proved to be feasible.

Juniors, by the age of nine, have attained a new level of independence and responsibility. They need a department assembly room where they can gather for directed worship with maximum spontaneity and participation. Adjacent to the assembly room should be the classrooms, just large enough for teacher and eight or ten pupils to sit about a table and engage in purposeful Bible study. The same provision should be made for intermediates, with separate classes for each age group, and with boys and girls separated during the Bible study period. Again, where there are sufficient numbers of juniors and intermediates, individual assembly rooms for each age or grade are often used.

Department assembly rooms should likewise be provided for young people and adults. Here brief services of worship and fellowship will be held preceding the teaching of the lesson. Classrooms may be somewhat larger, yet rarely larger than to accommodate more than twenty-five or thirty persons. With increased numbers, there should be multiple departments and additional classes, graded so as to maintain congeniality in accordance with the changing interests and needs that come with maturity.

Many churches are recognizing that the hour of Bible teaching is not enough. To this service they are adding a program of training that follows as exactly as possible the age groupings of the Sunday school. Just as there is a teaching service preceding the morning hour of worship, so there is a training service preceding the evening hour of worship. To this hour of training all members of the family are invited and for each age group provision is made as in the Sunday school. Since somewhat larger groups than in Bible study will be desirable, folding doors may be placed between two Sunday school classrooms so that the larger space will be available for the training hour. Otherwise the same facilities will be used both morning and evening for both teaching and training.

In addition to use on Sunday, the educational building should provide for weekday activities. Churches are experimenting with a weekday teaching service, utilizing the building after school hours for school children and on week nights for young people and adults. The "family night" midweek service may bring to the church large numbers of its members of all ages for a meal together, and then for group study and activities.

Obviously all this calls for a building carefully designed for educational purposes, a multi-use type of structure, adaptable to the program of each agency of the church.

## EQUIPMENT THAT FACILITATES TEACHING AND LEARNING

Every aspect of the building and its equipment should be tested by the question: Will it facilitate teaching and learning? For the little children, there should be educational toys and other play equipment that will engage them in happy activities that constitute an essential part of their learning. Much use should be made of appropriate recorded music and the best obtainable pictures. Window ledges, chairs, tables, and all other furniture and fixtures should be suited to the age of the children. Musical instruments in the departments should be of good quality and kept in tune. Cabinets for materials should be provided and audio-visual teaching aids made available. In the teaching of the greatest book for the highest ends in the noblest of all institutions, the best curriculum materials should be sought.

Sometimes the building committee will make a serious mistake in the matter of equipment. Costs of the building will be determined and the money raised with little account being taken of the necessity for adequate furnishings and facilities. If a church takes seriously its teaching commission, it should be just as concerned to see that the building is provided with adequate equipment as with the finished building itself.

## PLANNING THAT FORESEES FUTURE GROWTH

A church has to begin where it is and with what it has. In this respect, it is like every other growing thing. Those who plan the building may be confronted with severe limitations. Perhaps a small, modest building is all the church at first can afford. It is of utmost importance that the beginning be made with a view to future growth and expansion. Wise planning of the building calls for an over-all design that may require many years to attain. This design will envision successive units to be added as the church grows. Such a long-range master plan will foresee the time when the church school will have an enrollment of three hundred, then five hundred, then a thousand or more. For the realization of this expectation, there must be enough land space, including off-street parking. As each unit is added, it should be with minimum disturbance of the existing building and as a unitary entity. When eventually the total building stands complete, it will have architectural symmetry and maximum functional utility.

Thus will be justified all the time and effort, the thought and planning, the money and life that have gone into the building of the house of God, where the example of Jesus may be fully followed, who "went about . . . preaching . . . teaching. . . ." Thus will be fulfilled the word of the Lord of hosts to the prophet: "Consider your ways. Go up to the mountain, and bring wood, and build the house; and I will take pleasure in it, and I will be glorified, saith the Lord" (Hag. 1:7, 8).

## FOR FURTHER READING

Conover, Elbert M. *Building the House of God.* New York: Methodist Book Concern, 1928.

Dobbins, Gaines S. *Building Better Churches.* Nashville: Broadman Press, 1947.

Flake, Arthur. *Building a Standard Sunday School.* Nashville: Sunday School Board, 1922.

Fletcher, Banister. *A History of Architecture.* New York: Charles Scribner's Sons, 1950.

Harrell, William A. *Planning Better Church Buildings.* Nashville: Broadman Press, 1947.

Lambdin, J. E. *Building a Church Training Program.* Nashville: Sunday School Board, 1946.

Ruskin, John. *Seven Lamps of Architecture.* New York: E. P. Dutton & Co., 1932.

Smart, James D. *The Teaching Ministry of the Church.* Philadelphia: Westminster Press, 1954.

Tralle, Henry Edward, and Merrill, George Earnest. *Building for Religious Education.* New York: Century Co., 1926.

Vogt, Van Ogden. *Art and Religion.* New Haven: Yale University Press, 1951.

Washburn, A. V. *Outreach for the Unreached.* Nashville: Convention Press, 1960.

*Chapter 21*

# FINANCING CHRISTIAN EDUCATION IN THE LOCAL CHURCH

### Norman S. Townsend

To some Christians, the idea of planning for financing Christian education in the local church may seem mercenary or commercial or perhaps even carnal; for there has developed a concept of spiritual living and church administration that deemphasizes anything that deals with financial planning. It is supposed that to prepare and promote a financial program is to limit the freedom of the individual Christian or to restrict the liberty of the Spirit in doing His work in the church. This is both unscriptural and impractical. The New Testament is very clear in its teaching of stewardship and finances, with Paul summarizing it all in I Corinthians 16:1, 2: "Now concerning the collection . . . upon the first day of the week let every one of you lay by him in store, as God hath prospered him."

If the church is to progress in better curricula, improved facilities, more adequate equipment, and a greater outreach in Christian education, there must be a practical financing program. In fact, any consideration of Christian education is incomplete without the teaching value of good stewardship in financing through giving.

## THE SCOPE OF THE CHRISTIAN EDUCATION FINANCE PROGRAM

If there is in some circles a deemphasizing of the subject of finances in the work of the church, there is in others a similar attitude toward Christian education in the over-all financial budget of the church. There are

---

The late Norman S. Townsend, M.A., was at the time of his decease a member of the extension staff of Scripture Press, Wheaton, Illinois.

those who fail to give Christian education its proper place of importance in the total program. One prominent church in the United States, with a million dollar building and an annual budget of nearly two hundred thousand dollars, lists Christian education in a miscellaneous category, along with allotments for flowers and postage.

To finance the program of Christian education properly, there must be an understanding of its scope in the total program of the church. Then the planning should include a consideration of the following areas of activity:

### TEACHING AND TRAINING MATERIALS

These should include the Sunday school and youth curricula, with provision for both teachers' and pupils' manuals, with additional supplementary instructional materials. In most progressive churches, this also includes a budget item for the library each year, thus providing a continual supply of current periodicals and books that will increase the resource references available to the non-professional Christian worker.

Because no educational program can survive and develop without adequate leadership training, provision should be made for the purchase of textbooks and supplementary material. Even among those churches in which the participants in such training courses purchase their own personal copies, there should be a budget allotment for the initial purchase, thus guaranteeing the proper selection and the proper direction by the responsible committee.

### AUDIO-VISUAL MATERIALS

To avoid a hit-or-miss approach to this vital part of the over-all ministry, a long-range purchasing plan should be adopted. This will include the purchase and maintenance of equipment, such as motion picture, filmstrip-slide, and opaque projectors, screens, and tape recorder, as well as the regular audio-visual teaching materials needed. Many churches feel that such a provision is beyond their meager financial abilities; yet with a careful purchase policy, with even modest but regular allowances for this part of the total program, an acceptable audio-visual library of equipment and materials can be built up. In one rural church a provision of just four dollars a month over a period of five years resulted in a most complete audio-visual library.

### MISSIONARY PROJECTS

As part of the church's New Testament responsibility, missions is an imperative part of the Christian education ministry. In a recent survey conducted among Sunday schools from all parts of the United States, 77 per cent contributed something to missions, either in separate projects, or as part of the total church missionary budget. Therefore, the financing of any Christian education program must include provision for the missionary responsibility of this department of the church.

## Seasonal Activities

Vacation Bible school, summer camping, winter retreats for Sunday school staff and/or youth come under the responsibility of the Christian education department and need careful fiscal planning to be of the greatest value. These seasonal activities have many detailed costs that should be taken into budgetary consideration. This avoids last-minute "crash planning," and the necessity for special project begging from the platform, or in individual solicitation.

## Outreach

To avoid stagnation, a church must plan for growth through its Christian educational outreach. This involves paying the bills for Sunday school and youth promotion in the community, materials for visitation among absentees and new prospects, and for whatever type of transportation program is adopted by the church. Whether the investment is little or much in this field, it needs to be planned for in an orderly fashion, so that those participating will be guided as to how much is available for their part of the ministry.

## Miscellaneous Activities

Any financial planning for Christian education must be flexible enough to allow for miscellaneous expenditures to cover such items as Christmas, Easter, Rally Day programs, convention expenses for delegates, and socials.

Undoubtedly this scope of activities could be broadened in some local situations, but these are listed to indicate the need for a fuller consideration of Christian education in a church budget.

## SOURCES FOR THE FINANCE PROGRAM

How shall the money be raised to meet the demands of such a wide Christian education ministry as indicated by the scope just outlined? "Where will we get the money?" is a cry heard in large and small churches.

To help find the answer to this question, a survey was conducted among representative churches in every part of the United States, with the following results:

*Question:* From what source do you derive finances for the Sunday school?

*Answers:* 67 per cent indicated that the only source was through free-will offerings; 22 per cent reported the use of Sunday school weekly offering envelopes; 11 per cent were included in a unified budget plan. Some added to their income by special projects, individual subscriptions, and emergency aid from the church treasury, but this number was negligible.

*Question:* Is the Sunday school a separate organization in your church, with a separate treasurer, budget, and treasury?

*Answers:* 64 per cent of those replying answered "yes," while 36 per cent said "no."

*Question:* What is the average weekly offering in your Sunday school?

*Answers:* The average offering was listed as $50.95. This figure includes schools of all sizes, therefore no significant tabulation could be made as to the relative value of the different means of raising funds.

*Question:* Do you have a Christian education building fund at present or within the past twenty-four months?

*Answers:* 38 per cent said "yes" and 62 per cent said "no." Of those answering "yes" there was an almost equal division of those enlarging present facilities and those constructing new buildings.

As indicated in the answer to the first question in this survey, there are three general sources for the financing of the Christian education program in the local church: free-will offerings, specific weekly envelopes, and inclusion in the unified budget of the church.

FREE-WILL OFFERINGS

Undoubtedly this method is the most painless, and requires the least work. There are no records to keep, no envelopes to be opened, and no expenditures for materials. In some churches, this encourages people to give anonymously, and sometimes, because of human nature, to give more generously. One pastor reported that after ten years of using envelopes and keeping records, his staff abandoned the entire system in favor of "no-pressure" loose offerings. The average of less than fifteen dollars weekly skyrocketed to over seventy-five dollars through free-will offerings. In this case, people felt more willing to give when there was no intrusion on their personal affairs, and the office staff was able to invest its time and energy in other responsibilities.

For every one who favors this system as the best source of financing the Christian education program, there is at least one who will raise his voice against it. Some would say that churches represented by the example cited have not been given proper stewardship education, or that the envelope system was not properly used. One of the most vocal opponents of the loose offering system was the late Dr. Clarence H. Benson. He quoted Bert Wilson in the latter's *Know Your Church* as saying: "A wise committee knows the life history of loose collections. It was conceived in stinginess and nurtured in ignorance. It is pure fiction for members to say that they will pay without pledging; that they will 'drop into the loose collections.' People do not give adequately in loose collections. That alibi does not stand the test."[1]

In summary, the advantages and disadvantages of using loose offerings as a source of financing the local Christian education program are:

*Advantages:*

Allows more personal freedom in giving anonymously, thus more generously.

It requires less office work, thus allowing the staff to concentrate on other more important record keeping.

It is less expensive to initiate and to operate.

It allows more flexibility in the introduction of special projects or emergency needs during the year.

*Disadvantages:*

It allows a person to become irregular in his giving.

It does not provide any record for tax deductions.

Its saving in operational expense is negligible in comparison to the increase of giving under other systems.

Its "flexibility" allows too much opportunity for repeated "special appeals," thus undermining systematic order in the church's business life, and often marring the church's testimony in the community.

Weekly Envelopes Designated for Christian Education

In order to help those Sunday schools and Christian education departments that are separate from the regular church organization, many have found that the use of specially designated envelopes is the best means of raising funds for the operation and extension of the ministry. This system has several variations: the separate Sunday school envelope; the duplex or triplex envelope, with one portion designated for Christian education; the record envelope that provides spaces for noting attendance, prepared lesson, Bible brought, offering given, etc.; and the individual envelope that has the various church ministries listed, with Christian education being one that can be checked as the designated recipient of the money enclosed.

[1]Clarence H. Benson, *Techniques of a Working Church* (Chicago: Moody Press, 1946), p. 222.

*Advantages:*

Concentrates specific giving for Christian education, thus allowing those who wish to designate their gifts to do so.

Encourages weekly giving in a systematic manner.

Provides a means of regular giving, even when pupil is absent from Sunday school.

Avoids any possible embarrassment, as the amount of offering is concealed in the envelope.

*Disadvantages:*

Encourages the "isolation" of Sunday school or Christian education from the total program of the church.

Makes visitors and nonmembers feel embarrassed, as they do not have any regular envelopes to use. (Some schools have "extras" for such persons to use.)

Allows slackers to appear cooperative in giving, when in reality they can turn in blank envelopes.

Takes too much time and effort on the part of the staff.

THE UNIFIED BUDGET

There is an increasing trend among churches to use this source of finances for the total program, of which Christian education is a part. While, according to the survey, it is still in the minority, those using it are high in their praise of it.

The principle is simply that all offerings, whether loose or in envelopes, are apportioned to the various departments of the church, according to the budgetary allotments. Christian education, as one of the departments, receives a certain percentage. Thus, whether a person gives in Sunday school, morning or evening worship service, in youth meeting, or at the midweek service, a certain percentage of his gift will go to missions, music, the ministry, or maintenance.

*Advantages:*

Allows a broad freedom for those who want to give either through envelopes or in loose offering.

Coordinates the total ministry of the church as a unified whole, not fragmented parts.

Abolishes "pet projects" supported with partisan favor.

*Disadvantages:*

Limits the opportunity for any person to help in the event of a budgetary "inequity" in any one area of ministry.

Makes giving so impersonal and general that prayerful interest in specific projects and ministries (e.g., the Sunday school) ultimately dwindles.

Encourages concentration of power and authority under one head, thus hindering the full liberty of individual action.

The arguments against the unified budget, however, grow out of a self-centered concept of Christian living and giving. Certainly in any Scripturally-based, Spirit-guided church the unity and diversity of the Body of Christ (I Cor. 12 and Eph. 4) is the pattern for action and cooperation, even in the matter of finances.

Whichever means is used, it is important that the local church set up a budget for Christian education, whether separate, or as part of the whole church program of finances. There are basic steps to be taken in doing this.

1. Have the officers examine the budgets of other schools and/or churches. If a representative from one of the other churches can be present to explain the motives and methods of procedure, this will be very helpful.

2. Set a date (preferably a month or two before the annual business meeting) for the annual budget meeting involving the responsible committee. (This committee will be determined by local or denominational organization.)

3. Require the divisional or departmental heads (e.g., children, youth, adult divisions of the Christian education program) to prepare and submit proposed budgets for the coming year at this meeting.

4. After prayerful discussion, prepare the budget for presentation to the proper group which has executive power in such matters.

5. Above all, present the budget as part of the spiritual responsibility of the Christian, corporately and individually. This involves stewardship education.


SUGGESTED BUDGET PLAN No. 1

*Children's Division*

Teaching supplies

Sunday school                                $. . . . . . . . . . .

Youth groups                                  . . . . . . . . . . .

Weekday programs                              . . . . . . . . . . .

V. B. S.                                      . . . . . . . . . . .

Day camp                                      . . . . . . . . . . .

Audio-visual equipment and supplies           . . . . . . . . . . .

Library books                                 . . . . . . . . . . .

Special handcraft needs                       . . . . . . . . . . .

*Youth Division*

Teaching supplies
  Sunday school
  Youth groups . . . . . . . . . . .
  Weekday programs . . . . . . . . . . .
  V. B. S. . . . . . . . . . . .
Audio-visual equipment and supplies . . . . . . . . . . .
Seasonal projects
  Summer camping
  Winter retreat . . . . . . . . . . .
Library books . . . . . . . . . . .
  . . . . . . . . . . .

*Adult Division*

Teaching supplies
  Sunday school
  Evening study program . . . . . . . . . . .
  V. B. S. . . . . . . . . . . .
  Leadership training . . . . . . . . . . .
Audio-visual equipment and supplies . . . . . . . . . . .
Library books . . . . . . . . . . .
  . . . . . . . . . . .

*Special Projects*

Socials
Missions . . . . . . . . . . .
Publicity . . . . . . . . . . .
Visitation . . . . . . . . . . .
Convention delegates . . . . . . . . . . .
Transportation . . . . . . . . . . .
  . . . . . . . . . . .

SUGGESTED BUDGET PLAN NO. 2

Sunday school materials
Training hour supplies     $. . . . . . . . . . .
Summer ministry . . . . . . . . . . .
  V. B. S.
  Camping . . . . . . . . . . .
Audio-visual . . . . . . . . . . .
Transportation . . . . . . . . . . .
Publicity . . . . . . . . . . .
Library literature . . . . . . . . . . .
Conventions . . . . . . . . . . .
Missions . . . . . . . . . . .
Socials . . . . . . . . . . .
Visitation . . . . . . . . . . .
  . . . . . . . . . . .

Miscellaneous                                    . . . . . . . . . . . .
and any other items that fit the local needs for the Christian educational program.

The first outlined budget is set up according to the usual division in the Christian education board, and the general main divisions of Christian education's total church program. The second one is presented by various items as they may be included in the program of Christian education in a local church. Of course, there are items and areas of activity that will be added or subtracted, according to the needs of the local or denominational organizational plan. The important thing is to have some sort of budget that best meets the needs and represents the entire scope of the program.

It is recommended that the budget, when completed and adopted, be duplicated and distributed to everyone concerned, so that prayerful consideration of it can be given preparatory to participating in the actual giving to its support. Then, whether an every-member canvass, a budget Sunday, or a direct-mail campaign is conducted to solicit the support of the people in meeting the budget, the results will be based upon intelligent understanding and prayerful consideration, not "railroading" or high-pressure motivation.

## THE SERVICE OF FINANCING THE PROGRAM

The service of finance is more than the necessary providing of adequate funds to pay bills, meet payrolls, and secure materials and supplies. There is a definite Scriptural stewardship and educational value to it.

One Sunday school, visited some time ago, was conducting a special missionary project in the nursery department among two- and three-year-olds. When first mentioned, this seemed a bit extreme, for what could such young children know and understand about missions, in the first place, and in ministry of giving, in the second place. It was a revelation, therefore, to see the manner in which the children were taught to give by an exceptional teacher. She prepared the children for the monthly missionary offering by referring weekly to a special offering box she had made. A slit was cut in the top side of the box with a picture of the missionary family pasted beside the slot. On one side of the box was a picture of an ocean liner. ("The missionaries are going on a big boat.") On the second side was a picture of an open Bible. ("They are taking God's Book, the Bible, with them.") On the third side was a picture of Japanese children. ("They are going to a place where children look like this.") On the fourth side was a picture of Jesus. ("They are going to tell these children that Jesus loves them. . . . It takes a lot of money to take such a long trip, and our money will help them to get there and to teach the Japanese children about the Lord Jesus.") On the last Sunday of the month each child was given an envelope with the next Sunday's date printed on it and an explanation of the purpose of the offering. The envelope was then returned on the first Sunday of the month. Apart from the total given (it amounted to about seven dollars each month), the value of this offering was the instruction the children received. How different from the traditional dropping of coins in the plate (or on the floor!) that characterizes many schools!

The value of considering finances as an opportunity to teach is that it contributes to the spiritual growth of the pupils. The child who is instructed in the reason for giving—not just to pay bills or build a church, but to perform God's revealed will and to promote God's work and to propagate God's Word—will grow up to be an intelligent, productive member of the church and community.

From the pulpit, in the Sunday school class, during youth groups, in business meetings, through direct mail, in special classes, financial stewardship should be presented as a threefold responsibility.

### 1. Systematic—"upon the first day of the week"

The plan involves weekly giving. The principle laid down is that of regular and systematic giving. Like prayer, Bible reading, public worship, and other duties, giving is not to be a matter of impulse, not occasional, but systematic. If the Christian is paid weekly, he should set aside the Lord's portion weekly. This is the easiest method for the average Christian to make His gifts.

### 2. Personal—"everyone of you"

The plan makes stewardship a personal affair. The church must insist that every member give for himself. Every Christian who has committed himself to the church has assumed a personal responsibility for financing its activities.

### 3. Proportionate—"as God hath prospered him"

The proportion to be put aside is not mentioned. It may be less or more than the tithe, but it is to be computed and contributed as a special per cent of the income. Giving is to be in proportion to ability and is to be measured by the gains God makes possible. The man of large income is not to discharge the obligation by giving the widow's mite. In order to make it possible for the individual member to have a practical means of demonstrating this law, churches today issue the duplex weekly envelope. It serves as a constant reminder that Christians when they receive their income are to set aside God's portion in these envelopes.[2]

Christian giving and Christian living are related. It is only as the individual Christian recognizes this that any program will succeed. The key, therefore, to successful financing of the Christian education ministry in the local church is found in the words of our Lord:

"Lay not up for yourselves treasures upon earth, where moth and rust doth corrupt, and where thieves break through and steal: but lay up for yourselves treasure in heaven, where neither moth or rust doth corrupt, and where thieves do not break through or steal: for where your treasure is, there will your heart be also" (Matt. 6:19-21).

## RECOMMENDED READING

Benson, Clarence H. *The Sunday School in Action.* Chicago: Moody Press, 1948. Chapter XIV.

———. *Techniques of a Working Church.* Chicago: Moody Press, 1946. Part 5.

Bramer, Jr., John C. *Efficient Church Business Management.* Philadelphia: Westminster Press, 1960.

Brooks, Lawrence E. *Better Church Finance.* Anderson, Ind.: Warner Press, 1960.

Byfield, Richard, and Shaw, James. *Your Money and Your Church.* Garden City, N.J.: Doubleday and Co., 1959.

Cashman, Robert. *The Finances of a Church.* New York: Harper & Bros., 1949.

Ellis, Hallett W. *Christian Stewardship and Church Finance.* Grand Rapids: Zondervan Publishing House, 1953.

Gable, Lee J. *Christian Nurture Through the Church.* New York: National Council of Churches of Christ in the U.S.A., 1955. Chapter IX.

Grindstaff, Wilmer E. *Developing a Giving Church.* Westwood, N.J.: Fleming H. Revell Co., 1954.

Holt, II, David R. *Handbook of Church Finance.* New York: Macmillan Co., 1960.

Lansdell, Henry. *The Sacred Tenth.* Grand Rapids: Baker Book House, 1955.

Linamen, Harold F. *Business Handbook for Churches.* Anderson, Ind.: Warner Press, 1957.

Pendleton, Jr., Othniel A. *New Techniques for Church Fund Raising.* New York: McGraw-Hill Book Co., 1955.

Powell, Luther P. *Money and the Church.* New York: Association Press, 1962.

[2]*Ibid.,* pp. 231, 232.

An important part of any summer camp program is the daily session of Biblical instruction.

(Courtesy of Honey Rock Camp of Wheaton College)

# PART FIVE

*Agencies of Christian Education*

*Chapter 22*

# WEEKDAY YOUTH CLUBS

Eunice Russell

## THE IMPORTANCE OF SEVEN-DAY-A-WEEK IMPACT

A T WHAT POINT is the local evangelical church touching the pagan world in which it finds itself today? How is it getting into the hearts and lives of thousands of persons who are generally ignorant of the claims of Christianity? True, a certain percentage of unbelievers attend morning worship services as a matter of perfunctory duty. But to a large majority of people outside the church, the message it bears carries no dynamic appeal.

To combat this situation, some churches have resorted to worldly means in order to attract the unsaved—music with rhythm and harmony resembling that of the contemporary medium, theatrical-type productions in young people's services where extraordinarily talented youth are exploited, and high-geared publicity stunts resulting in numerical growth but little permanent spiritual value. Obviously, this attempt on the part of the church to reach the pagan must repulse rather than attract him. The world does not expect or want the church to imitate its ways.

Other churches have fallen into the peril of a dualistic program. Alongside distinctly spiritual activities—Sunday school, worship services, prayer meeting and choir—have been placed unrelated activities as a means of baiting the unwary outsider. Church socials, bowling leagues, and secular youth clubs as sponsored by some churches are examples of these. This is not to condemn the use of parties and athletic events within the local church, but it is to point up the danger of having such programs unrelated to the spiritual purposes of the church program.

---

Eunice Russell, M.A., is director of publications of Pioneer Girls.

What is the answer? If the morning worship service is our only point of contact with the unbelieving world, and if this contact is insufficient to reach all the church must reach if it is fulfilling its proper place in a community, then that church must examine its weekly program to determine how it can best reach out to these persons in the community. The average church has hundreds of families within its immediate neighborhood which have no true knowledge of God. How can the church bridge the gap that exists between such persons and vital Christianity?

The answer lies in the church's total week-long program. It also lies in the daily lives of church members who touch their non-Christian neighbors all week long in casual contacts at home and in places of employment. But the church can also help strengthen these informal between-Sunday contacts by serving the homes of the unreached; and it does well to start with the children in these homes, although it will not neglect their unchurched parents.

Also, of equal importance is the necessity of providing opportunities during the week for the spiritual growth of Christian children and adolescents. Not only does the church have a responsibility for reaching unsaved young people with the gospel, but it must make every provision for young Christians to grow in Christ and become useful in His cause.

A church examining its own needs with reference to its adolescents will likely find the greatest drop-off in attendance somewhere between the seventh and the tenth grades. "Seventy-five per cent of . . . [the] boys and 65 per cent of . . . [the] girls drop out between the ages of thirteen and sixteen."[1] It is the junior high schooler who begins to assert his independence in matters of church attendance and loyalty. Since this is also the age of greatest change physically, socially and emotionally, it ought to alarm the church that, when the young person most needs the stability and guidance of the church, he is most apt to flee its fellowship as a symbol of his rebellion against all forms of authority. Those who stay are often compelled to do so by their parents. The tug of the world outside is beginning to be felt, and the peer-conscious adolescent prefers to be with his friends from school rather than to attend church with his family.

> The adolescent is especially sensitive to the status he holds among his associates. The urge for friendship, recognition, status, or approval is undoubtedly strong during these years. . . . Conformity to the crowd seems . . . to be the one law to which . . . boys and girls yield implicit obedience.
> . . . [Consequently,] it is very important that boys and girls of this

[1]Clarence H. Benson, *Sunday School in Action* (Chicago: Moody Press, 1948), p. 42.

age should have the chance of satisfying group fellowship with those
of their own kind within the church setting. Unless this vital need
is met by the church, these growing boys and girls are very apt to
throw their interests and their loyalty where they can find this social
need satisfied.[2]

Must this adolescent exodus continue? Hundreds of parents and youth
workers will answer, "It doesn't need to happen!" And they have large
groups of teen-agers in their church programs to prove it. The problem
voiced by so many adolescents has been this: "Christianity had no relationship to my personal life." Many felt that the church was not interested in their social and personal lives—primarily because it did not
offer anything to meet these needs. Others had tired of listening to
familiar truths taught in conventional or trite ways with an authoritarian
approach. They had deep-seated questions which required thoughtful
answers expressed in language they could understand. Where were
the youth leaders who could effectively communicate the workability of
Christianity in teen-age experience?

Christianity insists that it be demonstrated in action. God Himself
chose to send Jesus Christ as a life-sized demonstration of what God is
like. The very nature of the Christian life requires that it be *lived* and
made a part of everyday actions and reactions. It is not enough to tell
young people on Sunday morning how to live; they must have *examples*
of the virtues we teach. This creates the need for a weekday activity
program, a laboratory of Christian living, as it were.

> Any leader who has struggled along with a group of uproarious
> boys or indifferent, giggly and bored girls knows what magic is
> sometimes accomplished by a simple, informal get-together in one's
> own home or at a campfire party out in the open. Such occasions are
> often the beginning of intimate, informal, happy group associations,
> which are so influential for growing adolescent personalities. They
> furnish bewildered leaders with a more intimate insight into the real
> persons they see sitting before them on Sunday morning.[3]

Herein lies the unique advantage of the weekday activity program
within the local church. Here Christianity is *caught* as well as *taught*.
Here the leader is forced to practice what he preaches—or lose his audience!

> It is impossible to teach effectively the things of religion apart
> from the things of daily life. A few hours on Sunday devoted to re-
> ligious matters cannot be expected to affect very seriously conduct

[2]Lucile Desjardins, *Building an Intermediate Program* (Philadelphia: Westminster
Press, 1939), pp. 25, 17.
[3]*Ibid.*, pp. 67, 68.

and character if divorced almost entirely from weekday interests and emphasis.[4]

Weekday activity provides an effective way for the local church to reach out and touch the lives of pagan youth around it. This program is a medium the unsaved understand. What young person between the ages of nine and seventeen doesn't belong to a club or group of some kind? Current North American culture has made the teen-ager and pre-teener very club conscious. "Belonging" is all-important. Why should it not be a Christian club—both for young people in the church and for the adolescent outside whom we want to reach for Jesus Christ?

## VITAL ELEMENTS OF A WEEKDAY ACTIVITY PROGRAM

Nothing effective merely "happens" without conscious effort. If the weekday activity program of the church is to fulfill its purposes—that of touching the lives of outsiders and winning them to Jesus Christ and developing Christian young people into steadily growing persons with a vital experience of spiritual reality—the church must think carefully about the elements which comprise the activity. A "basic seven" are suggested here:

### PERSONAL CONTACT

The club program is a natural place for informal personal contact between leader and young person. The leader reveals his real self in the course of a lively softball game or songfest. The genuineness of his Christianity is tested by the exertion required in a project to renovate the church nursery furniture, by his mental alertness in a crisis on a camping trip, by his reaction to failure or frustration at the craft table. Small wonder then that the club leader frequently becomes counselor as well. A properly conducted weekday activity will provide ample opportunity for personal counseling.

Still this individual attention involves effort on the part of the leader. He must make opportunities and then exercise his initiative in using them. The club is a gang, and rightly so. The leader attempts to be accepted as a part of this gang on the same basis as the others. When he is "in," his friendship and counsel will be sought in the more important areas of life where his maturity and understanding are valued.

This kind of personal contact is essential if individual needs are to be met, and if the goals of the weekday activity itself are to be fulfilled.

[4]G. S. Dobbins, *Working with Intermediates* (Nashville: Sunday School Board of Southern Baptist Convention, 1926), p. 18.

In order for the experience of conversion and growth to be meaningful, there must be adequate preparation of the individual; there must be thorough understanding of the step being taken; finally, wise personal counseling is necessary for progressive Christian growth. All three of these factors imply work with *individuals*, for everyone's rate of growth is different. Have Christian programs and their leaders been in such a hurry that the individual nurture of each life has been neglected?[5]

Each person has his own rate of maturing, his own independent needs based on his personality make-up. It is vital that the club leader recognize this and major on personal contact as a means of touching the lives of adolescents. He must be aware that mere numbers being reached by the club program are not the significant factor. It is the individual growth taking place which measures the success of the program.

## GROUP DYNAMICS

Relationships with other persons occupy an absorbing proportion of everyone's time and thought. In the weekday activity program, these are paramount. There is opportunity for constant interaction between members as they plan and play and study together. This makes grouping within the program very important.

The principle of grading applies here. The wise church will provide programs geared to the age level of the club members. This will mean several programs instead of one or two. The church must first study age and grade characteristics and ability levels. It must consider the grading in both secular and Sunday school. It will then establish programs for the grade groupings according to evaluation of the factors involved.

Time must be spent on consideration of the advantages of the single sex in contrast to coeducational grouping. The decision here is of vital importance. Many churches feel the coeducational approach is the more natural one; girl attendance is assured thereby at certain ages; and it may reduce the leadership problem. Advocates of separate club programs for the sexes maintain that: (1) Boys and girls have widely differing interests and needs based on varying maturity rates and basic sex differences (true somewhat at all age levels, but more true at some than others). (2) Boys need men as their leaders and girls are best led by women. (3) The type of program desirable in a club requires separate programs if girls are to obtain the leadership training and experience they need and if they are to be participants rather than spectators of activities. (4) Both sexes need some activities apart from the other to develop ideals and standards to prepare them for coeducational contact— an opportunity for which the club is uniquely adapted.

[5]Eunice Russell, "The Development of Pioneer Girls' Philosophy" (unpublished Master's thesis, Department of Christian Education, Wheaton College, 1959), p. 10.

Whichever choice is made, the church must be willing to bear responsibility for the decision. If the club work is to be coeducational, the activity will require twice as much effort to make it effective. Those who decide upon a single sex grouping will have to meet the needs of teen-agers for boy-girl association through other church agencies or by occasional combined activities.

## LEADERSHIP AND SERVICE TRAINING AND EXPERIENCE

Some teen-agers in a southern community who dropped out of church when they reached high school age declared, "There wasn't anything in the church for us to do." If young people are to be held within the church, they must be given progressive responsibility as they grow older. Yet it is unfair to give responsibility without the necessary training and experience under supervision.

The weekday club program can be an invaluable training ground for future leadership in the church. Not only is there an atmosphere of freedom in the club, but leadership can be learned in many different areas: how to plan a camping trip efficiently, how to take part in a discussion, how to keep accurate records, the importance of thorough preparation for a craft project, or a trip to an old people's home. In the club program an adolescent is important not just for spotlight talent, such as singing or playing an instrument, but also because he faithfully assists the leader in putting the equipment away after making a pair of bookends.

## USE OF GOD'S WORD

A young person's contact with the Scriptures should always be vital—related to his daily life. But this more easily occurs when he is guided in applying Biblical truth to common everyday experiences. The activities of the club program—which may appear to be secular in nature to the casual observer—provide a unique opportunity for living out the truth of the Word in practical ways. Memorization of Scripture can be meaningful in a setting like this. One verse applied to life is worth ten which never get beyond the stage of mental recall.

Another advantage of the club medium lies in the ease of member participation in discussions and Bible exploration. The atmosphere of informality is conducive to free expression and to individual exploration of the Bible for God's answers to life problems.

## INTEGRATION OF SPIRITUAL AND SECULAR

Wholeness of life is achieved through uniting all of life around a common center. For the Christian, there can be no center other than Jesus Christ. Although this truth may be taught in theory on Sunday morning, it takes the practical outworking through the week to show the growing young Christian the implications of this integration of life. The diagram following shows the contrast between the secular and Christian weekday activity program in presenting a balanced integrated life.

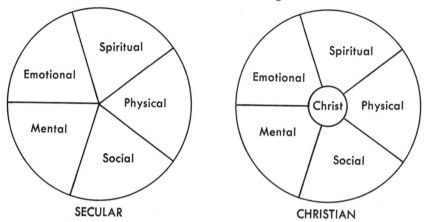

SECULAR                                        CHRISTIAN

How is this integration demonstrated effectively? In part, it is communicated by the example of Christ-centered Christians. The Biblical principle expressed by these verses—"God . . . giveth us richly all things to enjoy" (I Tim. 6:17); "All [things] are yours; and ye are Christ's; and Christ is God's" (I Cor. 3:22, 23); and "I am come that they might have life, and that they might have it more abundantly" (John 10:10)—gives to the believer a fullness of life because he can enjoy all of God's gifts freely as he dedicates them to God's glory. This makes the Christian's life a broad, rich panorama rather than a narrow, circumscribed path. The world of recreation, music, literature, nature, sciences, and art all belong to the Christian first, because God gave man these gifts and the capacity to enjoy them. Man must exercise spiritual and intelligent insight into the use of these gifts, for Satan has his counterpart to every good thing God has given. For this reason, young people must be guided into mature and wise appreciation of music, literature, art, etc., so that his view of these things and all of life is truly Christian.

The whole program of weekday activity is one of the most effective means of demonstrating this integration of secular and spiritual aspects. It is at this point that many programs falter, offering a kind of dualistic approach: combining the two elements but failing to integrate them. There must be an attempt to relate the activities which might be termed secular to those which are more obviously spiritual. Is baseball a Christian sport? Would playing Bible baseball make it more Christian? Baseball becomes a helpful Christian activity when a Christian plays and demonstrates Christlike attitudes. Is it valid for a Christian to appreciate good music? Is music only glorifying to God when it carries words which express definite spiritual concepts? Is not some gospel music actually more worldly in rhythmic patterns and tempo than some of the great classical music?

Through a carefully planned weekday activity program, young people can be guided to appreciate all of life as a gift from God, and to participate in all phases of it to glorify God and enjoy Him. In developing such an attitude, there will come true integration of life around the center—Christ.

CREATIVE ACTIVITY

For the young person, activity attracts. His whole being craves action. How important it is that God's temple of the human body be developed through wholesome recreation to be strong and useful. Variety of activity is also important, lest we stereotype young people into athletes or craftsmen or musicians. Christian youths should develop skills in various fields just as much as the non-Christian. By so doing he is broadening and strengthening his potential contact points with the pagan world. Through a mutual interest in tennis or art or aeronautics, the believer and unbeliever may be brought together in friendship, and the way paved for winning the unsaved person to Jesus Christ.

CHURCH RELATIONSHIP

Any continuing work for God must be an integral part of the total church program to be both permanent and balanced. A weekday activity program is a supplement to other phases of the church program but it is not a substitute. Without direct control and tie-in with the over-all educational plan it is apt to become the latter.

> Instead of an educational program as a whole, consciously prepared from the standpoint of ministering to the full development of the individual who is the object of all our teaching, we have a series of partial programs, often competing with each other for the time of the same individuals, each seeking to secure attention practically regardless of the contributions made by others.[6]

The weekday program will certainly feed other agencies of the church, but it can never take their place. Young persons who accept Christ through the club program need consistent follow-up, particularly those having unsaved parents. If the weekday activity program is properly administered and integrated, it will help maintain a balanced church pro-

[6]Osgoode H. McDonald, *A Church and Only a Church* (Philadelphia: Judson Press, 1936), p. 26, quoting B. S. Winchester, *The Teaching Work of the Church*, p. 196.

gram. Otherwise it may become an orphan on the side, or it may threaten to engulf the other aspects of the church program.

## OUTWORKING OF ELEMENTS IN AN ACTUAL PROGRAM

To discuss principles is one thing; it is quite another to put these principles into practice in an actual program. To demonstrate how this may be done, the programs of Pioneer Girls and Christian Service Brigade[7] have been selected as illustration.

### PERSONAL CONTACT

Aside from the casual counseling which occurs constantly, both Pioneer Girls and Brigade have built-in opportunities through their programs which require the girl or boy to come to their leaders to pass achievement tests. Leaders are encouraged to relate the skill learned with Christian attitudes, and in some cases the club member is asked to define a Scriptural principle involved in a given activity. In the requirements which send the boy or girl into actual exploration and memorization of God's Word, there are valuable opportunities for spiritual counsel.

### GROUP DYNAMICS

The entire program of both organizations emphasizes grouping. The program is separate for each age level (three in Pioneer Girls, two in Brigade with specific differences for older boys in the second division). Within each club the group is again divided into small groups led by boys or girls chosen from among the members themselves. By this means, boys and girls share in the planning and conducting of their own club programs.

### LEADERSHIP AND SERVICE TRAINING AND EXPERIENCE

By dividing the club group into workable units of five or six persons, it is possible to place leadership into the hands of the members themselves. They conduct their own business meetings, coach members on achievement work, and lead their own groups in brief devotions. The Brigade squad and Pioneer Girls council are basic units and discipline is easily maintained by working through the squad leader or council pilot.

In addition, formal leadership training is available to older Pioneer Girls and Brigadiers through achievements majoring on leadership,

[7]Brother and sister organizations having their headquarters in Wheaton, Illinois. These interdenominational organizations have weekday activity programs which become an integral part of the local church.

through annual area leadership conferences, and through a definite counselor-in-training course in the summer camping program.

## Use of God's Word

Leaders encourage teen-agers to develop the habit of personal Bible study. Often this is instigated by leading the group in Bible exploration together, allowing much participation by the group. Because the club atmosphere is informal, a spirit of freedom makes discussion easy—and honest.

There is memorization in the achievement program, but an attempt is made to make it meaningful rather than to emphasize quantity. A progressive program of acquaintance with the Bible exists in the achievements, but knowledge is not separated from its use in daily life. For example, a girl earning her sports badge ponders the meaning of I Corinthians 9:25a: "And every man that striveth for the mastery is temperate in all things." In this way members learn to relate Biblical truth to their lives.

## Integration of the Spiritual and Secular

The programs of both organizations are permeated with spiritual emphasis. The achievement system, the weekly club meeting, the summer camping program, all present a balanced program for developing young people physically, socially, mentally, and emotionally, as well as spiritually. The example of the leader is relied on to convey this integration as much as it is spelled out to the teen-ager. The program itself speaks of this integration by including recreation, skill accomplishment, leadership development, and Bible teaching purposefully throughout.

## Creative Activity

Through the achievements a variety of skills are taught—woodworking, canoeing, embroidery, music appreciation, citizenship, gardening, campcraft, etc. (boys' and girls' achievements are separate, as are their entire programs). The boy or girl is free to choose the fields in which he is interested, yet introductions to new areas in the weekly meeting stimulate him beyond the confines of his present experience. Outdoor life is emphasized through an extensive camping program—from overnight to long-term camps.

## Church Relationship

Church loyalty and participation are emphasized in achievements, but the strongest factor here is the direct relationship of both organizations to the local church. The church exercises initiative in accepting the programs, and then has control as it chooses the way in which the basic framework and principles of the programs are used.

## STRUCTURE OF THE WEEKDAY ACTIVITY PROGRAM

PASTOR, CHRISTIAN EDUCATION DIRECTOR AND CHRISTIAN EDUCATION BOARD

Those responsible for the Christian educational program of the church investigate the need for a weekday activity program and select one from among those available. Once the program has been adopted, these persons oversee the coordination of the weekday activity program and leadership training pertaining to it with other aspects of church programing. They act in an advisory capacity in the selection of leadership and formulation of policies affecting the total church. Periodically they should assist in evaluation of the program in relationship to the goals of the total church program.

### PLACE OF COMMITTEE

This committee has the direct supervisory responsibility for the weekday club programs. A girls' work committee and boys' work committee are formed, with representation from each on the Christian education board. These committees recruit and train leadership in accordance with the leadership standard of the church and of the programs approved. They are responsible for public relations, interpretation of the programs to the church constituency, promotion of the clubs among young people and the community, and education of adult prayer partners to specific prayer needs and methods of follow-up in homes. Into the hands of the committee is placed responsibility for the mechanics of the programs—finances, transportation, equipment, and facilities. This releases the leadership for their exhausting responsibilities in direct contact with adolescents.

### FUNCTIONS OF LEADERSHIP

The tasks of leadership are:
1. Planning the week-to-week program on a long-range basis.
2. Conducting each meeting and activity of the group.
3. Giving assistants and junior leaders in-service training.
4. Counseling the club members.
5. Evaluating the program with assistants and committee.
6. Relating the program to other aspects of the church program under the direction of the committee and Christian education board.

7. Establishing and maintaining a relationship to outside groups: the homes of unchurched club members, the community in general, the area and national organization of which the club unit is one part.

A weekday activity program structured on this basis will have provision for integration with the church program and for achieving an effective ministry with young people in the church and neighborhood. Unless the structure is carefully thought through and tied in definitely with the total Christian education program, the success of the program will be limited.

## IMPACT MADE BY WEEKDAY ACTIVITY EMPHASIS

The proof of the imperative nature of a weekday activity program within the local church is pointed up by the growth of interdenominational weekday activity programs in the past two decades. At least three such programs are in existence: Pioneer Girls and Christian Service Brigade (independent organizations developed side by side), and the Awana Youth Association for boys and girls. Both of these combinations use single sex grouping.

There has been a parallel development of denominational programs such as Trailblazers for Covenant youth, and Christian Youth Crusaders for Free Methodist young people (both coeducational). Increasingly the question seems to be, not, "Shall we have a program?" but, "Which one shall we adopt?"

## CRITERIA FOR SELECTION OF A WEEKDAY ACTIVITY PROGRAM

In determining its choice of a program, the church must answer five questions about the program under consideration:

1. Is its philosophy Scripturally and educationally sound?
2. Is its tie-in with the church program solid and inherent in its structure?
3. Is its organizational framework sound?
4. Is its program adequately developed with a balanced emphasis?
5. Are leadership training opportunities and program materials available?

The answer of the church to the needs it faces with regard to its young people is a crucial point. Will it face the needs squarely and courageously? If it dares to do so, it will admit that a gap exists between vital Christianity and the average young person's daily life. Will it supply the missing link by an effective bridge, one which takes into account teen-age interests and needs? It cannot isolate itself by pretending the problem does not exist. It must present Christ pre-eminent in every phase of life—between Sundays as well as on the Lord's day.

## BIBLIOGRAPHY

Bayne, Stephen F. "The Spiritual Aspects of Play," *Recreation,* XLVI (November, 1953), pp. 326, 446.

A secular leader's viewpoint on integration of secular and spiritual.

Benson, Clarence H. *Sunday School in Action.* Chicago: Moody Press, 1948.

*Blueprint for Christian Boys' Work.* Wheaton: Christian Service Brigade, 1964.

A guide to local church committees in organizing and maintaining an effective Christian boys' work program.

*Boys for Christ—Leaders' Manual.* Wheaton: Christian Service Brigade, 1962.

A handbook for leaders of boys relating to Brigade, but applicable to all boys' leaders.

Coughlin, Joseph W. "Professional Leadership Education for Christian Boys' Work." Unpublished Master's thesis, Department of Christian Education, Wheaton College, 1959.

Sets up a leadership standard for training the professional in boys' work.

Desjardins, Lucile. *Building an Intermediate Program.* Philadelphia: Westminster Press, 1939.

Dobbins, G. S. *Working with Intermediates.* Nashville: Sunday School Board of Southern Baptist Convention, 1926.

Gibbon, F. P. *William A. Smith of the Boys' Brigade.* London: William Collins Sons & Co., 1934.

Beginning of the church-sponsored weekday club movement.

*Guiding Girls.* Wheaton: Pioneer Girls.

An extensive "encyclopedia" of helps for the leader of girls relating specifically to Pioneer Girls' leadership but applicable to all girls' leaders.

Mayer, Herbert C. *The Church's Program for Young People.* New York: Century Co., 1925.

McDonald, Osgoode H. *A Church and Only a Church.* Philadelphia: Judson Press, 1936.

*Organizing Guide.* Wheaton: Pioneers Girls.

Instructions as to proper organization of girls' work in the church, bearing directly on the Pioneer Girls' program, but universally applicable.

Peacock, R. S. *Pioneer of Boyhood.* Glasgow: The Boys' Brigade, 1954.
History of this church-sponsored club movement.

*The Pioneer Girls Guide.* Wheaton: Pioneer Girls.
Basic leadership training for a Pioneer Girls' leader. Obtainable only in connection with the *Organizing Guide.*

Russell, Eunice. "The Development of Pioneer Girls' Philosophy."
Unpublished Master's thesis, Department of Christian Education, Wheaton College, 1959.
Points up basic principles and elements in a weekday activity program, using Pioneer Girls' historical development as illustration.

Steeves, Dimock. *Reaching Boys with a Christian Program.* Chicago: Moody Press, 1954.

# Chapter 23

# THE SUNDAY SCHOOL

## Edward D. Simpson and Frances F. Simpson

IT IS IMPOSSIBLE to overestimate the political and religious results of the Sunday school movement. One historian goes so far as to state that it was the Sunday school, together with the revival of Wesley and White-field, that spared England from the horrors of the French Revolution."[1] Such a statement underlines to the thoughtful person the need of a further study of this agency which is credited with having had such a powerful influence.

## *ORIGIN*

The origin of the modern Sunday school movement may be given in three scenes. The setting of the first is Gloucester, England, in the year 1780. This picture represents the birth of an idea. The second may suggest the realization of this idea, and the third, the transplanting of the idea to the virgin soil of the new world.

### BIRTH OF AN IDEA

Across the backdrop of imagination, sketch a businessman dressed in high fashion of the eighteenth century, for Robert Raikes was known as a dandy. See him in knee breeches, silver buckled shoes, white linen shirt, black long-tailed coat, and tall black hat. From his vantage point at the corner of Sooty Alley, peer with him down the street. See ramshackled hovels; dejected people; ragged, dirty children pursuing their favorite activity—fist fighting—this Sunday afternoon, their one free day from the hard labor of the week.

---

[1]Clarence H. Benson, *A Popular History of Christian Education* (Chicago: Moody Press, 1943), p. 128.

---

Edward D. (Th.D.) and Frances F. (D.R.E.) Simpson are associate professors of Christian Education at Fort Wayne Bible College, Fort Wayne, Indiana.

Robert Raikes believed such squalor and filth were preventable and that ignorance could be overcome. He determined to begin with the child. In 1780 he established his first Sunday school. People called him Bobby Wild Goose and his boys, the Ragged Regiment, for they did not appreciate his efforts to disturb the status quo. However, by 1783 the work had shown signs of success. Robert Raikes looked with a degree of satisfaction on this experiment, and promoted it through the paper he edited, *The Gloucester Journal.*

### The Realization of an Idea

Let imagination draw the picture of the second scene which took place several years later. See Robert Raikes in the rear of the kitchen of Mrs. Critchley, the Sunday school teacher. Observe his pleasure as he scans the rows of pupils, scrubbed clean for class (this was required), listening with varying attitudes to their teacher as she was seeking to help them learn to read. For many this school brings opportunity for study of the Bible which they learn to read. Some learn to love the Lord and obey His Book. Satisfaction is reflected from the master's face, for he is seeing the fruit of his idea.

### The Transplanting of an Idea

The third picture finds its setting in Oak Grove, Accomack County, Virginia. It is a Sunday evening in 1785. The major figure in the picture is William Elliott, credited with founding in the new world the first Sunday school with a pattern like that of Robert Raikes's school. With joyful anticipation he observes the goodly number of children who have joined his own on the broad porch of his spacious mansion on this typical southern plantation. They are seated on benches or squatting with comfortably knotted legs on the floor at his feet. In his hand is that precious Book he will be helping them learn to read.

Not all historians agree that these schools represent the beginnings of the modern Sunday school movement. Some would trace it back to the catechetical schools, others to the Bible study groups of the Waldenses and Albigenses, or to the Bohemian Brethren. To some, the great reformers Luther, Calvin, Zwingli, Knox and others are considered to be the fathers. In this study, Robert Raikes has been named as the originator because there seems to be a measure of continuity in the movement from his work forward.

## DEVELOPMENT

During this early period John Wesley's support contributed immeasurably to the popularity of the Sunday school, for he insisted that one be established wherever there was a Methodist Society. He introduced many practical features, such as a voluntary staff, monthly teachers' meetings, organized classes, graded curriculum, music, libraries, and government by a Sunday school society.

## ORGANIZATION DEVELOPED

The First-day or Sunday-school Society was organized in Philadelphia in 1791 for the purpose of promoting the establishing of Sunday schools. This was the forerunner of the American Sunday-School Union which was founded in 1824, an organization which has had a tremendous influence on the growth of the movement in the United States. Its record indicates that it established an average of three schools a day for over sixty-five years. Stephen Paxson, one of its missionaries, is said to have established over 1,200 schools with more than 83,000 pupils. The dedication of this man, who was both lame and tongue-tied, continues to be a challenge to Christians who seek to make a mark in time that will affect eternity.

## POPULARITY INCREASED

In the early days of the Sunday school movement, many of the established churches opposed these classes which met on Sunday, even though they studied the Bible. But starting with the Methodist Episcopal Church in 1827, denominations organized Sunday school societies. Soon the need for interdenominational endeavor contributed to the calling of the first national Sunday school convention in 1832. Laymen directed the movement from the beginning until 1907, when the International Sunday School Association was founded, and subsequently the leadership moved into professional hands. These conventions provided instruction on very practical problems and were sparked by a high level of enthusiasm.

## PROBLEMS NOTICED

Two major problems which continually faced Sunday school leaders were the need for trained teachers and for a satisfactory curriculum. John H. Vincent, a bishop of the Methodist Church who was a leader in the Sunday school movement, sought to answer the first problem in 1860 by establishing institutes for teacher training. This led to the Chautauqua program, which was originally a two-week institute held annually for Sunday school teachers, to instruct them in proper procedures.

Curriculum had been a thorny problem for many years. B. F. Jacobs, a leader in the Sunday school movement who later, at the third international convention, became chairman of the international executive committee, promoted the idea of uniform lessons. He suggested a lesson committee be established to select a Scripture passage and a golden text for each Sunday of the year. These selections were to be adapted for use of each age level and were to be used in the various denominations. The plan was adopted at the convention in 1872, and subsequently the International Uniform Lessons were published using this plan. In 1896 optional primary lessons were published to meet a growing need for graded lessons, a need which has continued to manifest itself ever since. In addition, denominational differences and theological divisions have contributed to the complexity of the problem.

PROGRESS EVALUATED

By the time the Sunday school movement had passed the hundred-year mark certain values had moved into clear focus. Regular study of the Bible as the authoritative Word of God contributed to the spiritual growth of participants. Multiplied opportunities for laymen in Christian service encouraged the development of a vigorous, active church leadership. The emphasis of the Sunday school on reading developed a demand for Bibles and religious literature, which led to the formation of the British and Foreign Bible Society and the Religious Tract Society. Growth in the program of missions at home and abroad has been closely associated with the Sunday school movement. The significance of these contributions of the Sunday school validate its existence as an important part of the program of the church.

## TWENTIETH CENTURY TRENDS

DECLINE

Statistical records give evidence of a decline in Sunday school enrollment in the United States, with a sharp drop of 12.6 per cent during the period 1916-1940. Though there were many factors contributing to this loss, of significance were (1) the change of leadership; (2) the new emphases in curriculum; (3) the teacher training program.

*Leadership.* Dr. James DeForest Murch explains a change in leadership which affected the movement.

> In this year [1922] the Council of Evangelical Denominations and the [International Sunday School] Association were merged to form the International Sunday School Council of Religious Education, now known as the International Council of Religious Education [new name: Commission on General Education of the National Council of Churches]. This action resulted in the loss of the freedom and enthusiasm which characterized the old lay leadership and opened the door to certain unevangelical influences which had come to dominate modern denominational leadership.[2]

[2]James DeForest Murch, *Christian Education and the Local Church* (Cincinnati: Standard Publishing Co., 1943), p. 86.

The "unevangelical influences" to which Dr. Murch refers were the leaders of the Federal Council of Churches, which had been organized in 1908 and was reorganized in 1950 as the National Council of Churches. The original purpose of this organization was to manifest the oneness of the Christian churches of America and promote the spirit of fellowship. In practice it has maintained open doors in membership and followed an inclusive policy, but there has tended to be an exclusive policy in leadership.[3] Those of liberal theological persuasion have been maintained in top posts. Beyond a doubt this theological liberalism had had a deadening effect on the total program of the church, for it represented a reversal of spiritual values and motivation.

*Curriculum.* The curriculum material produced by the leadership reflected the new viewpoint. In the interest of alleged intellectual acceptability, religious educators borrowed from secular leaders in the areas of philosophy, psychology, and pedagogy. When concepts from these areas were in conflict with the Scriptures, it was considered necessary to adopt them nevertheless in order to be intellectually respectable. Moreover, there was limited Bible content during those years when experience-centered teaching was popular.

However, there has been a change in this position since the International Council of Religious Education's 1946-1947 study of Christian education, and it is now assumed that experience and content are both important ingredients of curriculum. Therefore, some denominations are revising their curriculums. The Protestant Episcopal Church has set about to define what the church must teach. When the work is complete, these findings will be spelled out by age-level specialists in curriculum materials.[4] The United Presbyterian Church in the U.S.A. has a completely revised curriculum, the Christian Faith and Life Series, which seeks to relate content to experience. However, these materials are not structured to contribute to a vigorous evangelical witness—the spirit which characterized the Sunday school movement during its "golden days."

*Teacher training.* The Standard Course that was used widely for teacher training reflected this same emphasis on secular areas and was characterized by a lack of Bible content. Undoubtedly the viewpoint of the leadership was revealed in the type of curriculum material produced and in the requirement established in the teacher training program.

Since all these factors militated against the evangelical witness in the Sunday school, many leaders felt impelled to action which would preserve and propagate the viewpoint which they held dear. Undoubtedly

[3] James DeForest Murch, *Cooperation without Compromise* (Grand Rapids: Wm. B. Eerdmans Publishing Co., 1956), p. 41.
[4] D. Campbell Wyckoff, *The Task of Christian Education* (Philadelphia: Westminster Press, 1955), p. 130.

the efforts of these people have contributed to the revival which has been developing in the Sunday school movement.

RESURGENCE

Evangelicals have recognized the need to provide leadership, satisfactory curriculum materials, and a teacher training program for their constituency.

*Teacher training.* The Southern Baptists have demonstrated the value of a teacher training program in the use they have made of it. As a result of the challenge made by the denomination's president, Dr. J. B. Gambrell, the Southern Baptists in 1900 adopted a slogan, "A certificate for every teacher." The teacher training program was inaugurated in 1902 when the denomination had 10,404 schools and 712,012 pupils. By 1916 there were 18,175 Sunday schools with an enrollment of 1,760,802 pupils— an increase of 250 per cent in enrollment in fourteen years. Between 1916 and 1926 the Southern Baptists gained one million pupils. Evidence of the popularity of its teacher training program is the fact that 566,000 diplomas and 1,356,000 seals were awarded by the year 1935. Benson states that the reason for its success is the simplicity of its requirements and the enthusiasm with which the training program has been promoted.[5]

An interdenominational association for the promotion of teacher training among evangelicals was organized in 1931 under the leadership of Dr. Clarence H. Benson. Called the Evangelical Teacher Training Association, it maintains a primary emphasis on the Word of God. It provides a training curriculum which is academically sound, with basic courses in psychology of various age levels, pedagogy, and administration.

*Curriculum.* Since many of the denominational materials reflected the viewpoint of liberal theology and of secular education, Sunday school materials written for evangelicals were needed. Several independent publishers prepared materials which would meet the need of this group. They sought to provide literature which was theologically evangelical, educationally sound, and attractive in format. In addition, the National Sunday School Association has prepared the Uniform Bible Lesson Series for its evangelical public. The healthy growth in distribution of these materials, which have no denominational subsidy, reflects the fact that they meet a great need effectively.

*National Sunday School Association.* Concerned because of the decline in Sunday school attendance previously mentioned, the Sunday School Commission of the National Association of Evangelicals called for a meeting of evangelical leaders interested in Sunday school. As a result of this meeting, the National Sunday School Association was formed as an affiliate of the National Association of Evangelicals, and held its first

[5]Benson, *op. cit.*, p. 240.

convention in Chicago in 1946, dedicated to "revitalizing the Sunday schools of America."

Its efforts to accomplish this objective have resulted in the organization of fifty Sunday school associations on local, state and regional levels. Special emphases are observed annually, such as National Youth Week, March to Sunday School in March, National Family Week, and National Sunday School Week. Six commissions have been activated to expedite development in the total field of Christian education: Youth Commission, Research Commission, Camp Commission, Commission for Denominational Secretaries, Publishers Commission, and the National Association of Directors of Christian Education. Much instructional and promotional literature has been produced. Annual conventions, emphasizing inspiration and instruction, have attracted representation from ninety-one denominations. Dr. Clarence H. Benson highlights the importance of this organization in his statement that the NSSA was the greatest single force among those which added two million members to the nation's Sunday schools in 1953.[6]

Validation of Sunday school growth from 1945 to 1960 may be secured in the statistics of the *Yearbook of American Churches for 1962*, published by the National Council of Churches. The yearbook states on page 280 that enrollment almost doubled in this period, increasing from 21,426,453 to 41,197,313. The *International Journal of Religious Education* confirms the fact that this growth was "outside the denominations belonging to the National Council of Churches."[7] Undoubtedly the National Sunday School Association has made a significant contribution to this growth. Moreover, the sacrificial ministry of the executive director of this organization, Dr. Clate Risley, provided direction and impetus to the association.

The United States has been more successful than any other country in fostering this movement. However, it is of interest to observe the growth on the international level.

> Sunday church work now engages more leaders and learners than any other form of educational enterprise. Speaking in round numbers, there are some five million workers and fifty million pupils in the world's five hundred thousand Protestant Sunday church schools. . . . There is something like one Sunday church school member for each fifty persons in the world's population.
>
> In relation to other agencies, the Sunday church school not only reaches the largest number of persons, it also represents the most highly developed form of Christian educational endeavor with the longest background of experience. It has the most carefully worked

[6]David Olson, "Mr. NSSA," *Today*, VIII (July 17, 1955), p. 2.
[7]*International Journal of Religious Education*, XXXVII, No. 4 (December, 1960), 4.

out curricular materials and provides the most elaborate leadership education program. It is the most universally understood and fully recognized form of Christian educational endeavor.[8]

Among many factors contributing to Sunday school revitalization, the most prominent are teacher training, adequate materials for teachers and pupils, and an association to guide the total movement.

## SIGNIFICANT CHARACTERISTICS OF AMERICAN SUNDAY SCHOOLS

In looking at contemporary American evangelical Sunday schools, it is important to consider objectives, standards, program, organization, and promotion. Attention to sound policies in these areas produces vigorous schools.

### OBJECTIVES

An objective is an aim accepted by a group as a desired outcome of its endeavor. In the varying statements of objectives drawn up by evangelical Sunday schools, four common factors are usually found: evangelism, spiritual development, training for service, and recruiting and enlisting in service.

### STANDARDS

It is important that objectives be considered in relation to local conditions and that they be implemented through a statement of standards. "A standard is a printed statement of the qualities of an 'ideal school' with provision for measuring the various features of an actual school in relation to the ideal."[9] Self-evaluation according to such measuring sticks has led many schools to improvement in attaining their goals in the areas of curriculum, leadership, organization, and equipment.

### PROGRAM

A sound educational program in the church should have a balance in the opportunities it affords for participation in the various spiritual exercises the Scriptures underline as important: worship (John 4:24), teaching (Matt. 28:19, 20), training (Mark 1:17), service (Rom. 12; I Cor. 12; Eph. 4), and fellowship (Acts 2:42). Though it is expected that each agency of the church might major in one of these areas, yet it is true that one agency can provide experiences in all these exercises. The Sunday school should be structured to provide for experiences in all these

[8]Ralph D. Heim, *Leading a Sunday Church School* (Philadelphia: Muhlenberg Press, 1950), p. 22.
[9]*Ibid.*, p. 313.

areas, but concentrate on the teaching ministry. The success of the Sunday school has been and will be dependent on the effectiveness of its teaching program. Evangelicals insist that this teaching be Bible-based, Christ-centered, and life-related. It should be so presented that the pupil will be challenged to act upon the truth presented. Only when the truth has been incorporated into the life habits of the pupils is the teaching-learning process complete. Obviously, such teaching depends on teachers who know the Word of God, have a growing experience with Christ, understand their pupils, and are versatile in using the tools (methods) of teaching to help them accomplish their objective.

Organization

Generally, American Sunday schools are organized by departments. This provides the structure through which the personnel can administer the program.

*Departmental structure.* I Corinthians 13:11 suggests that children and adults differ in their abilities to think and understand. Accordingly, most Sunday schools group their pupils into age or grade levels within three major divisions: one each for children, youth and adults. These divisions may be subdivided into departments, and each department may include a number of classes. There is wide variation in the grouping of adults, but many accept the following plan for grading children and youth.

| Division | Department | Class (age) |
|---|---|---|
| YOUTH | College–career | 18-25 |
| | Senior high | 15-17 |
| | Junior high | 12-14 |
| CHILDREN | Junior | 9-11 |
| | Primary | 6-8 |
| | Kindergarten | 4-5 |
| | Nursery | 2-3 |
| | Cradle roll | Up to 24 months |

*Personnel.* The most important officers in the total structure of the Sunday school are the pastor and Christian education director. One of their most important responsibilities is that of developing leadership for the school. Those who implement this program include the superintendent (chief administrator of this agency), assistant superintendent (supervisor of visitation in addition), general secretary, treasurer, librarian, departmental superintendents, departmental secretary-treasurers, choristers, pianists, ushers, teachers and assistants for the various classes. Success in the school is in great measure determined by the proper administration and instruction of this staff.

*Administration.* Guidance for the Sunday school comes through three groups: the board of Christian education, Sunday school cabinet, and workers' conference. Major problems or policies affecting all educational agencies of the church are presented to the board of Christian education. This body, representing all educational agencies, correlates the church's total educational program. As the Sunday school is represented on the board, it is enabled to work more effectively in the framework of the total church program.

The cabinet, composed of pastor, Christian education director, general superintendent, secretary, treasurer and departmental superintendents, is the executive group for the Sunday school.

The workers' conference provides information, instruction, and inspiration for the total staff, and may be followed by departmental meetings. Correct departmental structure, with skilled and devoted personnel, administered through proper channels can go a long way in producing an effective Sunday school.

PROMOTION

After a sound educational program has been instituted, a school may well focus attention on a promotional thrust using records, visitation, advertising, and contests.

*Records.* A reliable system of records is essential in motivating the staff to seek to improve on past achievements. When they are kept accurately, presented graphically, and interpreted wisely, they can be an effective means of promotion.

*Visitation.* It is the school's responsibility to visit its absentees, prospects and the unchurched in the area with a view to winning them to regular participation. There are multiplied ways of organizing a program of visitation, but success will depend largely on faithful implementation.

*Advertising.* It is important that Sunday schools project a good program of advertising to bring those in the area under the sound of Bible teaching. There are many means which can be used, such as radio, newspapers, posters, dodgers, direct mail, telephone brigades, skits, highway billboards.

*Contests.* Attitudes toward the use of contests in Sunday school work vary widely. It is admitted that they can foster non-Christian attitudes and that some of the gains are but short-term humps on the attendance graph. However, there are gains! *Christian Life* reported an increase of 170,000 persons on Sunday school rolls in its 1956 contest. In the eight years it has fostered such contests there has been an increase of 1,250,000 persons in Sunday school attendance.[10]

These are some significant factors which can be used in building Sunday schools: clearly defined objectives, statement of standards, balanced program, sound organization, and good promotion.

## EVALUATION

An attempt should be made to evaluate this institution which has been in existence for almost two centuries and which has been a significant part of the total educational structure of the church for many decades, influencing many millions of people who have been touched by it.

### VALUES

It would be impossible to provide a detailed list of all the accomplishments of this agency, but consideration is given to certain contributions it has made to the individual, the home, the church, the nation, and the world.

*To the individual.* The Sunday school is effective as a character-building agency, evangelistic effort and educational institution. It "stimulates good impulses, gives moral guidance, and develops character, integrity, idealism, which are our best guarantee of the best kind of success."[11] The validity of this statement is further endorsed by the assertion that "98 per cent of all Sunday school trained boys and girls never get into serious trouble or crime."[12]

An additional value for the individual is found in the multiplied areas of Christian service which are open to lay people in the Sunday school program. In this agency there is opportunity for the individual to develop skills and talents, and to grow in spiritual stature.

*To the family.* Parents concerned lest their children be involved in juvenile delinquency might profit from the assistance of the Sunday school, as indicated in J. Edgar Hoover's statement: "Crime among youth would become practically negligible if the young people of America attended Sunday school regularly during their formative years."[13] No other success can substitute for the failure in the responsibility of providing spiritual nurture for one's children. A major value the Sunday school offers the home is that of spiritual growth at each age level.

*To the church.* The findings of studies indicate that the Sunday school provides the church with 60 per cent of its evangelistic opportunities, and

[10]"Greatest Results in Contest History," *Christian Life,* XVIII (March, 1957), p. 63.
[11]*Do You Need Our Sunday School?* (Harrisburg: Evangelical Press, n.d.), p. 3.
[12]*Would You Cheat Your Child?* (Chicago: National Sunday School Association, n.d.), p. 2.
[13]J. Edgar Hoover, "Why I Believe in the Sunday School," *United Evangelical Action,* X (September, 1951), p. 5.

80 to 85 per cent of its members.[14] In addition, the Sunday school trains leadership for administrative and official positions.

*To the nation.* Sunday school has been the instrument of reforms which have affected the nation. The interest of Robert Raikes and other Sunday school leaders in the welfare of children has encouraged social reform in child labor laws. The movement has stimulated provision of public education for children and youth. It was the Sunday school which championed the temperance movement. This agency helps to reduce crime, sanctify the home, promote Bible study, and produce the type of character which makes a nation great.

*To the world.* There is no race or creed which has a barrier dense enough to prevent the Sunday school from reaching hearts for Jesus Christ. Mission Sunday schools have multiplied in this country and in lands where missionaries have gone with the gospel. It is significant to observe that 90 to 95 per cent of all ministers, missionaries, and other full-time Christian workers come through Sunday school endeavor.[15]

## LIMITATIONS

In contrast to these values, it is necessary to recognize that there are needs and limitations in the various ministries of the Sunday school program.

*To the individual.* One of the most serious criticisms of Sunday school is its frequent failure to relate the Bible lesson to the daily life of the individual. There is certainly sufficient power in the Word of God to meet the needs of each pupil. But the claims and privileges offered in the Bible must be focused on the area of need in the pupil's life.

*To the family.* In many schools an emphasis on church-home relationships is largely lacking. "Let the school provide training for the mind, the Sunday school supply religious instruction, and let the home offer physical provisions of food, clothing and shelter." This is the compartmentalized type of living to which some people are exposed. But such an approach is far from Scriptural.

*In the church's total educational program.* Two types of institutional limitations with regard to the Sunday school may be observed: (1) weaknesses which are within the framework of the Sunday school itself; (2) those which are apparent in its interrelationships with other agencies of the church.

Those in the first category include: (1) failure to define objectives which would give sufficient direction; (2) failure to adopt standards which would help eliminate inadequate housing, grab-bag curriculum,

[14]*Our Most Indispensable Institution* (Chicago: National Sunday School Association, n.d.), p. 1.
[15]*Ibid.*, p. 1.

poor teaching procedures, etc.; (3) failure to provide long-range plans which would contribute to a balanced program; (4) failure to train leaders; (5) failure to maintain a vigorous program of promotion.

In the second category additional problems may be observed: (1) It has often built a spirit of loyalty to the Sunday school in competition with other church agencies. (2) It has developed the Sunday school budget at the expense of other agencies. (3) It has sought to maintain Sunday school personnel in its organization instead of evaluating each person's abilities in light of the total church's need for his service. (4) It has failed to make long-range plans which would obviate the scheduling of activities in competition with other church agencies.

*To the nation.* Moral decay in this nation means that Sunday schools are not reaching many Americans today. For example, there are thirty-seven million youth under the age of twenty-five without any kind of religious instruction. The majority of the adult population of America is unreached. This is the need which challenges the Sunday school today.

*To the world.* Is it necessary to underline the importance of a more vigorous program in the Sunday school in the light of the tremendous need in every country of the world? This is the task to which Christians were commissioned (Acts 1:8), and yet there are more unevangelized people in the world today than at the time that commission was given.

## BIBLIOGRAPHY

*Benson, Clarence H. *The Sunday School in Action.* Chicago: Moody Press, 1947.

———. *A Popular History of Christian Education.* Chicago: Moody Press, 1943.

Brown, Arlo Ayres. *A History of Religious Education in Recent Times.* New York: Abingdon Press, 1923.

Brown, Marianna C. *Sunday-school Movements in America.* New York: Fleming H. Revell Co., 1901.

*Building with the Bible in the Home.* Chicago: National Sunday School Association, n.d.

Cummings, Oliver DeWolf. *Christian Education in the Local Church.* Philadelphia: Judson Press, 1942.

*Do You Need Our Sunday School?* Harrisburg: Evangelical Press, n.d.

*Fant, David, and French, Addie Marie. *All About the Sunday School.* New York: Christian Publications, 1947.

Ferguson, Edmund Morris. *Historic Chapters in Christian Education in America.* New York: Fleming H. Revell Co., 1935.

"Greatest Results in Contest History," *Christian Life,* XVIII (March, 1957).

Greene, Samuel H. *The Twentieth Century Sunday School.* Nashville:
Sunday School Board of the Southern Baptist Convention, 1904.

Hakes, J. Edward. "Symposium: 'What the Sunday School Means to
Me,'" *Baptist Outlook*, VI (Fall Quarter, 1955).

*Heim, Ralph D. *Leading a Sunday Church School.* Philadelphia: Muhlenberg Press, 1950.

Hoover, J. Edgar. "Why I Believe in the Sunday School," *United Evangelical Action*, X (September, 1951).

*International Journal of Religious Education.* XXXVII, No. 4 (December,
1960).

Landis, Benson Y. *Yearbook of American Churches.* New York: Office
of Publication and Distribution of National Council of Churches of
Christ in U.S.A., 1959.

Lawrance, Marion. *My Message to Sunday School Workers.* New York:
Harper & Bros., 1924.

*Leavitt, Guy S. *Teach with Success.* Cincinnati: Standard Publishing
Co., 1956.

*———. *Superintend with Success.* Cincinnati: Standard Publishing Co.,
1960.

Michael, Oscar S. *The Sunday School in the Development of the American Church.* Milwaukee: Young Churchman Co., 1904.

Miller, Randolph Crump. *Education for Christian Living.* Englewood
Cliffs, N.J.: Prentice-Hall Inc., 1956.

*Murch, James DeForest. *Christian Education and the Local Church.*
Cincinnati: Standard Publishing Co., 1943.

———. *Cooperation Without Compromise.* Grand Rapids: Wm. B. Eerdmans Publishing Co., 1956.

*Our Most Indispensable Institution.* Chicago: National Sunday School
Association, n.d.

*Person, Peter P. *An Introduction to Christian Education.* Grand Rapids:
Baker Book House, 1958.

*Raffety, W. Edward. *The Smaller Sunday School Makes Good.* Philadelphia: American Sunday-School Union, 1927.

Russell, J. Elmer. *The Up to Date Sunday School.* New York: Fleming
H. Revell Co., 1932.

Sherrill, Lewis Joseph. *The Rise of Christian Education.* New York:
Macmillan Co., 1950.

*Sunday School Encyclopedia.* Chicago: National Sunday School Association, 1959. (Published annually for ten years.)

*Swanson, Lawrence F. *Build an Approved Sunday Bible School.* Chicago: Baptist Conference Press, 1957.

Vieth, Paul H. *The Church School.* Philadelphia: Christian Education
Press, 1957.

———. *Improving Your Sunday School.* Philadelphia: Westminster Press, 1930.

*Would You Cheat Your Child?* Chicago: National Sunday School Association, n.d.

Wyckoff, D. Campbell. *The Task of Christian Education.* Philadelphia: Westminster Press, 1955.

*Yearbook of American Churches for 1962.* New York: Office of Publication and Distribution, National Council of Churches of Christ in U.S.A., 1961.

*Recommended reading for practical helps.

*Chapter 24*

# DEPARTMENTALIZATION

## James DeForest Murch

ORGANIZATION OF THE CHURCH SCHOOL along departmental lines logically follows the generally accepted principle that the course of study must provide in a systematic way for each successive stage of life's unfolding, from early childhood to full maturity.

Most curriculum materials follow a regular gradation of studies and work from the nursery or beginner classes, with their simple exercises and stories, through primary, junior, intermediate, high school, college age and adult classes where mature men and women study together the weightier problems of theology and the Christian life. The organizational approach to the problem of effective teaching and nurture becomes one of providing a graded structure through which unity of purpose and program can be achieved and educational progress can be measured.

A thoroughly organized and graded school should have three general divisions. The first of these, the children's division, will include the elementary departments, ages one to twelve. The second, the youth division, comprises the secondary departments, ages thirteen to twenty. The third, the advanced classes or departments, ages twenty-one on through adult life.

The following schedule summarizes the organization in teaching and nurture groups which has become traditional through long experience in the educational life of American churches, though there may be variations in some quarters:

*Children's Division*
    Cradle Roll—birth to 2 years
    Nursery Department—2 and 3 years

---

James DeForest Murch, M.A., D.D., Litt.D., cofounder of Cincinnati Bible Seminary and former Managing Editor of *Christianity Today*, is a free-lance writer living in Chevy Chase, Maryland.

Beginner or Kindergarten Department—4 and 5 years
Primary Department—6 to 8 years or grades 1 to 3
Junior Department—9 to 11 years or grades 4 to 6

*Youth Division*

Intermediate or Junior High Department—12 to 14 years or grades 7 to 9

Senior or Senior High Department—15 to 17 years or grades 10 to 12

Young People's Department—18 to 20 years

*Adult Division*

Young Adults
Middle Adults
Older Adults

The variations in this pattern should be considered. The above classification of pupils is made somewhat arbitrarily by chronological age. Such a plan seems practical because the average church school has no strict educational requirements by grades on which promotions are made. Conflicts and embarrassments may occur because the pattern does not conform to that used in public schools. With young people and adults it is difficult to fix exact dividing lines. Since departmental and class organization must facilitate the aims and the program of the church school, it is wise to make whatever exceptions may be necessary in terms of the human equation. It should always be remembered that Christian education in the local church is a purely voluntary operation and in this respect it is not exactly comparable to the strict disciplines of formal education either public or private.

Another problem involving departmental organization arises from inadequate personnel and facilities for the educational program of the average church. Shall we maintain departmental machinery merely for the sake of conformity to an ideal pattern? If the church school class is perforce the only practical unit for all activities, departmental organization as such is likely to become obsolete. The size of the church building and its accommodations may well determine the extent to which departmental organization is feasible. But an adequate program of Christian education cannot be built on mere expediency. There must be ideals and norms and a determination to move toward the achievement of the highest possible educational goals. It is with this in mind that the following ideal departmental pattern is set forth.

## DIVISIONAL SUPERVISION

The effective functioning of the departmental system presupposes its proper integration with the administrative leadership of the church school and with the program of the church itself. This relationship is best assured by a strong panel of division superintendents who will have general supervision over the departments. There will be three—children's, youth, and adult. They will not direct with a heavy hand. They will lead, counsel, and cooperate with the departmental superintendents, who should be relatively free to develop their particular phase of the educational task. It is only in this spirit that a great church school can be built and maintained.

This further word of caution is applicable here, and is relevant to the whole administrative structure: There should always be a clear definition of the function of each leader so that overlapping and friction may be avoided. There should be a large measure of freedom and authority for the performance of assigned tasks. Strong lines of communication and fellowship should be constantly maintained between all members of the church school staff so that the highest leadership potential may be attained.

## CRADLE ROLL DEPARTMENT

The cradle roll department helps to meet the initial needs of the child, through the parents, from birth to two years of age. The infant is enrolled by departmental callers who periodically provide parents with literature designed to help them direct the child's life in channels which will insure his reverence for God and direct, in a Christian way, his growing consciousness of others.

Workers in this department include a superintendent, a secretary and callers. In addition, a qualified nurse should supervise the infants in the church nursery while parents are in classes and in worship service. All workers should be persons who show the love of God for babies and for parents. The cradle roll often becomes a means of reaching unchurched homes for Christ and establishing lifelong relationships between families and the church school.

## NURSERY DEPARTMENT

The nursery department ministers to the child two and three years old, providing group nurture and training, with adequate equipment and regularity of procedure.

The departmental superintendent should be a woman who loves children, knows how to deal with their parents, has a clear concept of departmental aims and techniques, and can direct the departmental program wisely and effectively. A husband-wife team, possessing these abilities, could also serve as co-superintendents. There should be a secretary to keep records, and teachers and assistants to be responsible for directed play, nurture and instruction. If possible, all personnel should have kindergarten training.

A simple standard for the department will consist of (1) maintaining purposeful contacts with each child and his parents, (2) providing educational services for the child's early religious nurture, and (3) keeping alive effective social contacts between the church and the home.

The nursery department should provide an attractive class-and-play room for the children.

## BEGINNER DEPARTMENT

The general aim of the department will be to establish habits of conduct which will cause four- and five-year-old children to love, trust, and reverence the heavenly Father, to identify Him with His Son Jesus Christ, to act according to God's will, and to please Him through prayer, praise, and acts of kindness to others.

The superintendent will give direction to the departmental program and cooperate with the teachers in achieving departmental objectives. The secretary will have charge of enrollments, attendance records, offerings, and departmental equipment. Periodic meetings of the staff should be held for discussion and planning.

The children should be grouped in two grades—the four-year-olds forming the first-year classes, the five-year-olds the second-year classes. The instruction period will involve worship, storytelling, recreation, and audio-visual aids.

The rooms for the department should be light, airy and attractive, and easily accessible to both children and parents. An assembly room and separate classrooms should have furniture suited to the age groups. Sand tables, audio-visual equipment, and appropriate pictures should be provided.

## PRIMARY DEPARTMENT

Children of ages six, seven, and eight have been enrolled in the public schools and are considerably advanced in mentality. They more or less consciously believe in God and have intuitive instincts for spiritual things. Their thinking can now be directed, attitudes formed, and conduct guided.

Departmental leadership focuses in the teaching staff. Each teacher should meet rigid educational qualifications, including a knowledge of the Bible and of her religious heritage. She should be loyal, cooperative, dependable, and thoroughly Christian. The superintendent will plan programs, supervise and unify the work of the department, handling all administrative details with intelligence and understanding. The secretary will keep all records and be responsible for all lesson materials, pictures, and equipment.

The pupils are grouped in three grades—one for each age. Each group should not include more than twelve children. Best teaching results are usually achieved if boys and girls are allocated to separate classes.

The Sunday morning schedule will include worship, varied use of the Bible, storytelling, expressional projects and other forms of instruction, and friendly recognitions which encourage social life in the orbit of the church.

A large area with class circles or separate classrooms are conducive to effective work. The quarters should be light and airy with furnishings in light attractive colors specially fashioned for this age group.

## JUNIOR DEPARTMENT

Juniors nine, ten, and eleven years of age are usually in the fourth, fifth, and sixth grades in public school. They are much more advanced mentally than others in the children's division. From the responsively changeable child, the junior is developing in a world of purposeful activity and beginning to make his own decisions. His interests in people, nature, play, reading, dramatization, collecting, instruction, and exploration create new educational problems and opportunities.

Beginning with the junior department men should also be utilized in leadership. The superintendent and the teachers should have special aptitudes for dealing with the age group. They should know the children's problems, interests, attitudes, emotional reactions, habits, and questions. Their knowledge of the Bible should be impressive and effectively related to the needs of juniors. Enrollment, recording and absentee secretaries and a chorister would complete the departmental organization. Monthly conferences of personnel would be of great value.

The children are grouped in three grades—nine-year-olds in Grade I, ten-year-olds in Grade II, and eleven-year-olds in Grade III.

Juniors are old enough to be recognized in departmental leadership, possibly through class organization with the usual officers—president, vice-president, secretary and treasurer. Special projects related to their lessons or their social interests will develop initiative and build character. Expressional activity now assumes an important role in the course of training. Impressional work should emphasize Bible reading and study, and utilize supplementary memory courses. Workbooks and audio-visual aids have a special appeal.

A general assembly room flanked by classrooms which provide teaching privacy, all provided with modern furniture and equipment, are essential to departmental efficiency.

The junior church with its separate graded worship services has been found an effective adjunct to the educational program in many churches.

## INTERMEDIATE OR JUNIOR HIGH DEPARTMENT

Early adolescence—twelve, thirteen, fourteen years—represents a time of crisis in the developing person. Startling changes are taking place in the lives of the boys and girls. Adjustments are often so difficult that they leave the church, feeling that it has no relevance to their problems.

Special care should be given to the choice of teachers and leaders, as intermediates are more apt to study their personalities than their lessons. Adolescents are quick to discern the slightest hypocrisy, and if they fail to observe a high moral or spiritual standard operative in the leader's life they become immune to instruction and guidance.

Many successful departments are headed by a young husband and wife combination in the superintendency. This arrangement has the important value of ministering effectively to the peculiar problems of each sex. This team should be thoroughly consecrated and disinclined to worldliness, able to discipline with firm and kindly reasonableness, and lead in lively constructive activities which have a ready appeal to young people. When the size of the department warrants, there should be an enrollment secretary, recording secretary, absentee secretary, a worship director, and a chorister. Where strong class organizations can function, the necessity for centralized departmental personnel is lessened.

There should be three grades in the department—one for each age. Local conditions will determine whether or not classes are to be separated by sex. Mixed enrollment is advisable for more adequate social expression and Christian fellowship. Class organization is valuable as a means of developing latent talent and achieving worthwhile objectives. The educational program must include both impressional and expressional phases, with strong emphasis on the latter. Youth groups and societies with regional and national relationships are valuable auxiliaries to a well-rounded program.

## SENIOR OR SENIOR HIGH DEPARTMENT

Fifteen to seventeen-year-olds are no longer fledglings and expect to be treated with the same respect as the young people in the eighteen to twenty age group just ahead of them in the church school. The average high school in America is as advanced as the college of fifty years ago, but the partial immaturity of seniors justifies the maintenance of a separate department for them.

The same type of husband-wife superintendency suggested in the junior high department is valuable here. There will be need not only for teachers of classes but also for sponsors of expressional groups. Personnel should be of the highest quality, possessing poise, optimism, enthusiasm, a sense of humor, and above all a sound grounding in the Christian faith. A word about sponsors: government by adults only will be distasteful to seniors since they believe they are thoroughly capable of running their own affairs. They will cooperate with adult advisers who are understanding and respectable, provided there is recognition of the more spiritually and socially mature youthful leadership in the department. A happy combination will produce splendid results. Where the size of the department warrants, there should be enrollment, recording, and absentee secretaries, but in the average church these functions may well be committed to class organizations.

Balanced impressional and expressional educational programs are essential to this as well as to the junior high and young people's departments.

## YOUNG PEOPLE'S DEPARTMENT

This department is made up of youth between the ages of eighteen and twenty, sometimes extended to those unmarried twenty-one to twenty-five. Many of these are no longer in school, but have taken their places in factory jobs, business, professional and domestic life. Many, however, have not completely decided what ideals will dominate their adult life, nor have they chosen their lifework. College and university youth offer a special problem and should be dealt with in a specialized program.

The young people's department must have a superintendent, but it is not always feasible to build a strong departmental organization. The tendency is to develop separate classes with highly organized promotional and social programs which may cooperate to some degree in projects of common concern. The superintendent should be an adult who has a youthful outlook and commands the respect of all. He will stand ready to motivate, support, counsel, guide, suggest, and place resources at the disposal of the young people, and to help them evaluate and plan realistically. There should be a shared responsibility in planning, but the actual work of the department should be in the hands of the youth themselves. The relationship between the church and the department should be so cordial and real that youth leaders of demonstrated ability should be invited to enter classes in leadership training and later to take places of responsibility in the life of the church organization.

In a large school there may be a youth council, consisting of representatives of all classes and groups within the department. The number of classes and the basis of membership will be largely determined by local conditions. There may be special classes for young businessmen, young businesswomen, young married people, or college groups. The council may coordinate and integrate certain phases of the class programs, such as worship (providing for a united departmental service), recreation, fellowship, promotion and publicity. Members of the youth council should all be active members of the local church and be approved by the church and church school. The superintendent of the department should be recognized as adviser. Such representative organization will not only elicit a deeper and more active interest in the departmental program on the part of the young people themselves, but members of the council will thus be trained in the type of work done in the church and be prepared to assume larger leadership in years to come.

Organized classes can be the undergirding strength of the young people's department. The later years of this age group require special attention. Early marriages, calls to military service, economic problems, and other developments force many to assume adult responsibilities. Such youth want to be recognized as adults and do adult things in adult ways. Creating of special organized classes meets their needs. These groups can follow the pattern of adult department classes.

## ADULT DIVISION OR DEPARTMENT

The church school that provides an educational program only for children and young people is failing in its task as the educational arm of the church. The modern revival of adult education in the secular world should point the opportunities of the church in this important area of its life. The enrollment of the ideal church school should be at least 50 per cent adult.

In some large churches there is an adult division with at least three adult departments—young adult, middle adult and older adult—but the usual organizational pattern consists of an adult department with specialized classes each separately organized as a cooperative unit of the whole.

There should be as many classes or groups as may be necessary to meet the educational needs of the church. Young married people's groups are becoming increasingly popular. The organized couple's class offers Christian fellowship, the sharing of mutual experiences, the discussion of social problems, help in life's crises, and a clean, wholesome program of recreation. Men's Bible classes and women's Bible classes have long been a vital part of church school organization. They partake somewhat of the nature of men's and women's clubs, offering opportunity for study, discussion, cooperative effort, and providing social and recreational activity. Older adults set up golden age classes, which not only study the Scriptures but provide hobby and craft programs, recreation, fellowship, and entertainment. The possibilities offered by the organized adult class idea are limitless.

Beyond the Sunday school's morning session the adult department can be responsible for Sunday-night and week-night classes in Christian stewardship, personal evangelism, church history, religious cults, Christian growth, Christian missions, social reform, personal faith and experience. Enrollment would be open to all, with new courses of study being offered each quarter.

The organized class has many advantages as a means of attaining adult education goals. It offers a channel through which latent leadership talent may be developed. It divides and distributes work and suits the right task to the right person. It distributes leadership among a large number of people over a period of years. It delegates responsibilities for particular tasks to particular persons and gets things done. It provides a responsible medium for reaching the unreached for Christ. It develops the service instinct through projects to help the weak and lift up the fallen. It provides close Christian fellowship and mutual understanding in the work of the kingdom. A well-rounded organized class program will include worship, Bible study, evangelism, missions, enlistment, fellowship, leadership, service, recreation, and benevolence. In planning an organized class program, the definite goals of the church and the church school should be borne in mind and full cooperation maintained.

This departmental system of organization is a neat package. It is based on good theory and under favorable circumstances is practicable in every particular. But it must be borne in mind that the church is a living organism and does not yield readily to being straitjacketed into preconceived molds. The people who compose the church school are human individuals who often resent and challenge changes in patterns to which they have become accustomed. After all, it is their spiritual welfare which must have priority. It is the divinely revealed purpose of the church which must be served. Churches themselves differ from one another, and each in its peculiar field has its unique problems with which organization must deal. All these factors must be taken into consideration in applying the basic departmental principle. Local church school leadership must therefore ultimately determine what organization will best meet the needs of their particular church.

## BIBLIOGRAPHY

Armstrong, Hart R. *Sunday School Administration and Organization.* Springfield, Mo.: Gospel Publishing House, 1950.
Brewbaker, Charles W. *The Adult Bible Teacher and Leader.* Cincinnati: Standard Publishing Co., 1943.

Chamberlin, J. Gordon. *The Church and Its Young Adults.* Nashville: Abingdon-Cokesbury Press, 1943.

Clay, Daisy J. *The Junior Leader.* Chicago: Moody Press, 1951.

Faris, Lillie A. *The Primary Teacher and Leader.* Cincinnati: Standard Publishing Co., 1953.

Flake, Arthur. *Sunday School Officers and Their Work.* Nashville: Convention Press, 1952.

Griffeth, Ross J. *The Intermediate Bible Teacher and Leader.* Cincinnati: Standard Publishing Co., 1949.

Grogg, Evelyn L. *The Beginner Bible Teacher and Leader.* Cincinnati: Standard Publishing Co., 1942.

Harner, Nevin. *Youth Work in the Church.* Nashville: Abingdon-Cokesbury Press, 1942.

Jones, Orabelle C. *The Nursery Department of the Sunday School.* Nashville: Sunday School Board of the Southern Baptist Convention, 1946.

*Leadership for Improving Instruction.* Washington: Association for Supervision and Curriculum Development, 1960.

Lentz, Richard E. *Making the Adult Class Vital.* St. Louis: Bethany Press, 1954.

Little, Lawrence C. (ed.). *The Future Course of Christian Adult Education.* Pittsburgh: University of Pittsburgh, 1959.

Lotz, Philip Henry (ed.). *Orientation in Religious Education.* Nashville: Abingdon-Cokesbury Press, 1950.

Murch, James DeForest. *Christian Education and the Local Church.* Cincinnati: Standard Publishing Co., 1943 (revised 1958).

Taylor, Marvin J. (ed.). *Religious Education: A Comprehensive Survey.* Nashville: Abingdon Press, 1960.

Thompson, Jean A., Klein, Sara G., and Gardner, Elizabeth C. *When They Are Three.* Philadelphia: Westminster Press, 1946.

Welshimer, Mildred. *The Young People's Bible Teacher and Leader.* Cincinnati: Standard Publishing Co., 1939.

Zeigler, Earl F. *Christian Education of Adults.* Philadelphia: Westminster Press, 1958.

*Chapter 25*

# SUNDAY EVENING YOUTH GROUPS

## Roy Zuck

Y OUNG PEOPLE, with their immeasurable potential and innumerable problems, are to the church today one of the greatest challenges for Christian education.

They are needed for leadership in spirituality, for stewardship of possessions, for vision of opportunity, for courage to undertake the difficult tasks, and for moral and financial support of the total Christian enterprise.[1]

Challenging teen-agers to full commitment to Christ, involving them in the total church program, and training them to be church leaders are problems of concern to youth workers, parents, and pastors. One answer to these problems is a well-functioning, purposeful Sunday evening young people's group. Properly conducted, it can attract, hold, and influence the lives of young people for the cause of Jesus Christ.

### HISTORY

In the first part of the nineteenth century the Sunday school movement in America had its origin. In 1851 the first Y.M.C.A. in the United States was founded, following the beginning of this organization in England in 1844. Its purpose was to care for the religious welfare of young men neglected by church organizations. Other efforts to reach young people were also made outside the local churches.

In 1867 Dr. Theodore N. Cuyler, of Brooklyn, organized a number of local youth groups together in what was called the Young People's

[1]John R. Mumaw, "Introduction," Ada Zimmerman Brunk and Ethel Yake Metzler, *The Christian Nurture of Youth* (Scottdale, Pa: Herald Press, 1960), p. vii.

Roy Zuck, Th.D., is editor of Training Hour Materials of Scripture Press, Wheaton, Illinois.

Association. This society developed a pledge, held weekly devotional meetings, and worked through various committees, such as devotional, visiting, and temperance committees, and a committee on entertainment.[2]

Other organizations sprang into being to strengthen the ministry of local churches among young people and to provide fellowship for youth on a wider scale. One such organization was the Young People's Baptist Union of Brooklyn, founded in 1877.

Christian Endeavor was organized in 1881 by Francis E. Clark in the parsonage of the Williston Congregational Church, Portland, Maine, of which he was pastor. Its purpose was to provide training in Christian service, to cultivate the devotional life, to promote church loyalty, Christian service, fellowship, and citizenship.[3]

The name Christian Endeavor was chosen because the society aimed to assist young people in *endeavoring* to live the Christian life. Other Christian Endeavor groups were soon founded. In four years the membership numbered more than 10,000. Today there are thousands of local Christian Endeavor societies in almost eighty different denominations and in practically every country of the world. The International Society of Christian Endeavor adopted as its slogan the phrase "For Christ and the Church."

Because Christian Endeavor was interdenominational, several denominations began their own youth organizations. The Brotherhood of St. Andrew (Episcopal) was formed in 1883. In 1889 the Methodists in the North founded the Epworth League at Cleveland, Ohio. Five years later the Epworth League began in the South. Since 1939, however, the name Epworth League has been replaced by the term Methodist Youth Fellowship.

Youth work among the Baptists began on a nationwide scale with the organizing of the Baptist Young People's Union (B.Y.P.U.) of America in Chicago in 1891. Many Southern Baptist churches organized B.Y.P.U. groups and affiliated with the national movement.

In 1895, in the interest of having their own youth organization, Southern Baptist leaders founded the B.Y.P.U. Auxiliary to the Southern Baptist Convention.[4] Because this organization expanded to include a program for every age, its name was changed in 1934 to Baptist Training Union.

[2]J. M. Price, James H. Chapman, L. L. Carpenter, and W. Forbes Yarborough, *A Survey of Religious Education* (New York: Ronald Press Co., 1959), p. 252.
[3]*Christian Endeavor Essentials* (Columbus: International Society of Christian Endeavor, 1956), p. 12.
[4]J. E. Lambdin, *The Baptist Training Union Manual* (Nashville: Convention Press, 1952), p. 145.
For a more complete description of the historical development of the B.Y.P.U. see William W. Barnes, *The Southern Baptist Convention 1845-1953* (Nashville: Broadman Press, 1954), pp. 183-191.

The B.Y.P.U. in the North has been known as the Baptist Youth Fellowship since 1941.

In the 1890's the Walther League was organized for the youth of the Lutheran Church, Missouri Synod. The Luther League of America was founded in 1895. In 1896 the Unitarians formed the Young People's Religious Union, and the Episcopalians founded the Junior Daughters of the King. As recently as 1958 the United Presbyterian Youth Fellowship (founded in 1889) merged with the Westminster Fellowship of the Presbyterian Church, U.S.A. (which began in 1943).

In the last few decades more and more denominations have established organizations for promoting youth work in their local churches. Many denominations provide literature for weekly programs for their young people, training for local youth workers, and regional and national rallies and conventions.

## PURPOSE

Youth workers—and young people themselves—should be aware of the purpose for which Sunday evening youth groups meet and should structure the groups to accomplish that purpose. As Newby has indicated:

> Perhaps the primary reason for any lack of effectiveness has been the limited understanding and conscious awareness of our basic objective. Many factors, including the theological climate, educational philosophy, and the lack of adequately trained leaders, have made it possible in many instances for youth groups to become just another social clique or club without an awareness of any distinctive purpose.[5]

Do youth groups exist for the purpose of entertaining young people with light, novelty-type programs? Is the goal merely to give teen-agers a good time? Is the purpose only to provide fellowship? Should youth groups be a second Sunday school, for Bible study? Should they be for training youth in Christian growth and leadership?

It is an educational axiom that pupils' needs determine aims or purposes. Therefore, to determine the purpose of youth groups, the needs of young people should be considered.

Young adolescents (ages 12-14, junior highs) go through a period of spurting, spasmodic physical growth. They are confused by their boundless physical energies, their strong emotional fluctuations, and new social adjustments to school life and the opposite sex. Spiritually they are aware of their imperfections and are sensitive to deep-seated spiritual needs. Therefore, youth programs for young teens should channel their energies,

[5]Donald O. Newby, "The Churches' Ministry to Youth," *Religious Education: A Comprehensive Survey* (New York: Abingdon Press, 1960), pp. 124, 125.

help place their personal problems and frustrations in "flying formation" under the control of Christ, aid them in achieving emotional and social balance, and satisfy their spiritual hunger.

Middle adolescents (ages 15-17, senior highs) face problems relating to conduct in dating, getting along with parents, maintaining an effective Christian witness at home and school, cultivating habits concerning their personal spiritual life. Therefore, youth programs for senior high young people should give them Christian guidance in matters of dating, home life, Christian living, witnessing, personal devotions, and the like.

Later adolescence (ages 18-24) is a period when significant life choices are made. The older young person faces major decisions, such as whether or not to go to college and, if so, what college to attend; what vocation to enter; and how to find God's will in marriage. Therefore, youth programs should guide older youth into an understanding of God's perspective and will regarding these decision areas.

Harner summarizes the needs of adolescence by pointing up the fact that young people need to find God, themselves, a lifework, a life mate, their relation to society, and their relation to the church.[6] Narramore explains how teen-agers are interested in fun, friendships, parents, education, personality development, looks, manners, communication, dating, military service, marriage, and spiritual issues.[7]

Young people, with their varied interests, conflicting standards, and numerous problems, need practical guidance in formulating a Christian outlook, or philosophy, toward life. They need to develop their spiritual gifts and abilities. They need to progress in their knowledge and use of the Word of God, in their personal spiritual devotion to Christ, and in their ability to serve Him effectively.

Youth groups ought to exist primarily for the purpose of helping Christian youth grow and mature in Christ through considering God's answers to life's perplexing problems. They should *train* and develop youth for dynamic spiritual living. As Mumaw has stated, "The church's work with youth is essentially a matter of guidance to help them achieve maturity."[8]

The effective youth group provides training not only for Christian living, but also for Christian leadership. Young people gain maturation in leadership skills through serving as officers or committee chairmen, working on committees or projects, and participating in the programs and various church activities.   Training through expressional activities has been the purpose toward which many denominations and churches have geared their Sunday evening youth organizations. The Southern

[6]Nevin C. Harner, *Youth Work in the Church* (New York: Abingdon-Cokesbury Press, 1942), pp. 31-32.
[7]Clyde M. Narramore, *The Psychology of Counseling* (Grand Rapids: Zondervan Publishing House, 1960), pp. 141-142.
[8]Mumaw, *op. cit.*

Baptists incorporated this objective within their organizational title—the Baptist Training Union. Baptist Publications, an independent Baptist publishing house in Denver, Colorado, has the Baptist Training Union; and the Scripture Press Publications Inc., of Wheaton, Illinois, publishes Training Hour material for youth programs. In other groups the objective of training is included among several other purposes. The Christian Workers' Service Bureau, of Redondo Beach, California, for example, states that youth meetings exist for training, expression, and fellowship.[9]

The purpose of youth groups is separate and distinct from the Sunday school, in that the Sunday school seeks to communicate God's truth (through Bible study and exposition), whereas youth groups seek to train youth in Christian living and leadership on the basis of truth received.[10]

Youth meetings afford more opportunity than Sunday school classes for expressional activities, for informality, for initiative and experience, for increased time for participation and projects, and for maximum personal and group involvement.[11] As Henry has indicated:

> The traditional Sunday school was organized for Bible study. This must still be its chief concern. Through the years, however, experience has shown that the total educational task of the church is much broader. Young people's societies with specialized expressional functions were set up to meet the needs of a limited age group.[12]

Such methods as panels, debates, interviews, buzz groups, reports, skits, brainstorming, and symposiums comprise a large part of the methodological approach in interesting youth programs. While the Sunday school may have relatively little time for similar methods of study, creative Sunday school teachers often use some of these methods in their classes.

In other words, the distinction between the Sunday school and the young people's meeting lies in objective, not in methodology. To think of the morning session as the time to use the teacher-give-lecture method, and the evening session as the time for the youth-read-parts method is to lose sight of the proper objectives and methods of both organizations. Rather, both sessions should be built around a self-contained curriculum, utilize a variety of creative methods, and be based squarely on the Word of God.

[9]George F. Santa, *Youth Leader's Handbook, No. 1* (Redondo Beach, Calif.: Christian Workers' Service Bureau, 1955), pp. 5, 6.
[10]Roy B. Zuck and Fern Robertson, *How to Be a Youth Sponsor* (Wheaton, Ill.: Scripture Press, 1960), p. 5.
[11]Louise B. Griffiths, *The Teacher and Young Teens* (St. Louis: Bethany Press, 1954), p. 95.
[12]Carl Henry, "Pastors and Christian Education," *Christianity Today*, III (August 31, 1959), p. 20.

Top-quality youth programs incorporate maximum participation on the part of the young people to create greater interest and to accomplish greater training. Involvement, Tani says, places youth "on the highest learning level."[13] But while sponsors are keenly eager that their youth participate in planning, preparing, presenting, and evaluating programs, they should be equally concerned that the programs help youth come to grips with life problems. As Bowman emphasizes, "The question is not what the young people did in this unit, but *what the unit did to the young people.*"[14]

Caution must be exercised in youth work so that the teens do not simply "put on programs." The meetings should be directed toward helping youth reach a verdict![15]

## ORGANIZATION

For a more effective program, young people should be divided into three age groups which parallel the stages of early, middle, and later adolescence. These are the junior highs (sometimes called intermediates or young teens), ages 12, 13, and 14, in grades 7, 8, and 9; the senior highs, ages 15, 16, and 17, in grades 10, 11, and 12; and older youth, ages 18 to 24, in college or careers.

Some churches divide the junior highs and senior highs into two-year groupings. According to this plan, the 7th and 8th graders comprise the junior high groups, the 9th and 10th graders comprise the middle high groups, and the 11th and 12th graders comprise the senior high groups. In some areas of the nation, 7th and 8th graders are the junior highs, and 9th, 10th, 11th, and 12th graders are in the senior high group. Each plan for groupings has its advantages and drawbacks. The 2-2-2 arrangement takes into account the relatively advanced status of the 9th grader and provides, in larger churches, some similarity in program and activities for the older groups of middle highs and senior highs, although it keeps them separate.[16]

Many churches find it advantageous to divide their youth groups according to the school grades of their youth rather than their ages. However, it is generally deemed wise not to grade youth closely into groups for each school grade, because of the informal and creative nature of, and the Christian fellowship afforded in, the youth meetings.

It is best not to have the junior highs and senior highs meet together, because of the wide range between their interests and needs. Small

[13]Henry N. Tani, *Ventures in Youth Work* (Philadelphia: Christian Education Press, 1957), p. 32.
[14]Clarice M. Bowman, *Ways Youth Learn* (New York: Harper & Bros., 1952), p. 89.
[15]*Ibid.*, p. 135.
[16]Tani, *op. cit.*, p. 19.

churches are wise in seeking to form at least two youth groups as soon as possible—when as many as six or eight can be in each group and as soon as adult leadership is available.[17]

The youth groups themselves are variously organized. In addition to cabinet officers for the entire group, such as president, vice-president, secretary, and treasurer, there are usually a number of committees, commissions, or study groups, in order to involve every young person in some activity related to his interests and abilities.

Denominations and churches affiliated with the United Christian Youth Movement usually organize their youth societies into five "commissions." These are the major areas of program and study covering the basic needs and concerns of youth. They are Christian faith (which includes areas such as beliefs, personal commitment and growth, conduct, the Christian heritage, and church membership), Christian witness (which includes evangelism, stewardship, churchmanship, and Christian vocations), Christian outreach (which includes home missions, foreign missions, ecumenicity, interchurch aid, and peace and world order), Christian citizenship (which includes service to the local church and community, intergroup relations, industrial relations and economic issues, and social problems), and Christian fellowship (which includes the local church activities, Christian home life, boy-girl relations, recreation, interchurch relations, leisure time, creative arts, and military service).[18]

Each young person in a youth society is assigned to a commission of his interest. Each commission then is responsible for the evening programs which relate to its areas of concern and for other activities and emphases in the local church that pertain to the commission. The socials, for example, are planned by the Christian fellowship commission, and spiritual-life retreats are organized by the Christian faith commission.

The advantages of this plan are these: broader scope of emphasis, easier placing of youth into committees that match their interests, and integration of emphasis throughout the church program for youth.

Many groups, however, would find it difficult to follow such an organizational plan because of these disadvantages: the possibility of all youth in a group not being equally involved and, therefore, not equally

[17]Following the trend established by the Southern Baptists, and the desire for augmenting the limited time of the Sunday school hour, churches are expanding their evening youth hour to include programs for children and adults. Thus they have a training program for every member of the family, paralleling the Sunday school in departmental and class organization. The adult evening hour provides opportunity for Bible-related elective studies, leadership training, and creative adult study and projects. The children's hour is used in a few churches for music education (children's choir practice and church music appreciation), whereas in many churches it is used for creative study of topics related to areas of Christian living and church leadership not considered in the Sunday school curriculum.
[18]"The Plan for Common Commissions in Christian Youth Work" (New York: United Christian Youth Movement, n.d.), pp. 2, 3.

interested in program planning; and the danger of some areas of concern within a commission being neglected because of the overly broad scope of the commissions.

A second type of organization used by some groups—particularly those of forty or more youth—is the multicommittee plan, with committees such as program, worship, library, social, missions, membership or enlistment, music, publicity, etc. Each young person is appointed to one of the committees for a designated number of months. The major difficulty in this plan is the heavy responsibility of the program committee for planning all the weekly programs for the duration of the committee membership.

A third plan of committee organization which has been used successfully for years and which engages every person in youth activities and programing is the "planning group" or "planning team" arrangement. In this method each young person is appointed to a smaller group (of three to eight persons, depending on the size of the youth organization), responsible for planning and presenting one program a month. Thus one group is responsible for the program on the first Sunday of each month, another is responsible for the second Sunday, etc.

This plan has a number of advantages: (1) It distributes program-planning responsibility to all youth, rather than just a select few on a program committee. (2) It encourages maximum participation. (3) It helps guarantee program variety. (4) It stimulates competition among planning groups and thus increases quality in the group programs. (5) It does not conflict with the need for other group officers or committees.[19]

The Baptist Training Union in the South utilizes this plan but dovetails into it a number of committees. Each person is on a planning group and a committee. The committee members are distributed so that each planning group has at least one representative from the five committees: program, membership, Bible reading, missionary, and social.[20] Each youth group is called a union. Each union is divided into two, three, or four groups, which are headed by group captains.

Perhaps one of the most functional types of organization is a combination of planning groups and a minimum of cabinet officers and committees. A social committee, a missionary committee, and an enlistment committee may be the only ones necessary for the effective functioning of many youth groups. Each planning group may also constitute one of the committees. For example, one planning group may be the social committee; a second planning group may be the missionary committee, etc.

---

[19]See Zuck and Robertson, op. cit., pp. 17, 18, 27-30, for further details on how this plan works.

[20]E. E. Lee, The Baptist Intermediate Union Manual (Nashville: Convention Press, 1946), pp. 21-23.

Larger groups (of forty or more young people) may wish to have half their members serve on planning groups and the other half serve on committees.

This planning-group arangement is equally workable among junior high groups. However, the term of office for junior highs should usually be only six months, whereas senior highs may efficiently serve for six months or a year. For junior highs, short-term appointments for projects to be done are better than long-term offices or committees. For example, rather than electing a social committee to plan several socials over a long period of time, it is better to choose a few interested young teens to plan the next immediate social. Then when that job is completed, the project group should be disbanded. This is better for junior highs, because "the early adolescent mind does not see an 'organization,' or view a year's program. He does visualize an immediate job to be done: a trip to be taken, a play to be given, a newspaper to be produced."[21] Bowman supports this thought by stating that young teens' "interests are more volatile, shorter-term."[22]

How should the Sunday evening youth group be related organizationally to the rest of the church program for youth? In smaller churches, where adult leadership is not available and extensive grouping is impossible, an organizational pattern, called by Hayward and Burkhart the "church department" plan,[23] is utilized. In this plan the youth society is related to the Sunday school by means of the same teacher-sponsor and the same set of youth officers. For example, the secretary of the senior high Sunday school class is also the secretary of the evening youth group. This is workable in small church situations where there are very few activities for youth other than the Sunday school and evening youth hour.

The "youth fellowship" plan, fully expounded by Cummings,[24] is now in vogue in many churches. In this setup the young person who joins the church becomes a part of the youth fellowship, which embraces all the activities and agencies for youth in the church.

If he is in the Sunday school, he is in the youth fellowship "at study." If he is in the morning worship service, he is in the youth fellowship "at worship." If he is elected an officer of the youth fellowship, such as vice-president, for example, he is the vice-president of all the youth agencies. This reduction of leadership opportunities is one of the drawbacks of the plan, along with the fact that each youth agency tends to lose its single identity as it is swallowed into the more embracive "youth

[21]Griffiths, op. cit., p. 97.
[22]Bowman, op. cit., p. 56.
[23]Percy H. Hayward and Roy A. Burkhart, Young People's Method in the Church (New York: Abingdon Press, 1933), pp. 177-184.
[24]Oliver DeWolf Cummings, The Youth Fellowship (Philadelphia: Judson Press, 1956).

fellowship." Furthermore, this plan tends to make the youth work in the church a separate fellowship within a fellowship, or a youth church within a church. However, it does have the merits of affording coordinated planning and leadership and making youth feel a part of a unified program.

A workable pattern now utilized by average-size and large-size churches is the youth council plan. A youth council consists of youth officers or representatives from each youth organization or agency (including Sunday school, the evening youth group, youth choir, weekday youth clubs, camp, etc.), along with a teacher, a sponsor, a church board member, and the pastor (and the director of Christian education, if the church has one). These persons meet to plan and coordinate the youth activities. Not a policy-making group, this council marks out the church's entire youth program and seeks to avoid conflicts of schedule, to prevent overlapping of curriculum emphases, and to formulate the details of a balanced program for the church's youth.[25]

The youth council is responsible to the subcommittee on youth work, which in turn is part of the board of Christian education. In most church situations this is the ideal pattern for youth organization because it unifies the total church program, it provides a central clearing house for all youth activity planning, it is a means of expediting the details of a balanced program, and it creates greater interest on the part of the young people and adults who are on the council.

Most youth groups meet on Sunday evenings, one hour before the evening church service, or immediately after the service. Other groups, however, choose to meet on a week night and combine a recreational program along with the youth program.

## CURRICULUM MATERIALS

Different types of curriculum material are available to sponsors and youth groups. Some program materials are printed in book form, with the intention that sponsors select from them those ideas that are suitable for their groups. However, most program books have been found to be inadequate for establishing any kind of extensive, purposeful curriculum. Program materials published by denominational or nondenominational publishing houses are released in annual "kits"; others are produced quarterly, with program ideas for each of thirteen Sundays; and some material is produced monthly. Perhaps the most common form of publication is quarterly. In some publications the program ideas are dated for each Sunday.

Some materials are printed in loose-leaf or perforated form, so that "parts" can be distributed to program participants (e.g., Christian Workers'

[25]Hayward and Burkhart, op. cit., pp. 184-88.

Service Bureau). Other publishers suggest that each person have a copy of the complete program in the quarterly guides (e.g., Scripture Press Publications, Inc. and Southern Baptist Convention). A few publishers provide separate materials for sponsors, whereas most publishers include helps for sponsors within the program ideas which go to the youth. Most published material contains ideas written each quarter by several writers, but a few publications furnish program ideas written by only one or two persons. Very few materials make any attempt to relate the evening curriculum to the Sunday school curriculum.

Program materials are structured in three ways: (1) one general topic or subject for thirteen consecutive Sundays; (2) a different subject each Sunday; or (3) the "unit" plan, in which one general subject is considered for two or three Sundays (with variety in each Sunday's program, of course). Several publishing houses follow the third approach because it provides adequate concentration on a topic of concern to youth without dulling their interest. Bowman calls these units "journeys of growth."[26]

A curriculum for youth may be established in many ways: (1) Follow a prescribed course of published materials. (2) Determine the interests of the group through an "interest finder," and use only those printed materials which match these determined interests. (3) Undertake projects which relate to the Sunday morning Bible study. (4) Use the first Sunday of each month for a "chain" of related programs, the second Sunday for another "chain," etc. (5) Allow the programs to go as they will, according to the whims and wishes of the youth. It is generally considered best to follow, to some reasonable extent, regularly released printed materials, so that there will be some order, or sequence, and so that both overlapping and overlooking of teen-agers' needs may be avoided.

No program material should be used slavishly. Adaption to local needs is always necessary. Curriculum materials must be altered to suit the present needs of the youth group. Local situations or problems may need to be introduced, some ideas extracted, and other new ideas incorporated.

Criteria for selecting curriculum materials should include the following: adequate coverage of subject matter; variety in methodology and approach; maximum pupil involvement; ease of adaptability; a wealth of creative, workable ideas; adequate sponsors' helps; a warmly evangelical tone; and loyalty to the Bible, God's infallible Word.

## LEADERSHIP

Youth sponsors have an important role in the proper functioning of their groups. They must be men and women who know Christ as Saviour,

[26]Bowman, op. cit., p. 59.

who love young people, who have a burning sense of dedication to youth, who maintain a vital, exemplary, Christlike life, and who are willing to cooperate with their total church program. They must know young people in order to work "with the grain" of youth characteristics, not against it. Youth sponsors need to strike a medium between being bystanders in the youth meeting and being dictators.

> He must play the middle course between the mother-hen baby-sitter type, who sits in the back row to keep the group from getting out of hand, and the dominating dictator type, who sits in the front and controls with an iron fist.[27]

Perhaps the best way to describe the function of youth sponsors is with the word *coach*.[28] As such, sponsors motivate, demonstrate, assist, and guide their youth in Christian activity.

It is questionable that youth sponsors should have any other heavy, equally demanding responsibility in the local church in addition to sponsoring a youth group. Though some leaders feel that they can best coordinate their youth work by having the Sunday school teachers also sponsor the evening youth groups, it seems more feasible to recruit more leaders, with no one overloaded, and with all planning done in utmost cooperation.[29]

Having two or three married couples sponsor a youth group reduces the leadership load for each adult and makes possible an adult adviser for each planning group. Trained lay leadership is essential for good youth programing. Sponsors may be trained through workshops, seminars, conferences, literature, personal consultation, and the experience of in-service training. If a church has a director of Christian education or a youth director, he should attempt to train the lay sponsors, rather than do the direct sponsoring of youth groups himself.

## PROBLEMS AND REWARDS

Youth work is not without its problems. Some of the problems to be found in the educational ministry of youth in local churches are as follows: (1) How to maintain the interest of youth over a sustained length of time. (2) How to insure good attendance, meaningful participation, and spiritual benefit from youth meetings. (3) How to meet the needs of older youth. More attention should be given to those in the college-age bracket, where major life decisions are made.[30] (4) How to recruit and train capable lay leadership for youth sponsoring. This is perhaps one

[27]Tani, *op. cit.*, p. 46.
[28]Zuck and Robertson, *op. cit.*, pp. 12-14.
[29]Bowman, *op. cit.*, p. 41.
[30]Peter P. Person, *An Introduction to Christian Education* (Grand Rapids: Baker Book House, 1958), p. 113.

of the most neglected areas in all youth work. (5) How to maintain an effective program for youth in a small church. Miller suggests combining groups from two or three smaller churches.[31] (6) How to guarantee that the evening youth group is properly correlated with the rest of the church program for youth. (7) How to guarantee that youth programing will make an impact on the lives of youth and that the truths discussed will carry over into the daily living of Christian youth.

Admittedly, youth work is work, but the rewards are numerous. It is rewarding to have a part in helping youth discover and exercise their spiritual gifts; become skilled in spiritual exercises, such as Bible study, prayer, and witnessing; grapple with the implications of God's truth for their daily lives; and dedicate themselves to Christian service.

## BIBLIOGRAPHY

Bowman, Clarice M. *Ways Youth Learn.* New York: Harper & Bros., 1952.

Brunk, Ada Zimmerman, and Metzler, Ethel Yake. *The Christian Nurture of Youth.* Scottdale, Pa.: Herald Press, 1960.

*Christian Endeavor Essentials.* Successor to and revision of *Expert Endeavor* by Amos R. Wells. (5th rev.) Columbus: International Society of Christian Endeavor, 1956.

Cummings, Oliver DeWolf. *The Youth Fellowship.* Philadelphia: Judson Press, 1956.

Griffiths, Louise B. *The Teacher and Young Teens.* St. Louis: Bethany Press, 1954.

Harner, Nevin C. *Youth Work in the Church.* New York: Abingdon-Cokesbury Press, 1942.

Hayward, Percy R., and Burkhart, Roy A. *Young People's Method in the Church.* New York: Abingdon Press, 1933.

Henry, Carl. "Pastors and Christian Education," *Christianity Today,* III (August 31, 1959), 20-21.

Lambdin, J. E. *The Baptist Training Union Manual.* (Rewritten.) Nashville: Convention Press, 1952.

Lee, E. F. *Baptist Intermediate Union Manual.* Nashville: Convention Press, 1946.

Miller, Randolph Crump. *Education for Christian Living.* Englewood Cliffs, N.J.: Prentice-Hall, Inc., 1956.

Narramore, Clyde M. *The Psychology of Counseling.* Grand Rapids: Zondervan Publishing House, 1960.

Newby, Donald O. "The Churches' Ministry to Youth," *Religious Education: A Comprehensive Survey.* New York: Abingdon Press, 1960.

[31]Randolph Crump Miller, *Education for Christian Living* (Englewood Cliffs, N.J.: Prentice-Hall, Inc., 1956), p. 309.

Person, Peter P. *An Introduction to Christian Education.* Grand Rapids: Baker Book House, 1958.

"The Plan for Common Commissions in Christian Youth Work." New York: United Christian Youth Movement, n.d.

Price, J. M., Chapman, James H., Carpenter, L. L., and Yarborough, W. Forbes. *A Survey of Religious Education.* (2nd ed.) New York: Ronald Press Co., 1959.

Santa, George F. *Youth Leader's Handbook No. 1.* Redondo Beach, Calif.: Christian Workers' Service Bureau, 1955.

Tani, Henry N. *Ventures in Youth Work.* Philadelphia: Christian Education Press, 1957.

Zuck, Roy B., and Robertson, Fern. *How to Be a Youth Sponsor.* Wheaton: Scripture Press, 1960.

## FOR FURTHER READING

Bowman, Clarice M. *Guiding Intermediates.* New York: Abingdon Press, 1943.

Cummings, Oliver DeWolf. *Guiding Youth in Christian Growth.* Philadelphia: Judson Press, 1954.

Flake, Arthur. *Baptist Young People's Union Administration.* (Rev. in 1942 by J. E. Lambdin. Rev. in 1952 by R. Maines Rawes.) Nashville: Convention Press, 1952.

Gesell, Arnold L., Ilg, Frances L., and Ames, Louise Bates. *Youth: The Years from Ten to Sixteen.* New York: Harper & Bros., 1956.

Hall, Kenneth F. *So You Work with Senior High Youth.* Anderson, Ind.: Warner Press, 1959.

Harris, Philip B. *The Director of Youth Work.* Nashville: Convention Press, n.d.

Hoglund, Gunnar, and Grabill, Virginia. *Youth Leader's Handbook.* Wheaton: Miracle Books, 1958.

Hoiland, Richard. *The Young People's Meeting.* Philadelphia: Judson Press, 1943.

Joiner, Verna. *What Teens Say.* Anderson, Ind.: Warner Press, 1962.

May, Rollo. *The Art of Counseling.* Nashville: Cokesbury Press, 1939.

Mayer, Herbert C. *Young People in Your Church.* Westwood, N.J.: Fleming H. Revell Co., 1953.

Moon, Allen. *The Christian Education of Older Youth.* New York: Abingdon Press, 1943.

Remmers, H. H., and Radler, D. H. *The American Teenager.* Indianapolis: Bobbs-Merrill Co., 1957.

Soderholm, Marjorie Elaine. *Understanding the Pupil. Part III, The Adolescent.* Grand Rapids: Baker Book House, 1957.

# Chapter 26

# VACATION BIBLE SCHOOLS

## Mavis Anderson Weidman

SUMMERTIME AND CHILDHOOD provide the church with one of its richest opportunities in the teaching and training of millions of boys and girls each year. Over the past fifty years church leaders have been taking advantage of this free time to share with youth the deepest teachings of the Christian faith in a program known as vacation Bible school, or vacation church school.

## HISTORICAL BACKGROUND

The vacation Bible school movement had its beginnings in the late nineteenth century and, like the first Sunday school, was organized to meet the needs of neglected children. As early as 1866 the First Church of Boston became interested in using the summer vacation period to provide religious instruction for children.

An organized school in Montreal, Quebec, was held in the summer of 1877, which included in its program hymns and songs, Bible reading and memory work, military drills, calisthenics, manual work and patriotic exercises.

"In the little town of Hopedale, Illinois, Mrs. D. T. Miles, the wife of the Methodist pastor in that town, established what appears to be one of the first vacation church schools in the United States."[1] Thirty-seven boys and girls attended the school in mid-May, 1894.

In the summer of 1898 a pious Baptist woman, Mrs. Eliza Hawes, grew concerned about the hordes of children idly roaming the streets of New York City and asked permission of her pastor to round up some of these

[1]Gerald E. Knoff, "Fifty Years and a Future," *International Journal of Religious Education*, XXVII (January, 1951), p. 6.

Mrs. Mavis Anderson Weidman, for the last eleven years the National Sunday School Secretary for the Christian and Missionary Alliance, recently was appointed National Director of Christian Education for the Alliance.

children and bring them into the church for some Bible teaching. This became a missionary project of the church and was called the Everyday Bible School.

In 1901 an executive secretary of the New York Baptist City Mission, Dr. Robert G. Boville, started daily vacation Bible schools which were the beginning of a movement later organized into the International Association of Daily Vacation Bible Schools. The denominations soon took over this work begun through lay leadership, and now there are more than 100,000 vacation Bible schools in existence, attended by approximately 9,000,000 pupils. Thus, after little more than a half century, Christian leaders have come to recognize the vacation Bible school as one of the most worthwhile agencies of the church for the Christian training of youth.

## OBJECTIVES

"The original purpose of vacation Bible schools was to use 'idle students' and 'idle churches' to teach 'idle children' the Word of God."[2] Today's schools have broadened their purposes and objectives considerably to include—

1. Supplementing the Sunday school's ministry. Children, if they attend regularly, receive fifty-two hours of instruction in Sunday school, as against 180 days in public school each year. The additional twenty-four hours in a concentrated block of time provided by a summer Bible school offer the Christian educator a setting for new learning experiences not possible in the Sunday school. Gene Getz has stated that "more than any other single agency of the church, the vacation Bible school offers a balanced program of Christian education—opportunities for instruction, worship, fellowship, and service."[3]

2. Providing a concentrated Bible study course with a predetermined aim. The teacher can build day by day on what has already been taught. He can observe the results of his work in the lives of his pupils and discover where additional help and instruction may be needed. There is enough time to teach, to put into practice what has been taught, to illustrate, to evaluate the learner's response, and then to set new goals.

3. Evangelizing not only those who regularly attend Sunday schools but new children of the community who perhaps never have attended Sunday school or church and who may be of other faiths.

No greater value is afforded by a vacation Bible school than that of winning boys and girls to Christ. Day after day consecrated

[2]Charles F. Treadway, "The Vacation Bible School," *Christianity Today,* IV (February 29, 1960), p. 12.
[3]Gene Getz, *The Vacation Bible School in the Local Church* (Chicago: Moody Press, 1962).

workers have opportunity to guide the child toward considering this most important decision. . . . No pressure is put upon the children, but after the claims of Christ are presented they are given opportunity publicly to declare their acceptance of Christ as Saviour.[4]

4. Building the church by its outreach in the community, the results of which are multiplied continuously as one family reaches another. The properly promoted vacation Bible school makes the church known in its locality.

## DEVELOPMENTS

MATERIALS

At first materials were very limited and the course of study was dependent upon the experience and ingenuity of the teachers. Mrs. Hawes' program lasted for two hours each day, six weeks each summer, and included worship, Bible stories, drawing, memorizing, nature study, games and the salute to the flag, and cooking and sewing for the girls. An editor for a leading publisher tells of the dramatic change in the picture today:

> Now there are nearly fifty publishers providing vacation Bible school materials. Nearly every denomination has its own course of study. The teaching techniques and general attractiveness of the present-day materials, in most cases, is up to the standard of textbooks used in public schools. Workbooks for the pupils are carefully graded to the age level. Beautiful full-color pictures, pre-cut figures, activity books and craft items are provided. Complete programs are given in detail and Bible and missionary stories are provided.[5]

SCHEDULE

Vacation Bible schools are often held as soon as public school closes for a period of two weeks, as one pastor said, "to get it over with." But more and more the trend is to wait several weeks until boys and girls have had a chance to get far enough away from school routine to be looking for an organized activity. Some churches have tried a one-week school. Regarding this practice, Rev. C. W. Denton, national secretary of Assemblies of God, states:

> Although we have experienced somewhat of a trend toward one-week vacation Bible schools, we are strongly encouraging two weeks. The first curriculum material for a vacation Bible school prepared by the Assemblies of God was designed for a three-week school. Our material now is prepared for ten sessions of three hours each. I feel decisions to shorten a vacation Bible school are usually made

[4]Treadway, op. cit., p. 12.
[5]Gladys McElroy, "The Vacation Bible School," The Defender, April, 1959.

on the amount of work for adults and not from the standpoint of the children's needs.

This is what Dr. Victor E. Cory, of Scripture Press, had to say regarding one-week and two-week vacation Bible schools:

A one-week school is definitely a step backward. Vacation Bible schools present an unprecedented opportunity of reaching the children of an entire community for Christ. Two weeks are a minimum, and there are some pastors who feel it should be at least four weeks.

### Evening Vacation Bible Schools

Evening schools have been tried with good results. Rev. Lawrence F. Swanson, secretary of the Baptist General Conference, reports:

Special Bible schools for the whole family are slowly replacing vacation Bible schools just for children in the Baptist General Conference. These schools are usually held in the evenings from 7:00 to 9:00 p.m. with departmentalized sessions. The largest attendances are often in the youth and adult ages. There is more of a concentration on Bible study with some of the other activities being dropped.

Certainly one of the advantages of an evening Bible school is that provision is made for the whole family to attend. It also helps to solve the problem of transportation.

Not all vacation Bible school leaders endorse the evening school. Rev. A. H. Orthner, pastor in the Western Canadian District of the Christian and Missionary Alliance and successful administrator of a vacation Bible school of more than a thousand pupils, makes the observation that in the evening school it is difficult to reach the nursery age. Mr. Orthner says:

The Sunday school growth potential is from the nursery children. With many of these little tots, vacation Bible school is their first connection with the church, and because they like it they will respond to an invitation to begin Sunday school.

One plan tried by Pastor Orthner which has worked very well is to have a school for nursery through primary in the morning, and junior through adult in the evening.

### Types of Vacation Schools

Various types of vacation Bible schools have been developed to meet local needs: (1) the individual church school, staffed and supported by the local church; (2) the cooperative denominational school where two or more churches of one denomination jointly plan and share in the responsibilities; (3) the interdenominational school where various denominations work together; and (4) the community school.

While there has been a growing tendency toward cooperative schools, the Southern Baptists, under the direction of Dr. Homer L. Grice, began as early as 1926 to emphasize the value of church-centered promotion.

> The individual church school is promoted, operated and financed by a single church. It has many advantages over the union school. It is likely to be more permanent. It can be built into the program of the local church as a permanent, correlated unit. It yields far greater dividends to the church that holds it, that is, it does more to enrich the life and increase the efficiency of the church that promotes it than an interdenominational school would to the same church.[6]

However, care must be taken that the local church program does not overshadow the missionary outreach of vacation Bible school to the unchurched children of the community.

## ORGANIZATION AND ADMINISTRATION

The responsibility for organizing a vacation Bible school may be committed to the board of Christian education, the advisory board, the deacons board, the elders, or the Sunday school executive committee. In any event, the vacation Bible school should be looked upon as the church's responsibility and should be considered an integral part of the total church program.

A special vacation Bible school committee should be appointed and the general superintendent of the school chosen. Upon his shoulders rests the main responsibility of the school and its corresponding success or failure. He should be a person of vision who has a burden for the community which he relates to the vacation Bible school. The other members of this committee should be selected from the top leadership of the church. The pastor, of course, is a member of this committee and in many cases he may be the superintendent. If the church has a director of Christian education, he is usually the superintendent of the vacation Bible school. The vacation Bible school committee must in turn select a leader for each department, teachers, pianists, secretaries, assistants, helpers, a janitor, and other personnel.

A good administration will begin systematic planning at least four, five or six months before opening date. Leaders can then have time to choose and prepare materials, build church interest and cooperation,

[6]Sibley C. Burnett, *Better Vacation Bible Schools* (Nashville: Convention Press, 1957), p. 11.

plan a promotional campaign, arrange facilities and equipment, and train personnel.

Where to find trained leadership for a vacation Bible school is perhaps the most vital, widespread and persistent problem to be faced. Some have sought to solve it by seeking outside help.

> The teachers are largely recruited from theological seminaries, Christian colleges, and missionary training schools. . . . When schools are sponsored by a conference, students are engaged for the entire summer session. The schools are staggered so that the team of teachers travel about like circuit riders.[7]

Although this may be a source for staff members in some denominations, a survey of one denomination reveals a continual decrease in the number of churches who use students and other outside paid personnel.

> The vacation Bible school is geared into the Sunday school from the standpoint of organization, objectives and curriculum; hence, the director of the vacation school and its teachers are largely from the Sunday school personnel.[8]

It would seem that the best solution is for each church to develop its own leaders over a long-range period. Effective forms of training consist of observation, workshops, week-end clinics, institutes, rallies, Saturday training classes, workers' conferences, and the like. Since much of the training of this volunteer staff is a matter of self-preparation, the choosing of enthusiastic, dedicated, Spirit-filled workers is a prerequisite to a well-staffed school. Helpers are usually young people who have an aptitude for arts and crafts, music, sports, or recreation.

There are many other problems to be worked out by the administration, such as: (1) scheduling the dates of the school for maximum participation of pupils and workers without conflicting with other programs on the church calendar; (2) balancing the daily program; (3) using leadership, time, space, and equipment to best advantage; (4) grading; (5) financing the school; (6) publicity and promotion; (7) reports and evaluation (to parents, to the churches, and to the denomination); and (8) planning for a series of training meetings for the staff.

It cannot be too strongly emphasized that the vacation Bible school ministry must be on the hearts and minds of the pastor and Christian education leaders early in the year. First, interest in the school must be built up throughout the church so that every member is keenly aware of its program, its objectives, and the part he can have in making the

[7]Peter P. Person, *Introduction to Christian Education* (Grand Rapids: Baker Book House, 1959), p. 147.
[8]Harold C. Mason, *The Teaching Task of the Local Church* (Winona, Ind: Light and Life Press, 1960), p. 51.

school known throughout the community. The promotion of vacation Bible school should not be a last-minute affair but a gradual acceleration of interest and participation which involves the whole church. In the early part of the year a report could be given concerning the concrete gains in Sunday school from vacation Bible school contacts made the previous summer. Dates for the new school should be announced as early as possible. After the director and general committee are appointed, a more concentrated promotional campaign can be undertaken in the form of posters, special announcements, newspaper ads, a parade, etc. Systematic announcements in the bulletin and from the pulpit will keep members informed and conscious of the needs and their responsibility to the school.

Another vital reason for early planning is the necessity of prayer support. The work can have no eternal value unless it is totally committed to God in its every aspect. A special prayer meeting series should be planned that will make it possible for every member to support the work in this way.

These two elements—prayer and promotion—are necessary to realize the potential of the school and to capitalize on the effort put into the work.

## CHOOSING THE CURRICULUM

The material to be selected should be judged objectively on the basis of Bible content, type of experiences it provides, evangelism, stewardship, service, fellowship, and worship.

Curriculum should be thought of as not just a text but "a planned block of guided experiences that are directed toward reaching a goal." The needs of the pupils should be the primary factor in choosing the text—particular needs as well as basic needs. It is important to discover what the pupils have been studying in Sunday school before selecting the course. Although vacation Bible school is a means of missionary outreach, its program and curriculum should be planned around the existing core of pupils to whom the church ministers.

## METHODS

Education and psychology affirm that a pupil learns best when he has a chance to practice; that growth comes as he has opportunity to develop his own talents and potential abilities; that a teacher cannot give learning to a pupil, for he learns only by his own activity and to the degree to which he wholeheartedly participates.

"Any teacher's manual can become a taskmaster or a tool, according to the skill of the teacher. Using a text creatively is a part of good teaching."[9] Many teachers need help to get out of the educational rut and learn to *use* materials rather than to be a slave to the materials.

In training sessions teachers should be encouraged to try methods that take advantage of the concentrated blocks of time; of the relaxed atmosphere of the vacation school as compared with the more confining Sunday school atmosphere; of the value of a well-balanced program. They should be reminded that the method is the means to an end *only*. It is an instrument in the hands of the teacher to accomplish his purpose. No teacher will be able to use every method equally well; however, the choice is wide and many a teacher will discover a new joy in teaching when he finds a live, reacting pupil at the other end of his effort. All methods cannot be outlined here but a few which employ the "learn by doing" principle are mentioned:

*Creative writing.* Children love to write poems, stories, prayers, choruses. All of these give insight into the child's spiritual understanding.

*Art.* Some pupils are able to express themselves through drawing. Supply crayons, chalk, art paper, modeling clay, etc., for these "artists."

*Dramatization.* Some will like to act out the story, use their imagination and pretend to be a certain character. Puppets may also be used in dramatizing the story.

*Newspaper.* The junior high group are particularly interested in facts and like to report things, to set up the information in orderly form and make it available to others.

*Field trips.* When planned in relation to the lesson, field trips can be a means of broadening and strengthening the pupil's understanding of a particular lesson.

## SPECIAL EVENTS

Most vacation Bible schools conclude with a program to which parents and friends are invited. The boys and girls under the guidance of their teachers plan their part in this program and exhibit their handcraft.

Other ways of sharing experiences can be provided which will build on the work accomplished during the school days. In one school the fourth, fifth and sixth graders invited the primary group to be their special guests while they dramatized a story that Jesus taught. The primaries were greeted in the hall by their hosts and ushered to the best front-row seats. Dried raisins were the only refreshment and were given out as part of the play. To the primaries this was a special event of vacation school, and it was even more special to the group who entertained them. In another school nursery mothers were invited to a tea

[9]Ruth Elizabeth Murphy, "The Vacation Church School," *Orientation in Religious Education*, ed. by Philip Henry Lotz (New York: Abingdon-Cokesbury Press, 1950), p. 269.

in the afternoon at which teachers and children shared with the mothers the work of the department.

During vacation Bible school many boys and girls experience the most important special event that life can hold for them when they receive Jesus Christ as their personal Saviour and commit their lives to Him. An opportunity should be given them to express their new faith publicly in the vacation school or in an opening service of their particular department of the Sunday school.

## FOLLOW-UP

As much as the days, months and weeks previous to vacation Bible school determine the success of the school, in the same measure that which is done to conserve the results in the weeks that follow the sessions will determine the worth of the entire effort. This has been a weak spot in administration and it is for this reason that much of the value of vacation Bible school is not as permanent as it could be if greater emphasis were placed on planning for follow-up.

The worker can play an important role in follow-up as an analyst. For this purpose a comprehensive questionnaire should be prepared. Every phase of the program, both in its adequacies and inadequacies, is included for the evaluation. The questionnaire should be sent to the workers immediately after the close of the school, with an appropriate letter of appreciation and an invitation to attend the evaluation meeting.

As an integral part of the total church educational program the work accomplished in vacation Bible school should be made a matter of record for both church and denomination. The report may be brief but should include: dates of the school, enrollment and average attendance, number of teachers and officers, course of study, those who attended from other churches, those who were unchurched, and any other vital statistical information. Charts and graphs interpreting the data will help to evaluate the effectiveness of publicity, of geographical outreach, of the wisdom of providing transportation, and of relative costs.

Future planning will be simplified if leadership personnel records are kept. These include leadership responsibilities, special talents, achievements, training and routine information as to address and phone number. This will also be used by the board of Christian education as a source of leadership in the total program of the church. Guidance in planning the budget for next year will be available if there are itemized lists of the cost of the school, itemized lists of sources, of finances, and the cost of the school per pupil. Time and money will be saved the next year if a public relations folder has been compiled with publicity items, newspaper clippings, announcements, posters, and a file of leftover materials.

All these records will be exceedingly helpful, but of most vital concern should be the follow-up of persons. Elsie Miller Butt brings this out forcibly:

> Careful attention to records and reports grows out of our concern for persons. It is strange indeed to see a church school keep strict account of money while neglecting to account for persons. The Christian fellowship and ongoing program of the church are available privileges, but the boys and girls and their parents may need help in becoming vitally interested. Careful records not only help prevent loss of persons to the Christian fellowship but conserve and develop the talents and achievements of people.[10]

This concern for persons will be reflected in the way in which the unchurched are planned for in the follow-up work. All new contacts should be added to the prospect Sunday school records. Information should be as complete and helpful to the visitor as possible. If the school has been the missionary outreach in the community that it should be, many unchurched boys and girls will have heard the way of salvation for the first time. The names of new converts should be recorded separately and plans made to see that they have all the special care and nurture that can be given them as new-born babes in Christ. A personal letter should be sent to each one encouraging him in his new-found faith and paving the way for a visit to the home. If the child attends another church, extra care should be given to see that he has a Bible and knows how to use it. His pastor should be informed of his decision for Christ and his parents encouraged to help him grow in the Christian faith.

The plans for follow-up should include letters to the parents. The first letter is mailed right after the close of the school to thank the parents for sending their children to the school. A further letter includes a cordial invitation to them to attend the Sunday school if they are not already members elsewhere.

The achievements of the vacation school can be conserved by planning a vacation Bible school Sunday in Sunday school in the early fall. This provides an opportunity for those who missed the school because of summer activities to share in what has been accomplished; for those who attended the school to recall the learning experiences and to give testimony of faith in Christ; and for leaders to relate the work of the vacation school to the Sunday school.

Adequate follow-up procedures help to correlate the work of the school with other educational agencies of the church and provide the means for the improvements needed in long-range planning.

[10]Elsie Miller Butt, *The Vacation School in Christian Education* (New York: Abingdon Press, 1957), p. 147.

## BASIC APPROACH TO FUTURE VBS PLANNING

The development of vacation Bible school in the educational program of the church will probably emerge from the following:

1. *Scheduling.* Instead of scheduling a vacation Bible school because "we have always had it," or selecting a time because "we always have ours early in the summer so we can get it over with," a church will study and evaluate the possibility of an evening vacation Bible school if it best meets the needs of the constituency; it will study the summer activities schedules of the community and of the majority of the church families to discover whether early summer or mid-August would reach the largest number.

2. *Programing.* More and more there is less emphasis on "VBS for boys and girls" and a stronger approach to the possibilities of involving the whole family in planning for both curriculum and leadership.

3. *Correlation with the total educational work of the church.* Although some attempt is now being made to choose the vacation Bible school curriculum with the Sunday school course of study in mind, there is very little mutual support between the various agencies of the church. This is coming to the attention of leaders and there will be more study given to the contribution being made through the total educational work of the church to the spiritual growth of individuals.

4. *Holding the interest of teen-agers.* Each year it becomes increasingly difficult to keep young people coming to vacation Bible school. A number of legitimate reasons can be given: they find summer jobs; parents do not urge them to go as much as they do the younger children who are underfoot; the young people feel that for the most part the program is for "kids"; ringleaders of the group may influence still others to stay away. To counteract these tendencies church leaders will consider the possibility of either an evening family school or, as has proved very satisfactory, a school in the morning for children and an evening school for teen-agers and adults.

To further stimulate young people to a realization that they are needed, the school can use those who are available as helpers in the children's school in the morning. Where the school is combined, care will be taken not to mix the program and activities of the upper graders with that of the children. Planning for youth will demand more and more attention in the total educational program of the church.

### BIBLIOGRAPHY

Burnett, Sibley C. *Better Vacation Bible Schools.* Nashville: Convention Press, 1957.

Butt, Elsie Miller. *The Vacation School in Christian Education.* New York: Abingdon Press, 1957.

Getz, Gene A. *The Vacation Bible School in the Local Church.* Chicago: Moody Press, 1962.

Knoff, Gerald E. "Fifty Years and a Future," *International Journal of Religious Education,* XXVII (January, 1951).

Mason, Harold C. *Abiding Values in Christian Education.* Westwood, N.J.: Fleming H. Revell Co., 1955.

———. *The Teaching Task of the Local Church.* Winona Lake, Ind.: Light and Life Press, 1960.

McElroy, Gladys. "The Vacation Bible School," *The Defender* (April, 1959).

Murphy, Ruth Elizabeth. "The Vacation Church School," *Orientation in Religious Education,* Philip Henry Lotz (ed.). New York: Abingdon-Cokesbury Press, 1950.

Person, Peter P. *Introduction to Christian Education.* Grand Rapids: Baker Book House, 1959.

Treadway, Charles F. "The Vacation Bible School," *Christianity Today,* IV (February 29, 1960).

## FOR FURTHER READING

Blair, W. Dyer. *The New Vacation Church School.* New York: Harper & Bros., 1939.

Colina, Tessa. *How to Conduct a Vacation Bible School.* Cincinnati: Standard Publishing Company, 1954.

Hall, Arlene S. *Your Church School.* Anderson, Ind.: Warner Press, 1957.

Latham, Mary E. *Vacation Bible School, What, Why, and How.* Kansas City: Beacon Hill Press, 1954.

LeBar, Lois E. *Education That is Christian.* Westwood, N.J.: Fleming H. Revell Co., 1958.

Ristine, Ethel. *The Vacation Church School.* New York: Abingdon-Cokesbury Press, 1947.

*Chapter 27*

# RECREATION

## Marion L. Jacobsen

FOR CENTURIES, sober-minded people—including Christians—looked upon play as evil. Whatever was entertaining, they reasoned, *must* be sinful. This Puritanical condemnation, however, gradually gave way to acceptance of play as a more or less necessary fleshly indulgence.

At different times and by different groups, recreation has been variously defined as any pleasant activity done for its own sake without any future benefit in view; the aimless expenditure of exuberant energy; a safety valve or outlet for excess vitality or accumulated tensions; a means of self-expression, especially when essential elements in life experience are lacking; and a re-creation in the sense that it rests, relaxes, and refurnishes for the business of life.

Carpenter declares that play "must be thought of primarily as an educational method rather than as recreation."[1] Tully summarizes the development of the concept of play: first sinful, then tolerated as a normal activity, and more recently used as a tool of learning and development.[2]

Today play is everywhere recognized not only as a legitimate activity but as an important factor in moral as well as physical and social development. Yet some Christian groups have been slow to assign recreation the significant place it deserves in their programs, and condone it primarily because all children play and most adults need recreation. Much present opposition or indifference grows out of a lack of a proper conception of the worthwhile objectives of recreation in the field of Christian education.

[1]L. L. Carpenter and associates, "Social-Recreational Agencies," *Survey of Religious Education* (New York: Ronald Press Co., 1940), p. 274.
[2]Bob Tully, "Play and Recreation," ed. by Philip H. Lotz, *Orientation in Religious Education* (Nashville: Cokesbury Press, 1950), p. 173.

Marion L. Jacobsen, B.A., is a housewife and author living in Wheaton, Illinois.

In itself, play is a potent teaching-learning method. Indirectly, it is a means of bringing and keeping people within reach of direct Christian training.

If Christian education is concerned merely with the imparting of religious information, recreation has little to contribute. But the goals of Christian education in the home, the Sunday school, and the church are to bring individuals into vital relationship with Jesus Christ, and to build a personality pattern and lead to life investment within a framework of Christian concepts and ideals.[3] Secular educators utilize recreation in the development of personality and character. Christian educators, because their aims are distinctively spiritual, will find it necessary to adapt their use of recreation accordingly.

## RELATION OF RECREATION TO SPECIFIC CHRISTIAN EDUCATION GOALS

In Christian education, recreation may not be thought of primarily as a means of enlistment and enlargement.[4] This value of play, however, is of some importance in the recreation program of the church, and no apology need be made for it. An effective program of social activities plays a significant part in increasing church attendance and attracting outsiders to the church and its affiliated organizations. Whether the play activity be a sand table in the beginner department or a fish-fry for teenagers, recreation helps hold the interest of people who are already attending services or are enrolled in classes. This may be a lesser function of a recreation program, but it helps to keep the spiritually immature within reach of further Christian instruction. No teacher can give the Word of God to class members who are not present, and a good social program helps to keep them coming until they find higher motives for attendance.

A good recreation program is also a proved tool for reaching those who are as yet not affiliated with the church or its organizations. They may not be interested in worship, Bible study, or Christian service, yet they will respond to the appeal of a pleasant experience of fellowship or creative leisure-time activity. Such social contacts bring these needy individuals within range of the more directly spiritual associations and ministries of the church, and help to keep them coming until they have made a personal response to the appeal of the gospel.

This goal of reaching the unreached should have a direct bearing on the kind and caliber of recreational program the church sponsors. Tactless, unintelligent, poorly focused, line-of-least-resistance planning will never fulfill this high spiritual purpose.

Exploiting the individual's desire for fun and fellowship as an incentive

[3]*Ibid.*
[4]Carpenter, *op. cit.*, p. 275.

for his attending church-sponsored activities is no more unworthy than the missionary's offer to teach the savage to read or farm or care for his sick, or the rescue mission's offer of food and shelter to human derelicts on the city streets. In each case the motive is not only to minister to an individual's lesser needs, but to find a point of contact that will facilitate the meeting of his deeper need of Christ and the Word of God.

A recreation program undeniably ministers in many different ways to an individual's physical, social, and emotional needs. Its most valuable function in the hands of Christian agencies, however, lies in the contact it may create and maintain between an individual and the person or organization that can minister to his essential spiritual need.

Once the learner has been brought into contact with one who is able to teach him the things of God (and this may well have been facilitated by a recreational event), play further serves this ministry by breaking down the barriers that keep people apart. The teacher must know the needs of his pupil, and only by intimate personal contact can he gain this knowledge. Home visitation is good, but playing baseball together or sharing a cookout may be even better. Teacher and learner must find their way across the no-man's land of age difference and unfamiliarity to a point of facile communication. There the learner's need will be revealed, and the teacher—either in private counseling or group study—may present Christ as the meeting of that need. Sutton says:

> The teacher who finds out the type of play activity in which the child is most interested, who manifests an interest in this game, and if possible takes part in leading the child into mastery of the sport, has gained an open sesame into the heart and life of the child that will enable him to direct the moral forces that go to build the right kind of character.[5]

In the process of a spiritual education of his own child, playing together helps a parent bridge the gap created by age difference and dissimilarity of experience.

Play, then, is more than a method of teaching—it helps produce the climate for all kinds of Christian learning.

Play is one of the Christian educator's best methods for molding character. "Man's conduct is more dependent on his feelings than upon his thought,"[6] says Tully. Play arouses emotions—enthusiasm, ambition, loyalty, cooperation—and so is a strong ally to the learning process. These feelings create attitudes which, in turn, build character. The effective teacher will not fail to utilize this method of developing character—that part of personality that involves moral qualities.

[5]Willis A. Sutton, "Character Education Through Play," *Playground and Recreation*, XXIV (February, 1931), p. 592.
[6]Tully, *op. cit.*, p. 173.

In play, character is built by imitation, suggestion, and instruction.[7] The playmate will imitate the example of the play leader, or will respond to suggestion and counseling from one whom he admires, respects, and enjoys. Instruction is most effective when associated with the happy or impressive activities that play can provide.

Recreation under adequate leadership will develop wholesome social qualities and consideration for others—courtesy, kindness, generosity, friendliness, unselfishness—characteristics so conspicuously lacking among the self-seekers and opportunists of our day.

Only the home exerts a greater influence over individual conduct than the play group. Yet some of the more costly disciplines of life may be better learned on the playground than at mother's knee—courage, tolerance, democracy, fair play, self-control, perseverance, determination, self-sacrifice, forgiveness. When through play we teach respect for the rights of others, how to get along happily with people, and the importance of obeying rules, we are laying important foundations for good citizenship, healthy world-mindedness, dedication to Christian living, and service.

Through well-chosen recreational activities, the teacher may help develop in the group sturdy qualities essential to progress and success—self-reliance (rightly related to dependence upon God), ingenuity, ambition, loyalty, aggressiveness, thoroughness, enthusiasm, and reliability. Cooperative endeavor through group interaction, recognition of the individual's contribution to the group, development of leadership ability—all these may be vigorously learned on the playground.

Carpenter tells us that play "is not only a possible but inevitable factor in the formation of character," and goes so far as to say that "character is not only tested by play, but largely made during play."[8] Luther H. Gulick, the American philosopher for the play movement, adds, "If you want to know what a child is, study his play; if you want to affect what he will be, direct the form of his play."[9]

The church is primarily concerned with the individual's spiritual need. It is not indifferent, however, to other personal needs—physical, economic, and social. Good medical care, for example, is important to the individual. Usually the church does not undertake to supply it; but in times of emergency, or in parts of the world where medical care is not otherwise available, Christian agencies may decide to enter this field. They may play a large part in meeting the need, legitimately using such an auxiliary ministry to open a door for the presentation of the gospel.

Some people may object that the need of the individual for recreation is not the concern of the church. Yet where this need is unmet, or where

[7] Ibid.
[8] Carpenter, op. cit., p. 263.
[9] Ibid.

the right kind of recreation is not available, and insofar as the church is equipped to undertake the responsibility, a wisely-conceived program of leisure-time activity is in order. Such a program may augment, rather than conflict with, the other goals of Christian education. However, it is important that the fellowship aspect of recreation not be allowed to eclipse the large contribution play may make in achieving distinctly spiritual goals.

Christians are finding recreational facilities outside the church increasingly distasteful, unprofitable, and often harmful. Increasing responsibility therefore falls upon the church to help meet the social need of its people. Social gatherings in the home include only a select group and cannot be depended on to supply the social need of every member of the church family.

For people of all ages, it is true that they can't be human in social isolation. Children need the fellowship and individual friendship of other children. Young people are in special need of Christian social contacts. In their transition from dependence upon the home to independence sufficient for establishing homes of their own, they are increasingly influenced by friends rather than by family. Out of such casual contacts the life partner is often chosen.

Christian fellowship and friends figure largely in the spiritual as well as social development of adults of all ages. Believers too are largely influenced by their associates. Attendance at worship and teaching sessions of the church does not adequately meet this need and should be augmented by social gatherings of church groups. Even the first-century Christians met for "love-feasts," which were not synonymous with the observance of the Lord's Supper.

Trends in modern society have accentuated the need for compensating activities in the recreational area. Industrialization with its assembly-line techniques tends to rob the individual of such essential elements of experience as adventure (new experiences), liberty to choose goals, sense of achievement, social acceptance, status, growth, and inner joy. All of these may be experienced in varying degree in natural play and in creative use of leisure.

The use of leisure is receiving increasing attention today. Smaller families, shorter working hours, and improved mechanical equipment for household tasks have combined to give people more free time than ever before. A community of 10,000 people has about 25 million hours of leisure per year. Although some of this time may be justifiably spent in undirected activity, intelligent, adequate planning of recreational opportunities is warranted. The Christian educator in the home, church, or school cannot ignore this vast potential for personality and character building.

Everyone needs the relaxation and renewal play provides. Even mature Christians do not outgrow their need for recreation any more than they outgrow their need for food and sleep. Christian workers especially, in their devoted service to Christ, often have to learn that they cannot afford to burn the candle at both ends—omitting rest, vacations, and other forms of recreation.

The cost of a recreational program is justified by the large contribution it makes to high spiritual goals, to personal development, to the meeting of human need, and to the growth and effectiveness of the church. Recreational activities deserve adequate allocation of funds in the budget of the church and its subsidiary organizations. However, participants may sometimes be asked to pay their own way in church social activities, and parents should be willing to contribute to play projects for their children. Materials and refreshments may be brought as a donation, and the Christian worker may well invest some of his own benevolent moneys directly in the social expense of the group he leads. Sunday schools may permit an adult class to withhold a percentage of its weekly offerings for class promotional purposes, which would include social activities.

## LEADERSHIP

The fruitfulness of play in Christian education depends largely on proper supervision. Without adequate leadership, the character-building value of recreation will be purely accidental, its function in enlargement uncertain, and its ministry to personal need limited.

Parents must take the initiative in providing planned play for the family, teachers and parents for the school. In the church, recreation often depends on volunteer leadership—the director or sponsor of a youth group, the teacher or social chairman of a Sunday school class or other subsidiary organization. Supervision of recreation activities may be included in the appointed duties of an assistant pastor, youth worker, or Christian education director employed by the church. Few churches hire a full-time director of recreation, though such leadership in a large church could have a richly productive ministry.

The play leader should be a cheerful, friendly individual who enjoys life and people. For spiritual effectiveness, he should be a Christian who has the kind of personality that "is born of a light that shines within, and which shows itself on the outside in a radiant face, a lively enthusiastic voice, and a buoyant spirit."[10] He must have an understanding of the

[10]Marion Jacobsen, *Good Times for God's People* (Grand Rapids: Zondervan Publishing House, 1952), p. 136.

deep-seated feelings of sorrow, sympathy, love, hate, fear, anger, loyalty, and other factors which underlie conduct.

Of crucial importance is the leader's need to know the high spiritual goals of recreation in Christian education. The participant may be interested in recreation merely as an end, but the leader views it both as an end and as a means.[11] The Christian education program is no less than a method by which individuals are reached for Christ and developed to be like Christ. Such goals give spiritual quality and incentive to the leader's social planning.

Even the professional recreation expert may need training in distinctly Christian goals and methods of play. Denominational or interdenominational workers' conferences or recreation institutes may offer such instruction. Christian camps and colleges with a truly Christian emphasis also offer suitable training courses. Certainly every church library should contain leadership training material in the field of recreation.

Only genuine devotion to Christ will enable the play leader to discharge his responsibility with a fine sense of the spiritual value of his work. In this area, as in other fields of Christian service, he will depend on the enabling of the Spirit of God and will know how to pray over the most practical matters. Because he renders this service "heartily, as to the Lord, and not unto men" (Col. 3:23), he will delight in it even when men fail properly to appreciate his efforts.

The work of the church recreational director, chairman, or committee should include:

1. Becoming thoroughly familiar with local recreation needs, interests, and available personnel and facilities.

2. Making a broad study of all types of play activities, especially those that go beyond the usual recreation routines.

3. Coordinating the social activities of the church and affiliated organizations. A posted official calendar schedule in the church office is a practical arrangement.

4. Considering the specific aims in view for each organization, and determining what type of recreational program will achieve those aims.

5. Leading all-church social activities, such as the annual Sunday school picnic and the watch-night service social hour.

6. Training recreation workers and teachers, emphasizing the spiritual goals of social activities and the use of play techniques in teaching.

7. Setting up a supply of source materials in the church library or a special recreation library; providing equipment for supervised play.

8. Arranging for recreation leaders to attend recreation institutes, including help with expenses where needed.

[11]*Recreation and the Church* (New York: National Recreation Association), p. 28.

9. Considering and working out the financing of recreational activities.

10. Carefully evaluating the success of each play activity or recreation program in the light of its objectives.

Knowledge of the characteristics of the age group involved is also essential to effective leadership. This involves familiarity with the attention span, physical capabilities and limits, special interests, preference for large- or small-group play, for more or less strenuous activity, for indoor or outdoor fun, at each age level. Juniors, for example, play better in smaller groups, while intermediates and seniors enjoy larger groups and a wider range of social activities.

In all the actual process of play, be it games, sports, parties, or hobbies, communication between the leader and those who participate is essential to the process of Christian education. The leader must by example, suggestion, or instruction let the players know what is acceptable conduct and what is not. This he does by recognition and praise, and also by disapproval and admonition. Without preaching, the leader must point out the character-influencing effect of certain acts and attitudes and their immediate and long-range results; he must show that what we do determines, to a large extent, what we will be.

Only in this way can the leader develop, in those he directs, such moral qualities and Christian graces as honesty, courtesy, unselfishness, kindness, fairness, generosity, obedience, loyalty, and cooperation.

Rules must be enforced promptly and privileges given without partiality. During play, the alert leader will find frequent opportunity for personal counseling, prompted by the revealing conduct and attitudes of those he directs on the playground.

Executive leadership is important in the recreational leader—the ability to enlist, organize, and direct others in the recreation program. However, sharing and delegating responsibility must be accompanied by careful follow-up on the part of the leader. He must make sure that delegated responsibilities are promptly and thoroughly discharged.

Originality is also a desirable and potent quality in a recreation director. However, one not endowed by nature with fresh ideas and ingenious methods can compensate largely for his lack by knowing where to look for them and making it his business to find them.

## HOW TO PLAN

The goals of a recreation program determine the direction of recreation planning. These objectives are the key not only in planning what to do but, later on, in evaluating what has been done. Much social activity in Christian circles, though harmless, is fruitless because it was not planned with definite, worthy objectives in view.

More than 250 years ago Theophilus Dorrington, rector of Wittersham in Kent, wrote his *Regulations of Play.* One of the principles he laid down was the importance of having better reasons for play than merely having fun, and the importance of not forgetting these goals during play.

Long-range planning is essential. The all-over program of an organization's recreation activities should be laid out a year in advance, determining at least the general character of each event. The season of the year will suggest the advisability of indoor or outdoor functions.

An annual banquet is usually best scheduled for the fall months. Not only is there prospect of larger attendance, but an outstandingly successful social event at the beginning of the organizational year provides promotional impetus for the months that follow. When an annual dinner takes place in the spring it makes a glorious climax, but much of its promotional value is lost in the summer slump that often follows.

The recreation chairman or supervisor may do most of the general planning himself, and delegate the working out of details to others. Or he may delegate the planning itself, providing he gives his assistants thorough supervision.

An individual or a group may be given responsibility for planning or working out details for one particular social event. It is often easier to get workers to assume responsibility for a single recreational activity than to take over the entire program of the year. Responsibility for the single function may also be shared with others, some planning for the entertainment or games, others planning decorations, food, or transportation.

A spirit of adventure and energetic consecration will never follow the line of least resistance in recreational planning. Ambitious, though not necessarily elaborate, plans are more effective in reaching the goals of play than those that are indifferent and mediocre. Whatever is involved, whether a simple Sunday morning breakfast for the men of a Sunday school class or an extensive program of sports for a summer camp, should be well done in every detail. Each event should, in its own way, be outstanding. Slipshod planning has rendered many a recreational project completely fruitless.

General party planning is concerned with a theme for the occasion as well as with the time, place, and participants. The theme is a matter of vital importance. It immediately gives character to the whole affair, and it eases the planning of invitations, publicity, games, decorations, and refreshments.

Detailed planning should include some pre-party activity to put first-comers at ease; games that function as mixers, enabling guests to learn each other's names; other activities that can be adjusted to fill the period allotted to play; an effective climax to complete the program; and refreshments suited in some way to the theme of the occasion so as to be an integral part of the whole.

The recreational program is not to be thought of as a duplicate of the spiritual preaching and teaching ministry of the church, but rather as augmenting that ministry. For this reason, recreational planning should be primarily geared to fun and fellowship rather than to direct instruction. However, it is easy to lead the group through its experience of fellowship and its feeling of unity into a brief period of inspirational experience with God.

A deft devotional touch, suited to the situation or theme of the occasion, is important; but no one should be allowed to turn a party or picnic into a prayer meeting. Usually the social event should be designed to attract the unspiritual participant to the group and its basic program of essentially spiritual activity, rather than to convert him on the spot.

Variety of activity is essential to successful recreational planning. This is as true of a single game party as of the play program for a series of vacation Bible school sessions. A change of pace stimulates interest and attendance and their spiritually significant by-products. Therefore effective recreational programing will utilize diverse forms of play—sandbox, water sports, progressive dinner, sight-seeing trip, week-end discussion retreat.

The successful play leader must have access to fresh, stimulating ideas for recreational planning—either his own or someone else's. Workers' conferences, at least on the interdenominational level, should occasionally offer courses in Christian recreation. Bible institutes and Christian colleges usually include such studies in their curriculums.

Most public libraries offer a good selection of recreation material, and the alert leader will find in newspapers and magazines, on radio and television valuable help regarding what to plan. Certainly every church library should contain volumes on such recreation activities as games, crafts, and camping.

A card file or loose-leaf notebook of ideas for camp activities, party themes and favors, mixers and ice-breakers, games, outdoor activities, decorations, refreshments, stunts, songs, hobbies, crafts can be the leader's greatest material asset. Here he has access to the cream of his own recreational training and experience, as well as to the tried methods of others. It is unwise to depend upon memory to reproduce the details of a game, stunt, or party.

Proper activity balance is important in recreation planning. Whether the project in hand involves an extended series of play periods or one single session, good balance must be kept between different forms of activity—indoor and outdoor, active and quiet, physical and mental, those in which all participate and those in which some are spectators.

Thorough recreation planning must also give careful attention to such details as making proper reservation of the facilities to be used, arranging good publicity for social activities, starting and ending the play program promptly according to schedule, and attending to financial matters involved in play projects.

## RECREATION PROGRAMING

A successful recreation program involves not only proper goals, adequate leadership, and careful planning, but also right content. The type of activity used will be determined by the nature of the goals in view.

If a Sunday school teacher wants to get to know the members of his class better, he may invite them by ones and twos, or as a group, to his home for dinner or a snack. Or he may schedule an overnight hike or cookout. If a scout leader discovers need for status and acceptance in one of his boys, he may schedule a recreational activity that will give the lad an opportunity to do what he does best; for instance, a session devoted to stamp collecting, music, or tennis.

It is said that only 10 per cent of possible play activities are utilized in 90 per cent of Christian recreation programing. This fact challenges the Christian play leader to familiarize himself with *all* recreation program elements rather than confine himself to the more stereotyped forms of play.

Hobbies, which may be promoted by a Christian organization but are carried on largely at home, give opportunity for creativeness. The creative arts, especially drama and music, may be included among the Christian educator's tools. Group play reading, acting out Bible stories, the spontaneous acting out of the end of a partly told story, action songs and rhythm bands—all can be used to promote learning. The aim should be fun and the joy of creating, not perfection.

Christian education in the home will make use of games, sports, trips, hobbies, crafts, and such devices as a weekly family night, to build family unity and develop right attitudes and moral choices.

The Christian school will utilize available gymnasium and playground facilities; will schedule parties, dramatics, and outings; and will organize clubs to reinforce its spiritual training.

Play is a strong partner of the church in Sunday or weekday classes, youth groups, choirs, social affairs, and agency clubs such as Scouts or Boys' Brigade, vacation Bible schools, camps, and conferences.

Simple social events may be strategically important. For example, a morning coffee for cradle roll mothers, held at the church where there are adequate nursery facilities, will serve to bring mothers who do not attend church services into fruitful contact with the church and the department superintendent.

Reading and discussion groups, talent or fun programs, breakfasts, luncheons, dinners, hikes, camping, a library for recreational reading, films, are all both pleasant and profitable. A church family night, including the evening meal, promotes fellowship and, by careful coordination of activities, relieves members of the congregation of coming to the church for committee and study sessions several nights a week.

Carpenter says, "There are great moral and spiritual values to a good old-fashioned Sunday school picnic."[12] This is true only when the church families who attend are kept more or less close together geographically and when the outing is carefully planned to the smallest detail.

Evangelicals, stressing as they do the highest spiritual objectives in Christian education, should excel in the energetic and intelligent application of contemporary recreation techniques in the home, the school, and the church. Though in the past play may have been merely tolerated as a sort of concession to the flesh, let it be recognized and employed today as a proper and fruitful method of Christian education.

## BIBLIOGRAPHY

Hutchinson, J. L. *Principles of Recreation*. New York: A. S. Barnes and Co., 1951.

Jacks, L. P. *Education Through Recreation*. New York: Harper & Bros., 1932.

Lotz, Philip H. (ed.). *Orientation in Religious Education*. Nashville: Abingdon-Cokesbury Press, 1950.

Mitchell, Elmer D., and Mason, Bernard S. *Theory of Play*. New York: A. S. Barnes and Co., 1934.

Neumeyer, M. H. *Leisure and Recreation*. New York: A. S. Barnes and Co., 1936.

Price, John Milburn, Chapman, James H., Tibbs, A. E., and Carpenter, L. L. *Survey of Religious Education*. New York: Thomas Nelson & Sons, 1959.

*Recreation and the Church*. New York: National Recreation Association.

*Recreation for Community Living*. Chicago: Athletic Institute, 1952.

Slavson, S. R. *Recreation and the Total Personality*. New York: Association Press, 1949.

Sutton, Willis A. "Character Education Through Play," *Playground and Recreation*, XXIV (February, 1931).

[12]Carpenter, *op. cit.*, p. 269.

Taylor, Marvin J. (ed.). *Religious Education*. Nashville: Abingdon Press, 1960.

## BOOKS ON RECREATIONAL PLANNING

Anderson, K., and Carlson, M. *Games for All Occasions*. Grand Rapids: Zondervan Publishing House, 1951.

Eisenberg, Helen. *The Omnibus of Fun*. New York: Association Press, 1956.

Harbin, E. O. *Fun Encyclopedia*. Nashville: Cokesbury Press, 1940.

———. *Games of Many Nations*. Nashville: Abingdon Press, 1954.

———. *Gay Parties for All Occasions*. Nashville: Abingdon Press, 1950.

Jacobsen, Marion L. *Good Times for God's People*. Grand Rapids: Zondervan Publishing House, 1952.

Jones, Anna May. *Leisure Time Education*. New York: Harper & Bros., 1946.

Macfarlan, Allan A. *New Games for 'Tween-agers*. New York: Association Press, 1958.

Royal, Claudia. *Storytelling*. Nashville: Broadman Press, 1956.

Smith, C. F. *Games and Recreational Methods*. New York: Dodd, Mead and Co., 1947.

*Chapter 28*

# CAMPING AND CONFERENCES

## Robert K. Bower

### INTRODUCTION

C AMPING IS RAPIDLY BECOMING one of the major facets of the church's
Christian education program. Young people and adults are finding
that camp experiences can be richly rewarding, despite the lack of modern conveniences at many camp grounds. Church camps give opportunity
for the spiritual development of the individual. In properly arranged programs, there are times reserved for the camper to read his Bible and to
commune with God. If the camper has not previously committed his life
to Jesus Christ as his Saviour, if he has never been challenged to "take
up his cross and follow Jesus," the opportunities afforded by a church
camp may well bring these matters into sharp focus so that the camper
will make decisions which will affect his life for time and eternity.

In the event that a board or director of camping has been assigned the
responsibility of planning a church camp (which may be a weekend or
an entire summer in length), there are two general objectives to be considered, one more important than the other. The supreme objective for
a church-related camp should always be the spiritual growth of the
camper. Nothing should supersede this. The second and subordinate objective, but nevertheless an important and necessary one, is that of gaining
experiences in outdoor living.

There may also be other objectives more specific in nature which can
serve as guidelines for the group or the person planning the camp. For
example, under the general objective of the spiritual development of the
individual, there will be such aims as accepting Jesus Christ as Saviour,
learning more about the Bible, learning how to pray, and learning how to

Robert K. Bower, Ph.D., is professor of Christian Education at Fuller Theological Seminary, Pasadena, California.

apply Biblical principles to everyday living. Then, too, there will be specific objectives related to camping itself. Learning how to swim, discovering the rules for hiking, developing skill in baseball, volleyball, tennis, and other sports, are examples of specific camping objectives.

There is no need, however, to divide a camping program into (1) spiritual activities and (2) outdoor camping activities, for they should be a unit, even as life should be a constant unified experience in living for Jesus Christ. Whether one shares in devotions or participates in a group game, he should be constantly aware of the fact that each experience is part of the totality of Christian living.

DEFINITION OF CAMP

Whenever we think of camping we think of outdoor activities such as those in which Boy Scouts and Girl Scouts engage. Because there are various degrees of outdoor living—ranging from sleeping in a bed roll in the woods to spending a week in mountain cabins equipped with hot and cold running water—it is difficult to draw a sharp line of demarcation between camping, retreats, Bible conferences, and other experiences often referred to as camping. Generally, if the primary emphasis is on preparing oneself for leadership in the church, it is a conference or retreat; if the primary emphasis is on experiences in the out-of-doors, it is camping. A church camp, however, will usually involve preparation for church leadership and also outdoor experiences (perhaps in the form of recreation). For the purposes of this chapter, therefore, the term "camp" will include conferences, retreats, and general outdoor experiences in Christian living.

KINDS OF CAMPS

There are several types of camps which may be planned by a church. Some of these are:

*Resident Camps.* This type of camp usually has permanent structures consisting of cabins, dining hall, chapel, and various recreational facilities. Most resident camps are administered by denominational or interdenominational agencies. Camps which conduct an adult Bible conference program generally provide camp facilities for the children of those who attend. The children in most cases are located on the same property as the conference, but sufficiently far away so that they may engage in a program graded to their own age level.

*Family Camps.* These are camps in which families from a church or a group of churches camp out for a weekend or more. The purpose is to bring family members closer together in a Christian atmosphere, thus creating stronger family ties. The program is designed so that a limited number of joint meetings for the participants is scheduled. This permits a flexible program in which families may share in such activities as hiking, swimming, boating, fishing, tennis, shuffleboard, volleyball, baseball, hobbies, and discussions designed to help parents better understand their children and to help children better understand their parents.

*Day Camps.* The day camp provides a child with camping experiences without the cost of resident camping and without the emotional tension of being separated from his parents for a protracted period. The typical program begins at nine or ten in the morning with a bus trip of thirty to forty minutes to the camp site. There the campers and their counselors participate in hiking, eating (and possibly preparing) their noon meal, games, studying nature, listening to Bible stories, and the development of simple skills (such as wood carving and weaving). The campers normally return home between three and five in the afternoon. The camp should be a week or more in length if it is to be called a camp, otherwise it should be termed a social or recreational activity.

*Bible Conferences, Retreats, and Institutes.* The general purpose of camps classified in one of these ways is to prepare the individual for leadership in his church. Weekends and occasionally an entire week will be spent at study and in training. Accompanying the intensive study sessions are periods for relaxation and for recreational activities. College campuses, church camps, and private camp grounds are frequently used, especially during holiday periods in the fall, winter, and spring seasons.

## PERSONNEL

### BOARD (OR CAMP COMMITTEE)

Most camps or camping programs require a policy-making body, usually known as a board of trustees. A church board of Christian education or a church camp committee may also function in this capacity. The basic functions of a board are to formulate policy, approve the selection of personnel, evaluate the effectiveness of the organization which it governs, and keep the supporting constituency informed. The general objectives, the program, and the means for implementing policy must all be approved by the board.

Since a great deal of knowledge and help are necessary for setting up a camp program, it is inadvisable for one person (e.g., the director) to attempt this without a board or committee to assist him. Moreover, any project that involves large financial expenditures should be governed, under most circumstances, by a board or policy-making body. One church known to the author, for example, purchased its own camp, with assets of approximately $250,000 and an annual operating expense of $75,000. Obviously, this is a large undertaking and requires not only financial but also legal and other administrative knowledge. Even a weekend camping experience of fifty young people may involve the handling of $500 to $1,000. The director of a camp, therefore, should have the advice and support of a board (or committee) as he attempts to administer the affairs of a camp program, regardless of the size of the camp.

DIRECTOR OF CAMP

The director is the official administrative head of the camp. It is his responsibility to *execute* the policies formulated by the board. In addition, he is expected to work out the general operational plan for the camp and submit it to the board for approval. This means that he must have a comprehensive grasp of general administrative principles and also ability to convince the board that his plan is workable and of real value. Although he is not expected to know how to repair automobile engines or tennis rackets, he must know administrative techniques and how to apply these at the level of detail. Thus, if there is a discipline problem in one of the groups he must know how to handle it. If there is first aid that must be administered, he must know exactly what steps should be taken to obtain prompt medical assistance. To fail at the level of detail is to fail, ultimately, in the whole program.

The director should be the executive officer responsible for all operations, including the business and financial activities. One of the fatal mistakes a board can make is to establish a camp organization and appoint two persons to direct separate parts of a camp program. This violates the principle of administrative unity (which states that any operation irrespective of its importance should be assigned to *one* person). Whenever there are two persons at the head of a camp, there will be uncertainty and inefficiency in management. Unity of management, therefore, should characterize a camp organization from the highest to the lowest level.

COUNSELORS

For children and teen-age campers it is necessary to provide adult supervision at all times. One unfortunate incident in which a child is injured or contracts an illness due to neglect, can do untold damage to the reputation of a director, of a camp, or of a church. It is imperative, therefore, that reliable, mature, and adequately prepared adult counselors be provided for church camps.

How many counselors should be procured? What should the ratio be between the number of counselors and campers? The usual recommended ratio is between four to twelve campers for each adult counselor,[1] with one counselor for each group of eight campers being the average found

[1]Julian H. Salomon, "Planning the Physical Plant of the Camp," *Administration of the Modern Camp*, ed. Hedley S. Dimock (New York: Association Press, 1952), p. 254.

by Lehmer.[2] As soon as the number exceeds twelve per counselor, there is the possibility that a camper may drop out from his group unnoticed, for perhaps twenty minutes to an hour—enough time to become lost or to fall into some unfortunate situation.

The recruitment of counselors, most of whom participate on a voluntary basis, is perhaps the most difficult task in setting up a camp. Nevertheless, there are dedicated Christians who are willing to sacrifice time and money and oftentimes a part of their vacation periods to assist young people in finding Christ as Saviour and in growing toward spiritual maturity. If there is sufficient planning and a face-to-face recruitment program, the number of required counselors should be available at the time camp begins.

## CAMPERS

Though most churches and camp directors would like to believe that campers have elected to attend a church camp for the purpose of growing spiritually, it is perhaps more realistic to recognize the camper's purpose as that of having a good time. Since the philosophy we have stated is that all activities should be permeated by Christian principles, we believe it is possible to arrange a camping program that is pleasant and wholesome and in which the campers *do* find enjoyment and also grow spiritually. Bible reading, grace at meals, and evening devotions can contribute to such growth if they are made a natural part of the program and do not appear to be forced into the schedule.

In order that campers may find a program that genuinely appeals to them, it is necessary that counselors and camp administrative personnel become acquainted with the needs, the problems, the interests, and the general characteristics of the campers. For example, counselors should be aware of the different scale of values held by upper and middle class young people and those who are generally from the lower class. As Davis has pointed out:

> Lower class culture, white or Negro, organizes adolescent behavior with regard to aggression, sexual relationships, age roles, and family roles, to mention only a few of the basic types of relationships, into patterns which differ radically from those of middle-class adolescents. . . . In middle-class, aggression is clothed in the conventional forms of "initiative," or "ambition," or even of "progressiveness," but in lower class it more often appears unabashed as physical attack, or as threats of and encouragement to physical attack. . . . The lower classes not uncommonly teach their children and adolescents to strike out with fist or knife and to be certain to

[2]D. Lehmer, "A Recommended Program of Counselor Training for Christian Camps" (Unpublished Master's thesis, Department of Christian Education, Fuller Theological Seminary, 1960), p. 45.

hit first. Both girls and boys at adolescence may curse their father to his face or even attack him with fists, sticks, or axes in free-for-all family encounters. Such fights with fists or weapons . . . occur sooner or later in many lower-class families. They may not appear today, nor tomorrow, but they *will* appear if the observer remains long enough to see them.[3]

If counselors and other camp personnel, therefore, are given sufficient background data concerning the characteristics of the campers who will be under their supervision, an effective program can be planned and the necessary steps taken to assure the discipline, the health, the safety, and the spiritual development of the campers who attend.

## ADMINISTRATION

If one is to keep all of the parts of an organization functioning effectively, he must be aware of those principles which will help him achieve this goal. The camp director, in a sense, is to be compared to an executive in a business firm. He has employees (campers), supervisors (counselors), administrative staff (camp staff), and a board of trustees (board or camp committee). The director may have as many as 100 to 500 under his jurisdiction at one time. He should, then, be acquainted with some of the principles of administration as they apply to the camp as an organization.

### ORGANIZING

In order for an institution or group to operate efficiently, its individual members should understand what authority each possesses and what his duties and relationships are in reference to other members. If one has doubt concerning the scope of his job, he may attempt to do too much or too little. If he attempts too many things, he will probably find himself duplicating the work of another, which is a waste of manpower; and if he does too few things, then certain essential tasks may lie undone. Moreover, tensions often develop between the person who feels that *he* has a responsibility for task "x" and the individual who is working on the same task because of vagueness about his duties and responsibilities.

Sometimes there is confusion over the matter of responsibility to a superior. For example, if a boy at camp is told by his counselor to perform a certain job but the dining hall supervisor insists that he perform an entirely different one, to whom should the camper give priority? This is a problem of authority and of the relationships which exist between two supervisory camp members. Without clearly defined lines of authority

[3]Allison Davis, "Socialization and Adolescent Personality," *Adolescence,* forty-third yearbook of the National Society for the Study of Education, Part I (Chicago: University of Chicago Press, 1944), p. 209.

and without the duties of camp personnel being described (usually in written form), conflicts of this nature will develop again and again. What is needed is a picture of the vertical and horizontal relationships that exist between all camp members. The picture may be a mental one, but preferably it should be visual in nature. "One picture," we have heard it said, "is worth a thousand words." An organizational chart, posted in the director's office or published in a camp manual, should help to clarify many of the relationships that are so often obscure and vague to the personnel of a camp.

Two cautions should be observed in organizing camp personnel: (1) the vertical relationship of a person to those above him should reflect the principle of unity of management or command[4] so that an individual is not responsible to two persons but only to one; and (2) all camp personnel should feel that their interests and concerns will never be sacrificed for the sake of an organization, but that the individual is more important than any organization or any set of rules.

PLANNING

As an administrative process, planning may be defined as that activity which involves a study of the history of an organization or institution in order to predict and establish its program for the future. A church camp would, then, examine past camping experiences and plan its future camp program in the light of its findings. A church launching its first camping program ought to make a study of camps already in existence and then, after considering all the circumstances surrounding the church, develop its own program accordingly.

How does the director go about planning? What does he do first? What steps should be taken for good planning to occur?

1. First of all, the policy-making body (board of trustees, camp committee, or board of Christian education) that is responsible for the camping program should decide on the dates for the camps, the site or sites of the camps, how each camp is to be financed (some churches subsidize campers, others do not), and the general objectives of the camps.

2. Once the decisions in step one have been made, the director for the camping program should be selected. This is usually the minister or director of education or an interested layman.

3. If the camp is to be a rather large one, then speakers and musicians should be contacted six to nine months in advance, since outstanding speakers and church musicians are usually in great demand and difficult to obtain on short notice.

[4]Louis H. Blumenthal, "The Functions and Principles of Camp Administration," *Administration of the Modern Camp*, ed. Hedley S. Dimock (New York: Association Press, 1952), p. 51.

4. A calendar should be prepared indicating the work to be done in promotion and recruitment in the six-month period prior to the opening of camp. Thus in January the director will begin to sign up the key personnel. Working from the top of the organization downward, he will recruit those to be in charge of the six general areas of camping: (a) counseling, (b) programing, (c) health and safety, (d) finance, (e) nutrition, and (f) property maintenance.

The director himself will probably arrange for the recruitment and selection of counselors, but he will need someone early in the year to start planning the camp program activities. He will also need a doctor, nurse, or first-aid specialist for the health and safety supervision of the camp; a business manager for handling financial matters; a chief cook for meal planning; and a property supervisor for the maintenance of the grounds if the camp site is owned by the church or church group. The earlier these key persons can be recruited the easier it will be for them to do their planning and for the director to plan the other aspects of the program as the opening date of camp approaches. Other details in the program should have deadlines, some in February, some in March, some in April, etc., until the day that camp opens.

5. Pre-registration should take place at the church one to two months before the camp starts. Postcards should be sent all pre-registrants immediately after their pre-registration, informing them of the dates of the camp and that a letter with additional information will be sent them a week or two before the camp begins. The letter should indicate: where the camp is located (use a map for this purpose with *accurate* directions for reaching the camp); the rules campers are expected to follow when they arrive at camp; and what items are to be taken, such as bedding, toilet articles, Bible, and other materials. The letter should also give directions in regard to the time and place from which the campers will leave, and the time and place to which they will be returned.

6. Transportation may or may not be a problem. If a church bus is to be used, it should be in good repair so that the lives of the campers will not be placed in jeopardy. If private cars are to be used, it means the recruitment of enough drivers to carry the group both up to and back from the camp. Whether a bus or private cars are employed, insurance should be taken out on all adults and children, to cover them from the time they leave home until they return. Occasionally the fees charged by a camp include travel and camping insurance, but this should be confirmed in writing before pre-registration begins.

7. Camp registration, the payment of fees, and the assignment of cabins should be conducted immediately upon the camper's arrival at camp. This should be followed by an orientation lecture and possibly a hike over the

camp grounds to acquaint the campers with the general plan and facilities of the camp. The more campers and staff personnel there are in a camp, and the more varied and comprehensive the camp program is, the more important it will be to do long-range planning—which may involve setting up engagements sometimes two to three years in advance.

## Staffing

Many camp staff personnel who are on a salary basis come from Christian colleges and high schools, with others coming from a camp's constituent churches. Since there is some remuneration connected with permanent staff positions, it is not as difficult to recruit personnel for these jobs as it is for cabin counselor positions. Where and how can counselors be recruited? Moreover, what should their qualifications and training be?

The general qualifications for counselors are: (1) a personal knowledge of Jesus Christ as Saviour; (2) mental, moral and emotional maturity; (3) nineteen or twenty years of age or older; (4) an understanding of the characteristics of the age group with which they will be working; and (5) some knowledge of, and liking for, camping activities.

In respect to the recruitment of counselors, the director should understand that this work ought to begin early in the program—before people have planned their vacations. Christians will frequently reserve time for church work if they are informed of a need at an early date. Parents of campers, Sunday school teachers, youth group sponsors, Christian college students, seminary students, and sometimes public school teachers and community agency workers can often be persuaded to give a part or an entire week of their vacation to counseling at a camp.

Application blanks for prospective counselors are usually sent out by the camp director (especially of a large camp) to the participating churches far in advance of the camp period. But if it is a local church program of camping in need of only five or ten counselors, then application blanks may not be required. In either case, however, if the person responsible for camping will visit prospective counselors in *their homes*, and explain the objectives and program of camping to them, the recruitment problem, the author is convinced, will largely be solved.

What kind of training should the counselors receive before they assume their responsibilities? This varies, of course, with the nature of the camp, the length of time campers and counselors remain at the camp, and a number of other factors. However, counselors should be given printed materials that describe the camp's objectives and philosophy, the rules governing campers and staff personnel, the general program for each day of the camp period, a clear statement of the duties of the counselor, a description of the counselor's authority and his relationship to other staff members. Instruction may be planned for counselors for a single evening in the case of a limited short-term camp experience. But for a summer camp where counselors may serve for a week or longer, instruction may be given on several nights in a church located near the homes of the counselors. Additional training may be scheduled for a day or more at the camp itself, prior to the arrival of the campers. Handbooks, charts, lectures, motion pictures, filmstrips, socio-dramas (or role-playing), case studies, and other means may be employed for the pre-training of counselors.

The general responsibility of a counselor is to provide supervision and guidance for the campers assigned to him. He should plan to have his meals with them, sleep in their cabin, conduct devotions with them, care for their health and safety, and generally give guidance in all activities of the program. For assuming this kind of responsibility, he may or may not receive remuneration. Lehmer[5] reports that out of some thirty-one camps contacted, seventeen did not pay any of their counselors, while seven did provide remuneration. Six gave remuneration to some counselors but not to all. There appeared to be a definite relationship between the salary received and the time spent at camp. If only a short period was involved, there appeared to be no remuneration. If, however, counselors remained for the summer or a large part of the summer, they apparently received a salary, though it undoubtedly was modest in nature.

Coordination

Along with the proper organization of personnel and an explanation of the objectives of a camp—both of which are basic to coordination—there is also the need for high morale among staff members and campers. There are many ways of achieving this. For example, the use of a democratic philosophy in the administration of the camp will contribute to keeping morale on a high level. When everyone realizes that each person is a part of the Body of Christ and that each has his respective function in an organization and, furthermore, that each, regardless of how insignificant his task might seem to be, is an integral and necessary part of the organization, then a spirit of teamwork,[6] of cooperation, and of understanding is the result. If, in addition, councils, committees, counselors, and campers can freely express themselves with respect to the purposes, program, and policies of the camp, the whole process of coordination should be greatly facilitated.

Evaluation

No camp program is complete unless there are records maintained

[5]Lehmer, op. cit., p. 45.
[6]Blumenthal, op. cit., p. 52.

which permit an assessment of the number of campers, the program, the financial condition, and the general success of the camp. The director as well as the board should be interested in the evaluation of a camp, for it permits the identification of areas which need improvement and provides a basis for sound planning in the years to follow. But without records and without a careful examination and interpretation of records, an improved and well-planned program is almost impossible. Records, therefore, must be kept, and evaluation should be considered as an integral part of the total administrative task.

## PROGRAMING

The hour-by-hour and day-by-day activities at the camp site comprise the camp program. Although it should be well planned, this does not imply that every minute must be occupied with a scheduled activity. The program should be characterized by flexibility so that campers do not feel rushed and under tension. On the other hand, counselors and program directors should always prove resourceful so that campers are not restless, having idle time on their hands because planning has been poorly done.

Since each camp is different, no daily schedule can be recommended for every situation. The example below, however, should serve as an indication of the kind of daily programing that may be conducted at a planning conference:

```
Rise .............................7:00 A.M.
Breakfast ........................7:30-8:15
Cabin clean-up ...................8:15-9:00
Planning period I ................9:00-9:50
Break ............................9:50-10:00
Planning period II ...............10:00-10:50
Recreation .......................10:50-12:00
Lunch ............................12:00-1:00 P.M.
Rest and relaxation ..............1:00-1:30
Planning period III ..............1:30-2:20
Planned games, hikes, etc. .......2:20-5:30
Dinner ...........................6:00-6:45
Executive committee ..............6:45-7:30
Reports on planning ..............7:30-8:15
Devotional period ................8:15-9:00
Free time ........................9:00-10:00
Cabin devotions ..................10:00-10:30
Lights out .......................10:30
```

In addition to a daily routine, there should be plans for different occasions, opening and closing day programs, camp traditions, banquets, indoor programs (in case of rain), tournaments, and other events which lend variety to the camp program.[7]

## CONCLUSION

Church camping can be a valuable and unforgettable experience. It should provide an atmosphere for coming into a closer relationship with God and with His Son Jesus Christ. Foremost in the thinking of any camp director, therefore, must be the spiritual value which the individual camper can gain in the time that he attends camp. If Christian principles are joined to sound administrative theory, and if prayer and dependence on the Holy Spirit are exercised, then the camper's spiritual growth should be such as to result in decisions that will glorify Jesus Christ our Saviour.

## BIBLIOGRAPHY

Blumenthal, Louis H. "The Functions and Principles of Camp Administration," *Administration of the Modern Camp,* ed. Hedley S. Dimock. New York: Association Press, 1952.

*Camp Director's Handbook.* Wheaton: Scripture Press, 1959.

Davis, Allison. "Socialization and Adolescent Personality," *Adolescence,* forty-third yearbook of the National Society for the Study of Education, Part I. Chicago: University of Chicago Press, 1944.

Ensign, John and Ruth. *Camping Together as Christians.* Richmond: John Knox Press, 1958.

Goodrich, Lois. *Decentralized Camping.* New York: Association Press, 1959.

Hammett, Catherine T., and Musselman, Virginia. *The Camp Program Book.* New York: National Recreation Association, 1951.

Ledlie, John A. (ed.). *Young Adult and Family Camping,* Monograph No. I in Monographs on Camping. New York: Association Press, 1951.

Lehmer, D. "A Recommended Program of Counselor Training for Christian Camps." Unpublished Master's thesis, Department of Christian Education, Fuller Theological Seminary, 1960.

Ott, Elmer F. *So You Want to Be a Camp Counselor.* New York: Association Press, 1946.

Reimann, Lewis C. *The Successful Camp.* Ann Arbor: University of Michigan Press, 1958.

[7]One of the finest books on camp programing is the one by Catherine T. Hammet and Virginia Musselman, *The Camp Program Book* (New York: National Recreation Association, 1951). It provides information on the mechanics of programing, instructions regarding camp craft skills, hikes, waterfront program, emergencies in camp, sports program, dramatics, storytelling, formal and informal discussions, special camp programs, banquets, and tournaments.

Salomon, Julian H. "Planning the Physical Plant of the Camp," *Administration of the Modern Camp*, ed. Hedley S. Dimock. New York: Association Press, 1952.

Tead, Ordway. *Democratic Administration*. New York: Association Press, 1945.

Welch, Emily H. *It's Fun to Be a Counselor*. New York: Association Press, 1956.

*Chapter 29*

# THE CHRISTIAN DAY SCHOOL MOVEMENT

## Mark Fakkema

C HRISTIAN DAY SCHOOLS exist and thrive today because the current aims of public school education do not correspond with the educational aims of many evangelical Christians. This disagreement over the ends of the educative process did not always exist in this country. During the last century and a half significant changes have taken place in the philosophy of state-sponsored, tax-supported education which have brought about the divergence. As Vivian Thayer has said about the public school, "Originating as a private and sectarian school, it evolved slowly into, first, a nonsectarian school for Protestants, and finally, the secular institution of today."[1]

### HISTORICAL BACKGROUND

In the past, in Western society it was the church more than the state which was concerned with the education of youth. During the Middle Ages, education, what little there was of it, was by the church and for the church.

Popular education began shortly before the Reformation. The Brethren of the Common Life as early as the fourteenth century established a system of elementary schools in northwestern Europe which was free from both state and church control. Their educational program was a "common life" project with the parents of the community serving as sponsors.

[1]Vivian T. Thayer, *Religion in Public Education* (New York: Viking Press, 1947), p. 41.

---

Mark Fakkema, B.A., LL.D., is General Manager of Christian Schools Service, Inc., Chicago.

Generally speaking, however, popular education conceived of as a Christian enterprise dates back to the Reformation. The religious doctrines which were basic to the Reformation necessitated a popular educational program. In fact, the idea of a common elementary school was a most important by-product of the Reformation.

The Reformation produced two profound changes in the life of the comman man, both of which called for the establishment of popular education.

First, the Protestant Reformation shifted religious authority from the church to the Bible. The all-important question for Protestantism became not, What saith the church? but, What saith the Scriptures? To know the Scriptures one had to be able to read. Hence, schools became essential to produce literacy among the masses.

Second, religious responsibility was transferred from the priest to the common man, from the church to the home. The clergy, according to Protestantism, has no monopoly in the ministry, for there is a "priesthood of believers" which includes all those who are rightly related to God in Christ by faith. To assume this responsibility intelligently, one must have some minimal education. Thus, education, which had been the prerogative of the clergy, must be extended to all men.

Accordingly, the spread of the Reformation carried in its wake the spread of general popular education. The early settlers who colonized the northeastern section of what eventually became the United States were in this Reformation tradition. Therefore it was to be expected that they would champion popular education. And, since the church and state were united in early New England, state-supported education was under the control of men who were committed to the Christian faith.

The result of this church-state alliance was most evident in the kind of textbooks used in the public schools of pre-Revolution New England. According to Rian, "the textbooks, more than anything else, made plain that Christianity and the Bible were indispensable to the welfare and the teaching of the pupil."[2]

The *New England Primer* was the leading text. More than three-fourths of its content was taken from the Bible, and even the remainder was explicitly Christian. In teaching the first letter of the alphabet a small picture of the fall of our first parents was presented. Opposite the picture were the words: "In Adam's fall we sinned all." All of the other letters were introduced by moral or Biblical references. The last letter, "Z," pictured a man in a tree with the words, "Zacchaeus, he did climb a tree his Lord to see." The *Hornbook*, another widely used text, gave

[2]Edwin H. Rian, *Christianity and American Education* (San Antonio: Naylor Co., 1949), p. 18.

approximately half of its contents to a consideration of the Lord's Prayer.[3]

The religious homogeneity of New England society during the colonial period made such a situation possible. Not only was a public school curriculum saturated with Christian doctrine tolerated, it was made mandatory by the state. In 1642 the Massachusetts court ordered the towns of the colony to structure curriculum so that children could "read and understand the principles of religion."[4]

By the end of the Revolution, however, all of this had changed substantially. Rian describes the post-Revolution scene as follows: "The influence of the church and religion gradually diminished and the civic authorities assumed support and control. The aim of education slowly acquired the emphasis of training for democratic living, for social efficiency and for useful pursuits in the world at large. Religion was no longer the center of the curriculum; in fact, it was eliminated altogether or reduced to a minor place in the course of study. The secular or the civic control of education gained the ascendancy, with the aims and the curriculum predominantly nonreligious."[5]

This change did not occur without turbulence, however. The storm which erupted in Massachusetts just before the midpoint of the nineteenth century was violent. The person about whom the tempest raged was the secretary of the Massachusetts Board of Education, Horace Mann.

Actually, the trend toward the secularization of the public schools began before Mann's election to the position of secretary in 1837. Ten years before, the Massachusetts legislature passed a law concerning town school committees which ordered that "said committee shall never direct any school books to be purchased or used, in any of the schools under their superintendence, which are calculated to favor any particular religious sect or tenet."[6] While this statute forbade sectarianism, rather than all religion, in the public schools, it did express a principle upon the basis of which religion *per se* was eventually eliminated from the curriculum of the tax-supported schools.

Mann became involved in what became a most bitter controversy through his now famous *Reports* to the Massachusetts Board of Education. As Culver has pointed out, Mann, in his first *Report*, "does not say that revealed religion cannot be taught, but that the school committees have not found any books on revealed religion the use of which would not violate the law of 1827."[7] In other words, revealed religion

[3]Donald E. Boles, *The Bible, Religion, and the Public Schools* (Ames, Iowa: Iowa State University Press, 1961), p. 8.

[4]Renwick H. Martin, *Our Public Schools—Christian or Secular* (Pittsburgh: National Reform Association, 1952), p. 47.

[5]Rian, *op. cit.*, p. 46.

[6]Raymond B. Culver, *Horace Mann and Religion in the Massachusetts Public Schools* (New Haven: Yale University Press, 1929), p. 22.

[7]*Ibid.*, p. 43.

could not be taught in the classroom, not necessarily because of an anti-religious bias, but because all textbooks available for the purpose of teaching religion were adjudged sectarian in outlook.

To add fuel to the fire, the various groups within the Christian church were, at this same time, contending with one another for recognition as *the* correct expression of the Christian faith and objecting to any other than their own tenets being taught. Then, to worsen an already bad situation, Mann, according to one of his biographers, was "in harmony with Unitarian optimism and at variance with Calvinistic pessimism. He believed that man was essentially good, and rejected the doctrine of human depravity and the necessity of conversion."[8] It is small wonder, then, that Mann has been considered to be the chief villain in the tragedy of the secularization of American public school education.

What happened in Massachusetts set off a chain reaction throughout the nation. In 1872 the Cincinnati Board of Education banned Bible reading; in 1890 the Supreme Court of Wisconsin ruled that Bible reading in public schools was unconstitutional; and the Supreme Courts of Nebraska, Illinois and Louisiana, during the 1902-1915 period, declared that Bible reading and hymn singing in public schools conflicted with their respective state constitutions.[9] This trend has continued until, more recently, the United States Supreme Court on June 17, 1963, in Abington School District vs. Schempp and Murray vs. Curlett, held that local laws requiring either Bible reading and prayer in tax-supported public schools are forbidden by our national constitution.

The current situation is summed up by the American Council on Education in this statement: "Public education in the United States is committed by federal and state law to the general principle that sectarian religious instruction must be excluded from the curriculum."[10] And since evangelical Christianity is deemed by the courts to be a sectarian religion in our pluralistic society, it is thereby excluded.

## CRITICISMS OF THE PRESENT SITUATION

Many people, including numerous friends of public school education, have expressed alarm over a nonreligious, secularized education for America's children and young people. Luther A. Weigle, dean emeritus of Yale Divinity School, has said, "When the state, through the Supreme Court, threatens to take all religion out of tax-supported schools and colleges and commit them to atheism, the religious freedom of American citizens is gravely endangered."[11] Nicholas Murray Butler, former presi-

[8]*Ibid.*, p. 64.
[9]Thayer, *op. cit.*, p. 38.
[10]*The Function of the Public Schools in Dealing with Religion* (Washington, D.C.: American Council on Education, 1953), p. 377.
[11]Martin, *op cit.*, p. 16.

374 AN INTRODUCTION TO EVANGELICAL CHRISTIAN EDUCATION

dent of Columbia University, has protested, "Our schools turn out intellectual giants and moral pygmies."[12]

Yet the trouble with public school education lies at a deeper level than this situation created by court decisions. The very *philosophy* of education which is predominant in the public schools today is at odds with the revealed Christian faith. As Rian has well said, "The most prevalent philosophy underlying modern American education is that of experimentalism. . . . Experimentalism not only challenges dogma and external authority, but also claims that these can never exist."[13]

It is the basic antithesis between the secular and the Christian world and life views which has caused an increasing number of evangelical Christian parents to become disenchanted with the public schools. If God is the Author of *all* truth, as Christian revelation indeed insists that He is, then *all* subjects in the school curriculum, whether history, sociology, science or literature, need to be presented within the framework of this philosophical position. This the public schools, by their own admission, cannot do.

## THE CHRISTIAN SCHOOL SOLUTION

Agreeing in substance with Milton's classic statement that "the end then of learning is to repair the ruins of our first parents by regaining to know God aright, and out of that knowledge to love Him, to imitate Him, to be like Him . . . "[14] increasing numbers of evangelical Christians, acting corporately as churches or as special societies, have tried to create a school situation in which truly Christian ends may be achieved by the educative process. This has required the founding and maintenance of Christian day schools.

The rationale for the existence of distinctly Christian educational institutions, side by side with public schools, has been summarized thus by Berkhof: "The education of our Christian youth may not be merely physical and intellectual, nor merely physical and intellectual with a small ingredient of surface morality added to it. It should be very decidedly religious, and the religion included should not be of the modern, naturalistic variety—which is little more than a superficial morality with a religious tint—but the religion that is taught in, and is required by, the Word of God; the religion of the grace of God in Jesus Christ; the religion that functions properly only when it is rooted in a regenerate life."[15]

[12]*Ibid.*, p. 24.
[13]Rian, *op. cit.*, p. 71.
[14]Kendig B. Cully (ed.), *Basic Writings in Christian Education* (Philadelphia: Westminster Press, 1960), p. 195.
[15]*The Christian School, The First Line Trench* (Chicago: National Union of Christian Schools, 1938), p. 7.

Or as Machen put it, "The Christian life cannot be lived on the basis of antichristian thought. Hence the necessity of the Christian school."[16]

## CHRISTIAN SCHOOL ORGANIZATION

Every local Christian school project calls for some type of organization. Evangelical schools tend to fall under one of three classifications:

1. The *parochial* school. In this type the school is a church project, carried on by the church board. Some churches, however, realize that education is a parental responsibility and that interested parents should have a share in the management of the school. In this situation the local church usually appoints a school committee which is responsible to the church board. Such a school is *semiparochial.* The Lutheran schools are parochial in character.

2. The *parent-society* school. In this case parents, often of different local evangelical churches, form an autonomous local Christian school organization. This society then draws up its own constitution and elects out of its membership a school board which assumes the duties of establishing and operating a local school. Policies are set at "society meetings" and at the end of each year the school board submits a report to the society, makes its proposals regarding the school program, and presents a budget for adoption by the society. The schools of the National Union of Christian Schools are in this category.

3. The *private* school. Control here is in the hands of one person or, more usually, in the hands of a self-perpetuating board of trustees. As a rule, such a school advertises its facilities and informs the public concerning the educational opportunities it offers, its curriculum, tuition charges, and other pertinent information. Frequently these are boarding schools and are on a secondary level. There are a number of excellent private schools in the evangelical school movement.

## SCHOOL AFFILIATIONS

According to government statistics, the nonpublic elementary and secondary schools now total over 17,000. At present, private school pupils number 48,100,000.

Lutherans have outstripped other Protestants in sponsoring day schools. However, many other denominations are doing a commendable work along this line.

In addition, there are two *non*denominational organizations with which many evangelical day schools are affiliated: the National Union of Christian Schools, organized in 1920, and the National Association of Christian Schools, created by the National Association of Evangelicals in 1947.

[16]*The Christian School, The Out-Flowering of Faith* (Chicago: National Union of Christian Schools, 1934), p. 18.

The steady increase in evangelical day schools and the phenomenal growth of individual schools indicate the keen concern and interest of Christian parents and educators in the sound, positive, well-rounded education of their boys and girls and young people. We cite one example of such growth: A school in the East was founded in 1950, beginning with kindergarten through fifth grade, two teachers, and fifty-five students. Today it offers complete education through high school, with a faculty of twenty and a student body of three hundred fifteen. This school is fully accredited by the Middle States Association of Colleges and Secondary Schools. Many more examples could be given.

### EVANGELICAL CHURCH-RELATED ELEMENTARY SCHOOLS
(K through Grade 8)
1963-64

Statistics in these three charts were provided by the Board of Parish Education, The Lutheran Church—Missouri Synod.

| Affiliation | Schools | Teachers | Enrollment |
|---|---|---|---|
| **Baptist** | | | |
| Texas Baptist Day School Association ........ | 24 | 173 | 3,507 |
| Los Angeles Baptist City Mission Society ...... | 28 | 160 | 4,194 |
| **Lutheran** | | | |
| American Lutheran Church ............... | 57* | 241 | 6,314 |
| Church of the Lutheran Confession .......... | 8 | 17 | 388 |
| Evangelical Lutheran Synod (Norwegian) .... | 12 | 14 | 278 |
| Lutheran Church in America ............... | 14 | 70 | 1,814 |
| Lutheran Church—Missouri Synod ...........1,378 | | 5,919 | 158,049 |
| National Evangelical Lutheran Church ....... | 3 | 9 | 228 |
| Synod of Evangelical Lutheran Churches ...... | 2 | 7 | 188 |
| Wisconsin Evangelical Lutheran Synod ...... | 224 | 853 | 24,068 |
| Mennonite Christian Day Schools .............. | 208 | ca.1,300 | 9,749 |
| Protestant Episcopal Church ................. | 204 | ca.2,000 | 19,357† |
| **Interdenominational** | | | |
| National Association of Christian Schools ..... | 176 | 1,291 | 18,710 |
| National Union of Christian Schools ........ | 228 | 1,692 | 45,507 |
| Totals ...............................2,566 | | 13,746 | 292,351 |

*69 additional congregations of the American Lutheran Church have separate kindergartens.
†227 additional separate kindergartens and nursery schools with an enrollment of 6,566.

### EVANGELICAL CHURCH-RELATED SECONDARY SCHOOLS (Grades 9-12)
1963-64

| Affiliation | Schools | Teachers | Enrollment |
|---|---|---|---|
| Baptist—Los Angeles City Mission Society ........ | 1 | 10 | 162 |
| **Lutheran** | | | |
| Church of the Lutheran Confession ............ | 1 | 2 | 26 |
| Lutheran Church—Missouri Synod ............. | 21 | 535 | 10,759 |
| Wisconsin Evangelical Lutheran Synod ......... | 8 | 121 | 2,471 |
| Mennonite ..................................... | 10 | ca.150 | 1,780 |
| Protestant Episcopal Church .................... | 24 | ca.600 | 6,160 |
| **Interdenominational** | | | |
| National Association of Christian Schools ........ | 17 | 152 | 2,240 |
| National Union of Christian Schools ............ | 28 | 410 | 9,685 |
| Totals ................................110 | | 1,980 | 33,283 |

## EVANGELICAL CHURCH-RELATED SECONDARY BOARDING SCHOOLS
### 1963-64

| AFFILIATION | SCHOOLS | TEACHERS | ENROLLMENT |
|---|---|---|---|
| Baptist—Southern Baptist Convention | 12 | 237 | 3,479 |
| Lutheran | | | |
| American Lutheran Church | 3 | 31 | 501 |
| Church of the Lutheran Confession | 1 | 5 | 57 |
| Lutheran Church—Missouri Synod | 11 | —* | 1,539 |
| Wisconsin Evangelical Lutheran Synod | 5 | 52 | 988 |
| Mennonite | 2 | ca.30 | 320 |
| Interdenominational—National Association of Christian Schools | 15 | 134 | 1,403 |
| Totals | 49 | 489 | 8,287 |

*Connected with colleges which train for church vocations.

## CONCLUSION

What of the future? Can we expect the current trend toward organizing more and more Christian elementary and secondary schools to continue?

Strong evangelical denominations will no doubt add day school instruction or expand their current programs as a matter of self-preservation. As Rian puts it, "Wherever a congregation supports a Christian school, controlled by the parents or the church, the faith and loyalty of that people are strong and intelligent."[17] These schools will tend to be parochial in character.

Individual evangelical churches, many of them having loosed their past ties with their denominations because of modernism, will want to avoid the leavening influence of secularism on the lives of their children, since they fear that this very influence was largely responsible for the defection of their "mother" denominations from the faith. Inasmuch as such churches will not be financially able to support their own schools, concerned parents within their memberships will need to enter into cooperative educational ventures with likeminded parents from nearby churches of similar evangelical persuasion. These will tend to be parent-society schools.

In addition, the private schools will probably continue to increase their enrollments in view of the waning popularity of the secular public schools. Parents who are alarmed over the possible influence of secular education on their children, but who live in areas where there are no local Christian schools, will find private boarding schools the solution to their problem.

As the last few vestiges of religion are eliminated from the public schools, as more and more parents become concerned about the effect of the educative process on their own children, as there is a continuing

[17]Rian, op. cit., p. 212.

upgrading of evangelical Christian day schools in physical facilities and personnel, and as there is a clearer enunciation of a truly Christian philosophy of education, the prospects of this movement are indeed bright.

## BIBLIOGRAPHY

Boles, Donald E. *The Bible, Religion, and the Public Schools.* Ames, Iowa: Iowa State University Press, 1961.

*The Christian School, The First Line Trench.* Chicago: National Union of Christian Schools, 1938.

*The Christian School, The Out-Flowering of Faith.* Chicago: National Union of Christian Schools, 1934.

Cully, Kendig B. (ed.). *Basic Writings in Christian Education.* Philadelphia: Westminster Press, 1960.

Culver, Raymond B. *Horace Mann and Religion in the Massachusetts Public Schools.* New Haven: Yale University Press, 1929.

*The Function of the Public Schools in Dealing with Religion.* Washington, D.C.: American Council on Education, 1953.

Martin, Renwick H. *Our Public Schools—Christian or Secular.* Pittsburgh: National Reform Association, 1952.

Rian, Edwin H. *Christianity and American Education.* San Antonio: Naylor Co., 1949.

Thayer, Vivian T. *Religion in Public Education.* New York: Viking Press, 1947.

## FOR FURTHER READING

Gaebelein, Frank E. *Christian Education in a Democracy.* New York: Oxford Press, 1951.

Romein, Tunis. *Education and Responsibility.* Lexington, Ky.: University of Kentucky Press, 1955.

Stokes, Anson P. *Church and State in the United States.* New York: Harper & Bros., 1950. 3 vols.

Taylor, Marvin J. *Religious Education: A Comprehensive Survey.* New York: Abingdon Press, 1960.

Whittemore, Lewis B. *The Church and Secular Education.* Greenwich, Conn.: Seabury Press, 1960.

*Chapter 30*

# THE BIBLE INSTITUTE AND BIBLE COLLEGE MOVEMENT

## S. A. WITMER

THE BIBLE INSTITUTE-COLLEGE MOVEMENT in America is now more than eighty years of age. It has grown steadily in the United States and Canada from a single school in 1882 to 250 in 1963. The movement embraces several of the largest and most noted Protestant missionary training centers in the world.

Bible institutes-colleges have contributed much to evangelicalism at home and abroad. They have given preparation to half or more of all Protestant missionaries from North America, and have helped to shape the lives of many eminent Christian leaders, including Wilbur M. Smith, Robert A. Cook, Billy Graham, and Ralph T. Davis. A number of evangelical bodies depend on Bible colleges to prepare men and women for positions of Christian leadership. But in spite of the dimensions and significance of the movement, little has been written about it.[1]

However, as the movement grows in self-consciousness, and the Christian and educational public becomes aware of its significance, professional as well as popular interest in Bible college education increases. A factual account of the movement was included in a report issued by a committee of the National Association of Evangelicals.[2] Several research studies have been conducted during the past decade by graduate students in preparation of theses and dissertations. Articles are beginning to appear

[1]A volume on the Bible institute-college movement in the United States and Canada was prepared by the author in 1962: *The Bible College Story: Education with Dimension* (New York: Channel Press).
[2]S. A. Witmer, "A New Form of American Education," *Christian Education in a Democracy* (New York: Oxford University Press, 1951), pp. 157-181.

The late S. A. Witmer, Ph.D., was at the time of his decease the executive director of the Accrediting Association of Bible Colleges.

in both religious and educational journals on the history and the philosophy of Bible institute-college education.

## CLASSIFYING BIBLE INSTITUTES-COLLEGES

What are Bible institutes-colleges? How does a Bible institute differ from a Bible college? What distinguishes the Bible college from the Christian liberal arts college? What place do these schools occupy in the pluralistic pattern of American higher education?

### NONCONVENTIONAL BEGINNINGS

The first Bible schools in America were purposely begun as nonconventional institutions. They came into being in response to Christian compassion for human need and for the practical purpose of implementing the Great Commission. A. B. Simpson, founder of Nyack Missionary College, was deeply concerned about the needs of masses without Christ in the cities of America and among the unevangelized people of other lands. While Dwight L. Moody, founder of Moody Bible Institute, moved many thousands in America and Britain in his evangelistic campaigns, yet he too was deeply concerned about the multitudes beyond his reach, particularly those in the urban centers of America. Conventional seminaries fell far short of preparing enough workers for the vast frontiers of human need at home and abroad. Further, the task was far too great to be undertaken by the professional clergy alone. There was an urgent need for many trained laymen. Even though A. B. Simpson was an able, seminary-trained scholar, he made the following plea in an editorial two years before Nyack Missionary College was founded:

> We want our best scholarship and talent in the mission field, but we want all who can go; and with a destitution so imperative, the Church of God should be willing to welcome the humblest "prentice hand," and dispense with full technical preparation wherever she finds other qualifications for humble usefulness.[3]

In Moody's historic address in 1886 on "City Evangelization," which initiated the steps that led to the founding of Moody Bible Institute, he issued the famous summons: "I believe we have got to have 'gap men,' men who are trained to fill the gap between the common people and the ministers."[4]

The first schools, therefore, were concerned primarily with equipping dedicated young people with the essential knowledge of God's Word and the practical skills necessary to become effective Christian witnesses in home visitation, city mission work, Sunday school teaching, and foreign

[3]A. B. Simpson, editorial, *The Gospel in All Lands* (May, 1880), p. 162.
[4]Richard Ellsworth Day, *Bush Aglow* (Philadelphia: Judson Press, 1936), p. 264.

missionary service. The great majority of students in the early days were admitted without high school preparation. Many were mature persons in their twenties and thirties. But in spite of their nonconventional academic standards, these schools met a need and were successful in training many hundreds of servants of Christ.

## Growing Academic Concern

The profound social changes of the twentieth century and the growing maturity of the movement eventually evoked concern over academic values and standards. Early in the history of the movement, students came to Bible institutes to seek more than lay training; some desired ministerial preparation. The general rise in education brought about by the democratization of the high school meant that many students came to Bible schools with a high school preparation. Eventually, the great majority were high school graduates. Since many wanted preparation beyond that obtainable in a Bible school, both faculties and students became concerned over the value of credits when students transferred to advanced institutions.

The problem of academic standing of Bible institutes-colleges raised the further question as to the place they occupy in the pattern of American education. Could nonconventional schools become educationally respectable? The critical issue was simply this: Bible colleges must either retain their distinctives and become a unique but respectable addition in the pattern of American education, or they must fit into one of the conventional categories and thus lose their identity and uniqueness. The latter course generally meant that Bible colleges must become liberal arts colleges. A small number of schools did take this alternative.

It can now be said that these issues have been faced and resolved. Leaders of the movement decided that the distinctive elements in Bible college education must be preserved at all costs and that academic recognition must be sought within the framework of specialized institutions. The Bible institute-college movement has become of age and now occupies a distinct place in American higher education.

The maturation of the movement came about largely through the Accrediting Association of Bible Colleges, which was established in 1947. It became the means by which Bible institutes and Bible colleges might achieve academic standing while preserving their central thrust of preparing young people for Christian service through a Bible-centered program of education. With the counsel of several distinguished educators, the Association formulated college-level academic standards in such areas as admissions, faculty preparation, curriculum, and library.

The Accrediting Association of Bible Colleges, which includes in its accredited list most of the older and larger Bible schools of the United States and Canada, is recognized by the United States Office of Education. It is a member of the American Council on Education and the Council on Cooperation in Teacher Education. A number of its schools are officially recognized as institutions of higher learning by their respective state boards of education and ranking state universities.

In the tenth year of the Association's history, Dr. Enock C. Dyrness, registrar of Wheaton College, noted the maturing development of the movement in the following tribute:

> May I offer my congratulations for the tremendous progress which has been made during the past ten years. Not only is this true of the schools that are members of the Accrediting Association, but also of those who have not as yet taken that step. With the establishment of the Accrediting Association of Bible Colleges, the Bible school movement has really come of age and achieved its rightful place in American higher education.[5]

Another educational leader, Dr. Frank E. Gaebelein, made the following appraisal a year later:

> Here is a story that needs telling, a chapter in the history of education that ought to be widely circulated. For it is not generally recognized that within the last six or seven decades a new and distinct form of education has been quietly and steadily developing in our country. . . . Almost ignored in the histories of education, they [Bible institutes and Bible colleges] have become, in their own right, a distinct educational genre. More than that, they have been exercising in their field a vital and, in some areas, as in the foreign missionary enterprise, a crucial influence.[6]

While the Bible college movement has made great advances in achieving academic standing, there is still ground to be gained. The stigma of second and third rate education is not easily removed. Unfortunately, the Biblical-theological field has been one of the areas in which diploma mill operators have carried on their fraudulent practices, and in the minds of the partially informed it has tended to raise a question regarding the integrity of all schools identified as "Bible."

The movement itself faces the challenge of preserving its spiritual vitality and dynamic evangelicalism while upgrading its academic standards. It has been demonstrated in a number of institutions that spiritual life and scholastic standards are not antithetical. The best in intellectual achievement goes hand in hand with the excellence that befits all endeavor in the name of Christ and for His honor.

[5]Enock C. Dyrness, "The Bible College and Accreditation," AABC Newsletter, II (May, 1958), p. 1.
[6]Frank E. Gaebelein, "The Bible College in American Education," School and Society, LXXXVII (May 9, 1959), p. 223.

DEFINITION OF BIBLE COLLEGE EDUCATION

With growing maturity, the Bible institute-college movement has had to define the precise function of Bible college education. The Accrediting Association of Bible Colleges gives the following definition:

> Bible college education is education of college level whose distinctive function is to prepare students for Christian ministries or church vocations through a program of Biblical, general, and professional studies. Included in the concept of Christian ministries are such church vocations as pastor, missionary, Christian service director, minister of music, and other specialized forms of Christian service by both lay and "professional" workers.[7]

It has also become necessary to differentiate between the Bible college and other types of Christian institutions of higher learning. The Bible college differs from the seminary in that it functions on the college or undergraduate level. The seminary, on the other hand, is a post-college or postgraduate institution. It majors in pastoral training while Bible institutes-colleges offer many varied programs for specialized ministries, the four most common being pastoral training, missionary preparation, Christian education, and music education.

The distinction between the Bible college and the Christian liberal arts college was made explicit in a policy statement adopted by the Accrediting Association of Bible Colleges in 1960. The statement, in part, follows:

> 1. *Similarities.* Both the Christian liberal arts college and the Bible college should be committed to a Biblical philosophy of education. In both, Christ should be the center of integration. Both are concerned with the personal development of students. Both seek to broaden and deepen the educational foundation of incoming students by general education.
>
> 2. *Distinctive objectives.* From this point the Bible college and the Christian liberal arts college become distinctive in their objectives. The liberal arts college goes on from a foundation of general education in the humanities and sciences to prepare students by liberal arts majors for many professions and vocations. The liberal arts therefore distinguish the chief subject matter of the liberal arts curriculum.
>
> Bible colleges, on the other hand, are specialized. Their distinctive function is to prepare students for Christian ministries and church vocations. This they do through a program of Biblical, general, and professional education. The Bible major therefore is at the heart of the Bible college curriculum. However, a Bible college may offer liberal arts majors provided these are in addition to and do not dis-

[7]*Manual* (Fort Wayne: Accrediting Association of Bible Colleges, 1960), p. 2.

place the required Bible major or alter the objectives of Bible college education.

3. *Central purpose.* The central purpose which characterizes Bible institutes and Bible colleges is to prepare students for Christian service at home and abroad either as full-time or lay workers. The first Bible schools in America were established for this purpose.[8]

One other distinction needs to be made—the difference between the Bible institute and the Bible college. Essentially, the two types belong to the same family of educational institutions, and the distinction in types has come to be more or less superfluous, as is the case with other types of college-level institutions of specialized education. Both seek the same goals and both are committed to a Biblical philosophy of education. Where there is a difference it is usually one of length of program. The Bible institute is generally a three-year, non-degree-conferring institution, while the Bible college offers four- and five-year programs leading to degrees. The longer period permits the Bible college to include one more year of general education than can be incorporated in a three-year program. The Accrediting Association of Bible Colleges recognizes that both types of schools can operate according to college-level standards, and so membership is open to both. This practice is similar to that of the regional accrediting associations, which accredit both junior and senior colleges.

## HISTORY

NYACK MISSIONARY COLLEGE

Nyack Missionary College, first known as the Missionary Training College for Home and Foreign Missionaries and Evangelists, has the distinction of being the first Bible college established in America. It was founded in 1882 by A. B. Simpson to implement his vision of taking the gospel to neglected peoples at home and abroad. However, many of the early American colleges were similiar to Bible colleges in nature when they were founded. In Europe, a number of training institutes were established prior to Nyack's founding. The Pietist movement in Germany gave rise to a number of independent and semi-independent missions organized to train and to send forth missionaries to foreign lands. The institution that influenced Simpson more than any other was the East London Institute for Home and Foreign Missionaries, established by Rev. H. G. Guinness. In presenting his plan for a training college, Simpson said:

> Many will be glad to know that in humble dependence on the guidance and help of God, it is proposed to open, in a few months, a

[8]Proceedings of fourteenth annual meeting of the Accrediting Association of Bible Colleges, 1960.

Training College for Home and Foreign Missionaries . . . fitted to give a specific and thorough preparation for Evangelistic and Missionary Work, to earnest and consecrated persons who do not wish to take a regular course of study in a Theological Seminary. It will be somewhat similar in character and design to the "East London Institute for Home and Foreign Missionaries" in London. . . .[9]

From a humble beginning in the old Twenty-third Street Theater in New York City, Nyack has grown until it is now one of America's leading missionary colleges, occupying a spacious campus on the west palisades of the Hudson River at Nyack, New York.

## MOODY BIBLE INSTITUTE

The school which was destined to become the largest and most renowned of all Bible institutes was established in 1886 by Dwight L. Moody and his associates—Moody Bible Institute. Following several years of planning and organization, a "full-fledged training school emerged, dedicated to teaching men and women the fundamentals of the English Bible and practical Christian work." The institute has grown into a multifunction institution carrying on a variety of Christian enterprises. Besides the day school of 1,000 students, an evening school of 900, and a correspondence school with 30,000 enrollees, the Institute propagates the gospel through Moody Press, Moody Literature Mission, *Moody Monthly* magazine, Moody Institute of Science, the Extension Department, and the Radio Division. Its 2,300 alumni in active missionary service constitute 10 per cent of the Protestant missionary force from North America.

## GROWTH OF MOVEMENT

The Bible institute movement grew somewhat slowly at first. Six of the extant institutions besides Moody and Nyack were founded in the nineteenth century—Western Baptist Bible College, Kansas City, Missouri; Johnson City Bible College, Kimberlin Heights, Tennessee; Toronto Bible College, Toronto, Canada; Northwest Christian College, Eugene, Oregon; Berkshire Christian College, Lenox, Massachusetts; and Azusa College, Azusa, California. Nine more Bible institutes-colleges were founded in the first decade of the twentieth century, seventeen in the second, and twenty-five in the third.

The great development in numbers of schools has taken place in the past three decades according to a survey conducted in 1960 by the Accrediting Association of Bible Colleges.[10] The survey identified 236 day Bible institutes-colleges in the United States and Canada; 37 per

[9]A. B. Simpson, editorial, *The Word, Work, and World* (July, 1883), p. 112.
[10]"Survey of Bible Institutes and Bible Colleges in the United States and Canada," *AABC Newsletter*, IV, (August, 1960), pp. 1, 8.

cent founded in the first five decades of the movement (1882-1929), while 63 per cent were founded in the three decades that followed. The peak development took place during the World War II period, for sixty-nine institutions were founded from 1940 to 1949. That the movement continues to grow is attested by the fact that at least fifty new schools were founded during the 1950-60 decade.

Of the 248 known schools, 194 are in the United States and fifty-four in Canada. The total day school enrollment of these schools is approximately 25,000, with Canadian schools accounting for 15 per cent of the total and United States schools, 85 per cent. Another 9,000 are enrolled in ninety evening schools, and more than 200,000 in thirty-two correspondence divisions.

Fifty-four per cent of the Bible colleges are denominationally related, while 46 per cent classify themselves as independent. Most of the largest schools both in the United States and Canada are independent of denominational control. In Canada these include Toronto Bible College, Prairie Bible Institute, and Briercrest Bible Institute. In the United States, Moody Bible Institute, the Bible Institute of Los Angeles, Philadelphia College of Bible, Barrington College, Columbia Bible College, and Multnomah School of the Bible may be cited.

## BIBLE COLLEGE PROGRAMS

Two basic principles have shaped the programs of Bible colleges. First, Bible college educators without exception hold that the Bible is the inspired, authoritative Word of God. From this premise, Bible colleges derive their theology, their philosophy of education, their methodology, and their system of values. The second principle has to do with the mission of the church. Bible colleges hold that the one supreme task of the church is embodied in the Great Commission: "Go ye into all the world, and preach the gospel to every creature" (Mark 16:15). The practical end of Biblical education, therefore, is to prepare recruits to implement this imperative order of the Lord Jesus Christ.

### Bible-centered Curriculum

All Bible schools place the Bible in the center of the curriculum. The Accrediting Association of Bible Colleges requires a minimum of thirty semester hours of Bible and Theology in all programs, and a minimum of forty hours in programs that prepare for Bible teaching and preaching ministries.

But far more is involved than a certain number of credits in Bible. The revealed truth of the Bible is regarded as the integrating principle for all knowledge. All disciplines, all fields of study, all knowledge find their

ultimate meaning in the Incarnate Word whom the written Word discloses. Thus the quest for an integrating principle is not ended by scientific discovery nor by philosophic reflection, but by *revelation*. It follows,
therefore, that Biblical truth has implications for psychology, for history,
for sociology, for physics and all the other sciences. For example, it takes
Biblical truth to disclose the real nature of man, even though psychology
and anthropology add much to our knowledge.

Dr. Frank E. Gaebelein made this observation of Bible college education:

> The central feature of the Bible college is well worth looking at,
> because it carries implications far beyond this one kind of institution.
> This is the kind of education that has solved for itself the perennial
> problem of educational philosophy—the identification of an integrat-
> ing principle for the entire curriculum. For it the Bible is, to use
> Lewis Mumford's brilliant figure, "a magnetic field at the center which
> will continually polarize each fragment that enters the field."[11]

A further reason for giving the Bible a central place in the curriculum
is that it is the divinely ordained instrument to mold and to shape the
character of Christian disciples. Through the transforming power of the
Spirit of God and moral responsiveness on the part of the student, the
Word transforms lives into the image of Christ. "All scripture," wrote
the apostle Paul, "is given by inspiration of God, and is profitable for
doctrine, for reproof, for correction, for instruction in righteousness: that
the man of God may be perfect, throughly furnished unto all good works"
(II Tim. 3:16, 17).

In modern times, a noted psychologist paid a similar tribute to the
Bible. Wrote Dr. Henry C. Link: "The greatest and most authentic
textbook on personality is still the Bible, and the discoveries which
psychologists have made tend to confirm rather than to contradict the
codification of personality found there."[12]

A further reason for giving the Bible first place in the curriculum is
that it contains the message of life which Christ's disciples are called
upon to teach and to preach. The Bible is God's message of salvation
to lost mankind. It follows that those who would transmit it must master
its contents and understand its truths.

GENERAL EDUCATION

General education in a Bible college is structured to conform the total
personality of the student to the image of Christ. It includes all those
experiences, both curricular and extracurricular, which contribute to the
growing maturity of students in their preparation for effective living as

[11]Gaebelein, *op. cit.*, pp. 223, 224.
[12]*The Return to Religion* (New York: Macmillan Co., 1936), p. 105.

Christians and citizens. The whole of college life—chapel services, field work, recreation, dormitory life, social life, student activities, athletics, job employment—should contribute to this central goal of Christian education.

Because the qualities of dedication, selflessness, spirit of service, reverence, prayerfulness, and self-discipline are critically important in the lives of Christian workers and because they are foremost in the hierarchy of Christian values, Bible schools stress the cultivation of the spiritual life. Formal arrangements include chapel services, devotional periods, individual guidance, spiritual life conferences, missionary activities aimed to inculcate missionary vision and passion.

General education in a Bible college also seeks to broaden and deepen the educational foundation of students by a soundly conceived sequence of courses in English composition, English literature, world literature, speech, history, sociology, psychology, philosophy, music, health, natural science, mathematics, physical education, and education. It aims to give students ability to communicate effectively, to give them a purview of history, an understanding of social institutions and principles, an understanding of the scientific method, appreciation of cultural values, and a knowledge of human nature.[13]

## TERMINAL PROGRAMS

The symbol of the Accrediting Association of Bible Colleges is a triangle with Christ at the center, "Bible" at the base, "general" at one side, and "professional" at the other. Practical or "professional" training for church vocations or Christian ministries completes the triad of Bible college education.

At this point, Bible colleges have many more specialized programs than do seminaries, which major in pastoral preparation. Just as modern technology has called for a large number of vocational and technical skills, so the adaptation of technology and science to the communication of the gospel has called for many specialties for service at home and abroad. In missionary preparation alone, training programs for the following specialized ministries will be found in Bible colleges:

> Missionary Medicine
> Missionary Nursing
> Missionary Education
> Linguistics
> Journalism
> Missionary Technical:
> Photography

13*Manual* (Fort Wayne: Accrediting Association of Bible Colleges, 1960), p. 11.

    Engineering
    Radio and Communciations
    Aviation and Mechanics
    Construction
    Printing
    Jewish Missions
    European Missions

In the homeland there are demands for parish workers, church secretaries, Christian social workers, ministers of music, writers of Christian
literature, directors of Christian education, youth leaders, camp supervisors and counselors. Most Bible colleges offer programs in the fields
of pastoral training, Christian education, general missionary work, and
sacred music, yet a number offer one or more of the more specialized forms
of training. Obviously, in some highly specialized fields such as aviation
the demand for skilled workers is too limited to require more than one
or two ably conducted schools.

A significant aspect of training for Christian ministries is practical experience in Christian service that has characterized Bible institute education since the time of Simpson and Moody. With rare insight into the
learning principles involved, they combined the practical with the theo-
retical. In a given year about 80 per cent of the students in Bible colleges
complete at least one semester of regular Christian service assignments.
A number of conferences on Christian service have been held in recent
years to study means by which this phase of education can become more
effective in the student's preparation.

PREPARATORY PROGRAMS

Since a considerable number of students plan to pursue graduate
studies, some Bible colleges have arranged suitable programs in which
there is a relatively large content of general education. In some cases
liberal arts majors are available to prepare students for related graduate
studies. A major in Bible is always required, to give the student a foundation in Christian faith and, in the case of a seminary goal, to give the
student sound pre-theological preparation.

## CHALLENGE

The population of the world, which should be viewed from the perspective of Calvary, is four times larger than when William Carey began
the modern missionary movement. In another twenty-five years living
persons for whom Christ died will number close to four billion and by the
end of the century, seven billion. The task to which Bible schools are
committed and to which they have contributed largely is so stupendous

that they cannot afford to strive for less than the best in quality of preparation.

"Bible colleges must never forget their origin and their heritage. They
must never yield to the rationalistic and cultural forces of declension that
have withered many movements born of revival. They should constantly derive their vision and dynamic from the fountain of eternal youth
that flows from the throne of God."[14]

## BIBLIOGRAPHY

Day, Richard Ellsworth. *Bush Aglow.* Philadelphia: Judson Press, 1936.
Dyrness, Enock C. "The Bible College and Accreditation," AABC *News-
letter*, II (May, 1958).
Gaebelein, Frank E. (ed.). *Christian Education in a Democracy.* New
York: Oxford University Press, 1951.
———. "The Bible College in American Education," *School and Society*,
LXXXVII (May 9, 1959).
Link, Henry C. *The Return to Religion.* New York: Macmillan Co.,
1936.
*Manual.* Fort Wayne: Accrediting Association of Bible Colleges, 1960.
McKaig, Charles Donald. "The Educational Philosophy of A. B. Simpson,
Founder of the Christian and Missionary Alliance." Unpublished doc-
toral dissertation, School of Education of New York University, New
York, 1948.
"Survey of Bible Institutes and Bible Colleges in the United States and
Canada," AABC *Newsletter*, IV (August, 1960).
Tozer, A. W. *Wingspread.* Harrisburg: Christian Publications, 1943.
Witmer, S. A. *The Bible College Story: Education with Dimension.*
New York: Channel Press, 1962.
———. *The Accrediting Association of Bible Colleges Looks Forward.*
Fort Wayne: Accrediting Association of Bible Colleges, 1960.
———. *Preparation of Missionaries in Bible Institutes and Bible Colleges.*
Fort Wayne: Accrediting Association of Bible Colleges, 1959.

## FOR FURTHER READING

Boon, H. W. "How It All Began," *Christian Life*, XXI (June, 1959).
Cable, J. H. *A History of the Missionary Training Institute.* Nyack, N.Y.:
Missionary Training Institute, 1933.
Crum, T. B. "Bible Colleges Today," *Christian Life*, XXI (June, 1959).
Cubberley, Elwood P. *The History of Education.* New York: Houghton
Mifflin Co., 1948.

[14]S. A. Witmer, *The Accrediting Association of Bible Colleges Looks Forward*
(Fort Wayne: Accrediting Association of Bible Colleges, 1960), p. 13.

Erdman, Charles R. *D. L. Moody: His Message for Today.* New York: Fleming H. Revell Co., 1928.

Feucht, Oscar E. *Leadership Through Bible Institutes.* St. Louis: Board of Parish Education, Lutheran Church—Missouri Synod, n.d.

Haggard, Cornelius P. "Spiritual Leadership: The Only Answer," *Christian Life,* XXI (June, 1959).

LeBar, Lois E. *Education That is Christian.* New York: Fleming H. Revell Co., 1958.

Moody, William R. *The Life of Dwight L. Moody.* New York: Fleming H. Revell Co., 1900.

Niebuhr, H. Richard, Williams, Daniel Day, and Gustafson, James M. *The Advancement of Theological Education.* New York: Harper & Bros., 1957.

Thompson, A. E. *The Life of A. B. Simpson.* New York: Christian Alliance Publishing Co., 1920.

Witmer, S. A. "How to Live in Two Environments," *Christian Life,* XXI (June, 1959).

———. "Bible College Education," *School and Society,* LXXX (October 16, 1954).

*Chapter 31*

# THE CHRISTIAN LIBERAL ARTS COLLEGE

## Enock C. Dyrness

E DUCATION AND LIBERTY have in a real sense been the heritage of the American people. The need for Christian higher education was early recognized in the New England colonies. Harvard College was founded in 1636 primarily for the training of Christian ministers. West Gate at Harvard bears this inscription:

> After God had carried us safe to New England and we had builded our houses, provided necessaries for our livelihood, reared convenient places for God's worship, and settled the civil government, one of the next things we longed for and looked after was to advance learning and perpetuate it to posterity, dreading to leave an illiterate ministry to the churches, when our present ministers shall lie in the dust.[1]

As the country expanded to the west, Christian colleges were founded for the training of Christian leaders. In many states, Christian colleges preceded the establishment of state universities. The history of many of these indicates that they were founded through the sacrificial efforts of earnest Christian people for the training of leaders. For example, Oberlin College in Ohio was founded in 1833 by a home missionary and a returned foreign missionary who were entirely destitute of means when they undertook the work. Mr. Shipherd owned a small one-story home in Elyria, and nothing more. Mr. Stewart had nothing. Mr. Shipherd, who is recognized as *the* founder, while preparing for college, is reported to have had a profound religious experience which as the frequent fashion

---

[1]William H. Crawford, *The American College* (New York: Henry Holt & Co., 1915), pp. 3, 4.

Enock C. Dyrness, LL.D., is registrar of Wheaton College, Wheaton, Illinois.

then was, beginning with conviction of sin, self-abasement, depression and severe struggle, issued at length in full assurance and pardon and consequent joy and peace.

The pattern was similar in many of the colleges founded during the pioneer days. The Christian liberal arts college has therefore been a part of the American scene from early colonial days. It has contributed much to the cause of higher education and has had a significant part in providing leadership for church and state.

The Christian liberal arts college occupies a strategic place in the evangelical cause. A survey of Christian leaders in America reveals that a high percentage of them have been trained in Christian colleges. The growing need for such leadership emphasizes the importance of Christian schools, and particularly the need for more evangelical liberal arts colleges. The future of the evangelical cause around the world will depend largely upon the leadership provided by these institutions which today face a challenge never before equaled in the history of the world.

## EDUCATION IN A STATE OF FLUX

Drastic changes have occurred in the field of higher education during the past century. One hundred years ago 75 per cent of all professional workers were engaged in four fields: theology, teaching, medicine, and law. Today there are 2,200 occupations requiring highly trained manpower and the number is growing each year. The atomic age has emphasized the importance of science, and has affected many areas of life. These changes are reflected in today's college curriculum.

Another change has been the rapid growth in population and the great increase in the number of young people attending college. In the fall of 1962, the U.S. Office of Education reported a total college and university enrollment of 4,206,672, an increase of approximately 800,000 in a period of three years.[2] Conservative estimates indicate that by 1978 there will be 9,200,000 students enrolled.[3] This would represent 40 per cent of college-age young people, while twenty years ago less than 16 per cent of college age were enrolled in institutions of higher learning.

This increase poses some very real problems for Christian colleges. A survey conducted in Ohio indicated that the privately controlled colleges of that state estimated that they would be able to increase their enrollment approximately 77 per cent by 1970.[4] If these figures stand up, it

[2]*Opening (Fall) Enrollment in Higher Education, 1962* (Washington, D.C.: Division of Educational Statistics, Bureau of Educational Research and Development, U.S. Department of Health, Education and Welfare, 1962), p. 3.
[3]*Collier's Encyclopedia 1962 Yearbook* (New York: Crowell-Collier Press, 1962), p. 208.
[4]Ronald B. Thompson, *Meeting Ohio's Needs in Higher Education—A Summary of the John Dale Russell Report.*

would mean that the publicly controlled universities in Ohio will be compelled to enroll four times the number of students that were enrolled in 1955!

For many years there has been a wholesome balance between privately supported institutions and public universities and colleges, with almost an equal number of students enrolled in each. Today 60 per cent of college students are enrolled in tax-supported institutions with the percentage rising year after year.[5] In the fall of 1962, only 763,829 students of the 4,206,672 in institutions of higher learning were enrolled in private liberal arts colleges, 70 per cent of which had an enrollment of less than 1,000.[6] Most of these were founded as "church schools" and many of them have some denominational affiliation. Unfortunately, many colleges that were founded as conservative evangelical institutions have slipped from their moorings and no longer promote the cause they once championed. Instead, many church-related colleges are actually undermining the faith of the young people sent to them by trusting Christian parents.

Finances have been a major problem for most private institutions and particularly for the Christian liberal arts college. As Dr. Gould Wickey has observed, "It appears that the denominations were long on founding schools and short on supporting them."[7] Tuition has never paid more than a fraction of the cost in accredited private colleges. Herbert Solow, writing in *Fortune* magazine, suggested raising tuition charges to more nearly meet costs.[8] This is the trend at present in many schools.

The rapid expansion of educational opportunities for youth has been very encouraging. However, as pointed out in *Christian Education in a Democracy:*[9]

> There are causes for concern. The church has lagged in developing its educational program. To be sure, individual Christian colleges have made striking progress in expanding their services to meet new needs. One of the bright aspects of the present educational scene is the growth of colleges committed to the evangelical faith. Not only have their enrollments mounted and equipment increased, but they have also in a number of cases gained full academic recognition through accreditation by regional and national agencies. Nevertheless, church colleges as a whole have slipped from the commanding position of fifty years ago. Many Christian institutions have not had the support needed to keep up with educational developments; others have hardly realized their shortcomings.

[5]American Alumni Council, *Commentary* (Washington, D.C.: A.A.C., 1963), October 28, 1963, p. 67.
[6]*Opening (Fall) Enrollment in Higher Education, 1962, op. cit.*
[7]Frank E. Gaebelein, *Christian Education in a Democracy* (New York: Oxford University Press, 1951), p. 152.
[8]"Colleges Are Too Cheap," *Fortune,* LVI, September, 1957, p. 163.
[9]Gaebelein, *op. cit.,* p. 136.

Recognizing the need to re-examine college objectives, the Fund for the Advancement of Education made grants to thirty-eight colleges for such a study during 1952-1954. In a summary of the findings published in 1959 entitled *Fortifying Higher Education—A Story of College Self Studies* by Robert S. Donaldson, the following quotation from Jonathan E. Rhoads, provost of the University of Pennsylvania, is typical:

> Every university, and probably every family, business or state, needs a periodic quickening of the pulse to avoid stagnation. It can come from wars or other catastrophes, and it can come from thoughtful self study, followed by thoughtful action. This is a known method to improve education, and if it produces some scars, it may be that surgery was necessary. The project was good for all of us at this university, and brought about constructive changes.

Inspired by this and similar reports many Christian colleges have greatly strengthened their program and effectiveness through self studies conducted by members of the faculty. It is to be hoped that more schools will benefit from such self-examination, and that Christian colleges will assume the leadership of which they are capable.

## WHAT CONSTITUTES A CHRISTIAN LIBERAL ARTS COLLEGE?

Obviously, having a denominational label or a Christian origin does not make an institution Christian in the true sense of that word. We would define a Christian college as an institution of higher learning offering a broad preparation for life, in which Christ is honored in the classroom of every department, in sports, in the social and extracurricular activities, and in the lives of the faculty, staff, and students.

*Christian Education in a Democracy* suggests the following criteria for a Christian educational institution:

> 1. A Christian educational institution must be built upon a thoroughgoing Christian philosophy of education.
> 2. It must have a faculty thoroughly committed to its distinctive philosophy.
> 3. The entire curriculum must be Christ-centered.
> 4. It must have a student body that will actively support its philosophy and aims.
> 5. It must recognize the two aspects of Christian education—the required and the voluntary.
> 6. It must actually do the truth through applying the Christian ethic in all its relationships.

The same writer goes on to point out:

> It is not external regulation that prevents independent colleges and

schools from wholehearted Christian education, but the reluctance of boards of trustees, administrators, and teachers to go all the way. . . . Another reason for timidity is the fear of losing caste among other institutions. . . . There are colleges and schools that, in this secular age, are making a real dedication of their resources to Christian education. They would also bear witness to the fact that very wonderful results attend the practice of the principles set forth. . . .[10]

Fortunately, there are a goodly number of Christian liberal arts colleges scattered throughout the country and there is evidence that these are being strengthened. The situation, however, is far from what it should be, and unless steps are taken soon by evangelical Christians to undergird the educational program, they stand in danger of losing the gains that have been made.

## THE CAUSE OF MORAL BREAKDOWN

Leaders in government and society are becoming alarmed by the moral breakdown which is apparent on every hand. Much of this may be attributed to the absence of any spiritual or moral instruction in the schools, and particularly in colleges which train teachers and leaders. Canon Bernard I. Bell, eminent Episcopal clergyman, in his book, *Crisis in Education*, states:

> We who have doubts of the competency of our schools and colleges and universities, our churches and homes, are all for a better education, all for an education more competently devised to do what an education is supposed to do; but we feel sure that much which today calls itself "education" is not only inadequate but has gotten clean away, in important and determining particulars, from doing what it is supposed to do. We believe, in short, that America is progressing toward uneducation, toward the prevention of education, toward injury to growing human beings, toward grave danger to cultural stability. . . . All the greatest thinkers since Plato have insisted that the formulation of a moral philosophy is fundamental to the education of the free man; and it is just here that the American colleges and universities with rare exception are falling down on the job. They assist very few of their students to discover what in the light of age-long experience the would-be wise man is to try to become. By their neglect they graduate into the citizenry throngs of muddle-headed men and women, many of whom, if they had not been submitted to malpractice, might have turned out to be truly gay and happy people, understanding and effective leaders of the commonalty. Instead, blind men are ejected into society to lead other blind men till both fall into the ditch.[11]

[10]Gaebelein, *op. cit.*, pp. 63, 64.
[11]Canon Bernard I. Bell, *Crisis in Education* (New York: Whittlesey House, 1949), pp. 10, 58.

At the 1960 annual conference on higher education sponsored by the National Education Association, the topic, "To What Extent Should the Study of Religion Be Included in the Curriculum?" was discussed by educational leaders. Dr. J. Edward Dirks of Yale University Divinity School stated:

> Historical considerations argue strongly for the study of religion. It had been an integral part of the major Western academic traditions and was transferred to American colleges and universities from their beginnings.
>
> Religion is included as an aspect and dimension of culture. Inasmuch, therefore, as education has the task of transmitting the cultural heritage, religion cannot be excluded. . . .[12]

He went on to state: "Ideally, a college or university which has resources and is legally free to do so, should provide for the study of religion. . . ."

In the same session, Dr. A. L. Sebaly, director of Student Teaching at Western Michigan University, stated:

> The next decade will be an exciting one for those who are interested in considering the extent to which the study of religion should be included in the curriculum. Among educators there is increasingly an openness of discussion about the area. There will be a change of emphasis in some of the disciplines as they are related to religion. For example, in the field of sociology there is an increasing interest in the study of the institution of religion. And certainly there is an increasing interest in the study of the place of religion in psychology. Study and teaching in the various disciplines, however, are not enough. There is need for experimentation and research if the gains of the past decade are to be furthered.[13]

It is our conviction that the answer to the problem will not be found by merely attempting to introduce courses in "religion" in secular schools, but rather by giving the Christian liberal arts college its rightful place in the educational program. This would involve strengthening existing institutions and establishing additional Christian colleges to provide the instruction which is so desperately needed in this day. As Dr. Elton Trueblood points out: "The right answer to the enormous demands involved in the increase in population is not to destroy our small colleges by making them big, but rather the decision to start new ones."[14]

[12]*Current Issues in Higher Education* (Washington: Department of Higher Education, National Education Association of United States, 1960), pp. 73 ,74.
[13]*Ibid.*, p. 75.
[14]*The Idea of a College* (New York: Harper & Bros., 1959), p. 11.

## SOME BASIC CONSIDERATIONS

To evaluate the Christian college adequately, some basic factors need to be considered:

1. *Who should go to college?* The first factor to be considered is the aptitude and interest of the student. Not all high school graduates will benefit from a liberal arts course. Those lacking interest and motivation should be encouraged to seek a trade or vocation suited to their aptitude. Others, showing a technical bent or interest should be encouraged to enter a technical or professional school. Some with a strong desire for college training may lack the aptitude as evidenced by their high school record or College Entrance Examination Board score. These should be encouraged to take further training in line with their interests and aptitudes. For some of these, a two-year terminal junior college course may serve better than a four-year course. Others will benefit from a professional or vocational course.

The liberal arts college provides a broad general education with an opportunity for limited specialization. To derive the greatest benefit from such a course, the student should have an adequate college-preparatory course in high school and should have satisfactory scores on standard tests such as those provided by the College Entrance Examination Board and the American Council on Education.

The mortality rate in colleges and universities is such as to suggest that greater care should be exercised in screening candidates for college entrance. Unless a student ranks in the upper two-thirds in high school, he is not likely to succeed in college. Occasionally, a student with high aptitude scores who has made a mediocre record in high school may succeed in college if properly motivated. Experience indicates, however, that study habits developed in early life persist in college, and the able student with poor study habits is likely to encounter difficulty in college. Even Christian young people with a serious purpose find it difficult to overcome poor study habits developed over a period of years.

The Christian college should properly seek to maintain high academic standards as well as high spiritual standards. To achieve this goal, careful selection of students is necessary. To admit those lacking in preparation or aptitude is to encourage lower standards and to invite failure. A college does not render a kindness in admitting a student who is likely to fail. It has a responsibility to the applicant and to the students already enrolled, and, in the case of the Christian school, to the Lord whom it professes to serve.

2. *The academic standing and accreditation of an institution.* These are important factors. They normally are clearly set forth in the college catalog and should give the prospective student an accurate idea as to

how the credits earned would transfer to other schools or meet certification and other requirements. Accreditation should be stated in very clear terms and should indicate the relationship of the school to regional accrediting associations, to the state department of public instruction, and to the state university.

There are six regional accrediting associations in the United States, covering among them every section of the country: the New England Association of Colleges and Secondary Schools, the Middle States Association of Colleges and Secondary Schools, the Southern Association of Colleges and Secondary Schools, the North Central Association of Colleges and Secondary Schools, the Northwest Association of Secondary and Higher Schools, and the Western College Association.

There are also various national accrediting associations concerned largely with professional areas, such as the National Association of Schools of Music, the National Council for Accreditation of Teacher Education, and similar associations in other professional areas. The National Commission on Accrediting with headquarters at 1785 Massachusetts Avenue, N.W., Washington, D.C., lists twenty-eight such agencies whose policies and procedures are acceptable to it. The Commission consists of seven constituent members (associations) and more than 1,100 colleges and universities throughout the United States.

The American Association of Universities for many years published a list of approved institutions but has now discontinued the practice of inspecting and adding names to the list. Institutions on the approved list are generally recognized as fully accredited by institutions throughout the world.

The U.S. Office of Education publishes a list of institutions accredited by nationally recognized regional and professional accrediting agencies under the title *Accredited Higher Institutions.* This publication is issued about every four years. It also issues an annual *Education Directory, Part III—Higher Education,* which includes all higher educational institutions accredited by regional agencies or by the recognized national professional associations, and other institutions whose course credits are fully accepted for transfer by accredited higher institutions.

If an institution does not make its accredited position clear in its published materials, such information may usually be secured from the state university.

3. *Faculty strength.* Although it may be assumed that an institution that is fully accredited will have an adequate faculty, the qualifications of the faculty as listed in the annual catalog are of significance. Unless a good percentage of the faculty hold an earned doctor's degree, the institution probably does not rate too high scholastically. It should be

noted, however, that good teaching does not necessarily follow because a teacher holds a Ph.D. degree. Frequently, gifted teachers without the doctorate excel their colleagues who hold such a degree. Many great teachers never acquired an earned doctorate. However, any school with only a small percentage of earned doctorates is likely to be among the weaker academic institutions.

Stability of the faculty measured in terms of years of service in the institution is another important factor in judging the strength of a college.

4. *The curriculum.* The liberal arts college is generally considered to be a non-vocational institution. However, it seeks to provide a practical four-year course, enabling its students to enter a profession such as teaching, or to take further specialized training in an appropriate graduate or professional school. The curriculum is so planned that it offers a well-rounded general education, preparing the student to take his place in society regardless of his field of specialization. As pointed out in *Christian Education in a Democracy*, "General education helps the student achieve a synthesis of ideas."[15] Former President Eisenhower's Commission on Higher Education defined general education as "those phases of non-specialized and non-vocational learning which should be the common experience of all educated men and women."

The Christian liberal arts college provides not only the basic courses for a general education but also areas of specialization appropriate thereto, plus training in Bible. To avoid weakening its program, a college must limit its offerings to such courses as contribute to its announced objectives and which can be justified by the demand of its students. This involves a constant re-evaluation of objectives and measuring their realization. No institution can offer all the majors to be found in liberal arts colleges, and expediency dictates that a school should limit its offerings to those areas in which it has the facilities, staff, and resources to do an acceptable piece of work.

5. *Guidance program.* Of growing importance in our colleges is the provision for an adequate counseling and guidance service. The day is past when deans of men and women serve merely as disciplinary officers. They now serve as counselors and guidance officers and devote most of their time to helping students with their personal and academic problems. Many schools offer a testing program which helps to guide the student in making an intelligent choice of a vocation. While the classroom teacher is a vital factor in the education of the student, the development of individualized programs emphasizes the need for qualified counselors. Such guidance is of particular importance in the Christian institution and its value and significance cannot be overemphasized.

[15]Gaebelein, *op. cit.*, p. 141.

6. *The extracurricular program.* This is an important part of the student's education and supplements classroom instruction. A well-planned educational program will include experience in various extracurricular activities, such as music, debate, athletics, and other forms of activity, including practical Christian work. While it is true that some of these factors can be overemphasized, their neglect could result in a serious weakening of the entire educational experience. A well-balanced program is highly desirable and there should be sufficient activities to meet the needs and tastes of every student. The demand for trained leadership in various recreational areas emphasizes the importance of preparing the students in our Christian colleges to assume such leadership on a part- or full-time basis after leaving college.

7. *Plant and facilities.* While some would define a college as Mark Hopkins on one end of a log and a student on the other, in our twentieth century we have come to recognize the importance of adequate facilities to carry out the educational program. Though buildings do not make the institution, they are an important factor. They need not be ornate or costly, but they should provide the space and equipment needed to enable the college to function efficiently. It is essential that an institution have facilities adequate to carry out the program announced. These include not only classrooms and laboratories, but adequate library facilities, dormitories, dining halls, health facilities, gymnasium, and extracurricular facilities. The size of the campus is an important factor as is the character of the community in which the institution is located. The educational facilities available in the immediate area also make their contribution to the total program of the school.

8. *Location.* There is much evidence to indicate that location is an important factor in the growth and development of a college. While some strong institutions have developed in areas "off the beaten path," such a location has in most instances proved to be a handicap. Some schools have thrived because of favorable climate, while others have succeeded in spite of severe climatic conditions. Other things being equal, however, the school with the most favorable location is more likely to attract and hold students.

Since it is impossible to operate a school in a vacuum, the surroundings have a direct bearing on the educational program. To be near a large industrial center may present hazards, but it also presents opportunities for training and service. Likewise, proximity to an educational or cultural center contributes to the breadth of training provided.

Transportation facilities, while not as important a factor as in former years, are nevertheless of significance to those considering a school and should be given appropriate attention.

9. *Costs.* While the item of expense will of necessity weigh heavily in many families, it would be a sad mistake to attempt to evaluate schools on this basis. Although there are exceptions, as is true in other fields, one usually gets what he pays for. While it is true that the item of expense should have careful consideration, it should be recognized that in most schools the opportunities for self-help are such that even the student of limited means may find it possible to acquire an education in a more expensive school. Today most institutions maintain generous scholarship and loan funds which enable the student of limited means to acquire an education without undue hardship. The federal government has also stepped into the picture in its Defense Education Program and provides generous loan funds to worthy students, giving special preference to those preparing for scientific fields and to those looking forward to the teaching profession. In the case of the latter, loan funds up to $1,000 a year are available with a provision that the amount owed at the end of the college course will be reduced at the rate of 10 per cent a year for the first five years of teaching in a tax-supported institution. This virtually means a 50 per cent scholarship to those selecting teaching as a profession.

Employment opportunities are also plentiful on many college campuses, and as a rule, the rate of compensation varies in direct proportion to the costs involved. Where the costs are high, the rate of compensation is also likely to be high, so that in actual hours it takes little more to acquire an "expensive" education than it does to acquire a cheaper one.

*Conclusion*

These are some of the basic considerations that merit the attention of those having an interest in the field of Christian education. It is our conviction that insufficient attention has been given by the Christian public to the significance of the role of Christian colleges in the world today.

In conclusion, it should be pointed out that the Christian liberal arts college offers a general education equal to or better than that of most secular schools, *plus* spiritual values of inestimable worth. Young people should be made aware that choosing a Christian college need not involve less than the best by any standard.

*BIBLIOGRAPHY*

Bell, Canon Bernard I. *Crisis in Education.* New York: Whittlesey House, 1949.

Blauch, Lloyd E. *Accreditation in Higher Education.* Washington, D.C.: U.S. Office of Education.

*Collier's Encyclopedia 1962 Yearbook.* New York: Crowell-Collier Press, 1962.

Crawford, William H. *The American College.* New York: Henry Holt & Co., 1915.

*Current Issues in Higher Education—1960.* Washington, D.C.: Department of Higher Education, National Education Association of United States.

Donaldson, Robert S. *Fortifying Higher Education—A Story of College Self Studies.* New York: The Fund for the Advancement of Education, 1959.

Dugan, Willis E. *Counseling Points of View.* Minneapolis: University of Minnesota, 1959.

Gaebelein, Frank E. *Christian Education in a Democracy.* New York: Oxford University Press, 1951.

Irwin, Mary. *American Universities and Colleges.* Baltimore: Williams & Wilkins Co., 1960.

Leonard, Delavan L. *The History of Oberlin.* Boston: Pilgrim Press, 1898.

McGrath, Earl J., and Russell, Charles H. *Are Liberal Arts Colleges Becoming Professional Schools?* New York: Teachers College, Columbia University, 1958.

McGrath, Earl J. *Liberal Education in the Professions.* New York: Bureau of Publications, Teachers College, Columbia University, 1959.

*Opening (Fall) Enrollment in Higher Education, 1962.* Washington, D.C.: Division of Educational Statistics, Bureau of Educational Research and Development, U.S. Department of Health, Education and Welfare, 1962.

Reeves, Floyd W., Russell, John Dale, Gregg, H. C., Brumbaugh, A. J., and Blauch, L. E. *The Liberal Arts College.* Chicago: University of Chicago Press, 1932.

Solow, Herbert. "Colleges Are Too Cheap," *Fortune*, LVI (September, 1957), p. 163.

Thompson, Ronald B. *The Impending Tidal Wave of Students.* Washington, D. C.: American Council on Education, 1959.

Trueblood, Elton. *The Ideal of a College.* New York: Harper & Bros., 1959.

*Chapter 32*

# THE HOME AS AN EDUCATIONAL AGENCY

MORRIS INCH

W HO IS TEACHING OUR CHILDREN? Fairchild and Wynn, after a carefully documented study involving 845 families in group interview situations and the completion of 1,000 questionnaire forms, comment: "Most dramatically during the last century general education has transferred from home to school."[1] The school is not the only institution acting *en loco parentis*. "Sociologists of the family almost universally speak of a decline in the religious function of the home and transfer of these functions to religious institutions."[2] In view of this trend, what can be expected of the home as an educational institution?

## *THE RESPONSIBILITY FOR EDUCATION*

It is of first importance to recognize God's educational standard for the home. For this purpose we consider:

> Hear, O Israel: The Lord our God is one Lord: and thou shalt love the Lord thy God with all thine heart, and with all thy soul, and with all thy might. And these words, which I command thee this day, shall be in thine heart: and thou shalt teach them diligently unto thy children, and shalt talk of them when thou sittest in thine house, and when thou walkest by the way, and when thou liest down, and when thou risest up. And thou shalt bind them for a sign upon thine hand, and they shall be as frontlets between thine eyes. And thou shalt write them upon the posts of thy house, and on thy gates" (Deut. 6:4-9).

[1] Roy Fairchild and John Wynn, *Families in the Church: A Protestant Survey* (New York: Association Press, 1961), p. 34.
[2] *Ibid.*, p. 36.

Morris Inch, Ph.D., is associate professor of Bible and Christian Education at Wheaton College, Wheaton, Illinois.

RESPONSIBILITY

"Thou shalt teach!" With these words was fixed parental responsibility, implied in the creation of the first family, commended by Christ's own example (Luke 2:51, 52), and taught by His followers (Heb. 13:4; I Tim. 5:14). Delegation of responsibility, as necessary or desirable as it may be under certain circumstances, is never abdication. The parent is held accountable for the training which his children receive.

RESPONSIBILITY TO GOD

In context it seems best to understand "the one God" as "the only God." There is no rival. As God is one, so the parents are charged to one (total) allegiance. With all affection, dedication, and concentration the only true God is to be served. Children are gifts from the Almighty. They belong to the father who sired them, the mother who bore them, but first and last to God who gave them. "The Christian, better than most, has the opportunity to spend his life for some purpose that will outlive him. The parent in a Christian family has an even greater challenge. There has been placed into his hands by the grace of God a child whose growth and life will be his to influence."[3]

In a deeper sense than we know, parents are God's representatives and representations to children. They appear godlike, and God seems to the child parentlike. Early childhood knows little of right or wrong, but much of what parents like or dislike. Eventually the child comes to realize that even these godlike persons fail and fall short. On these occasions the parent must be repentant and ask forgiveness. Thus the child "may learn that God is someone much better and more wonderful even than the parents. Secondly, he may learn that, when he has done wrong, he too must ask forgiveness of God, and of other people if he has done them wrong."[4] The parent is the child's first step toward God, but the decisive step is one of personal faith in Christ as Saviour.

RESPONSIBILITY FOR CHILDREN

"Teach diligently" means literally to "prick them in" so that the truth will remain indelibly upon their hearts. "Sitting . . . walking . . . lying . . . rising" seem to underscore the fact that subject material should be made a theme of living interest. From the references to morning and evening come the Jewish practice of repeating the *Shema* (composed of Deut. 6:4-9; 11:13-21; Num. 15:37-41) as if to launch the busy hours of the day and set apart the rest of the night with thoughts of God.

[3]Alexander DeJong, *The Christian Family and Home* (Grand Rapids: Baker Book House, 1959), p. 91.
[4]Leslie and Winifred Brown, *The Christian Family* (New York: Association Press, 1959), p .37.

The command to bind the words as a constant reminder was taken quite literally by the Jews. The *tefillin* were small cases containing Scripture attached to the head and left hand. The *mezuzah* was a case containing a parchment roll fastened to the right doorpost of the house. It became the custom for the faithful upon visiting a home to reach up, touch the *mezuzah* with the fingertips, and kiss the fingers as an act of devotion. This act provided a solemn reminder that the home was devoted to God and that nothing should transpire there which was out of keeping with this lofty ideal. Whether or not such literal observance was expected (commentators debate the point), its intended purpose is clear. Parents were to keep the law constantly before the memory of the child. By precept and example, reverence and love of the Almighty were to be instilled.

The basic personality is formed in the home. The child of school age is already old in terms of basic character. The infant is little able to choose his responses, but by trial and error finds those which will bring parental attention. He is amenable to the parent's design, the order soon becoming internalized. Allegiances may change, energies may be redirected, but one's basic personality tends to persist. The potentiality of the home as a teaching institution is staggering, and is the measure of the parent's responsibility. "Both parents and the child need to realize that the home is the most important factor in training the child for total Christianity. The home is 'the school of Christian living,' 'the most fundamental institution in the world,' 'the nursery of every generation,' 'the college of life,' 'the training ground of the child.' "[5]

## THE FAMILY IN TRANSITION

There is no lack of attention given to the home today; lack of insight— perhaps, but lack of attention—no. Conferences, commissions, agencies, and curriculum writers all pour materials onto the market. Criticism is perhaps as significant as the proposals: "Too much church literature betrays a wish for today's families to remain just as they were in the 1890's, not so much for the sake of the families' health as for the convenience of ecclesiastical *modus operandi*."[6] The family has changed. It "is no longer the basic unit of mass society . . . then the attempt to base Christian education on the recovery of this unit is both unrealistic and reactionary."[7] Even the moderate suggestions of church curriculum writers have met with less than enthusiastic reception if not at times utter frustration in the home. To understand the character of any family

[5] Oscar E. Feucht, *Helping Families Through the Church* (St. Louis: Concordia Publishing House, 1957), p. 244.
[6] Fairchild and Wynn, *op. cit.*, p. 15.
[7] Letty M. Russell, "The Family and Christian Education in Modern Urban Society," *Religious Education*, LVI (January-February, 1961), p. 48.

we need to observe it to be the result of (1) survivals from earlier forms of the family, (2) the existing social and economic situation, and (3) the prevailing and evolving ideology of the society.[8]

## SURVIVAL FROM EARLIER FORMS OF THE FAMILY

The Jewish home was patriarchal, that is, regulated by the father. He was priest, and responsible to God for the welfare and edification of the family members. Harry Golden reflects upon his early years: "The happiest memory of life on the Lower East Side was that Papa was boss. In the Jewish household, the father was a figure of authority."[9] The religious significance and the economic significance of patriarchal authority were interrelated. Not only blessing but survival depended on acquiescence to the father's decision. Rebellion was treated with severity: reproof, chastening, and even the death penalty could result (Deut. 21:18-21).

The home of Old Testament times was more exactly a household (*beth*), which included several marriage groups: sons and daughters-in-law, unmarried children, grandchildren, servants and their families. Each household was part of succeedingly larger circles of clan, tribe, and nation. Children were prized. "Lo, children are an heritage of the Lord: and the fruit of the womb is his reward. As arrows are in the hand of a mighty man; so are children of the youth. Happy is the man that hath his quiver full of them: they shall not be ashamed, but they shall speak with the enemies in the gate" (Ps. 127:3-5). With the arrival of the child came the obligation to teach: "Train up a child in the way he should go: and when he is old, he will not depart from it" (Prov. 22:6).

The early Christian community carried over the Jewish family order. Increased significance was given to the Scriptures, while decreasing emphasis was placed on ritualistic Jewish family observances. As Christianity spread itself over the extent of the commercially orientated empire and embraced Gentile stock, fundamental family concepts underwent strain. Nevertheless, Christians went on teaching the sanctity and responsibility of the home. A fact generally overlooked by those who review this period was the emphasis on Christian hospitality (Rom. 16:2; I Tim. 3:2; I Pet. 4:9). Hospitality shows strong kinship to the larger family circle of Judaism, and its willingness to accept others into its protective environ. Thus, even the homes which lacked the careful preparation of Jewish instruction drew strength from the greater family of God as it practiced hospitality.

Of great importance to the church of the early centuries was the rise

[8]Robert Winch and Robert McGinnis, *Selected Studies in Marriage and the Family* (New York: Henry Holt & Co., 1953), p. 39.
[9]Harry Golden, "Has the American Family Fallen Out of Love?" *Better Homes and Gardens*, XXXVI (July 28, 1960), p. 68.

of the catechumenate, an instructional for adult candidates for church membership. It showed considerable development during A.D. 200-325, reaching its peak in 325-450 but had lost its significance by 550. During this time the church passed through persecution to a place of favor in the empire. It was peculiarly a transitional period in home education with strains of Hebrew-Christian foundations, the rigors thrown on the home by persecution, and a new ease following conquest of and compromise with the pagan influences of the empire.

The next period can be characterized by the sacramentary. Overlapping the earlier period, further modifying the Christian purity which persisted, it laid stress on the sacramental bestowal of God's grace through the church. The church appeared content to think of God's grace as coming to children through the sacraments. Adult education left behind only its formulas, making persons catechumens symbolically through ritual. The medieval ideal was a Christian society, a larger Christian family. The importance of the home as an institution for Christian education waned. Folk religion, the combination of pagan traditions and Christian concepts, filled much of the vacuum vacated by parental instruction.

The Gulliver giant of the Renaissance was stirring by the fourteenth century, and quite awake by the sixteenth. In part it was a revival of learning. The Reformation is sometimes called the Renaissance of the North, and was particularly distinguished by its religious content. Where the Renaissance in general had little immediate influence on the average home, the Reformation lay heavy stress on parental responsibility for Christian education. A priesthood of believers required an instructed and active constituency. Luther typifies the concern: To bring up children well "is the big work of parents, and when they do not attend to it, there is a perversion of nature as when fire does not burn or water moisten." The Roman Catholic Counter-Reformation, while not as zealous for home instruction, soon outstripped Protestant educators in its use of school and pedagogy.

Commercial and industrial revolution marked the seventeenth century. Factory production replaced domestic industry. No longer did the family provide group earnings but employment was structured on an individual basis. Husbands, wives, and children all worked in different departments of the factory. Home tended to become only a shelter. The authority of the father weakened along with his capacity as chief breadwinner. The plight of the home is graphically portrayed in the Victorian reformers who yearned for a return to the feudal family system, and Marx and Engels who saw in class struggle and progress eventual emancipation and utopia for the masses.

The Bible and the plow symbolize the religious and rural orientation of colonial America. The home was patriarchal, instruction taken seriously, and the family ties close. By the nineteenth century movements and conditions were sapping the roots of the unified colonial times. "Preeminent among these forces were the spread of democratic ideas from political to social and family life, the rapid development of a new industrial order, the extension of the Western frontier by resolute pioneers, and the slow but continuous decline, after the middle of the century, in the influence of organized religion upon family and personal life."[10]

What has survived from the earlier forms of the family? The following seem evident: (1) The basic right of the home as responsible educator. The state recognizes the right of parental prerogative and intervenes only in cases of neglect. (2) An ideal of the home based on the Hebrew-Christian tradition as it is expressed in Western civilization. (3) The peculiar arrangement of this ideal in terms of the needs and goals of the new world. (4) The modification of the American arrangement by increased pluralism and the recent urbanization of life.

EXISTING SOCIAL AND ECONOMIC SITUATION

No longer is the dominant family image the closely knit rural home of colonial times, or even that of a generation ago. Nor is there a convenient mold into which all homes can be poured. In fact, pluralism of type is itself characteristic of the current situation. The home has become atomistic, each member absorbed in his own interests, and the home in turn isolated from its relatives. It is adaptable but unstable, adjusting readily but not always effectively. The pace is too rapid and the casualty rate too high. Technology is outracing interpersonal relationships. Each generation is being raised in an atmosphere significantly different from the preceding one. This fact produces increased tensions between youth and their elders. We may have little or no concept of where we are going, but there can be no doubt that we are getting there in a hurry.

The home as an economic unit faces the seriousness of a rising economy, and prediction of increased unemployment. The family income is increasingly the product of multiple wage earners. Cooperative family earning enterprise is the exception. The home is losing its independence and self-sufficiency. It "is no longer a self-sufficient unit. Children have become a luxury, and old persons and relatives find little place in a cooperative enterprise."[11] Nevertheless, the standard of living is high, and creature comforts are not lacking for the vast majority of families.

[10]Bernard Stern, *The Family: Past and Present* (New York: D. Appleton-Century, 1938), p. 215.
[11]Oliver E. Byrd, *Family Life Sourcebook* (Stanford: Stanford University Press, 1956), p. 229.

PREVAILING AND EVOLVING IDEOLOGY OF THE SOCIETY

Winch and McGinnis stated that in order to understand the family we must not only consider the survivals from earlier forms, the existing social and economic situation, but the prevailing and evolving ideology of the society. We consider the last of these factors under two topics: secularism and collectivism.

By secularism is not meant a purposive atheistic philosophy, but the result of certain forces centering the home's attention on that which is temporal rather than eternal. The deep concern of families

> for economic standing and monetary returns, their predilection for commercial entertainment, their practical atheism (they live as if there is no God) are indications of the widespread secularism of our time. It has been suggested that our values in this day are as if someone had sneaked into a department store during the night and changed the price tags from one item to another, so that expensive items have cheap price tags and valueless articles are priced exorbitantly high. Secularism is like that.[12]

Christopher Dawson has done us a service in exploding the myth of cultural pluralism in America. He says that we have a religious pluralism, but one culture and that "secular."[13] The secular ideology may not be an outgrowth of but is at least rationalized by an appeal to American democracy. This claim appears to be a distortion which stresses freedom from religion in order to propagate a culture in which the only real knowledge is concerned with naturalistic values.

At first glimpse the home of today looks more individualistic, more self-reliant than that of yesterday. However, we are apparently misled in this judgment. To be sure, individual initiative and risk-taking are involved, but the family "has been a collective experiment in the sense that the couples were acting under the stimulus of current criticisms of family life and were attempting to realize in their marriage the new conceptions of family living disseminated by the current literature, presented by the marriage of friends, or developed in discussion by groups of young people."[14] Conformity marks today's home as it does the individual.

This resumé provides us with a more realistic, if less optimistic, picture of the home we have to consider, and the Christian home is likely to have more in common with its cultural norm than its Biblical ideal. We have in mind, then, a home which has at least the following trends operative:

---

[12]John C. Wynn, *How Christian Parents Face Family Problems* (Philadelphia: Westminster Press, 1955), p. 24.
[13]Christopher Dawson, *The Crises of Western Civilization* (New York: Sheed and Ward, 1961), Chaps. 13-15.
[14]Winch and McGinnis, *op. cit.*, p. 41.

1. A conscience for something of the nature of the Judeo-Christian ideal: patriarchal, religious, responsible.

2. A mentality which is more or less secular: material goals, temporal satisfactions, pragmatic functions.

3. A sensitivity toward what is expected by the group: complacent, conformed, respectable.

Such a home values education, but more for its prestige and extrinsic possibilities than for its intrinsic worth for an abundant life. It feels incapable of taking religious leadership, and shies away from responsibilities elaborated by God. It wants "all this and heaven too."

## THE FAITH WHICH EDUCATES

When we think of a Christian home it is natural to do so in terms of grace at table, Scripture before bedtime, or mottoes on the walls.

> No mere book, be it said forthrightly, makes a home Christian. Even reading the Bible cannot alone accomplish so high a goal. The plain fact is that there are no techniques or formulas known that will bring about family living. It is just not to be achieved by good works alone. *The essential increment is the grace of God.* For the family, like the individual, is justified by faith.[15]

RIGHT RELATIONSHIPS

The Christian home is an act of grace. Christian marriage is a triangle with God at the apex. It is formed by partners who have experienced God's forgiveness in Christ, being born of the Holy Spirit. These relationships, to God and to one another, draw the sides of the triangle and realize a Christian marriage.

Children are God's gift, and become part of the parents' stewardship to God. Doris Grumbach comments on the unrest so often evident among homemakers who do not feel that they are doing something worthwhile in directing the affairs of people three feet tall. "If what psychology tells us is so, this is a far more complicated and more demanding activity than editing a magazine, selling a dress, meeting a business executive, doing research for an advertising agency, or even writing a book or painting a picture."[16] If what Scripture tells us is true, can there be a more significant role than that of the parent?

Paul provides a series of commands concerning family relationships: "Wives, submit yourselves unto your own husbands . . . husbands, love your wives"; "Children, obey your parents . . . and fathers, provoke not your children to wrath" (Eph. 5:22, 25; 6:1, 4). It is also interesting to

15Wynn, *op. cit.*, p. 9.
16Doris Grumbach, "A Woman's Place," *Commonweal*, LXXIV (April 28, 1961), p. 120.

note how these admonitions relate to Christ: wives are subject as unto the Lord; husbands love as the Lord loved His Church; children obey in the Lord; and fathers conversely bring up the children in the fear and admonition of the Lord. The measure of each relationship is Christ.

The relationship of husband and wife is one of complementing roles. A certain mutuality and equality seems to be expressed in the transition verse into this passage: "Submitting yourselves one to another in the fear of God" (Eph. 5:21). The husband is to love (*agapē*); not simply sexual love (*eros*) but divinelike love. Such love has the self-sacrificing character of the Christ who gave Himself for His Church. It is not conditioned by the attractiveness or response of the object loved, but overflows from the heart of the one who loves. The husband's example is Christ's love in that He who had authority came not to be served but to serve, not to receive gifts but to give. The wife's example is her reverence for, and desire to please and serve, Christ.

Children are charged with obedience to parents, who are held responsible by God not to provoke them to anger. The child is in a dependency relationship, the parent in one of responsibility. The goal for both must be the maturing of the young person who needs none but the Saviour, but who ministers to all in His name.

Rigorous Obedience

The Christian family "places all its life in harmony with the purposes and will of God. [It] lives by an intelligent and dedicated plan."[17] There are times when the child should be expected to follow the parent's decision with little or no understanding of the issues involved. These are the exceptions. Training in responsible choice comes through opportunity for and guidance in making right choices. Parents are concerned with the discipline which is internal, regulated by the Holy Spirit, responding to the will of God. They want for the child more than a carbon copy. "The mature Christian does not copy others. He continues to grow in his own way and according to his own abilities, for he is an individual."[18]

Refined Atmosphere

The Christian home should be characterized by the fruit of the Spirit: "love, joy, peace, longsuffering, gentleness, goodness, faith, meekness, temperance" (Gal. 5:22, 23). We reflect on the first two of these fruits by way of illustration. Brandt and Dowdy analyze the love components of

[17]Hazen Werner, *Christian Family Living* (New York: Abingdon Press, 1958), p. 30.

[18]Vera Channels, *The Layman Builds a Christian Home* (St. Louis: Bethany Press, 1959), p. 18.

I Corinthians 13 as patience, kindness, generosity, humility, courtesy, unselfishness, good temper, guilelessness, sincerity.[19] The children enter vicariously into the love which they sense between the parents, and they experience as well the love which overflows the marriage bond to them.

"There are happy homes which are not specifically Christian. There are those built solely on sound and well-established principles of mental hygiene."[20] There are Christian homes which lack the joy that we might expect. The contrast is only an apparent anomaly. Persons enjoy to varying degrees the benefits of God's providential care, the knowledge of His creation, and the residue of Christian ethics in our society, while some Christians have hardly begun to experience the fruits of the Christian life. Yet life with Him is infinitely worth living. It is "joy unspeakable and full of glory" (I Pet. 1:8).

The hope for home education lies in what the Christian home is by the grace of God. It is a dynamic, living unit, following prescribed guide lines. The home ideal is not to be found either by complacency (which we are apt to call dependency on God) or in frantic do-goodism, but by entering into the very life of God by the Holy Spirit's entering into the life of man. There are no simple rules which guarantee success; but if the family will courageously and prayerfully seek God's face, He will be found.

## HOME EDUCATION IN TODAY'S WORLD

Current interest in the home and its educational responsibility is well taken. However, the home today is not the well-knit, patriarchal design of the nineteenth century, but the atomistic, individualized norm of the twentieth. The temptation to sweep the problem under the rug by use of some devotional gimmick must be resisted. Nothing less than a vitally related, disciplined, and experiencing Christian family can cope with the complex times. There follow a series of suggestions for translating the ideal into twentieth century actuality.

1. Give the home a chance to breathe. Hawkins and Walters, in interviewing eighty-five families, found that the primary reason given for not being together more was simply a lack of time.[21] The church is one of the chief offenders in making "busy work" for the family. The church must go beyond feeling an obligation to employ the time of its families to the circumspect use of that time.

2. Revive Christian hospitality. This involves treating persons such as the boy whose parents are uninterested in spiritual things, the elderly

[19]Henry Brandt and Homer Dowdy, *Building a Christian Home* (Wheaton: Scripture Press, 1960), p. 10.
[20]Channels, *op. cit.,* p. 18.
[21]Wesner Fallaw, *The Modern Parent and the Teaching Church* (New York: Macmillan Co., 1946), pp. 25, 26.

convalescent, or the newly arrived couple in the community as honorary members of the family.

3. Go beyond evangelism of children and Christ-to-the-youth to families-for-the-kingdom. Energetic programs for reaching children and youth have become necessary because of our inability to cope with the family unit as such.

4. Evaluate the results of our mania for close grading practices. "Neither Scripture nor pedagogy support the iron-clad rule that individuals must be mechanically classified according to age."[22] We have, it seems, over-stressed verbal comprehension in teaching. There is still more caught than taught. The graded worship service lacks some of the educational values of the family pew, and removes one of the all too few opportunities for expressing family solidarity.

5. Tune in on a higher wave band. "Even church families, more than they realize, take their view of life more from Broadway, Hollywood, Wall Street, and the omniscient commentators of press and radio than from the New Testament and the pulpit."[23] The Christian must realize and compensate for the indoctrination provided so amply by sub-Christian society.

6. Carefully structure spiritual priorities in place of the temporal. "A man's life consisteth not in the abundance of the things which he possesseth" (Luke 12:15). The only thing that survives death is that which has become part of human personality.

7. Hold out for loving authority. "Children need friends, of course, but they need in a very special way *parents* who are parents."[24] If the current disrespect for authority and personal rights is to be checked, it will be done at the level God directed, in the home. "Honor thy father and mother; which is the first commandment with promise" (Eph. 6:2).

8. Recapture the nobility of work. We have dramatized the ideal of leisure time, and minimized the importance of productivity. "Six days shalt thou labor, and do all thy work" (Exod. 20:9). The bulk of commentaries has dealt with the following verse on Sabbath rest, but not to be overlooked is man's privilege to labor as God worked making "heaven and earth, the sea, and all that in them is" (Exod. 20:11a).

9. Put "loyalty" back into our vocabulary. The poor record of American P.O.W.'s in Korea seems to confirm measurably the Communist report that the American "had weak loyalties to his family, his community, his religion, and his fellow soldiers."[25] It is a threatening day when a mother's

[22]William D. Streng, "A New Plan—the Family Class," *International Journal of Religious Education*, XXXVI (May, 1960), p. 12.
[23]Paul Vieth, *The Church and Christian Education* (St. Louis: Bethany Press, 1947), p. 171.
[24]Channels, *op. cit.*, p. 73.
[25]Russell Kirk, *The American Cause* (Chicago: Henry Regnery, 1957), p. 2.

prayer, the unfurling of "Old Glory," or the sounding of a church bell fails to tug at the heart strings, make a man stand taller and walk straighter.

10. Recover our relatives, those who have been lost by our isolated and insulated existence. Dr. Margaret Mead of the American Museum of Natural History said: "The small isolated family of the U.S. is not the best unit to handle the confusing conditions of modern life."[26] She continued to plead for a new design for family life which would make the best creative use of space knowledge of the child and the adjustment knowledge of the grandparent.

In summary and preview the words of Phillips Brooks seem overwhelmingly applicable: "Do not pray for easy lives, pray to be stronger men; do not pray for tasks equal to your powers, pray for powers equal to your tasks."

## POSTSCRIPT: ACCENT ON PRACTICE

What is being proposed about realizing the potential of the home as primary educator? There follow a number of articles with brief synopses to give some indication of current thought in its most concrete form: specific suggestions for action.

Boll, Eleanor S., "Watch Your Table Talk," *Christian Living*, X (January, 1963). Thoughts about what we say, and what attitudes we express at mealtime.

"The Christian Home's Greatest Contribution to the World," *Christian Living*, X (May, 1963). Enthusiastic reports on the value of the Christian home.

Dreier, Mary E., "Friday Fun Night for the Family," *Hearthstone*, XIV (January, 1962). Making a family "ritual" out of Friday night by getting together just for fun.

Harwell, Jack U., "Pattern for Family Living," *Home Life*, XV (February, 1961). Just living the Christian life together, nothing new but made vital by the people who experience the promises of God.

Hendricks, Howard, "Worship—Family Style," *Moody Monthly*, LXIII (December, 1962). Fresh thoughts on the family altar.

Hill, Shirley, "Time Out of Joint," *Hearthstone*, XIV (January, 1962). An interesting technique, supplying an article for stimulation and two discussion directives for use in the home. The theme is family feeling for world citizenship, and could be adapted easily to missionary emphasis.

[26]"New Type of Family Needed," *Science News Letter*, LXXXIII (March 16, 1963), p. 168.

Inch, Morris A., "P.T.A. Goes to Church," *Sunday-School World* (November, 1963). Experience with parents taking a more direct responsibility for their children's education through a parent-teacher's program.

Jackson, Dorothy R., "Is the Church Breaking Up Your Happy Home?" *Christian Herald*, LXXXVI (July, 1963). A suggestion for family night at the church.

McEntire, Kathleen E., "We Planned a Family Life Week," *International Journal of Religious Education*, XXXIX (January, 1963). The development of a family week program for a local church from inspiration to finished product.

Merrifield, Mildred M., "We're All in This Together," *Home Life*, XV (July, 1961). The opportunity which sickness brings to delve into Christian resources and draw new perspective. The family tests its anchor-chain.

Silverman, Betsy M., "Can Three Generations Live Together?" *Parents' Magazine and Better Homemaking*, XXXVIII( April, 1963). A realistic appraisal of the problems and potentials of meeting obligations beyond the immediate family circle.

Streng, William D., "A New Plan—the Family Class," *International Journal of Religious Education*, XXXVI (May, 1960). The idea first experimented with in 1952 in the Holy Trinity Lutheran Church of Dubuque, Iowa, and since in several pilot programs in various denominations. Families study together in groups of two, three, or four.

Sydnor, James R., "Music in the Home," *International Journal of Religious Education*, XXXIX (November, 1962). Practical suggestions for revitalizing the role of music in the home.

"What Graduates and Parents Want to Know," *Moody Monthly*, LXIII (June, 1963). Stimulating question and answer session of value to Christian homes looking for counseling help.

Whiting, Mabel, "Our Family Goes to Press," *Christian Life*, XXIV (May, 1963). One "clan" found a way of "keeping in touch" by turning out a quarterly newspaper with information gathered by reporters from each family branch.

Widmer, Fredrick W., "A Family Vacation Bible School," *International Journal of Religious Education*, XXXVIII (April, 1962). The successful adventure of First Presbyterian Church of Atlanta with a family vacation Bible school.

## BIBLIOGRAPHY

Brandt, Henry and Dowdy, Homer. *Building a Christian Home*. Wheaton: Scripture Press, 1960.

Brown, Leslie and Winifred. *The Christian Family*. New York: Asssocia-
tion Press, 1959.
Byrd, Oliver E. *Family Life Sourcebook*. Stanford: Stanford University
Press, 1956.
Channels, Vera. *The Layman Builds a Christian Home*. St. Louis: Beth-
any Press, 1959.
Dawson, Christopher. *The Crisis of Western Civilization*. New York:
Sheed and Ward, 1961.
DeJong, Alexander. *The Christian Family and Home*. Grand Rapids:
Baker Book House, 1959.
Fairchild, Roy, and Wynn, John. *Families in the Church: A Protestant
Survey*. New York: Association Press, 1961.
Fallaw, Wesner. *The Modern Parent and the Teaching Church*. New
York: Macmillan Co., 1946.
Feucht, Oscar E. *Helping Families Through the Church*. St. Louis: Con-
cordia Publishing House, 1957.
Golden, Harry. "Has the American Family Fallen Out of Love?" *Better
Homes and Gardens*, XXXVI (July 28, 1960).
Grumbach, Doris. "A Woman's Place," *Commonweal*, LXXIV (April 28,
1961).
Kirk, Russell. *The American Cause*. Chicago: Henry Regnery, 1957.
"New Type of Family Needed," *Science News Letter*, LXXXIII (March
16, 1963).
Russell, Letty M. "The Family and Christian Education in Modern Urban
Society," *Religious Education*, LVI (January-February, 1961).
Stern, Bernard. *The Family: Past and Present*. New York: D. Appleton-
Century, 1938.
Vieth, Paul. *The Church and Christian Education*. St. Louis: Bethany
Press, 1947.
Werner, Hazen. *Christian Family Living*. New York: Abingdon Press,
1958.
Winch, Robert, and McGinnis, Robert. *Selected Studies in Marriage and
the Family*. New York: Henry Holt & Co., 1953.
Wynn, John C. *How Christian Parents Face Family Problems*. Phila-
delphia: Westminster Press, 1955.

## FOR FURTHER READING

Askew, Mary W. *Your Home: Today and Tomorrow*. Richmond: John
Knox Press, 1946.
Bossard, James, and Ball, Eleanor. *Ritual in Family Living*. Philadelphia:
University of Pennsylvania Press, 1950.

Duvall, Evelyn R. *Family Development.* Philadelphia: J. B. Lippincott Co., 1962.

Eavey, Charles B. *Principles of Personality Building for Christian Parents.* Grand Rapids: Zondervan Publishing House, 1952.

Fallaw, Wesner. "The Role of the Home in Religious Nurture," *Religious Education* (Marvin Taylor, ed.). New York: Abingdon Press, 1960.

*The Family and Its Christian Fulfillment.* New York: Foreign Missions Conference of North America, 1945.

Jacobsen, Margaret L. *The Child in the Christian Family.* Wheaton: Scripture Press, 1959.

Kerr, Clarence. *God's Pattern for the Home.* Los Angeles: Cowman Publications, 1953.

Marney, Carlyle. *Dangerous Fathers, Problem Mothers, and Terrible Teens.* New York: Abingdon Press, 1958.

Miller, Randolph Crump. *Education for Christian Living.* Englewood Cliffs, N. J.: Prentice-Hall, Inc., 1956.

Riley, John. *This Holy Estate.* Anderson, Ind.: Warner Press, 1957.

Rose, Arnold M. "Acceptance of Adult Roles and Separation from Family," *Marriage and Family Living,* XXXVIII (April, 1962).

Small, Dwight. *Design for Christian Marriage.* Westwood, N.J.: Fleming H. Revell Co., 1959.

Tyler, Wilfred and Frances. *The Challenge of Christian Parenthood.* Nashville: Broadman Press, 1954.

Wynn, John C. (ed.). *Sermons on Marriage and Family Life.* New York: Abingdon Press, 1956.

# INDEX